English Fiction of the Victorian Period

Longman Literature in English Series

**General Editors: David Carroll and Michael Wheeler
University of Lancaster**

For a complete list of titles see pages viii and ix

English Fiction
of the
Victorian Period
1830–1890

Michael Wheeler

Longman

London and New York

LONGMAN GROUP LIMITED
Longman House, Burnt Mill, Harlow
Essex CM20 2JE, England
Associated companies throughout the world

Published in the United States of America
by Longman Inc., New York

First published 1985

BRITISH LIBRARY CATALOGUING IN PUBLICATION DATA
Wheeler, Michael,
  English fiction of the Victorian period
  1830–1890.
  — (Longman literature in English series)
  1. English fiction – 19th century –
  History and criticism
  I. Title
  823'.8'09   PR871
ISBN 0-582-49236-X csd
ISBN 0-582-49235-1 ppr

LIBRARY OF CONGRESS CATALOGING IN PUBLICATION DATA
Wheeler, Michael, 1947–
  English fiction of the Victorian period.

  (Longman literature in English series)
  Bibliography: p.
  Includes index.
  1. English fiction – 19th century – History and
  criticism. I. Title.
PR871.W49 1985   823'.8'09   84-20125
ISBN 0-582-49236-X
ISBN 0-582-49235-1 (pbk.)

Set in 9/10 pt Bembo (Linotron 202)
Produced by Longman Singapore Publishers (Pte) Ltd.
Printed in Singapore.

Contents

Editors' Preface

The multi-volume Longman Literature in English Series provides students of literature with a critical introduction to the major genres in their historical and cultural context. Each volume gives a coherent account of a clearly defined area, and the series, when complete, will offer a practical and comprehensive guide to literature written in English from Anglo-Saxon times to the present. The aim of the series as a whole is to show that the most valuable and stimulating approach to literature is that based upon an awareness of the relations between literary forms and their historical context. Thus the areas covered by most of the separate volumes are defined by period and genre. Each volume offers new and informed ways of reading literary works, and provides guidance to further reading in an extensive reference section.

As well as studies on all periods of English and American literature, the series includes books on criticism and literary theory, and on the intellectual and cultural context. A comprehensive series of this kind must of course include other literatures written in English, and therefore a group of volumes deals with Irish and Scottish literature, and the literatures of India, Africa, the Caribbean, Australia and Canada. The forty-six volumes of the series cover the following areas: Pre-Renaissance English Literature, English Poetry, English Drama, English Fiction, English Prose, Criticism and Literary Theory, Intellectual and Cultural Context, American Literature, Other Literatures in English.

David Carroll
Michael Wheeler

Longman Literature in English Series

General Editors: David Carroll and Michael Wheeler
University of Lancaster

Criticism and Literary Theory

Criticism and Literary Theory from Sidney to Johnson
Criticism and Literary Theory from Wordsworth to Arnold
Criticism and Literary Theory from 1890 to the Present

The Intellectual and Cultural Context

The Sixteenth Century
The Seventeenth Century
The Eighteenth Century, 1700–1789
The Romantic Period, 1789–1830
The Victorian Period, 1830–1890
1890 to the Present

American Literature

American Literature before 1865
American Poetry of the Twentieth Century
American Drama of the Twentieth Century
American Fiction, 1865–1940
American Fiction since 1940
Twentieth-Century America

Other Literatures

Irish Literature since 1800
Scottish Literature since 1700
Indian Literature in English
African Literature in English
Caribbean Literature in English
Australian Literature in English
*Canadian Literature in English *W. J. Keith*

Already published

Author's Preface

Thirty years ago Kathleen Tillotson introduced her pioneering study on *Novels of the Eighteen-Forties* by announcing that it was too late to talk about 'Victorian novels', and that the time had surely come to 'break up "the Victorian novel" into manageable segments; not by novelists, or categories, or phases, but simply by concentrating upon a decade or so at a time'. Although most academic specialists have followed Professor Tillotson's lead in breaking up the subject into segments, more has been written since 1954 on individual novelists, categories, and phases than on single decades. A flood of books and articles on almost every conceivable 'aspect' of Victorian fiction has, however, reinforced one's sense of what Tillotson calls 'the insuperable difficulty of doing critical justice to the novels of sixty-three years in a single book'. Why, then, a single book on English fiction of the Victorian period, 1830–1890?

Firstly, the aim of this as of all volumes in the Longman Literature in English Series is to provide a critical *introduction*. I cannot hope to do critical justice to any one novel in a book of this kind, let alone to the *œuvres* of the major and minor novelists, or to specific sub-genres and phases of Victorian fiction. I can, however, attempt to provide the reader who is fairly new to the study of the fiction with critical guidelines, and offer suggestions for further reading. Secondly, there is still a need for a study which, while not attempting 'coverage' of such a large subject, introduces its salient features – methods of publication, forms and sub-genres, themes, motifs, and conventions – and tries to relate the fiction to its nineteenth-century context.

This study, then, is everywhere selective; and selection has been made with students in higher education in mind. The main body of the book is divided into four distinct chronological phases, each of fifteen years, the first beginning seven years before Victoria ascended the throne and the last ending eleven years before her death. Although these divisions are clearly more arbitrary in the case of some writers and traditions than of others, they represent distinct phases in the development of the novel, and the advantages of following such a scheme in my view outweigh the disadvantages. Each of the four chapters which follow the general introduction begins with a discussion of developments in the novel form and of the particular sub-genres – social-problem novels, sensation novels, and so on – which flourished at the time. Major novelists are then treated in more detail in separate sections of each chapter.

In the process of selecting individual authors, novels, and themes for more detailed discussion, there are bound to be some major omissions. I particularly regret not being able to say more about George Eliot's early work and the later novels of Trollope and Meredith. Henry James is to be treated as an American novelist in another volume in the series, but his absence from this book may seem a glaring omission. F. R. Leavis made James one of his great triumvirate of George Eliot, James, and Conrad in his highly influential book on *The Great Tradition* (1948), thus establishing a canon of English fiction which excluded most major Victorian novelists. The absence of James from my study allows more space for these other Victorian writers, some of whose reputations have not yet fully recovered from the stigma of a dismissive Leavisite footnote or aside.

No critical work can be totally objective and perfectly balanced in its emphasis, of course; and my own is no exception to this rule. A large selection of critical studies which offer alternative readings and approaches is therefore included in the *General Bibliographies*. These comprise three sections – (i) English fiction: history and criticism; (ii) Victorian background: historical, intellectual, cultural; (iii) Victorian fiction (further divided into five sub-sections). Each of the fifty entries in the notes on *Individual Authors* includes a summary of an author's career, with titles and dates of major novels, and a list of biographical and critical works on that author. Bibliographies in these appendices are limited almost exclusively to printed books rather than articles in scholarly journals. The *Chronology* sets out works of fiction, other works (literary and non-literary), and historical events, etc., in three parallel columns, offering a reference guide to the context in which individual works of fiction were published.

As in the appendices, dates given for novels in the text refer to first publication in volume(s) or in serial form: e.g. *Vanity Fair* (1847–48). References to specific passages in novels, and some other works such as novelists' autobiographies, are by chapter numbers in parentheses (16), or, where appropriate, by book and chapter numbers (v. 2). Where the first reference to a novel includes a reference to a chapter number it is given thus: (*Adventures of Philip*, 1861–62; 23). Raised numerals in the text refer to the notes at the end of each chapter.

Finally, I would like to thank the University of Lancaster for granting me a term's sabbatical leave during the preparation of this book; staff of the University of Lancaster library, and especially Thelma Goodman, for much patient assistance; Anne Dalton, Maureen Jex, and Joan Chesters for their skilful typing; the many undergraduate and postgraduate students with whom I have discussed Victorian fiction over the past eleven years, and especially Shirley Bradshaw and Brenda Abercrombie; Christopher Walsh for his valuable comments on early drafts; David Carroll for his advice and encouragement at every stage of the project; my wife Vivienne for understanding, and my children Joshua, Charlotte, and Emily for not understanding.

MDW
December 1983

For my parents,
David and Hilda Wheeler

Chapter 1
Introduction

The Victorian Age was not only the longest but also the greatest in the history of English fiction. It was an age of the novel in the same sense that the Restoration was an age of drama and the Romantic period an age of poetry. The past tense seems inappropriate, however, when one considers how much Victorian fiction is still in print, and is still read by the general reading public. The richness and variety of the fiction is well represented in the writers to whom I devote separate sections in this book: Dickens, perhaps the greatest novelist in the language; Thackeray, a brilliant satirist and realist; Charlotte and Emily Brontë, who wrote the two most famous modern romances in English; George Eliot, whose work marks the high point of an English realist tradition in which Trollope, Elizabeth Gaskell, and Gissing also figure; Meredith, the writer who extended the intellectual range of the novel through innovation and experiment; Hardy, a challenging and often controversial novelist in his own time, whose critical reputation has risen steadily in ours; and Stevenson, the leading figure in the late nineteenth-century revival of romance.

The 'greatness' of this age of fiction is not only qualitative, however – a matter of a galaxy of major talent – but also quantitative. For the work of a host of other writers, ranging from Wilkie Collins to Rider Haggard, from Disraeli to George Moore, and from Charles Kingsley to Mrs Humphry Ward, still lives in the sense that it is still read, and is also the subject of closer critical attention today than at any time since its publication. Quantity in this context has another, negative side to it, of course, and most of the tens of thousands of novels published during Victoria's reign (an estimate of forty thousand is sometimes quoted) are unquestionably buried, if not dead and quite beyond recall. They lie in the catacombs of the major libraries, to be disturbed perhaps once or twice a century by scholars who seek more representative views of the age than the most original creative writers generally offer, or more representative examples of specific sub-genres. These forgotten novels have gone the way of all minor examples of popular literature written to pass the reader's time and keep the writer's pot boiling, or to instruct the reader and get the writer's pet theory into print. In an age which delighted in the clutter of Gothic architecture and heavily ornamental interior design, novels were all too often not so much 'baggy monsters' as monstrous bags, into which almost anything could be crammed. Given that some kind of love interest was virtually a *sine qua non*, whether as the main theme, or as a side issue introduced for light relief, or, more interestingly, as a means whereby other themes – political, social, religious – could be domesticated, hundreds of minor writers published rambling novels in which every conceivable topic of the day was treated. Significantly, some of the writers of novels discussed in this book would not have described themselves as novelists, but turned naturally to the most popular literary vehicle available.

Under what conditions, then, were novels – major works of literature and pot-boilers alike – published in the nineteenth century? The fact that the Victorian novelist wrote for the reading public rather than for a patron meant in effect that he or she had several masters rather than one: these might include the publisher and his professional 'reader', the editor of a magazine, the proprietor of a circulating library, the bookseller, and, directly or indirectly, the reading public itself. An accurate picture of the complex relationship between Victorian novelists and the book trade has recently been drawn[1]; here I can only sketch in the outline. By the second decade of the nineteenth century, when Scott and Jane Austen were writing, novels were generally published in three or four volumes. Although three-volume novels, or 'three-deckers', sold at a standard price of half a guinea a volume, which put them beyond the means of most middle-class readers, they remained the staple form throughout our period. The remarkable staying power of the three-decker has been attributed to the fact that it was commercially safe. Its success, however, and eventual demise also coincided with the rise and fall of Charles Edward Mudie, the mogul of the Victorian circulating libraries.

Mudie started lending books in a shop in Bloomsbury in 1842, and rapidly expanded his empire into the country and abroad. Books were lent a volume at a time for a fee of a guinea a year per reader. Voracious readers who could not afford expensive three-deckers could borrow them for a fraction of the retail price, bound in Mudie's own boards. Many aspiring writers also benefited, in that Mudie's order of a couple of hundred copies often represented the difference between the launching of a literary career and oblivion. Furthermore, if a novel were particularly successful with the reading public, Mudie would buy in more from the publisher and reserve a large stock of the author's next work. Usurping some of the publisher's power, Mudie also acted as an unofficial defender of public morals, a spokesman for the mythical 'Mrs Grundy', that epitome of English propriety.[2] Mudie's own scrutiny of novels – a first level of screening – was supplemented by letters received from irate fathers and anxious clergymen complaining about books borrowed from his libraries, mainly by women, who made up the majority of the novel-reading public. The consequent withdrawal of titles sometimes had disastrous results for their authors.

Before the advent of radio and television, novel-reading, and particularly reading aloud in the family circle, were of course common middle-class leisure activities. That new titles were sometimes keenly sought for in the circulating libraries throughout the period is confirmed in anecdotes such as Mary (Mrs Humphry) Ward's in her *A Writer's Recollections* (1918; 12). One day in 1888 a lady jumped into Mary Ward's compartment in a train about to leave Waterloo station, delighted to have got hold of the first volume of *Robert Elsmere*, Mrs Ward's most famous novel. Breathlessly she informed a friend seeing her off that she would have been forced to wait for several weeks had she not seized a copy from somebody returning it to the library, even though it was promised to other readers. (Mary Ward recalls that she did not reveal her identity to the lady, but left her to plunge into the much-sought-after novel.) The story illustrates an obvious point which is nevertheless sometimes forgotten: that novels are written primarily to be read when new.

Although cheap reprints of three-deckers often came out some years after the first edition, and 'collective editions' of established novelists such as Dickens and Bulwer were to be among the reasonably priced 'railway' novels sold by W. H. Smith from mid-century, new fiction was not read by anything like its potential readership in the 1830s until the revival of the monthly part novel, initiated by the publication of Dickens's *Pickwick Papers* (1836–37). An improvised miscellany which later turned into a novel, and which sold in huge numbers after the introduction of Sam Weller, *Pickwick* set the pattern for most of Dickens's later novels, as well as for those of some of his rivals. Due to appear on the first day of every month, but in practice coming out the day before, each number was a slim paper-bound booklet, containing advertisements inside both covers and on the first and last of the thirty-two pages. Two expensively produced plates illustrated each number, which, at the price of a shilling, reached a wider readership than had been dreamt of before. Whereas readers of *Jane Eyre* could devour the whole novel on the day that they purchased it (and several literary figures recorded that they could not put it down), readers of twenty-part monthly serials usually had to wait for nineteen months to find out how they ended, the last issue being a double number. Each number had to end at a moment of tension or of rest, and in Dickens's case an idiosyncrasy or exaggerated physical feature of a minor character served partly as an *aide-mémoire*, often months after the character's previous appearance in a novel. Monthly publication of their early novels also allowed Dickens and Thackeray to keep just ahead of printers' deadlines, and to respond to the criticisms and suggestions of readers and critics as they wrote.

Monthly part publication was gradually superseded by serial publication in family and literary magazines (both weekly and monthly) as a major outlet for novelists, who sometimes had to respond to a hard-pressed editor's sudden demand to round off a story which was depressing the circulation figures. Weekly serialization, in magazines such as Dickens's own *Household Words* and *All the Year Round*, caused problems of compression which Dickens himself once described as 'crushing', while Hardy's dealings with the censorious editors of family weeklies contributed to his disaffection with the constraints of the Victorian novel. The Brontës, the only major Victorian novelists who never ventured into serial publication of any kind, were brought up on the prestigious monthly, *Blackwood's Edinburgh Magazine*, and made tiny versions of 'Maga' as children. The most successful monthly magazine, however, was the *Cornhill*, launched in 1860 under the editorship of Thackeray. The fact that the first issue, priced at a shilling, contained the opening chapters of novels by both Trollope and Thackeray himself helps to explain the sale of 110,000 copies. As in the case of monthly part novels, successful magazine serials were later published in volumes, often at a large profit and usually by the publisher who owned the magazine.

Clearly, then, we have to take cognizance of the form or forms in which Victorian novels were published. For although serial novels were reprinted in volumes, and, in the case of Hardy for example, were sometimes revised at that stage, the fact remains that most Victorian fiction was not originally written to be read throughout over a short space of time. Novelists' decisions on such matters as pace and the introduction of new characters were dictated partly by the demands of the specific form in which their work was to be serialized. The same is true for the writer of modern television drama. The Duke of Omnium's garden party in the first episode of Simon Raven's dramatization of the Palliser novels (BBC TV, 1974) provided a good televisual means of both showing off the new marvels of colour, and bringing together and introducing the numerous characters who were to figure in later episodes. (No such party exists in the novels themselves.) In contrast, Trollope himself could afford to begin slowly in the first monthly part of *Can You Forgive Her?* (1864–65), gradually unfolding the major *secondary* plot. The wedding of Plantagenet and Lady Glencora (a big event in the television version) is referred to only briefly and retrospectively in later numbers. In each case the material is adapted to the medium.

Conditions were right for the production of large numbers of novels in the Victorian Age, not least because the Industrial Revolution had expanded and strengthened the position of the middle classes, who made up the majority of the novel-reading public. Urban growth had been rapid in the early decades of the century, and by 1841, 48.3 per cent of the population of England and Wales lived in towns and cities.[3] By 1881 the figure had risen to 70.2 per cent. The combined effects of expansion in manufacture, commerce and overseas trade, increased movement of population, and improvements in transport systems, led to a broadening of the middle classes which now ranged from the lowly clerk to the captain of industry, and to considerable upward and downward social mobility, itself a favourite theme of the novelists. A vigorous working-class sub-culture, also the product of urbanization, supplied the needs of a social group which was less illiterate than is often imagined.[4] It was not, however, until Forster's Education Act of 1870 had produced a more ambitious generation among the 'lower orders' that novelists complained of the over-production of fiction to cater for this new readership. Broadly speaking, the English novel of the period everywhere reflects, while often also challenging, middle-class values.

The values, prejudices, and assumptions of the middle classes are often reflected more clearly in the specialized sub-genres of Victorian fiction, such as sensation novels, school stories, and Utopian fiction, than in the work of the major novelists, and in each of the following chapters I will discuss these sub-genres first. They are of special interest because their emergence and (often rapid) demise reflect broad cultural changes in the period. They also embodied the more extreme literary fashions, and explored in detail the most contentious contemporary issues. Conventions and ideas worked out in the various sub-genres provided the leading novelists with material with which to experiment, and one definition of major fiction in the period is that which transcends the categories of the sub-genres while treating similar themes, such as social issues, religion, and history. For example, this period of crisis threw up a sub-genre which has come to be known as the 'social-problem novel', in which conflicts between the classes, and between master and man, or male seducer and female victim, are dramatized. In a century in which the population of Britain almost quadrupled, and political thinkers became increasingly fearful that individual freedom might be sacrificed in the name of public opinion or of the growing number of the unrepresented masses, the major novelists also examined the shifting relationship between the individual and society, often adopting the themes, motifs, and symbols of the social-problem novel.

Many of the most burning issues in Victorian Britain were religious controversies, and again it is in the comparatively minor sub-genre of religious fiction – often narrow in focus and hortatory in style – that these issues were most directly addressed. Sectarian strife, or the challenge to orthodox belief of biblical criticism, materialist philosophy, and science, were also recurrent themes of leading writers from Dickens to Hardy, who adapted the stereotypes of the period's religious fiction, such as the portly rector, the thin, hypocritical dissenter, and the female philanthropist of High Church persuasions, to their own broader purposes. Social-problem and religious fiction reflect the seriousness with which mid-Victorian writers and readers approached the most pressing questions of the day, and we will see that the characteristic role of the authorial narrator in these novels is similar to that of the sage or prophet figures of Victorian non-fictional prose. Many novelists also rivalled historians like Carlyle and Macaulay, in the hugely popular historical novel, tending to see history either in terms of its great heroes, or of its broadly progressive sweep towards an enlightened present. In either case the Victorian historical novelist examines the past in order both to entertain and teach his or her own generation.

It was not until the last quarter of the nineteenth century that the idea that fiction should embody some kind of moral teaching was seriously challenged by the comparatively amoral novel of ideas, and by the documentary fiction of the new realists which shocked Victorian sensibilities in its frankness. Early in our period, however, all varieties of fiction – including the so-called 'silver-fork' novel of fashionable life, the 'Newgate' novel, which made the criminal its hero, marine, sporting, and Irish rogue novels – were all broadly described as 'romances', reflecting their lowly status as a literary form identified with escapism. The use of the word 'romance' also reflects the extremes of this early fiction. Wildly improbable plots, exaggerated social contrasts, glamorized villains and recklessly brave heroes all indicate the distance which separates romance (meaning, simply, fiction) from reality. By mid-century, however, distinctions between the romance and the novel became the subject of critical debate, and an aspect of a broader discussion concerning romance and 'realism'. As in all such discussions, critics found that the most original literature resisted categorization. Indeed, even the minor social-problem novelists of the period whose stated aim was accurate realistic description conveyed their ideas through romance plots. It is time, however, to look more closely at some Victorian definitions of these notoriously slippery terms.

In 1859 we find the critic David Masson discussing 'romance' and 'novel' as terms which had come to be used for convenience, to distinguish between two broad categories of fictitious narrative:

> A Romance originally meant anything in prose or in verse
> written in any of the Romance languages; a Novel meant a
> new tale, a tale of fresh interest. . . . now, when we speak of
> a Romance, we generally mean 'a fictitious narrative, in prose
> or verse, the interest of which turns upon marvellous and
> uncommon incidents'; and, when we speak of a Novel, we
> generally mean 'a fictitious narrative differing from the
> Romance, inasmuch as the incidents are accommodated to the
> ordinary train of events and the modern state of society.' If
> we adopt this distinction, we make the prose Romance and
> the Novel the two highest varieties of prose fiction, and we
> allow in the prose Romance a greater ideality of incident than
> in the Novel.[5]

Masson later uses two other terms which are related to the novel/romance distinction and to the subject of realism:

> Thackeray is a novelist of what is called the Real school;
> Dickens is a novelist of the Ideal or Romantic school. (The
> terms Real and Ideal have been so run upon of late, that their
> repetition begins to nauseate; but they must be kept, for all
> that, till better equivalents are provided.) It is Thackeray's aim
> to represent life as it is actually and historically. . . . He will
> have no faultless characters, no demigods. . . . Dickens, on
> the other hand, . . . has characters of ideal perfection and
> beauty, as well as of ideal ugliness and brutality. . . .[6]

Masson argues, however, that the 'Ideal or Romantic artist must be true to nature as well as the Real artist, but he may be true in a different fashion',[7] and we will see later (in Ch. 3) that Dickens proves to be the best illustration of this point. Creative writers are more wary than critics of labels, and Trollope's comment that 'a good novel should be both [sensational and realistic], and both in the highest degree' (*Autobiography*, 1883; 12) can be compared with Meredith's equally bluff statement of 1862: 'Between realism and idealism, there is no natural conflict. This completes that' (see p. 141 below).

Trollope's and Meredith's comments are useful reminders of the dangers of the kind of categorizing in which Victorian critics delighted. Yet although Victorian fiction is characteristically a mixed genre – and Masson acknowledges this even in the process of defining his terms – the specific convention of realism, in which writers attempt to engage directly and consistently with the complexities of human experience in the real world, is at the centre of all nineteenth- and twentieth-century critical discussion of English fiction. The rise of the novel in the eighteenth century was closely related to the emergence of a prosperous urban middle class, as Ian Watt has shown,[8] and the heroes and heroines of the English realist tradition are not kings and queens, or knights and ladies of the court, but ordinary people, often of middle and sometimes of lower rank, whose literary antecedents include Everyman and Bunyan's Christian in *Pilgrim's Progress*. Although all plots are variations on only a small number of archetypal stories, the very name of the novel asserts its newness, one aspect of which is its generating of numberless new characters who, whether major or minor, are thought worthy of our attention. The novel, which adopts and secularizes many of the conventions of Puritan spiritual autobiographies and exemplary 'lives' of the seventeenth century, also treats the individual 'soul', of whatever rank, as being inherently significant.

The philosophical roots of eighteenth-century realism are Lockean, and in one of the most important recent studies on the realistic imagination in the nineteenth century George Levine reminds us that realism is 'a mode that depends heavily on our commonsense expectation that there are direct connections between word and thing'.[9] The several different uses of the word 'realism' in mid-Victorian criticism, however, apply to a variety of literary categories.[10] In terms of subject-matter, for example, realism could mean simply the depiction of modern life (for Masson one defining characteristic of the novel itself). More specifically, and particularly later in the nineteenth century, realist novelists were those whose subject-matter was offensive. Alternatively realism meant a type of minute description, or simply the dull opposite of the imaginative in fiction. All these definitions are related to the writer's (impossible) attempt to depict everyday things as they are 'actually and historically', in Masson's terms – a concept which itself begs several philosophical questions.

David Masson's book, in which he contrasted the Real school and the Ideal school of nineteenth-century fiction, was published in the same year as George Eliot's first novel, *Adam Bede* (1859), so he could not include in his discussion the writer whose work represents the high point of Victorian realistic fiction. G. H. Lewes claimed that realism ennobled a low subject and best treated a high one, and in George Eliot's fiction the mundane is raised to a high level of sanctity, but – crucially – without reference to the supernatural. Her fiction investigates the problem of moral choice in a world without God; and the kinds of *selection* from 'reality' – now a more elusive concept – made by herself as author and by her characters, reflect the nature of that problem. Following her death, however, the so-called 'new realists' of the 1880s shifted the argument away from morality. Gissing and George Moore, literary artists whose primary concerns were aesthetic, emphasized the need for minute accuracy of detail and a willingness to portray the ugly in their defence of realism, while for the most part rejecting what they considered to be the brutalism of Zola's naturalism.

It was also in the 1880s that the romance revival, led by R. L. Stevenson, challenged the assumptions of the new realists, substituting vision (which George Eliot's realism had formerly preserved) for their observation, and, in tales of adventure, turning its back on modern life in Europe and setting sail for foreign parts. The critical debate between realism and romance in the Victorian period (the main subject of my last chapter) revives the issues discussed in the early years of the Victorian period (the subject of Ch. 2). For example, the honorific terms of the writers of romance in the 1880s – romanticism, idealism, imagination, wonder, vision – are strongly reminiscent of Carlyle's key words in his critique of Utilitarianism in the early 1830s, when he argued that the 'dynamical' in thought, religion, and education must be developed, thus redressing the current imbalance towards the 'mechanical' in human life and institutions, and that the 'unconscious' must be nurtured in a too conscious age. Behind Carlyle, and equally influential upon Victorian fiction, was Sir Walter Scott, the first fully professional British novelist, and the first to be honoured with a title. Scott is the prime example of a writer whose realism 'completes' his romance, in the presentation of both Highland individualism and Lowland law-abiding attitudes, or in the tension in his work between disruptive and restraining forces.[11] Certainly his central concern is with the moral decisions of individual members of a complex society, and in this he prepared the ground for Victorian realism.

Like Jane Austen's social comedies, which were to influence Trollope, Elizabeth Gaskell, and George Eliot later in the century, Scott's finest Waverley novels were published in the post-Revolutionary era of the Regency. The 'Romantic impulse' in Victorian fiction[12] is rooted not only in the prose of Scott and Carlyle, however, but also in the Romantic poetry of the first two decades of the century. John Speirs argues that the 'poetic imaginativeness' which distinguishes nineteenth-century novelists from those of the eighteenth century reflects the response of Victorian writers to Shakespeare and to Romantic poetry.[13] Moreover, the realism/romance bifurcation we find in Scott and Victorian fiction is also present in some of the seminal works of English Romantic poetry. Coleridge's account, for example, of his and Wordsworth's intentions in writing the *Lyrical Ballads* (1798), suggests more interesting parallels with Victorian fiction than with Victorian poetry: 'The thought suggested itself . . . that a series of poems might be composed of two sorts. In the one [Coleridge's], the incidents and agents were to be, in part at least, supernatural. . . . For the second class [Wordsworth's], subjects were to be chosen from ordinary life' (*Biographia Literaria*, 1817; 14). Wordsworth, the poet of common or ordinary life, and of domestic realism (as in 'Michael'), did not share Coleridge's enthusiasm for German supernatural tales, and even thought of removing his friend's 'Ancient Mariner' from the second edition of *Lyrical Ballads*, believing that it had adversely affected the reception of the first. At the heart of Romantic poetry's most famous collaborative experiment, then, is the dichotomy between realism and romance, between a poetic of common life and the Gothic,[14] which was also to characterize the fiction of the Victorian age.

Fiction, however, has always been a more popular form than poetry, and in the nineteenth century the novel was generally considered to be primarily for entertainment.[15] This helps to explain the opposition of Evangelicalism to the novel early in the century, and the slowness with which it was accepted as a serious literary genre. A second function – the novel as a vehicle for moral teaching – to some extent answered the Evangelical critics of the genre, and became the primary critical touchstone in the third quarter of the century. Moralism in Victorian fiction is conveyed largely through the commentary of authorial narrators and through judgements enacted in the plot, and particularly in the endings of novels. It is typified in Thackeray's and Trollope's descriptions of themselves as preachers to their own generation, and of their novels as (entertaining) sermons. In a period which produced its own prophets or sages, such as Carlyle and J. S. Mill, Ruskin and Matthew Arnold, George Eliot's own *Wise, Witty, and Tender Sayings* (1872) were published during her lifetime, and the intrusive authorial voice in fiction, which directly addressed the 'dear reader', was the subject of much critical controversy. The more astringent moralists among the novelists, such as Thackeray and Meredith, adopt Carlylean metaphors of stripping and laying bare in their judgements upon hypocrisy and corruption, and all three writers draw upon eighteenth-century satirical traditions in their writing. It is significant that actual trials in courts of law figure in many nineteenth-century novels, including *Paul Clifford*, *Pickwick Papers*, *Bleak House*, *Mary Barton*, *Alton Locke*, and *Felix Holt*. In his descriptions of Magwitch's trial in *Great Expectations* (1860–61), Pip places the judge's death sentence in a larger perspective by invoking the Last Judgement (see p. 102 below). In Pip's very act, however, of handing judgement of Magwitch over to the highest authority, Dickens still exercises authorial control over both his fictional narrator and Magwitch. In other words, he plays God in relation to his own creatures, a feature of Victorian fiction on which John Fowles comments in *The French Lieutenant's Woman* (1969; 12–13). I will return to this theme when I contrast novelists of the same period within the Victorian Age – *Wuthering Heights* is anarchically non-judgemental in contrast to *Jane Eyre*, for example – and when tracing the gradual shift later in the century away from George Eliot's higher morality and towards the comparative neutrality of R. L. Stevenson as authorial narrator. For by the 1880s the third broad concept of the novel's function – as a vehicle for ideas – had gained ground on earlier emphases upon entertainment and moral improvement.

The didacticism of earlier Victorian fiction was not simply moral and dogmatic, and here it is worth citing a critic whose statement in the *Prospective Review* of April 1853 also suggests further continuities between Romantic poetry and the nineteenth-century novel. Fiction, he writes, 'conjures up an ideal world in the midst of our prosaic realities, and men, absorbed in selfish interests, are awakened to more generous sympathies, and their hearts, severed in the turmoil of the world, find a bond of fellowship by the creation of the *poet*' (my emphasis).[16] Both Elizabeth

Gaskell and George Eliot consciously aimed to awaken their readers to more generous sympathies, and both believed in what Keats described as 'the holiness of the heart's affections'. The critic's words, however, apply most suggestively to Dickens, whose ideal women, for example, are often hard to stomach for the twentieth-century reader. What we must remember is that like many other novelists of his time, Dickens portrayed not only the kind of fallen human beings we know in ourselves and in those with whom we live, but also the kind of human being we might ideally be.

The severing of men's hearts in the turmoil of the world was a central Victorian theme, and, as I suggested earlier, successive generations of novelists addressed themselves to the changing relationship between the inner life of feeling and the outer world of action in society. In a newly industrialized age novelists examined the growing conflicts between the individual human will and socially determining factors such as heredity, class, and environment – the circumstances which modify the development of a single life.[17] Among early Victorian novelists, for example, Thackeray and Edward Bulwer argue that respectable law-abiding behaviour is the privilege only of those born into certain social classes. Dickens's social vision becomes increasingly deterministic. Whereas Mr Pickwick moves freely between towns and villages which are quite separate communities, and which together make up no identifiable society, the various settings in Dickens's novels of mid-career, although distant from each other topographically, are closely linked or even 'chained' together through symbolism and plot. In *Little Dorrit* (1855–57), for example, it is as if the nation itself is enchained and imprisoned; and the space in which the hero and heroine must attempt to live is terribly constricted.

Imprisonment – physical, psychological, or spiritual – is a central metaphor not only in Dickens's novels but in Victorian fiction generally, and is applied not only to social problems but also to personal relationships, in courtship and marriage, and in family life. In the Brontës' novels the physical confinement of the heroine often reflects her sense of spiritual imprisonment in a hostile environment which is shaped and controlled by men. Whereas Charlotte Brontë's female pilgrims in a barren land seek a limited freedom within the bounds of Christian doctrine and ethics, Emily Brontë's *Wuthering Heights* represents a more radical attempt to achieve liberation from a confining and (in Joseph's case) vindictively judgemental religious scheme. The ideals of George Eliot's heroines, on the other hand, are hampered by the accumulated constraints of the real, as they attempt either to redeem or to escape from the oppressive narrowness of the domestic environment which imprisons them. The characteristic pilgrim figure of Dickens, the Brontës, and George Eliot gives way in late Victorian fiction to the explorer figure, in a more dangerous and uncertain world. Gissing, for example, is a social explorer in the hell-on-earth that is the East End, where his characters are caught in a vicious circle or downward spiral of poverty, from which there can be no escape. Gissing's grim determinism can be compared to that of Hardy, whose tragic vision in his later novels is mediated through repetitive plots and images of confinement and enclosure, suggesting that the trapped protagonists inhabit a universe which is not neutral, but actively malevolent.

Whereas Dickens and the Brontës, Elizabeth Gaskell and George Eliot offer different and often extremely limited degrees of freedom and hope of transcendence, Gissing and Hardy are deeply pessimistic writers, working in a later period in which nations, and social groups and centres of power within nations, seemed increasingly intransigent in their antagonisms. The movement in Victorian fiction away from the mediation of social reality through the consciousness of a hero or heroine, whose fate is ultimately secure in the hands of a God-like author-narrator, and towards tragic schemes in which the universe is either neutral or hostile, reflects a decline in both individualism and the possibility of social salvation. Dickens's ironic treatment of Pip's social advancement in *Great Expectations* can be read as a critique of his own *David Copperfield*, in which the hero's apotheosis was blissful married life with a saint. Darwin's observations on the determining influence of environment on plants and animals had a profoundly disturbing effect upon later Victorian writers. In an age in which the word 'progress' encapsulated the secular teleology of historians such as Macaulay, of populist biographers such as Samuel Smiles, and of philosophers and social scientists such as the social Darwinists, the Victorian novelists' treatment of the individual and society constantly reopened the question: Progress towards what, and measured by whom?

This change from a providential scheme in a world of shared values, where the central character undergoes some kind of pilgrimage,[18] to a less stable world in which explorers venture into darkest Africa or darkest London, is reflected in the use of allusion and received literary and biblical models in the fiction. The linear plotting of *Jane Eyre*, for example, suggests parallels with Bunyan's *Pilgrim's Progress*; and the title of *Vanity Fair* is drawn from Bunyan's classic work, although the end of Thackeray's novel holds out no hope of a Celestial City as the destination for his puppets. Other Christian concepts and models, such as conversion, confession, and transcendence, are also adopted in both secular and religious fiction. Drawing upon the familiar texts of a shared Christian culture – the Book of Common Prayer, the Authorized Version of the Bible, the *Pilgrim's Progress*, and the better known passages in *Paradise Lost* – as well as Shakespeare's plays, Wordsworth's poetry, and translations of the *Arabian Nights*, most Victorian novelists before George Eliot and Meredith, wrote for the many rather than the few. But whereas the earlier novelists quoted or referred to works which were familiar to a wide range of readers, later novelists used allusion more self-consciously and uncertainly, and less directly.[19] Thus changes in the cultural, thematic, and structural uses of allusion reflect some of the changes in both the novel and the age which I have outlined in this introduction. In its many types and varieties, as well as in its greatest practitioners, the Victorian novel reflects the energy and vitality of an age which witnessed more rapid and disturbing social and intellectual change than any other period before or since, as I hope to show in the following chapters.

Notes

1. See J. A. Sutherland, *Victorian Novelists and Publishers* (London, 1976), to which I am indebted. This and other studies on readership, publication, and reception are listed on pp. 220–21 below.

2. In Thomas Morton's play *Speed the Plough* (1798), reference is often made to Mrs Grundy's views, although she herself never appears on stage.

3. C. M. Law's figures, quoted in Geoffrey Best, *Mid-Victorian Britain, 1851–1875* (1971; repr. Frogmore, 1973), p. 24.

4. See, for example, R. K. Webb, 'The Victorian Reading Public', in *From Dickens to Hardy*, edited by Boris Ford, New Pelican Guide to English Literature, vol. 6 (Harmondsworth, 1982), p. 206.

5. See David Masson, *British Novelists and their Styles: Being a Critical Sketch of the History of British Prose Fiction* (Cambridge, 1859), pp. 26–7.

6. Masson, pp. 248–9.

7. Masson, p. 250.

8. See Ian Watt, *The Rise of the Novel: Studies in Defoe, Richardson, and Fielding* (1957; repr. Harmondsworth, 1963), pp. 42–51.

9. George Levine, *The Realistic Imagination: English Fiction from Frankenstein to Lady Chatterley* (Chicago and London, 1981), p. 9.

10. David Skilton assembles a list of eight uses in *Anthony Trollope and his Contemporaries: A Study in the Theory and Conventions of Mid-Victorian Fiction* (London, 1972), pp. 149–52.

11. See Donald D. Stone, *The Romantic Impulse in Victorian Fiction* (Cambridge, Mass. and London, 1980), p. 12; Robert Kiely, *The Romantic Novel in England* (Cambridge, Mass., 1972), p. 151.

12. See Stone, *The Romantic Impulse in Victorian Fiction*.

13. John Speirs, *Poetry Towards Novel* (London, 1971), p. 11.

14. For George Eliot and Elizabeth Gaskell, Wordsworth was the great Romantic precursor. Yet both novelists refer to Mary Shelley's *Frankenstein* at crucial points in their fiction, and Levine makes this seminal Gothic novel the starting-point for his study of nineteenth-century realism (*The Realistic Imagination*, p. 24).

15. When examining the new seriousness and the emphasis on 'thought' in late Victorian fiction of the 1880s, Kenneth Graham adds: 'The idea of the novel as pure entertainment died hard, nevertheless.' *English Criticism of the Novel, 1865–1900* (Oxford, 1965), p. 10.

16. See Richard Stang, *The Theory of the Novel in England, 1850–1870* (New York and London, 1959), pp. 65–6.

17. See, for example, Raymond Williams, *The English Novel: From Dickens to Lawrence* (1970; repr. Frogmore, 1974) and Maurice Larkin, *Man and Society in*

Nineteenth-Century Realism: Determinism and Literature (London and Basingstoke, 1977). See also p. 68 below, on 'environment'.

18. See Barry V. Qualls, *The Secular Pilgrims of Victorian Fiction: The Novel as Book of Life* (Cambridge, 1982), and M. H. Abrams, *Natural Supernaturalism: Tradition and Revolution in Romantic Literature* (New York and London, 1971).

19. See Michael Wheeler, *The Art of Allusion in Victorian Fiction* (London, 1979).

Chapter 2
Pre-Victorian and Early Victorian Fiction

Fads and fashions

Social and political historians of Britain, like historians of English literature, find the 1830s difficult to place. A decade of invention and reform, the 1830s mark the transition between the end of the Industrial Revolution and the beginning of the Victorian Age. Signs of the times – the title of Carlyle's prophetic essay of 1829 – included Darwin's voyage on the *Beagle* (1832–36), the beginning of the Oxford Movement (1833), Fox Talbot's early experiments in photography (1835) and Brunel's *Great Western* crossing the Atlantic (1838). Yet those who lived in the decade which saw the beginning of the railway boom, soon to change the face of Britain, were still dependent upon older modes of transport; manners and fashions were still variations upon Regency themes; and many of the great changes which later generations were to see in their daily lives were as yet only in embryo.

British cultural life was also in a transitional state in the 1830s and early 1840s. Turner was still at the height of his powers as a Romantic artist when David Wilkie and William Mulready were developing what was later to be a flourishing 'genre' tradition of Victorian narrative painting, in which everyday life was realistically depicted. In architecture, the opposing forces in the so-called Battle of the Styles, which was to rage between Gothic and Classical schools throughout the mid-nineteenth century, were being drawn up. The early experimental work of the two greatest mid-Victorian poets, Tennyson and Browning, was strongly influenced by Keats and Shelley; and the early careers of Carlyle, J. S. Mill, Sterling, and F. D. Maurice were shaped partly by their different responses to the ideas of Coleridge. But there were also discontinuities. Although Scott's influence on Victorian fiction was profound, no Victorian successor was to approach him as a historical novelist. Jane Austen's influence upon *early* Victorian fiction was minimal. Indeed, the early work of Dickens represents a new start in nineteenth-century fiction. The re-emergence, however, of the monthly part novel, with *Pickwick Papers*, was not the only innovation in a period of experiment. For example, some of the most interesting experiments in prose narrative were published in *Fraser's Magazine* (founded 1830), including Thackeray's early stories and parodies, and Carlyle's *Sartor Resartus* (1833–34), a work which profoundly influenced the development of Victorian fiction. The Life and Opinions of Diogenes Teu-felsdröckh, a German professor, are mediated through a form of frag-mented spiritual autobiography, arranged in some sort of order by the Editor. *Sartor Resartus* explores themes which many later novelists take up, such as education, the idea of pilgrimage, the alienation of the individual in a modern society, and the plight of the poor. Ironically, Carlyle himself tried to persuade every novelist of any merit with whom he came in contact to give up writing fiction and concentrate on history and biography.

Carlyle can perhaps be forgiven for dismissing most of the fiction of the 1830s and early 1840s as inferior stuff, for, apart from the work of Dickens and Thackeray, this was a period of fads and fashions rather than of major developments in the novel. The variety of sub-genres of fiction in vogue – historical, silver-fork, Newgate and social-problem, marine, sporting, and Irish rogue novels – puts one in mind of Polonius's generic divisions and sub-divisions in *Hamlet*: 'tragedy, comedy, history, pastoral, pastoral-comical, historical-pastoral', and so on. The pedigrees of these sub-genres, however, were very short indeed when compared to those of Polonius's list of classical forms. Significantly, much of Thackeray's early fiction was revisionary in purpose and parodic in method, and his position *vis-à-vis* at least five of the sub-genres mentioned above is encapsulated in the famous burlesques published as 'Punch's Prize Novelists' (1847) at the end of this first phase of pre-Victorian and early Victorian fiction. On the whole one would rather take the burlesques to a desert island than the novels he parodies – a sad reflection of the quality of the minor fiction pro-duced over the previous fifteen or twenty years.

One of Thackeray's burlesques, entitled '"Barbazure", by G. P. R. Jeames, Esq., Etc.', parodies the hugely popular historical romances of the prolific G. P. R. James, whose works were read and indeed imitated by Marian Evans, later 'George Eliot', as a schoolgirl. Several features of James's romances, such as his ponderous archaisms and intense interest in costume detail, neatly captured by Thackeray in 'a surcoat of peach-coloured samite and a purfled doublet of vair bespoke him noble', and his predilection for executions by the axe (Thackeray: 'the hideous minister of vengeance, masked and in black, with the flaming glaive in his hand, was ready'), are shared by the equally popular historical romances of William Harrison Ainsworth. In *The Tower of London* (1840), for example, whose central figure is Lady Jane Grey, Ainsworth catered for the English history cult of the time.[1] His lurid tale of intrigue, rackings, and beheadings un-folds in the precisely documented setting of the Tower, whose history down to the nineteenth century is a major theme of the work. Although Ainsworth's fast-moving stories are tempered with this curious obsession for antiquarian detail, he is probably best remembered for the striking set pieces in the early works, such as Dick Turpin's ride to York on Black Bess in *Rookwood* (1834), a Newgate historical romance, or the descriptions of the plague pits and the Great Fire in *Old St. Paul's* (1841). A master of hyperbolic description and racy narrative, Ainsworth had no ear for spoken English, and the dialogue in his novels is stilted.

Although much more impressive than Ainsworth in his scope and

intellectual range, Edward Bulwer (later Bulwer-Lytton) is often as weak in
the rendering of direct speech, which is infected by the inflated mannerism
and encyclopaedic allusiveness of his narrative style. Bulwer's research into
the periods in which his romances are set was intended to improve on Scott
in the matter of historical accuracy, but the documentary density of his
work is achieved at the expense of clarity in the development of plot and
character. Like his contributions to other sub-genres, Bulwer's historical
romances are more significant as literary-historical documents than as living
fiction. Under the influence of Carlyle, Bulwer specifically focuses on the
tragic sacrifice of individuals in the broad scheme of the progress of Western
civilization, and, at a time when the old order was changing in England,
emphasizes the endings of historical eras. Consider, for example, *The Last
Days of Pompeii* (1834), *The Last of the Barons* (1843), and the final words
of *Rienzi* (1835): 'THE LAST OF THE ROMAN TRIBUNES'.[2]

Bulwer also played an important role in the development of the fashionable or 'silver-fork' novel, a sub-genre which flourished in the second
quarter of the century. The other main exponents were Disraeli, whose
Vivian Grey appeared in 1826–27, Theodore Hook, Lady Blessington, and
Mrs Gore, and their common theme was high-society manners, a subject
of great interest in a period of social mobility.[3] At a time when new specu-
lative money was in circulation among the rapidly expanding middle-class
nouveaux riches (also the subject of much of Thackeray's early fiction), Bulwer believed that the interest in this most popular sub-genre of the 1830s
was based on a combination of emulation and envy:

> In proportion as the aristocracy had become social, and
> fashion allowed the members of the more mediocre classes a
> hope to outstep the boundaries of fortune, and be quasi-
> aristocrats themselves, people eagerly sought for
> representations of the manners which they aspired to imitate,
> and the circles to which it was not impossible to belong. But
> as with emulation discontent also was mixed, as many hoped
> to be called and few found themselves chosen, so a satire on
> the follies and vices of the great gave additional piquancy to
> the description of their lives.
>
> *England and the English* (1833; IV. 2)

The elaborate discussions on the cultivation of *ton*, the detailed exactness
of the descriptions of furnishings, food, and fashions as guides to people's
position in high society, and the superficiality of the characters portrayed
in the silver-fork novel made it an easy target for critics and novelists who
had higher ambitions for English fiction. Bulwer's *Pelham* (1828) – chiefly
remembered as the novel which was said to have initiated the fashion of
black evening dress for men – was the butt of Carlyle's mockery in *Sartor
Resartus*. Missing both the irony of the novel and the earnestness of its hero,
Carlyle wrote a stinging parody entitled 'The Dandiacal Body' as part of
his treatment of the Philosophy of Clothes – Professor Teufelsdröckh's theory that all external forms are merely clothes, and thus temporary and

ultimately irrelevant. Again, parodies of the silver-fork novel, such as Thackeray's burlesque on Mrs Gore ('"Lords and Liveries", by the Authoress of "Dukes and Déjeuners", "Hearts and Diamonds", "Marchionesses and Milliners", Etc. Etc.'), and Dickens's extract from the fictitious 'The Lady Flabella', read to Mrs Wititterly by Kate Nickleby (*Nicholas Nickleby*, 1838–39; 28) are more enduring than the sub-genre itself. This brittle, artificial fiction of the *beau monde* did, however, provide material with which later novelists could work. One thinks, for example, of Dickens's portrayal of the 'brilliant and distinguished circle' that assembles at Chesney Wold, where 'all the mirrors in the house are brought into action' (*Bleak House*, 1852–53; 12), and of his recurrent assaults on snobbery and the development of a highly polished 'surface' as a symptom of Victorian hypocrisy. Later, Meredith's Sir Willoughby Patterne, the statuesque, dandified master of Patterne Hall in *The Egoist* (1879), is a living, or partly living example of that particular breed of the English male which emerged most prominently in the Restoration and the Regency, and in the silver-fork novel and Wildean drawing-room comedy, in which civilization withers into matters of taste and style.

Bulwer and Ainsworth also explored romance possibilities offered by the criminal classes at the other end of the social scale in their 'Newgate' novels, originally a term of critical abuse.[4] The romanticized criminal, and particularly the highwayman (an anti-establishment loner who did the city-dweller no harm), captured the imagination of readers brought up on the Gothic novel, and the dark shadow of the gallows in the background added a *frisson* for the morbidly curious. The sub-genre marks a revival of interest in the exploits of those who figured in the popular Newgate Calendar, including such notables as Dick Turpin and Jack Sheppard (both subjects of Ainsworth's novels), and of criminals like the eighteenth-century scholar-murderer Eugene Aram and the famous poisoner Wainewright, the subjects of Bulwer's novels *Eugene Aram* (1832) and *Lucretia* (1846).

Although Bulwer's novels have not stood the test of time, the fact that he strongly influenced several different sub-genres of fiction in the 1830s is certainly impressive, and his *Paul Clifford* (1830) was both the first Newgate novel and the first influential novel of our period with a social reforming purpose. Brought up in a low drinking house in London, the illegitimate Paul is wrongly imprisoned for picking the pocket of a barrister, William Brandon, who later turns out to be his father. Having made his escape from the Bridewell, our hero spends seven years as a highwayman, passes himself off as a member of high society, and wins the heart of Lucy Brandon, a young lady who proves to be his cousin. When finally arrested, Paul is sentenced to death by his father, now a judge, who dies soon after the trial, having learnt the identity of the criminal. All ends happily and improbably with Paul's sentence commuted to transportation and his marriage to Lucy in America. In later life Paul is wont to say: 'Circumstances make guilt, ... let us endeavour to *correct the circumstances*, before we rail against the guilt!' (36). Far more noble than the 'gentlemen' whose watches he steals, he epitomizes Bulwer's moral that 'there is nothing essentially different between vulgar vice and fashionable vice' (1840 Preface).

As a polemic against what Bulwer calls 'a vicious prison-discipline, and a sanguinary criminal code' the novel is limited, making its Godwinian point about circumstances only in the broadest way, and scarcely documenting low life or imaginatively entering the criminal mind at all. Although the mannered style of the narrative often registers class divisions with a wittiness which is sorely lacking in the heavyweight social-problem novels published twenty years later, its overall effect works against any sense of a serious engagement with the theme of crime and punishment. As in so many of Bulwer's novels, the leading ideas which prompted the writing of the book are in practice subordinated to romance plotting.

Bulwer's next Newgate novel, the popular *Eugene Aram*, became the main focus of the controversy surrounding the sub-genre, for its hero was a real murderer. The main assault on Bulwer came from *Fraser's Magazine*, initially in the hostile criticism of his work by the editor, William Maginn, and then in Thackeray's first long serialized work of fiction, *Catherine* (1839–40), written to shame his readers into recognizing the folly of romanticizing crime and the criminal by presenting them with the sordid reality. (Although *Oliver Twist* (1837–39) was later claimed to be similarly concerned with the 'miserable reality' of the life of thieves (1841 Preface), Thackeray considered that Dickens, like Ainsworth, had made his criminals too attractive.) Bulwer was still Thackeray's target in his *Punch* burlesque entitled '"George de Barnwell", by Sir E. L. B. L., Bart.'. Interestingly, however, as the idealist Bulwer himself looked back over the period in which the realist Thackeray had attacked him, he wrote: 'The true movement of the last fifteen years has been the progress of one idea, – Social Reform' (Preface to 1848 edition of *Paul Clifford*). This movement is reflected in the fourth important sub-genre of the period, the 'social-problem' novel.

The reformist measures which followed the first Reform Act of 1832, such as the Factory Act or 'Children's Charter' (1833) and the Poor Law Amendment Act (1834), were launched on a sea of paper: parliamentary reports, or 'blue books', political tracts, newspaper articles, and social-reform literature which pressed for reform and lamented the inadequacy of legislation actually brought in. The stock themes and conventions of the social-problem novel were adumbrated in the reformist poetry of the 1830s and 1840s by Caroline Bowles, Lady Caroline Norton, and Thomas Hood: the yawning gulf between rich and poor, the inhumanity of the new factories and workhouses, and the scandal of pauper burials; the abandoned 'fallen women', the worn-out sempstresses, and the beggar dying in the snow. Harriet Martineau's *Illustrations of Political Economy* (1832–34) are, as their title suggests, tales whose literary pretensions were subordinate to their author's main aim of instruction. It is, however, significant that Harriet Martineau is the third female writer of reformist literature mentioned so far, for women played a crucial role in the literary crusade against the exploitation of the working classes which characterized the English Industrial Revolution. In Frances Trollope's novel on the abuses of child labour, *Michael Armstrong, the Factory Boy* (1839–40), it is the wealthy Mary

Brotherton who investigates the evils of Sir Matthew Dowling's factories, and in *Jessie Phillips* (1842–43) the seduction of the sempstress heroine and the murder of her illegitimate baby typify the way in which the exploitation of women was presented by the social-problem novelists. This last theme recurs in *Helen Fleetwood* (1839–40) and *The Wrongs of Woman* (1843–44) by the earnest Charlotte Elizabeth Tonna, and in *William Langshawe, the Cotton-Lord* (1842) and *The Young Milliner* (1843) by the little known novelist Elizabeth Stone (*fl.* 1840–73), whose work influenced Elizabeth Gaskell's *Mary Barton* (1848); and it was later to become a central theme of much major Victorian fiction.[5]

These early novels and stories, however, tend to exaggerate the evils they expose by focusing exclusively on extreme cases, sometimes giving the impression that factories were piled high with human limbs wrenched off by machines or rapacious overseers. They tend to sentimentalize the poor, thus treating the working class monolithically, and are often documented with ponderous footnotes in the style of the blue book. Their significance lies in the fact that they began the process of educating middle- and upper-class novel-readers, many of whom had formerly been quite ignorant of what was going on in the manufacturing areas of Britain. Although extremely weak as imaginative works of fiction, they also prepared the ground for those novelists of the later 1840s and the 1850s – Disraeli, Elizabeth Gaskell, Charles Kingsley, and Dickens – who dramatically raised the standard of writing in the sub-genre, responding to Carlyle's warning in his long essay on *Chartism* (1839) that 'if something be not done, something will *do* itself one day, and in a fashion that will please nobody' (1).

Apart from the four main sub-genres of the first phase we are considering, much of the minor fiction of the time is characterized by a strong emphasis on action and adventure, often treated in a broadly humorous manner.[6] Captain Marryat wrote his tales of the sea in an era in which famous voyages of exploration and scientific research were made, such as those of Sir John Franklin and the young Charles Darwin, and in which Kinglake's *Eothen* (1844) and George Borrow's *The Bible in Spain* (1843) were published. Although there is simply too much incident crammed into too many short chapters in *Peter Simple* (1832–33), a novel concerned mainly with external events rather than the development of characters, the work is unique in the charming innocence of its first-person narrator, who is exposed to the rigours of life in the British navy. *Mr Midshipman Easy* (1836) was popular with young readers, and so *Masterman Ready* (1841–42) and the famous historical novel, *The Children of the New Forest* (1847), were written specially for them. The rivalry between the army and the navy of this period, and between the novelists who wrote about life in the two services, is nicely placed by Thackeray in 'The Tremendous Adventures of Major Gahagan' (1838–39), a ludicrously exaggerated account of the military and amorous exploits of an old Indian army hand, when the Major dismisses his adventures at sea in a single sentence: 'The writers of marine novels have so exhausted the subject of storms, shipwrecks, mutinies, engagements, sea-sickness, and so forth, that . . . I think it quite unnecessary to recount such trifling adventures' (1). Thackeray's brilliant *Punch* burlesque on Charles Lever's novels about the adventures of his roguish Irish heroes in the army – '"Phil Fogarty: A Tale of the Fighting Onety-Oneth", by Harry Rollicker' – was so devastating that poor Lever decided he could not repeat the formula of his highly popular works like *Harry Lorrequer* (1837) and *Charles O'Malley* (1840), and actually changed direction as a novelist, later writing provincial and historical novels on Ireland on the lines of Scott and Maria Edgeworth. The rollicking heroes of the early novels dash headlong into battle, not only in engagements with the enemy but also in their duelling and love-making, stumbling from one comic scrape to another. The jollity of Lever's work is matched by that of the sporting novelists, and especially of Surtees, whose *Jorrocks' Jaunts and Jollities* (1831–34) and *Handley Cross* (1843) have a limited comic appeal in their way. *Jorrocks* was the kind of sporting novel Dickens might have written instead of *Pickwick Papers*, had he agreed to write his text specifically to accompany the plates of Seymour, his first illustrator; and his early fiction is in general closer in tone to the broad humour of the sporting novel and the Irish rogue novel than to the bizarre ironic humour of *Sartor Resartus*, or the kind of corrosive satirical humour fostered in *Fraser's*. It is to one of that magazine's early staff members, Thackeray, that we now briefly turn.

Gamblers and speculators: early Thackeray

In the 1830s, a transitional decade in the history of English literature, the young Thackeray experimented with a variety of forms and techniques in the fiction and journalism by which he earned his living. He was already something of an expert in the subject of insecurity, both emotional and financial, in his own life, and spent much time abroad in this era of social and political change in Europe, later writing accounts of his tours in the form of travel books. He created characters in his early fiction whose main ambition is to change their lives through some kind of significant movement: to travel across land and sea, or to move up the social scale, in either case having an eye to the main chance. Thackeray portrays a world in which the conventions of speculation at the gambling table and in the marriage market are conflated, as the social climber rises and falls and the self-willed adventurer forces his way to fame and fortune.

Thackeray's experiments with different narrative techniques are more varied and inventive than those of his contemporaries, and suggest a sustained interest in observing the social hierarchy from a wide variety of angles.[7] In James Plush, for example, a semi-literate butler who makes and loses a fortune by investing in railway shares, Thackeray dramatizes the conflict between natural affection (his love for Mary Ann Hoggins) and a sense of social propriety (his view of what is expected of a 'man of rank'). James attends a dinner for one of the 'Welsh bords of Direction', and hears 'Pore Mary Hann' played on the Welsh harp: 'The clarrit holmost choaked me as I tried it, and I very nearly wep myself as I thought of her bewtifle blue i's. Why ham I always thinkin about that gal? Sasiety is sasiety, it's lors is irresistabl. Has a man of rank I can't marry a serving-made' (*The Diary of C. Jeames de la Pluche, Punch*, 1845–46). After ruin and imprisonment, James find happiness as landlord to the aptly named Wheel of Fortune hotel, married to his beloved Mary. In the course of his rise and fall, James both shares in and exposes the follies and pretensions of the world of the silver-fork novel.

Thackeray's first substantial serial work of fiction, *Catherine: A Story* (*Fraser's*, 1839–40) is more directly aimed at a popular sub-genre, the Newgate novel, in its stated purpose of exposing the sordid realities of one of the lives recorded in the Newgate Calendar. His subject is Catherine Hayes, burned in 1726 for the murder of her husband. We are introduced to the main characters at the Bugle Inn, a hostelry very different from the Merrie England snuggeries of *Pickwick Papers*. Count von Galgenstein, Captain of horse, and Corporal Brock, who sit refreshing themselves in the inn, are unceremoniously described as 'scoundrels', and the shrewish landlady, Mrs Score, and Catherine, the 'idle and extravagant' serving-maid, use all their wiles to entice customers to spend their money, rather than good-heartedly providing a welcome for their guests (1). When 'Cat' goes off with the Count to endure a miserable existence with this gambler and womanizer, Thackeray's persona, Ikey Solomons, who narrates the story, comments on the reading public's taste for rogues, and asks the ladies among his readers to bottle up their tears 'and not waste a single drop of them on any one of the heroes or heroines in this history: they are all rascals, every soul of them' (3). Having outlined the events surrounding the murder of John Hayes at the end of the narrative, dwelling on the fact that his severed head was 'much hacked and mangled' ('Another Last Chapter'), Solomons closes with the observation that his 'poem' has presented 'a scene of unmixed rascality performed by persons who never deviate into good feeling'.

'Good feeling' sounds the keynote to *The Great Hoggarty Diamond* (*Fraser's*, 1841), a work whose tone was consciously intended to be sweet after the harsh discords of *Catherine*. Samuel Titmarsh, a naive clerk who rises in his firm and in society on the flimsy basis of the diamond pin he is given by an aunt, witnesses the follies and corruption of those who serve mammon. Like James Plush, his thoughts constantly revert to his country sweetheart Mary Smith, as he himself rises in London society (1). After the inevitable fall, his marriage to Mary, and the death of their firstborn baby in the Fleet – a debtors' prison – Titmarsh positively welcomes the fact that his wife is able to work as a wet-nurse for Lady Tiptoff and thus support him (13). His response to his powerless position is grounded in love rather than pride and self-will.

A similar transformation is achieved in Thackeray's most ambitious early work, *The Luck of Barry Lyndon* (*Fraser's*, 1844), although here it is not until near the end of his life as an adventurer that the hero records the moment when good feeling overcomes his ambition, on the death of his nine-year-old son in a riding accident (19).[8] We learn in the last chapter that the narrator, now a broken and dying man, is writing in the Fleet. Throughout his narrative Redmond Barry has emphasized the strength of his own will, from the day when he left his native home in Ireland vowing that he would 'never re-enter the place but as a great man', adding 'and I kept my vow too, as you shall hear in due time' (3); in his experiences in the Seven Years War, when he preserved himself from the officers' canings by wearing a bullet around his neck for the man or officer who caused him to be beaten (6); and in his career as a professional gambler on the Continent with his uncle, and his later marriage to Lady Lyndon, whom he heartlessly courts in front of her dying husband, coolly admitting that 'it could not have been very pleasant to him to see a handsome fellow paying court to his widow before his own face as it were' (13). In a clear reference to the Irish rogue novels of Lever, Lover, and others, Redmond Barry points out that his intention to marry a fortune was 'what ten thousand Irish gentlemen have done before'(7). His energy, and the cleverness with which he exploits his devilish good 'luck',[9] are most interestingly portrayed in the middle section of the novel, in which he lives by his prowess at the gambling tables of Europe. Chapter 9, for example, charts in little a rise and fall in fortune within the narrative's overall scheme of a steady rise followed by a calamitous and irreversible fall. Barry and his uncle make a fortune gambling, and at one point accept a chariot in payment, on which they have the family crest painted, surmounted with 'an Irish crown of the most splendid size and gilding'. They then ignominiously lose to some beardless students, are drugged and robbed of everything but their clothes by a phoney count, and, after eighteen months, have to 'begin the world again'. The 'merits and energy' (16) which drive Redmond to begin the world again, and which carry him to the top of the social scale, ruthlessly exclude good feeling, leaving broken hearts and lives in their trail.

For Thackeray, the achievement of a hard clarity in his portrayal of Redmond Barry, the young Irish adventurer, prepared the ground for his creation of the female adventuress *par excellence*, Becky Sharp in *Vanity Fair*, his masterpiece, which will be discussed in the next chapter. By 1845 he had developed his own, often astringent comic style, with which he could expose the squalid reality behind the glamorous mask which the contemporary fictional rascal or adventurer presented to the world. Whereas the lesser writers of his day worked within the conventions of the fashionable sub-genres, such as the historical romance, the silver-fork novel, or the Newgate novel, Thackeray found his literary identity in working against these conventions. As in the careers of other major writers, including Fielding and Jane Austen, the nature of his realism was defined in the process of wrestling with the traditions of his precursors and his rival contemporaries. Characteristically, realism in Thackeray issues out of parody:

The privilege of chroniclers: early Dickens

Like Thackeray, Dickens put down his literary roots in his early days as
a journalist. But whereas Thackeray published much of his early fiction in
Fraser's and later in *Punch*, experimenting with authorial personae and the
use of fictional 'editors' in his work, Dickens made one bold innovation
in revitalizing the part novel in *Pickwick Papers* (1836–37), the form which
was to remain his favourite for the rest of his career. The fascinating story
of Dickens's seizing of the initiative in the planning of *Pickwick* after the
suicide of Seymour, the illustrator for whom the apprentice writer was at
first meant to supply copy, is too complex to recount here[10]; but it perfectly
illustrates Dickens's capacity to improvise, as does his development of Sam
Weller after the dramatic increase in sales which followed that character's
appearance in the fourth number. Dickens was also willing to drop ideas,
as, for example, when he quickly gave up the editorial apparatus of the
Pickwick Club, and later of the Master Humphry figure as the narrator of
The Old Curiosity Shop.
　　Writing much of his early fiction month by month, keeping just ahead
of printers' deadlines during the time that the last numbers of *Pickwick* and
the first monthly instalments of *Oliver Twist* in *Bentley's Miscellany* were
being written concurrently, Dickens established a unique relationship with
his large and increasing readership; and by 1845 he had produced six novels,
only one of which, *Martin Chuzzlewit*, in many ways the best, had proved
a failure with his public. The vitality and flexibility of Dickens's impressionistic prose, and the relish with which he exploited what he called the
privilege of 'chroniclers' to 'enter where they list, to come and go through
keyholes, to ride upon the wind, to overcome, in their soarings up and
down, all obstacles of distance, time, and place' (*Barnaby Rudge*, 9), are only
the most obvious signs of the kind of freedom of invention which took the
reading public by storm. Dickens's overcoming of all the obstacles of distance, time, and place in some of his early novels contrasts sharply with
the more controlled effects of Jane Austen, for example. Although Jane
Austen was clearly aware of encroaching social and political change at the
turn of the nineteenth century, her fictional world seems stable when
compared with that of Thackeray's and Dickens's early work written in
the 1830s and 1840s. The irony of the authorial narrator in her novels is
'stable' in Wayne Booth's sense, being intended, covert, fixed, and finite.[11]
The strata of her society are so precisely determined and universally known
that a young lady's fortune can be read off as an index to her proper rank
in the marriage market, though special beauty and social charm can also
promote her. Above all, however, it is Jane Austen's sense of place which
suggests stability, and particularly the setting of the action in a single family
house or a small number of such houses. Although she takes her characters
away from these houses to particular locations, such as the wilderness at

Sotherton, or Box Hill, or the Cobb at Lyme Regis, in order to show them reacting to some extraordinary set of events, and intruders also play important roles in unsettling households, most of the limited action in her novels occurs within the confines of fixed and comparatively stable *loci*, allowing her to concentrate on the inner lives and relationships of her characters.

It is significant that whereas Jane Austen learnt most from Richardson's epistolary novels, the young Dickens drew on his boyhood reading of other eighteenth-century English novelists, and particularly Smollett, who worked in the picaresque tradition of Cervantes's *Don Quixote* and Le Sage's *Gil Blas*.[12] 'We who have lived before railways were made', Thackeray once wrote, 'belong to another world',[13] and it is no coincidence that Dickens's novels which preceded *Dombey and Son* (1846–48), in which the new railways figure, are clearly definable as early Dickens, the Dickens of coach journeys, country inns, and coach offices. The loose picaresque structure of *Pickwick Papers*, a work which has been described as a 'miscellany',[14] allows the narrative to bowl along like the coaches it describes, leaving many of the proliferating minor characters of the work behind, as it were – economically placed by Dickens, usually by reference to some ruling passion or idiosyncrasy, but fixed and, perforce, undeveloped. Journeys are one of the most important controlling metaphors in Dickens's early novels. At first improvised, Pickwick's tours are later more directed and purposeful, and in subsequent novels Dickens adapts the fictional possibilities of the journey motif to a more direct treatment of the evils of the world.

On the first of Pickwick's five coaching tours he is accompanied to Rochester on his vaguely defined quest for knowledge of the world by the three younger members of the newly formed Corresponding Society of the Pickwick Club, Tupman, Snodgrass, and Winkle, and meets the loquacious itinerant actor, Jingle, an eccentric and brilliant conversational improviser. By the time he sets off on his second tour, to Eatanswill in Suffolk, Pickwick has visited Dingley Dell, engaged Sam Weller as his servant, and been discovered by his friends with the fainting Mrs Bardell in his arms. During the second tour, Pickwick and Sam actively pursue the impostor Jingle, and later make their third tour, to Ipswich, specifically in search of him. As Pickwick becomes increasingly engaged in trying to right wrongs which he at first encountered by chance, and to grapple with Mrs Bardell's crooked lawyers, Dodson and Fogg, Dickens develops the major sub-plot of Sam's below-stairs life which runs in parallel with his master's; and the three Pickwickians become less and less important. The fourth tour, to Bath and Bristol, is taken largely because the Pickwickians have not visited the area before, although important encounters occur on the tour. After his harrowing experiences in the Fleet prison, however, Pickwick agrees to pay his fines and leave prison so that he can make his final tour, to Bristol and Birmingham, for the purely altruistic purpose of soothing those characters who are angered by Winkle's elopement with Miss Arabella Allen. Having begun the novel as an innocent but wealthy man in retirement, with time, money, and a fund of benevolence at his disposal, Pickwick has journeyed from innocence to experience, accompanied by the much younger Sam Weller who, paradoxically, knew more of suffering and of evil than his master did before they met.

This paradox is highlighted in Chapter 16, when Pickwick leaves Mrs Leo Hunter's literary breakfast and sets off with Sam on the outside of a stage-coach headed for Bury St Edmunds, in pursuit of Jingle. As they ride along through pleasant countryside, Sam comments that the delightful prospect 'beats the chimley pots', and tells Pickwick how he was 'first pitched neck and crop into the the world, to play at leap-frog with its troubles' in London, and of the nadir of his young life when he slept rough under the dry arches of Waterloo Bridge. The dark reality of this period of Sam's life is referred to as something which has passed, and the 'mellow softness' of the present prevails. Characteristically, there is no hint of bitterness in Sam against his ineffectual father, Tony; rather, filial love reigns. When they arrive at Bury, Sam recommends a good night's sleep at the Angel hotel: 'There's nothin' so refreshin' as sleep, sir, as the servant-girl said afore she drank the egg-cupful o' laudanum.' Sam's black humour, inherited from his father, is another kind of accommodation of suffering and evil within a broadly comic scheme.

Again, it is paradoxically at the very moments when Pickwick and his companions seem most secure from the outside world, snugly eating and drinking in wayside inns or at Wardle's farmhouse at Dingley Dell, that they are told the most disturbing of the interpolated tales which are strewn through the narrative: tales of murder and revenge in families divided by hatred.[15] As the novel develops, however, and as Pickwick's benevolence is channelled towards those whom he encounters on his travels and, most starkly, in the Fleet prison, the confrontation between good and evil becomes overt. Yet the forces of what Thackeray called good feeling, and specifically the love of Pickwick, that 'angel in gaiters' as Sam calls him, for his fellow men, are never in danger of being brought down even by the rascally lawyers, whose comic treatment hardly allows of their being seen as forces of evil. It has been suggested that no novel could move further than *Pickwick Papers* towards asserting 'that it is possible to establish something that resembles the Kingdom of God on Earth'.[16] Pickwick's role as surrogate father to Sam and good uncle to the lovers in the novel is central from first to last, culminating in the marriage of Snodgrass and Emily Wardle from Pickwick's permanent retirement home at Dulwich. Sam is to remain Pickwick's servant. He is also to marry his sweetheart, whose name, like those other unspoilt young girls in Thackeray's early fiction, is Mary. Innocent love, handled with delightful comic touches in the flirtations at the Christmas celebrations at Dingley Dell, smiled at by the local clergyman (28), prevails throughout the narrative and is at last triumphant.

The raw world of Sam's childhood and of some of the interpolated tales in *Pickwick* is apprehended indirectly, through internal narratives of past events; but one's sense of unease at conditions in the Fleet is mitigated only by the gratuitous fact that Pickwick can effect his own release, and that of Jingle,

Job Trotter, and Mrs Bardell, by drawing on his apparently unlimited financial resources. Dickens's next novel, *Oliver Twist; or, the Parish Boy's Progress* (1837–39), is in certain respects more like Thackeray's early fiction than like *Pickwick*, being narrowly focused on the life of the hero, and presenting the young Oliver directly confronting a hostile world from birth. The early chapters of *Oliver* present the stark realities of the workhouses which were the product of the Poor Law Amendment Act of 1834, but Bumble and the workhouse board are later balanced by the benevolent fairy godfather and godmother figures in the novel: Mr Brownlow and Mrs Maylie. Dickens's description, however, of young Oliver's escape from Sowerberry the undertaker suggests the heartlessness and ignorance of the adult world in general. Oliver painfully limps his way towards London, sleeping rough in midwinter. Hardly able to crawl along, he waits at the bottom of a hill until a stage-coach comes up, and begs of the outside passengers:

> But there were very few who took any notice of him; and
> even those told him to wait till they got to the top of the hill,
> and then let them see how far he could run for a halfpenny.
> Poor Oliver tried to keep up with the coach a little way, but
> was unable to do it, by reason of his fatigue and sore feet.
> When the outsiders saw this, they put their halfpence back
> into their pockets again, declaring that he was an idle young
> dog, and didn't deserve anything; and the coach rattled away,
> and left only a cloud of dust behind. (8)

Rather than merely providing opportunities for digression and the proliferation of characters and action, as in *Pickwick*, the hero's journey and the coach incident in *Oliver Twist* focus attention on the message of Dickens's social parable. As an unimaginative adult world rattles past him, Oliver, always passive and vulnerable in the novel, proves easy prey to the young Artful Dodger, whom he meets in Barnet. When the road to London finally leads to Fagin's den, peopled by boy-thieves who smoke and drink spirits 'with the air of middle-aged men'(8), Oliver enters a world in which Dickens can investigate the paradox he only touched upon in *Pickwick*, where Sam Weller knows more of the world's evil ways than his older master.

The picture darkens further in *Martin Chuzzlewit* (1843–44), the last novel of this early phase of Dickens's career, in which another journey to London exposes the selfishness of the occupants of a coach. Commenting on the frosty-looking outside passengers on the coach, Mr Pecksniff, inside, observes to his daughters that it is 'always satisfactory to feel, in keen weather, that many other people are not as warm as you are' (8). This he considers to be 'quite natural, and a very beautiful arrangement; not confined to coaches, but extending itself into many social ramifications'. With tears in his eyes, and shaking his fist at a beggar who wants to get up behind, he develops his thoughts allegorically: 'What are we but coaches? . . . Our passions are the horses . . . and Virtue is the drag. We start from

The Mother's Arms, and we run to The Dust Shovel.' Pecksniff goes to sleep for three stages, under the influence of the contents of a bottle he has with him, and is annoyed to be awakened by the intrusion of old Anthony Chuzzlewit, who congratulates himself on getting a place inside for the price of an outside ticket, and his son Jonas, who flirts with Pecksniff's daughters. Each traveller on the broad road to The Dust Shovel is concerned solely with his or her own comfort. When they stop at a hotel, the contrast between their behaviour and that of Pickwick, Wardle, or Sam Weller is underlined as Jonas orders half measures of spirits in the hope of getting more out of the innkeeper than he would if the liquor were all in one glass, and as Pecksniff secretly slips off to the bar 'in order that he might refresh himself at leisure in the dark coach without being observed'.

Dickens's social analysis is as undeveloped as his moral observations are uncomplicated at this stage of his career. When Nicholas Nickleby arrives in the city by coach, after he has left Crummles's travelling theatre, he notices the sharp social contrasts in the 'noisy, bustling, crowded streets': 'life and death went hand in hand; wealth and poverty stood side by side; repletion and starvation laid them down together' (*Nicholas Nickleby*, 1838–39; 32). The ironic overtones, however, of the echo of Isaiah's prophecy of the Kingdom (Isaiah 11. 6–7) remain unexplored; the Cheeryble brothers merely dole out good cheer, rather than effecting reforms; and Dickens's reformist writing in the early chapters, where he describes Dotheboys Hall, takes up little space in the novel as a whole. Wackford Squeers is brought back into the London chapters only as a partner in crime to the evil Ralph Nickleby, a typically casual piece of plotting in the novel. Dickens is equally free in his brilliant improvisation of a strangely assorted range of characters: the Mantalinis and the Crummles; Miss La Creevy and Mrs Witterley; Sir Mulberry Hawk and Lord Frederick Verisopht; the Cheerybles, John Browdie, and Newman Noggs. In the final chapters he characteristically separates the sheep from the goats in a fictional last judgement: Ralph Nickleby hangs himself, Squeers is transported, Dotheboys Hall is broken up, and Gride is murdered; while Nicholas and Kate Nickleby make 'good' marriages, and Newman Noggs settles down near Nicholas and becomes a great favourite with his children.

The assumption, however, in early Dickens, that all will finally be well with his heroes and heroines becomes increasingly questionable. Indications of a more sophisticated treatment of character and motive in *Martin Chuzzlewit* include the fact that the journey of young Martin and Mark Tapley to a new Eden in America proves to be a false trail, and that old Martin, their secret guardian, is both a benefactor and a stern judge. Although the young women in the novels which follow Pickwick are finally rescued in some way, they are increasingly vulnerable, and threatened by a hostile world. Little Nell in *The Old Curiosity Shop* (1840–41), Madeline Bray and Kate Nickleby in *Nicholas Nickleby*, Mary Graham in *Martin Chuzzlewit*, and Dolly Varden in *Barnaby Rudge* (1841), are prey to the lust of Quilp, Gride, Sir Mulberry, Pecksniff, and Hugh; and Dickens dramatizes the plight of three of these characters by having their would-be seducers physically restrain them as they attempt to escape. Ultimately, Dickens exercises authorial control over the rescue of these women, although in *The Old Curiosity Shop* his handling of Nell's journey with her grandfather away from the threat of Quilp to the Midlands, and ultimately to her death, exposes one of the limitations of the novel and, indirectly, of his other early novels. In using the privilege of chroniclers to separate good from evil, thus preserving Nell from corruption, Dickens makes the static quality of his heroine more obvious, in sharp contrast to the manic energy of his fascinating villain. The contrast is perhaps most clear in their deaths. Dickens wept as he killed off Little Nell:

> They moved so gently, that their footsteps made no noise; but there were sobs from among the group, and sounds of grief and mourning.
> For she was dead. There, upon her little bed, she lay at rest. The solemn stillness was no marvel now.
> She was dead. No sleep so beautiful and calm, so free from trace of pain, so fair to look upon. She seemed a creature fresh from the hand of God, and waiting for the breath of life; not one who had lived and suffered. (72)

The endings of several later novels, including *David Copperfield* (1849–50), in which David's marriage to Agnes marks a regression to the world of childhood, are rooted in the same soil as this most idealized of death-bed scenes. Nell, one of Dickens's ideal little virgin women, who is never more than partially alive, is now in her natural state, implicitly resting in that other Dickensian ideal of a heavenly peace.

Contrast the death of 'dear, gentle, patient, noble Nell' with that of Quilp in the Thames off Quilp's Wharf, where he has his 'lair' or 'den'. It is like a grotesque Gothic finale:

> One loud cry now – but the resistless water bore him down before he could give it utterance, and, driving him under [the hull of a ship], carried away a corpse.
> It toyed and sported with its ghastly freight, now bruising it against the slimy piles, now hiding it in mud or long rank grass, now dragging it heavily over rough stones and gravel, now feigning to yield it to its own element, and in the same action luring it away, until, tired of the ugly plaything, it flung it on a swamp – a dismal place where pirates had swung in chains through many a wintry night – and left it there to bleach. (67)

The old analogy of the river of life flowing into the sea of eternity was to become one of Dickens's central symbols in later novels (see pp. 84–7 below), and his description of the Thames estuary looks forward to *Great Expectations*. In *The Old Curiosity Shop*, however, Dickens leaves the body of the dwarf whom he formerly described as an animal, now an inanimate 'it', in a kind of limbo. While Quilp's body bleaches in a dismal swamp, Little Nell is dying near consecrated ground and surrounded by a group of mourners. Whereas Quilp has indeed journeyed from The Mother's Arms to The Dust Shovel, Little Nell's difficult pilgrimage ends in the Eternal City. The lack of intersection between the two journeys is symptomatic of Dickens's separation of opposing forces which cannot be allowed to meet in the arena of real experience. This polarization is also evident, though less obviously, in his use of benevolent characters who rescue innocence from the clutches of evil in his other early novels.

The violence of Dickens's description of Quilp's death is also characteristic of much of his early work. Although a campaigner against public executions in the 1840s,[17] Dickens's morbid interest in hanging was not only that of a reformer. He sentences a number of characters to death by hanging. At the end of *Oliver Twist*, for example, the hero fades from view as Dickens works up the description of Bill Sikes's flight, and his jump from the rooftops in Jacob's Island, ending with 'a sudden jerk' and a 'terrific convulsion of the limbs' as a rope accidentally tightens around his neck (50); and he lingers over Fagin in the condemned cell, in the chapter entitled 'The Jew's Last Night Alive' (52). In *Barnaby Rudge* a chapter is devoted to the hanging of Rudge, Hugh, and, fittingly, Dennis the hangman (77).

Thus in overcoming the 'obstacles of distance, time, and place' in his early novels, Dickens creates a teeming world of sharp contrasts and divisions, of sweet virgins and pathological killers, benevolent uncle figures and scheming seducers, in which the black gallows stands 'in the full glare of the sun, with its black paint blistering, and its nooses dangling in the light like loathsome garlands' (*Barnaby Rudge*, 77). He exploits the privilege of chroniclers with extraordinary facility in the improvisation of plots and the proliferation of characters. Critics of the 1850s and 1860s agreed that the creative powers of Dickens the comic genius, the 'inimitable' entertainer, author of *Pickwick* and *Nicholas Nickleby*, declined as he grappled with more profound themes. The reversal of this judgement in our own century reflects a broad tendency in modern literary criticism to see tragedy as a higher mode than comedy, and to value seriousness and maturity in a novelist's handling of social issues rather than comic inventiveness. While acknowledging that the trial of *Bardell* v. *Pickwick* and the courtship of Mrs Nickleby by the 'Gentleman in the Small-Clothes next Door' are comic masterpieces, and that many of Dickens's most memorable characters belong to the early novels, I believe that his most significant use of the privilege of chroniclers is fundamentally evasive, particularly in the separation of good and evil and the consequent failure to examine them in the context of a complex social setting. Himself deeply divided, a fascinating example of Victorian suppression and neurosis, Dickens never lost his compulsive interest in sharp contrasts rather than subtle shadings. In his middle and later periods, however, he was to bring his invention more fully under control in the service of an imagination engaged in social and psychological themes which also challenged the major thinkers of the Victorian Age.

Notes

1. At Lady Jane's execution 'not an eye was dry' (42). Paul Delaroche's famous painting, *The Execution of Lady Jane Grey*, caused a sensation at the Paris Salon of 1834, and Roy Strong argues that in nineteenth-century England Jane Grey represented 'an obsessional female type: the victimized child-woman': *And when did you last see your father?: The Victorian Painter and British History* (London, 1978), p. 122. See also Andrew Sanders, *The Victorian Historical Novel, 1840–1880* (London, 1979), pp. 32–46.

2. See Allan Conrad Christensen, *Edward Bulwer-Lytton: The Fictions of New Regions* (Athens, Georgia, 1976), p. 113, *et passim*.

3. See Matthew Whiting Rosa, *The Silver-Fork School: Novels of Fashion Preceding Vanity Fair* (1936; repr. Port Washington, 1964), p. 17.

4. See Keith Hollingsworth, *The Newgate Novel, 1830–1847: Bulwer, Ainsworth, Dickens, & Thackeray* (Detroit, 1963).

5. When discussing an episode in the pornographic 'autobiography', *My Secret Life* (*c.* 1890), in which the narrator virtually rapes a field-girl, Steven Marcus comments that what had changed in the Victorian period was 'the consciousness with which these happenings were regarded; the Victorian novel was among the chief agents of that new and altered consciousness. For the first time in history it could be asserted . . . that persons of the lower social orders were not to be treated in this way.' *The Other Victorians: A Study of Sexuality and Pornography in Mid-Nineteenth Century England* (London, 1966), p. 138.

6. Recent studies on humour and comedy in the Victorian age include Robert Bernard Martin, *The Triumph of Wit: A Study of Victorian Comic Theory* (Oxford, 1974) and Robert B. Henkle, *Comedy and Culture: England 1820–1900* (Princeton, 1980).

7. Robert A. Colby writes, 'Thackeray's familiar literary devices – the intrusive narrator, the constantly switching perspectives, his alter egos, recurring characters . . . can now be recognised among the means by which he impresses upon us the complexity and relatively of truth': *Thackeray's Canvass of Humanity: An Author and His Public* (Columbus, Ohio, 1979), p. 36.

8. Chapter numbers cited are as in the revised (1856) and subsequent editions of *Barry Lyndon*.

9. The change of title from *The Luck of Barry Lyndon* (*Fraser's*, 1844) to *The Memoirs of Barry Lyndon, Esq.* (1856) was never approved by Thackeray. Anisman comments on this in his critical edition of the novel, saying that Barry's life, 'which makes him lucky in the eyes of society, is a far from happy one and he never has the fulfillment of a warm, happy family life that is so important to Thackeray': W. M. Thackeray, *The Luck of Barry Lyndon*, edited by Martin J. Anisman (New York, 1970), p. 17.

10. See, for example, Robert L. Patten's introduction to the Penguin English Library edition of *Pickwick Papers* (Harmondsworth, 1972).

11. See Wayne C. Booth, *A Rhetoric of Irony* (Chicago and London, 1974), pp. 1–7.

12. David Copperfield's list of childhood reading ('Roderick Random, Peregrine Pickle, Humphrey Clinker, Tom Jones, the Vicar of Wakefield, Don Quixote, Gil Blas, and Robinson Crusoe . . . the *Arabian Nights*, and the *Tales of the Genii*') was actually Dickens's own list, according to John Forster in his *Life of Charles Dickens* (1).

13. Gordon N. Ray, *Thackeray: The Uses of Adversity, 1811–46* (New York, 1955), p. 107.

14. Butt and Tillotson suggest that 'a quarter of the way through its course, *Pickwick* discovers its shape, with the emergence of Sam and the beginning of the action of Bardell v. Pickwick', but add that 'as it grew into a novel, *Pickwick* did not lose its character as a miscellany, with a "free range of English scenes and people", nor its loosely picaresque form'. John Butt and Kathleen Tillotson, *Dickens at Work* (London, 1957), pp. 71–2.

15. See Robert L. Patten, 'The Art of *Pickwick*'s Interpolated Tales', *ELH*, 34 (1967), 349–66.

16. Steven Marcus, *Dickens: from Pickwick to Dombey* (London, 1965), p. 51.

17. For a discussion of Dickens's ambivalent views on capital punishment see Philip Collins, *Dickens and Crime*, Cambridge Studies in Criminology, edited by L. Radzinowicz, 17 (London and New York, 1962).

Chapter 3
Mid-century Fiction

A Victorian identity: social-problem, religious and historical novels

We now come to a remarkably productive phase in the history of the nine-teenth-century English novel, and the first in which both the fiction and the 'shared culture' of novelists and readers can be characterized as specifically Victorian. For in many spheres of life and culture, from politics and religion to painting and fashion, the areas of controversy and development of later decades were marked out at mid-century, when writers, artists, and preachers addressed themselves to the issues confronting a newly expanded industrialized and urbanized society. For example, the Condition of England Question came to a head in the debates generated by the repeal of the Corn Laws in 1846 and by the Chartist uprisings of 1848; and the most influential social-problem novels of the century were written between 1845 and 1855, by which date much of the very worst poverty experienced in the Hungry Forties had been at least partially relieved. An awareness, however, of living in a divided society, and a consequent fear of revolution, were to remain the legacies of this mid-century period. The Oxford Movement of the 1830s and 1840s, and J. H. Newman's conversion to Roman Catholicism in 1845, left the Church of England deeply divided on High, Low, and Broad Church party lines in the 1850s. While anti-Papist feeling ran high among churchmen and nonconformists following the restoration of the Catholic hierarchy in England and the appointment of Nicholas Wiseman as Archbishop of Westminster in 1850, the more liberal Protestant thinkers were already registering the first tremors of the challenge to orthodoxy represented by science and German biblical criticism. Meanwhile regular religious observance and the maintenance of strict moral standards remained the norm in families of the dominant middle class. Against this complex background, religious fiction became a popular sub-genre in its own right.

Social, religious, and other controversies, such as the arguments generated by the foundation of the Pre-Raphaelite Brotherhood of artists in opposition to the Academy in 1848, were closely followed by a greatly enlarged reading public, with access to a wide range of newspapers and periodicals which were now cheap and easily available. Thus the 1850s, variously described by twentieth-century writers as the Victorian Noon-Time, Victorian Noon, and Victoria's Heyday,[1] saw the beginnings of mass participation, both directly, by means of rail travel to the Great Exhibition of 1851, the Academy exhibitions, or the launchings of Brunel's great steamships, and indirectly, by reading about the exploits of Palmerston in diplomacy and Livingstone in exploration, or the disastrous Crimean War and Indian Mutiny. Similarly, in the arts, prints of the most popular paintings of modern life sold in large quantities, as did the works of the new Poet Laureate, Tennyson.

The novel, however, was the most popular literary genre at mid-century. The expensive three-decker became much more widely available through Mudie's and other lending libraries; most of Thackeray's major novels appeared in the cheap monthly number form with which Dickens had already achieved a series of huge popular successes; and Dickens himself published fiction in serial form, including his own Christmas stories and *Hard Times*, Elizabeth Gaskell's *Cranford* and *North and South*, and stories by Wilkie Collins, in his weekly family periodical, *Household Words*, founded in 1850. Although conditions were ideal for the novel to flourish at mid-century, the fact that so many major and significant minor novelists came to maturity or began their careers at this time is partly a happy historical accident. In those *anni mirabiles* of English fiction, 1847–48, Thackeray's *Vanity Fair* came out in monthly numbers alongside Dickens's *Dombey and Son*, Disraeli completed his trilogy of novels with *Tancred*, and an impressive list of writers published their first novels: Emily Brontë, *Wuthering Heights*; Charlotte Brontë, *Jane Eyre*; Anne Brontë, *Agnes Grey*; Elizabeth Gaskell, *Mary Barton*; Anthony Trollope, *The Macdermots of Ballycloran*; Charles Kingsley, *Yeast*; J. H. Newman, *Loss and Gain*. The rich variety of form and subject-matter represented here is characteristic of the mid-century literary scene.

For all their differences, the major mid-century novelists also share certain common concerns. The life of the individual, in the family, in courtship, and in marriage, is related to larger historical, social, political, or spiritual themes. The figure of the vulnerable, innocent child, a legacy of the Romantic movement and a key Victorian symbol, haunts many of the major novels of the period: Dickens's Florence Dombey and David Copperfield, Thackeray's Henry Esmond, Charlotte Brontë's Jane Eyre, and Emily Brontë's Heathcliff are all memorable as children. Four of them are orphans, and Florence has lost her mother. Their yearning for emotional and spiritual fulfilment in a hostile world, and the effect it has on themselves and those they encounter in their adult lives, suggests interesting parallels with mid-century poetry, and especially Matthew Arnold's volumes of 1852 and 1853. As in the poetry of Arnold and Tennyson, the inner life is reflected in external objects and locations, and change and development in the individual is often related to external social change.

The reformist drive in much of the fiction of mid-century, evident in the social-problem novel and the broader vision of Dickens's major social novels, is often complemented by an attempt to place the changes of the present in the context of the historical past. Disraeli's political novels, for example, are informed by his reading of English history, and students of Victorian fiction should also examine the writings of contemporary historians such as Macaulay – extended prose narratives which often rivalled the novel in popularity. At a time of rapid change, both the historian and the novelist explored the central theme of progress. None of the major novelists, however, approached Macaulay in his optimistic reading of recent English history, and Charlotte Brontë's reference to the 'warped system of things' in the preface to the second edition of *Jane Eyre* (1847) is characteristic of a period in which many novelists attacked received views on the position of women, for example, and, with Carlyle, saw cash as the sole nexus in a highly acquisitive society.

The work of Thackeray, the Brontës, Elizabeth Gaskell, and Dickens will be discussed later in this chapter. (Trollope's novels are discussed in Ch. 4, which covers the most fertile period of his long career.). Before examining these individual novelists, however, I want to consider three of the most important sub-genres of the mid-century period, to which most of the major novelists also contributed: the social-problem novel, the religious novel, and the historical novel.

Jean-Paul Sartre wrote: 'It seems that bananas have a better taste when they have just been picked. Works of the mind should likewise be eaten on the spot.'[2] Although this statement is of doubtful validity it is certainly pertinent to reformist literature, written with an educative purpose for a specific readership at a specific time. The Victorian social-problem novel represented an 'appeal' not only in the broad Sartrean sense of a writer's creation finding its 'fulfilment' in the reading,[3] but also in the more specific sense of demanding a response of some kind, such as a change of attitude or behaviour. In 1845, which I am taking as the first year of the mid-century period in the development of Victorian fiction, the journalist and playwright Douglas Jerrold wrote a prospectus to his new shilling magazine in which he reflected the spirit of the age in his own aims as editor: 'It will be our chief object to make every essay . . . breathe WITH A PURPOSE. Experience assures us that, especially at the present day, it is by a defined purpose alone . . . that the sympathies of the world are to be engaged, and its support ensured.'[4] The immediate purpose of the mid-century social-problem novelist was still that of educating the middle and upper classes. In the same year as Jerrold's prospectus, Disraeli wrote of the rich and the poor being 'as ignorant of each other's habits, thoughts, and feelings, as if they were dwellers in different zones, or inhabitants of different planets' (*Sybil*, 1845; II. 5). In *Mary Barton* (1848) and *North and South* (1854–55), Elizabeth Gaskell describes a kind of class apartheid in early Victorian Manchester, where members of the middle class can walk the streets of the town without ever entering the slum districts, and thus indeed remain ignorant of poverty, in their own 'zone'. It is no coincidence that Dickens makes education itself one of his central themes in *Hard Times* (1854), set in industrial Coketown. In country areas too, the innocent aristocrat and the knowing farm labourer can look at the same village or house and see different things, as Tregarva the gamekeeper suggests in Kingsley's *Yeast* (1848) when he unwittingly echoes Carlyle in saying that 'a man's eyes can only see what they've learnt to see' (3).

Any critical assessment of a Victorian social-problem novel must necessarily include some kind of judgement on its ideology, and the way in which this shapes its diagnosis of social ills and ideas on possible cures. A strong authorial presence in the narrative is, of course, characteristic of Victorian fiction, but here it is of special significance, where novelists write as teachers, guides, and even prophets. Most obviously and commonly, an author-narrator will introduce a passage of commentary on some fictional episode, often writing in the style of the religious tract or the statistical 'blue book', or parliamentary report. But dialogue can also be weighted in such a way that the author's viewpoint emerges very clearly, as for example in Stephen Blackpool's interview with Mr Bounderby in Dickens's *Hard Times*, when they discuss divorce (I. 11).

This is not to say, however, that the social-problem novelists all wrote from positions which were fully worked out and strongly held. Indeed, the tensions within their novels betray the difficulties they faced as they analysed the Condition of England Question. Perhaps the most extreme case is *Alton Locke* (1850), in which the 'Parson Lot' side of Kingsley – radical, Christian Socialist, reformist – struggles with the establishment clergyman who admired the more heroic variety of English aristocrat. In the revisions he made to the Cambridge chapters (12–13) in the edition of 1862, removing the original passages which had criticized the university and its undergraduates, Kingsley showed how he had come to resolve at least one problem of this kind. Two years previously, in 1860, he had been elected Regius Professor of Modern History at Cambridge, and now wished to acknowledge what he called the 'purification' which had gone on in the university since he had been an undergraduate!

Perhaps the most interesting example of this kind of tension or conflict is Elizabeth Gaskell's *Mary Barton*, for here the writer's difficulties are related to the problems of form and plotting in social-problem fiction. The opening chapters of the novel are one of the best portrayals of working-class life in nineteenth-century fiction, representing the grey masses o^f .. alien class as a group of unique individuals, as different from each othei as members of higher social groups are. Whereas Elizabeth Gaskell's detailed, often harrowing realism engages the sympathy of the reader in the lot of the poor, and particularly of the Chartist and union man, John Barton, his daughter Mary, and their friends the Wilsons, her portrayal of the wealthy mill-owning Carson family is unflatteringly stereotyped. (*North and South* was written partly in order to correct this imbalance.) Having, however, sympathetically illustrated the plight of the oppressed Manchester weavers and explained their arguments for militant action, she draws back from the brink of finally condoning either their attitudes or their actions, preferring to preach mutual understanding and education between the classes as a social palliative. Similarly, the happy ending of the two-volume novel has been much criticized as a fudging of the issues raised in the first volume, for Mary Barton simply sails away to a new life in Canada, married to her worthy working-class lover Jem Wilson, leaving the stark realities of the Manchester slums behind her.

Elizabeth Gaskell's pious wish that worker and master might love one another in the spirit of the Gospels is as inadequate a solution to the problems she exposes as Disraeli's appeals to the English aristocracy and Kingsley's suggested programme of sanitary reform. Moreover, the limitations of her social analysis, as revealed in her plotting, also highlight other limitations of the social-problem novels of the period, for these mid-century novelists characteristically illustrate the general and unexceptional (in *Mary Barton*, the masters' exploitation of the workers and the workers' embittered response) through the particular and exceptional (John Barton's murder of his employer's son, Harry Carson, on behalf of the union).

Elizabeth Gaskell is typical in her use of a love plot to organize the particular and exceptional, and in her abnegation of the role of social analyst in the process of working out that plot in the second volume. In shooting Harry Carson as an enemy of the weavers, John Barton also unknowingly kills his daughter's would-be seducer. The wadding he uses in the gun borrowed from Jem Wilson is a piece of an old valentine from Jem to Mary, on the blank part of which Mary had once copied Samuel Bamford's poem entitled 'God help the poor' (9, 21–22). The police arrest Jem as the owner of the gun, knowing that he has recently had an angry exchange with Carson, his rival lover. They pursue the line of reasoning which, for the reader, is symbolically represented by the valentine greeting on the card. The motive of the actual murderer is symbolically represented by the Bamford poem: Barton avenges the poor. This contrived and over-elaborate plotting epitomizes the social-problem novelists' attempts to accommodate the threatening forces of class conflict within a romance scheme, to which the ethics of the New Testament can then be applied. In her later, more mature, and finished novel, *North and South*, Elizabeth Gaskell still makes the central love plot her main focus, Margaret Hale's eventual marriage to the Milton-Northern manufacturer John Thornton being the culmination of their mutual education. As in *Mary Barton*, the conflation of the love plot and what might be called the social-problem plot is the source both of the narrative strength and the social-analytical weakness of *North and South*. For all its obvious shortcomings, however, *Mary Barton* is perhaps the most compelling of the mid-century social-problem novels, a moving if at times highly melodramatic parable for the times, portraying early Victorian Manchester as the town of Dives and Lazarus, in which Lazarus becomes an avenger.

Disraeli's *Sybil; or, The Two Nations* is in places just as melodramatic as *Mary Barton*. Yet in many ways his reformist novels differ from those of Elizabeth Gaskell, Charles Kingsley, and the women novelists of the 1830s and 1840s mentioned in Chapter 2 (see pp. 18–19 above). He worked on a much larger canvas, for example, virtually creating the political novel in *Coningsby; or, The New Generation* (1844), whose theme is 'the derivation and character of the political parties' ('General Preface to Novels and Tales', 1870–71), and completing his ambitious Tory trilogy with *Sybil*, on 'the condition of the people', and *Tancred; or, The New Crusade* (1847), on 'the duties of the Church'. Disraeli's ideas on the history and destiny of the English nation, ideas with which he launched his bid for the leadership of his party, are worked out in the novels through symbolic confrontations, such as the clash between Coningsby's grandfather, Lord Monmouth (the aristocrat of the old order) and his enemy Millbank (the model self-made industrialist who takes care to consume his own smoke), and the marriage of the noble hero Egremont to Sybil, an 'angel from heaven' (II. 14), the daughter of a Chartist overseer who turns out to be of aristocratic descent. This use of plots concerned with private lives, and particularly love lives, as vehicles for some kind of social message typifies the social-problem novelists' technique of domesticating large social issues in personal terms. In Disraeli's case, however, the grand scale of some of his ideas can work against this effect. For example, characters are often portrayed as representatives of a whole line of racial, tribal, or national descent. The Rev. Aubrey St Lys in *Sybil* is 'distinguished by that beauty of noble English blood' – of 'the Norman tempered by the Saxon; the fire of conquest softened by integrity' (II. 11). Queen Victoria, 'fair and serene', has 'the blood and beauty of the Saxon' (I. 6). The two nations, rich and poor, must unite under the crown, and, as in so many reformist novels, it is specifically female sympathy and love which is seen as the social balm: 'Will it be her proud destiny at length to bear relief to suffering millions, and, with that soft hand which might inspire troubadours and guerdon knights, break the last links in the chain of Saxon thraldom?' (I. 6).

Disraeli works with a broad brush and bold colours, illustrating his ideas by dramatically bringing together the opposite ends of the social spectrum as part of his political strategy. He caricatures the poor in *Sybil*, and, when he treats the trade unions melodramatically, exploits the fact that these violent and secret societies were objects of terror. The creative energy, however, the fresh ideas, and the nice, albeit snobbish social touches of Disraeli's novels contribute to the liveliness of approach and lightly ironic tone which other novelists who worked in the sub-genre often lacked.

Although *Sybil, Alton Locke,* and *Mary Barton* are strongly religious novels in the sense that their polemics are rooted in the Christian social ethics of Young England Toryism, Christian Socialism, and Unitarianism, nobody would classify them as 'religious fiction' in the sense of being specifically about religion. The boundaries of religious fiction are often difficult to draw, however, as many Victorian novelists reflect the religious issues of the period in their work without actually addressing themselves to those issues. Elizabeth Gaskell's *Ruth* (1853) is included in the large Garland reprint series of Victorian 'Novels of Faith and Doubt' (1975) as a 'Novel of Dissent'[5]; for the heroine, an abandoned unmarried mother, is taken in by a dissenting minister and his sister, Faith, whose religion is portrayed sympathetically, in contrast to that of the Pharisaical Mr Bradshaw. Elizabeth Gaskell's main theme, however, is the broader social issue of the 'fallen woman', and therefore *Ruth* can also be classified as a social-problem novel. Also in the Garland series, and published in the same year as *Ruth*, is Charlotte M. Yonge's best-seller, *The Heir of Redclyffe*, listed under 'Tractarian and Anti-Tractarian Novels'; yet Charlotte Yonge's High Church position is manifested only indirectly in the novel, whose real interest lies in the intensity of religious feeling which informs its plot. Young Sir Guy Morville, the first heir of Redclyffe to come into his inheritance in the novel, clears his name of the false charges brought against him by his cousin, Philip, who himself becomes the next heir. As a Victorian version of the 'gentil parfit knyght', his true nature is revealed in a series of self-sacrificial heroic actions: his rescue of sailors shipwrecked on rocks off the beach at Redclyffe (23) and of his young wife as she hangs over a precipice during their wedding tour (30), and his fitting death of a fever caught from Philip, whom he has nursed back to health in Italy (31–33). (Philip lives on to inherit Redclyffe, 'a care-worn, harassed man', 44.) The novel ran through numerous editions and reprintings, largely, one suspects, because it was 'safe': the central characters are intense, upper-middle-class young people who read and talk in idyllic rural settings, and the author's moral judgements upon them are firmly based on a creed which remains unchallenged throughout.

It is therefore interesting to contrast Charlotte Yonge's use of the 'fever', a conveniently vague and yet dangerous illness contracted in many Victorian novels, with that of James Anthony Froude in his decidely unsafe and highly controversial *The Nemesis of Faith* (1849). For although Froude's plot also turns on the effects of a fever contracted in Italy in the last third of the novel, the circumstances and interpretation of the illness could hardly be more different. Like other religious novels of its kind, *The Nemesis of Faith* is organized around a series of spiritual crises. The hero, Markham Sutherland, becomes a sceptic, resigns his living as an Anglican clergyman, and falls in love with Mrs Helen Leonard on the shores of Lake Como. During a boating trip the preoccupied couple fail to notice that Helen's little daughter Annie has got wet, and they are thus indirectly responsible for her death when she develops a fever. Whereas Helen believes that this is a judgement upon her for having married a man whom she has never really loved, the shocked Markham refuses to act on her interpretation and take her away with him, seeing Annie's death as 'a punishment for the sin which he had wished to commit'.[6] (Helen enters a convent, where she dies peacefully two years later, whereas Markham dies in doubt and despair in a monastery, having been saved from suicide by the miraculous intervention of an English Roman Catholic priest who is clearly modelled on Newman.)

Unlike Charlotte Yonge's handling of the fever, Froude's is related to Markham Sutherland's earlier agonized soul-searching in which he wrestles with a more familiar mid-century problem of interpretation – that of the critical approach to Scripture and the creeds. For *The Nemesis of Faith* squarely tackles religious 'difficulties', as *Mary Barton* and *Alton Locke* tackle social problems, though the nature of Markham Sutherland's difficulties demands a quite different form to accommodate them. He describes his struggles with his own conscience over the Thirty-nine Articles, the creeds, and the great nineteenth-century stumbling block of the doctrine of everlasting punishment, in a series of ten letters to his friend Arthur in the first section of the narrative and, after Arthur himself has described his ordination and subsequent resignation in the third-person mode, in the lengthy

'Confessions of a Sceptic' which take up the middle third of the novel. Froude's main interest is in the spiritual and intellectual torments endured by himself and other young doubters of his generation, and the demands of plot and of the development of characters other than the hero are subordinated to the description of those torments.

Similarly, the spiritual life of Newman's Charles Reding in *Loss and Gain* (1848) remains the single narrow focus of the narrative throughout the novel, without generating a complex sense of relationship between the hero and his world. Unlike Markham Sutherland, however, Charles Reding defines and articulates his position on questions of doctrine by engaging in lengthy debates with other Christians – first his fellow undergraduates at Oxford and later a series of fanatics of miscellaneous persuasions – as he takes the long and painful road from the Church of England to Rome. The greatest English Christian apologist of his time, Newman wrote most of his major works as contributions to current religious controversies, and it is characteristic of him that *Loss and Gain* was written in response to another novel: Miss Elizabeth Harris's *From Oxford to Rome* (1847), a fictionalized version of its author's own route down that road and a warning to others against following her example. Newman had already published his *Essay on the Development of Christian Doctrine* (1845), in which he explained his position in the year of his conversion to Rome. The most moving parts of *Loss and Gain*, such as the descriptions of Charles leaving Oxford (III. 3) and of his first seeing the mass celebrated (III. 10) have the intensity of autobiography. But Newman also enjoys himself in this (for him) comparatively lightweight literary genre of the novel, and introduces passages of satire and broad humour into the narrative. For example, he catches the enthusiasm and hyperbole of the undergraduate in Charles's friend Sheffield, who bursts into his room on the first day of term to announce that Oxford has 'just now a very bad inside': 'The report is, that some of the men have turned Romans; and they say that there are strangers going about Oxford whom no one knows any thing of. Jack, who is a bit of a divine himself, says he heard the Principal say that, for certain, there were Jesuits at the bottom of it; and . . . he declares he saw with his own eyes the Pope walking down High Street with the priest' (I. 14). Typically, however, this flight of fancy is merely the prelude to a discussion on the stage Charles has reached on the road to Rome, and the chapter as a whole represents one more milestone on a journey which at times wearies not only the hero but also the long-suffering reader.

We have seen that Disraeli's analysis of modern English society is based on his reading of English history. Similarly, both Froude and Newman examine the spiritual life of their generation in the light of Church history. During Markham Sutherland's Tractarian phase, for example, he was 'readily induced to acknowledge that the Reformation had been the most miserable infatuation', though later his 'faith in Newman' was finally destroyed.[7] Following Newman's conversion and the restoration of the Roman hierarchy in England, Catholic and Protestant writers alike turned to the history of the early Church in their fiction in order to suggest the true significance of current events in England. The alternative title of

Charles Kingsley's *Hypatia; or, New Foes with an Old Face* (1853) is characteristically pugnacious, as is the muscular monk in the novel, Philammon, who proves to be handy in a fight. Kingsley's anti-Catholic views on celibacy figure largely in his treatment of Philammon's exposure to the life of Alexandria, where he meets the novel's heroine, Hypatia, a pagan teacher of Greek philosophy and literature. The physicality of the persecution of the Christians in fifth-century Alexandria and of the terrible 'sports' in the theatre (22), clearly fascinated Kingsley, and the climactic martyrdom of the converted Hypatia, naked at the high altar in the church, shocked even his more sympathetic readers and critics.

This powerful novel prompted two other leading English priests to write on the martyrdom of women. In an attempt to answer Kingsley, Cardinal Wiseman initiated a Catholic Popular Library series with a novel entitled *Fabiola; or, The Church of the Catacombs* (1854), whose excesses of physical horror have prompted critics to speculate on the psychology of its author. The twelfth work in the series, Newman's *Callista: A Sketch of the Third Century* (1856), also took up Kingsley's challenge, thus anticipating the later open debate between the two men in which Newman's position was stated in the form of the *Apologia pro Vita Sua* (1864). The martyrdom of the converted Roman heroine, Callista, is treated as a miraculous event, placed in a rapidly unfolding sequence of sacraments: baptism, confirmation, and the eucharist in custody (31) are followed by a public confession of her new faith (33). Her death on the rack, with limbs outstretched on a plank, at the place where slaves are buried outside the walls of the city of Sicca, suggests parallels with the crucifixion; and the novel ends, like *Loss and Gain*, with a mass, in this case for the soul of a martyr whose discarded body has lain in the sand, uncorrupted and untouched by wild beasts. *Callista* is a novel of set pieces, such as the justly famous description of the plague of locusts (15); and the development of character and plot is not sustained. In his contrast between the corrupt city with its violent mob and the cool caves in which Agellius and other converts secretly celebrate the mass, Newman succeeds in conveying his spiritual vision of the world and the Church, implicitly relating a distant period of persecution, when religion was literally a matter of life and death, to the recent history of the small Roman Catholic community in his own country.

Novelists who researched the history of the Church in order to write about the religion of their own times were working in an age in which 'sages' and historians also interpreted the past in relation to the present. The title of Carlyle's *Past and Present* (1843), a work in which he contrasted medieval and modern England, also struck the keynote of much of his other writing; and his seminal account of *The French Revolution* (1837) provided a historical foundation for his prophetic writings in the age of Chartism and an 'unworking aristocracy'. J. A. Froude adopted Carlyle's ideas on heroes and hero-worship in his *History of England from the Fall of Wolsey to the Defeat of the Spanish Armada* (1856–70), in which his highly topical anti-Catholic sentiments found full expression. Macaulay's magisterial *History of England from the Accession of James II* (1849–61) interpreted history as a story of progress towards the nineteenth century – 'the history of physical, of moral, and of intellectual improvement' ('Exordium'). In Macaulay's case this other major nineteenth-century form of extended prose narrative rivalled even Dickens's novels in popularity: almost 30,000 copies of the third and fourth volumes of the *History* were sold in the first three months of publication in 1855, for which Longman paid him the unprecedented sum of £20,000. The historical novelists of mid-century tended to be attracted to periods of English history in which change and development were rapid and violent, as in their own time. Ainsworth produced his *James the Second; or, The Revolution of 1688* in 1848, the year of European revolutions and Chartism in England; and Bulwer's *Harold, the Last of the Saxons* came out in the same year.

But perhaps the most interesting historical novel written from the perspective of the present is Kingsley's best-seller of 1855, *Westward Ho!*, a romance of adventure and of war with the dastardly Spaniards in the age of Drake and Raleigh. Like his close friend J. A. Froude, who was already working on the history of the period, Kingsley allowed his anti-Catholic feeling to distort his account of England's past. In portraying the bellicose Protestant Englishman as an imperialist with God on his side and a heroic liberator of the victims of the Spanish Inquisition, Kingsley also sublimated his frustrated urge to fight in the first year of the Crimean War, producing a book which was intended to 'make others fight'.[8] His religion is central both to his view of the war and his descriptions of the exploits of Amyas Leigh and his crew in the West Indies and against the Spanish Armada. In a letter of 1855 he writes that the soldier 'wants a faith that he is fighting on God's side; he wants military and corporate and national religion, and that is what I fear he has yet to get. . . . That is what the Elizabethans had up to the Armada, and by it they conquered.'[9] In *Westward Ho!* the old sailor Salvation Yeo comes to believe that fighting the Spaniards is 'really fighting in God's battle against evil, as were the wars of Joshua or David' (16). The conflict between Amyas Leigh, the young Devonian lion, and the main Catholic characters in the novel – his cousin Eustace, a priest and therefore a superstitious liar (3, 22), and the dark, handsome Don Guzman, who lures Rose Salterne, a lovely Devon girl, into marriage – provides the structure upon which Kingsley's stirring plot is constructed. Written in only seven months, the novel proved to be a great popular success with a reading public anxious about Catholicism at home and war abroad, and who also enjoyed a good yarn. Again, the fact that *Westward Ho!* is memorable mainly for a few set pieces of exciting narrative suggests the novel's limitations. (At the end of the novel, for example, Amyas's pursuit of Don Guzman's ship after the battle of the Armada ends in the Spaniard's shipwreck and the frustrated Amyas's blinding by a bolt of lightning, 32.) Fascinating as a grossly prejudiced period piece, the novel bursts fitfully into lurid but spellbinding life.

No new thing under the sun: Thackeray's major novels

Thackeray the novelist owed much to his training as an artist and journalist: his early experiments in fiction and burlesque, discussed in Chapter 2, were published mainly in *Fraser's*, from 1837, and in *Punch*, from 1844. Having mastered the art of the comic pen and pencil sketch, he went on to make his name as one of the leading writers of the day with the publication in monthly parts of *Vanity Fair* (1847–48), a long novel of panoramic range which still retained the freshness of an improvised series of sketches. The subjects of Thackeray's early work – ambition and the wilful hero or heroine, class and snobbery, money, speculation, and the marriage market – also recur later in his career, although they are treated more seriously as his satire broadens and deepens. Indeed, the sameness of much of his mature fiction in which characters reappear and themes are reworked in several novels, reflects his sense of the universal qualities of the human condition.

Another kind of continuity in Thackeray's career is his commitment to the portrayal of the real rather than the ideal. An example of this can be seen in the second monthly number of *Vanity Fair*, which opens with a description of William Dobbin's miserable schooldays. One sunny afternoon he is lying under a tree engrossed in his favourite book, the *Arabian Nights*, when the shrill cries of little George Osborne break the spell. Dobbin looks up to see the boy being beaten by Cuff, the bullying 'chief and dandy' of the school, who unfairly accuses him of drinking the rum-shrub he was ordered to fetch: 'The Princess Peribanou had fled into the inmost cavern with Prince Ahmed: the Roc had whisked away Sinbad the Sailor . . . far into the clouds: and there was everyday life before honest William; and a big boy beating a little one without cause' (5). This abrupt descent from romance to reality is characteristic both of Thackeray and of later writers in the Victorian realist tradition. Whereas the beaten child provided the social-problem novelists and Dickens with a figure who represented the oppressed in early Victorian society, Thackeray only interjects a brief admonitory statement concerning bullying. More significantly, his handling of the incident reveals his interest in the complexity of human motivation. Having previously shown Cuff taunting Dobbin about being the son of a mere grocer, Thackeray states that he does not know what Dobbin's motive was for springing up and screaming at Cuff to stop beating young Osborne: 'Perhaps Dobbin's foolish soul revolted against that exercise of tyranny; or perhaps he had a hankering feeling of revenge in his mind, and longed to measure himself against that splendid bully and tyrant.' Similarly, Osborne is not portrayed as the pure innocent, wholeheartedly grateful to his rescuer. When Dobbin challenges Cuff to a fight and tells Osborne that he must be his bottle-holder, he agrees rather reluctantly:

'for you see his papa kept a carriage, and he was rather ashamed of his champion'.

Thackeray often restated his intention to portray the world as it really is. Early in his career, he described the sordid realities of crime and rascality in *Catherine* and *Barry Lyndon*. Near the end of his life, in the *Adventures of Philip* (1861–62), he makes his narrator, Arthur Pendennis, say that 'if Philip's boots had holes in them' he has 'written that he has holes in his boots' (23). In the process of exposing the reality behind the social appearance or the wished-for ideal in his major novels, Thackeray constantly reaffirms his sense of the ambivalence of human conduct in a fallen world. Set in the early eighteenth century, *Henry Esmond* (1852) opens with a prefatory passage on 'Early Youth' written by the narrator, Esmond himself, in which he says that the Muse of History has hitherto worn a mask similar to that of her sister Muse of Tragedy, and that she 'busies herself with the affairs only of kings'. Recording that he once saw Louis XIV who, 'divested of poetry', was but a little old man with a great periwig, he wonders whether history shall ever 'pull off her periwig'. At the end of this introduction, in a passage which is reminiscent of Bulwer's comments on crime in *Paul Clifford* (see p. 17 above), Esmond comments on his own nature in relation to the Lord Mayor of London and the highwayman whom the Mayor condemns to death: 'I look into my heart and think that I am as good as my Lord Mayor, and know I am as bad as Tyburn Jack.' Depending on environment and circumstances he could have found himself in the place of either the alderman or the highwayman, the judge or the criminal. In pulling off the periwig of history, Thackeray portrays kings, aldermen, and criminals, the reader, the hero, and himself, in a state of undress.

As a clear-sighted moralist and satirist who often adopts the tone and stance of the preacher, Thackeray's most famous text is Ecclesiastes 1. 2 ('Vanity of vanities, saith the Preacher, vanity of vanities; all is vanity'), which he quotes in the final paragraph of *Vanity Fair*: 'Ah! *Vanitas Vanitatum!* Which of us is happy in this world? Which of us has his desire? or, having it, is satisfied? – Come children, let us shut up the box and the puppets, for our play is played out' (67). Bunyan echoed the keyword of Ecclesiastes, broadly meaning emptiness or futility, when he invented Vanity Fair in *Pilgrim's Progress*; but Thackeray's secular vision in the novel *Vanity Fair*, where there is no hint of a possible Celestial City for his characters in the closing chapters, suggests that for him both Ecclesiastes and *Pilgrim's Progress* were mediated by eighteenth-century satire: Johnson's *The Vanity of Human Wishes* and Hogarth's series of morality paintings and engravings, such as *The Rake's Progress* and *The Good and the Idle Apprentice*, for example. The vanity theme also recurs in the novels which follow *Vanity Fair*. When Henry Esmond has to tell Beatrix of the death of the Duke of Hamilton, to whom she is engaged, he comments that 'if a satire upon human vanity could be needed, that poor soul afforded it in the altered company and occupations' in which he found her (35). For she had spent the previous days liberally spending her future husband's money on such luxuries as a great chased salver on which the ducal arms and coronet were to be engraved. Esmond conveys the suddenness of Beatrix's fall in a detailed observation which requires no commentary from him: 'The next time Mr Esmond saw that piece of plate, the arms were changed: the ducal coronet had been replaced by a viscount's: it formed part of the fortune of the thrifty goldsmith's own daughter, when she married my Lord Viscount Squanderfield two years later.' One can imagine Hogarth producing 'Before' and 'After' illustrations, with the salver as the centrepiece.

Narrowly interpreted, a motto from Thomas à Kempis would have been appropriate to this episode on the vanity of human wishes: *Sic transit gloria mundi* ('How quickly the glory of the world passes away!', *Imitation of Christ*; cf. 1 John 2. 17). More central to Thackeray's vision, however, are the verses that follow the Preacher's words on the vanity of vanities:

> What profit hath a man of all his labour which he taketh
> under the sun? One generation passeth away, and another
> generation cometh: but the earth abideth for ever. . . . The
> thing that hath been, it is that which shall be; and that which
> is done is that which shall be done: and there is no new thing
> under the sun.
>   (Ecclesiastes 1. 3, 4, 9)

What differentiates Thackeray's major novels from his earlier fiction is his profounder interest in the nature of the universal human lot, irrespective of time and place; and his conviction that there is no new thing under the sun helps to explain both his lifelong interest in history and his impatience with Dickens's nagging concern with the specific social ills of his time.

This conviction surfaces in a number of recurrent preoccupations in Thackeray's fiction. Firstly, and most explicitly, there is his often world-weary sense that the plots of most individual lives are remarkable only in their predictability. For example, he refers to Harry Warrington's courtship of Lady Maria as 'An Old Story' in the title of Chapter 18 in *The Virginians: A Tale of the Last Century* (1857–59):

> Is not one story as stale as the other? Are not they all alike?
> What is the use, I say, of telling them over and over? Harry
> values that rose because Maria has ogled him in the old way;
> because she has happened to meet him in the garden in the
> old way; because he has taken her hand in the old way. . . .

The verse from Ecclesiastes is actually quoted in the 'Overture' chapter of *The Newcomes* (1853–55), where Thackeray answers his own question, 'What stories are new?', with the answer, 'All types of all characters march through all fables'; but although 'there may be nothing new under and including the sun', it 'looks fresh every morning, and we rise with it to toil, hope, scheme, laugh, struggle, love, suffer, until the night comes and quiet' (1). These words say as much about Thackeray as a writer as they do about us as readers. Like the Preacher in Ecclesiastes, Thackeray in his novels dwells on the idea of the inexorable wheel of time which brings all men to their deaths. He habitually emphasizes the universality of his theme by breaking into the narrative with authorial commentary or some kind of moral fable, as in the paragraph on the 'second-floor arch in a London house' in a chapter of *Vanity Fair* 'In which Two Lights [those of Mrs Sedley and Mr Osborne] are Put Out':

> That stair, up or down which babies are carried, old people
> are helped, guests are marshalled to the ball, the parson walks
> to the christening, the doctor to the sick-room, and the
> undertaker's men to the upper floor – what a memento of
> Life, Death, and Vanity it is – that arch and stair – if you
> choose to consider it, and sit on the landing, looking up and
> down the well!   (61)

Thackeray suggests the inevitability and universality of time's cycle ('A time to be born, and a time to die. . . . A time to weep, and a time to laugh', Ecclesiastes 3. 2, 4) by referring in this general way to the stages of life and to those who attend a family at various stages.

Thackeray's mature novels, then, relate 'Births, Marriages, and Deaths' (*Vanity Fair*, 67) as the 'old story'. Indeed, G. K. Chesterton suggested that *Vanity Fair*, *Pendennis* (1848–50), *The Newcomes*, and *Philip* are 'in one sense all one novel'.[10] When the historical novels *Henry Esmond* and *The Virginians* are also added to this list, it is clear, for example, that Thackeray delighted in tracing the lives of the few families who dominate the novels through a number of generations. We learn about the later lives of the Crawleys of *Vanity Fair* in *The Newcomes* (13), a novel which is ostensibly narrated by Arthur Pendennis, as is the later *Philip*. George and Harry Warrington, the twin brothers in *The Virginians*, are the grandsons of Henry Esmond; and their father is an ancestor of Pendennis's friend, George Warrington, who himself figures in both *Pendennis* and *The Newcomes*. Generations of young men – Esmond, the Warrington twins, Pendennis, Clive Newcome – share similarly high aspirations and make the same kinds of mistakes in love and in their professions. Thackeray's own illustrations and chapter heading vignettes indicate his indebtedness to the emblem tradition, which itself assumes that there is no new thing under the sun in terms of human folly; and his young men are often compared with stock biblical figures such as the Prodigal Son (e.g. *Pendennis*, 21) and the Good Samaritan: *Philip* is entitled 'The Adventures of Philip on his Way Through the World, Shewing Who Robbed Him, Who Helped Him, and Who Passed Him By'. Moving in middle- and upper-class circles, mixing with army officers, churchmen, and writers in the London clubs, bachelor lodgings, or more spacious town and country houses, Thackeray's men tend to get into debt and fall in love with an openness which makes it easy for the reader to treat them as Thackeray would have us treat Pendennis: 'Knowing how mean the best of us is, let us give a hand of charity to Arthur Pendennis, with all his faults and shortcomings, who does not claim to be a hero, but only a man and a brother' (*Pendennis*, 75).

Thackeray also reworks other themes and motifs in different novels.

Consider, for example, some of the echoes of *Vanity Fair* in *The Newcomes*, published six years later. In Chapter 13 we hear talk of 'Rebecca, Lady Crawley', Colonel Rawdon Crawley, and Sir Pitt, all major characters in *Vanity Fair*, and later in the novel 'all the vanities of the world' are said to be over for the dead Sir Brian Newcome (48). The theme of the marriage market in *Vanity Fair*, developed in Thackeray's portrayal of Amelia Sedley and her father (13), is treated more forcefully in *The Newcomes*, where Ethel Newcome strongly objects to the machinations of her grandmother, Lady Kew, on her behalf (28, 32). When Lady Kew dies, 'after fourscore years of lonely vanity', her funeral is reminiscent of old Sir Pitt Crawley's in *Vanity Fair* (41). Finally, genuine affection is shown in both novels when characters are made bankrupt and their friends buy back treasured possessions at the ensuing sales of house contents: three young stockbrokers buy some of Sedley's silverware for 'good Mrs Sedley' in *Vanity Fair* (17), and a friend of old Colonel Newcome's 'bought in for a few shillings those two swords which had hung . . . in the good man's chamber, and for which no single broker present had the heart to bid' (72). The treatment of the Colonel's sale is more sentimental than that of Sedley's, however. (The mellowness of *The Newcomes* finally becomes mawkishness in the famous death-bed scene, when the Colonel, at his old school, answers the heavenly roll-call with the word he knew as a boy, 'Adsum', and he stands 'in the presence of The Master', 80.) As in the case of Ethel Newcome and Amelia Sedley and the marriage market, Colonel Newcome's bankruptcy is a reworking of an earlier theme in a new context and therefore in a different tone. The similarities between the two novels, however, help us to understand Chesterton's further comment on the oneness of Thackeray's novels of nineteenth-century life: 'Certainly the reader sometimes forgets which one of them he is reading.'[11] And this sense of oneness reinforces Thackeray's central theme: that there is no new thing under the sun.

In his mature fiction, Thackeray returns again and again to the frailties of men and women recognizably like ourselves, living in the real world. There are no dramatic conversions of characters, of the kind we find in the work of Dickens, Elizabeth Gaskell, and other contemporaries. In view of the trials he endured in his own life, it is hardly surprising that Thackeray suggests few grounds for optimism concerning humanity. For Thackeray's art is fundamentally unheroic. *Vanity Fair* is subtitled 'A Novel without a Hero', and its characters include no idealized woman of the kind Dickens created. Thackeray's sense of an unheroic nineteenth century was based on a specifically anti-heroic reading of history which challenged Carlyle's influential views on heroes, great individual men who provided the driving force of a nation's history. Instead of being taken on to the battlefield of Waterloo in *Vanity Fair*, we are shown Jos Sedley making his ignominious retreat from Brussels (32). Only at the end of the chapter does Thackeray briefly mention the combat, and, in the final sentence, also the end of the ninth monthly number, tie it into the plot: 'Amelia was praying for George, who was lying on his face, dead, with a bullet through his heart.' As in *Barry Lyndon*, he challenges received ideas on how the historian should present a battle, in Henry Esmond's description of events during the Seven Years War:

> Esmond beheld . . . burning farms, wasted fields, shrieking
> women, slaughtered sons and fathers, and drunken soldiery,
> cursing and carousing in the midst of tears, terror, and
> murder. Why does the stately Muse of History, that delights
> in describing the valour of heroes and the grandeur of
> conquest, leave out these scenes . . . that yet form by far the
> greater part of the drama of war? (23)

Esmond's prefatory statement to the effect that he 'would have history
familiar rather than heroic' anticipates not only his accounts of war but also
his insider's view of public events. Seen from Esmond's point of view the
'great' figures of his time tend to be cut down to size, as when the Prince
of Wales is drawn to Castlewood in amorous pursuit of Beatrix at the time
of Queen Anne's death, when his supporters look to him to seize power
(41–42). Here is that old story of ogling flirtation played out in an earlier
time and at a more elevated level than in either *The Virginians* or *The Newcomes*, and still suggesting that there is indeed no new thing under the sun.

I will now examine this central theme in Thackeray's two finest novels,
Vanity Fair and *Henry Esmond*, in rather more detail, and consider how he
adapts his analysis of human motives to the demands of historical settings,
the first in the recent past of the Regency and the second in the more distant
early eighteenth century.

Seven years before writing his comic play, *Money* (1840), Edward Bulwer
claimed that the first thing that strikes the moral inquirer into the English
social system is 'the respect in which wealth is held', and that 'with us,
Money is the mightiest of all deities' (*England and the English*, II. 1). In the
secular world of Victorian realist fiction, money and financial problems are
major themes, not only in the sense of being much talked about in novels,
but also of providing a staple for plots. The allegorical representation of
Greed or the intervention of the *deus ex machina* of earlier literary forms are
now scaled down to a moment of weakness at cards or the reading of the
will of an aged relation. As in the novels of his admirer, Anthony Trollope,
the crises in Thackeray's plots are often specifically financial crises in the
lives of his main characters. In *Vanity Fair* the characters' social ambitions
and financial difficulties are seen in the context of two kinds of wealth: the
new money of the stock-market, in which poor Mr Sedley, the stockbroker, 'dabbles on his own account' (13) and is declared a bankrupt; and
inherited land, which comes down to old Sir Pitt Crawley from an Eliza-
bethan ancestor in the form of the large estate of Queen's Crawley, Hants.
Significantly, however, Sir Pitt is also a speculator himself, and his legal
battles keep him in debt (9). By the time he dies, the house is almost deserted and the timber has been ruthlessly thinned.

Thackeray was writing in the mid-century period in which huge fortunes were made and lost very rapidly, especially in the new railway in-
vestments of the 1840s, and other novelists of the period also used the
financial crash as the catastrophe in their plots: Dickens has Dombey's
mercantile firm collapse in *Dombey and Son*, published at the same time as

Vanity Fair, and shows how hundreds are ruined when Merdle's financial empire folds in *Little Dorrit* (1855–57); Miss Matty is ruined when her bank stops payment in Elizabeth Gaskell's provincial novel, *Cranford* (1852–53). Thackeray, of course, satirizes the world of a previous generation in *Vanity Fair*, which is set in the years between 1813 and 1830. This historical distance frees the novel from the local controversies of contemporary satire, suggesting the Fair's temporal universality and thus complementing our sense of its spatial universality when, for example, we find its booths erected in Brussels as well as London (28). Far from being able to crow over the satire of his Regency parents or grandparents, the Victorian reader is implicated both in a general way and with reference to specific institutions. For example, Thackeray has one eye firmly fixed on his own generation when he demonstrates that relationships between his characters are conducted like those between an employer and an employee, or a banker and a client; and also when he refers to the London Stock Exchange, and shows how the wealth of both the nation and many of its individual citizens is based on dealings there.

The contrasting social ambitions of the two female protagonists in *Vanity Fair*, Rebecca Sharp and Amelia Sedley, are related to the two different kinds of wealth mentioned above. In an improvised monthly part novel with little other coherent overall organization, Thackeray provides a firm plot structure in his skilful development of the parallel careers of these two girls, who leave Miss Pinkerton's academy in Chiswick Mall together in the opening chapter. Becky Sharp is the vivacious and scheming daughter of a penniless artist, now alone in a world in which she must rely on the sharpness of her own wits, whereas for the more beautiful and conventional Amelia, the stockbroker's daughter, the world seems 'new, fresh, brilliant' (2). Both girls are married much earlier in the novel than is usual in Victorian fiction: Becky to Captain Rawdon Crawley, a Guards officer and the son of a baronet, Sir Pitt Crawley; and Amelia to Rawdon's fellow officer, the dashing George Osborne, son of a wealthy merchant who cuts him off for marrying the daughter of a bankrupt. Near the middle of the novel, in the eighth monthly part, Becky's and Amelia's paths cross on the eve of Waterloo, when George Osborne, who has carried on a 'desperate flirtation' with Becky, plans to run away with her, and passes her a note, 'coiled like a snake', in a bouquet (29). Following George's death in the battle, Amelia spends the second half of the novel as a doting widow, to be disabused by Becky herself in the climactic final chapter, when she in effect frees Amelia to marry the devoted William Dobbin by flinging the love note into her lap.

In this novel without a hero, the wilful Becky is the main driving force behind the action, rather than Amelia, the character who is announced as 'the heroine of this work' (2). Becky is described as a 'little adventuress' (41) and, when she revisits Queen's Crawley where she used to be a governess, she congratulates herself on having risen above her humble origins because she has 'brains', and 'almost all the rest of the world are fools' (41). She has applied the drive of the speculator to the business of acquiring the 'good name' of Crawley and of thus gaining access to the world of the corrupt old aristocracy.

Although unremarkable in looks, being small and slight, pale and sandy-haired (2), she uses her 'very large, odd, and attractive' eyes on a series of men in the course of the novel, including her father-in-law, old Sir Pitt, and Rawdon's earnest elder brother, Pitt, who succeeds to their father's title; Amelia's husband, George, and her brother, Jos Sedley; and the obnoxious, leering Lord Steyne, whose attentions bring about her catastrophic exposure. In the fifteenth number, when 'Colonel' Rawdon Crawley, now virtually a professional gambler and billiard player, is imprisoned for debt in Mr Moss's sponging-house, Becky writes him a note claiming that she is unwell and cannot raise money until the morning. In fact she is entertaining Lord Steyne at home and has large gifts of money from him secreted in her desk. Rawdon is released by his sister-in-law, Lady Jane, and returns to the house in Curzon Street to discover a compromising scene, though Becky protests her innocence. After Rawdon has left Becky, Thackeray ends the chapter and the monthly number with a crucial paragraph in which he abnegates his authority as an omniscient narrator,[12] asking, 'What *had* happened? Was she guilty or not? She said not; but who could tell what was truth which came from those lips; or if that corrupt heart was in this case pure?' (53). There are many hints concerning Becky's promiscuity elsewhere in the novel, and it seems quite probable that she and Steyne were indeed lovers, although Thackeray himself earlier describes her as 'guiltless very likely' (44). What really matters, however, is that Becky's 'credit', with her long-suffering husband and with society at large, is no longer good: 'All her lies and her schemes, all her selfishness and her wiles, all her wit and genius had come to this *bankruptcy*' (my emphasis). For years she and Rawdon have been 'living well on nothing a year' in Curzon Street (36–37). In other words, like some financiers in the City, they have lived on credit and confidence, running up large debts at the expense of the 'fools' who make up the rest of the world, such as shopkeepers and their landlord, Raggles, the retired butler who, thanks to them, ends up in the Fleet prison (37). Now Becky's moral bankruptcy leads to the bursting of this more mercenary bubble, and the Crawley household breaks up in disarray, with Rawdon accepting the Governorship of the aptly named Coventry Island, where he dies of yellow fever (67), and Becky leading a vagabond existence on the Continent as an exile from English society (64).

Although Becky bears the full force of Thackeray's moral outrage at several points in the narrative, she remains a tantalizingly attractive figure, attractive in the very features which are unladylike in the eyes of society, and which in terms of the history of fiction represent a strong challenge to the conventional idea of a heroine: her energy and self-sufficiency, her frankness and iconoclasm, and even her siren-like quality. Yet Thackeray implies that although she is unique, many of the characteristics which she displays vividly and openly are common to mankind, but are generally concealed. For example, he prefaces his description of how Becky and Rawdon lived well on nothing a year with a passage in which nomenclature suggests the universality of his theme: 'I suppose there is no man in this Vanity Fair of ours so little observant as not to think sometimes about the worldly affairs of his acquaintances, or so extremely charitable as not to wonder how his neighbour Jones, or his neighbour Smith, can make both ends meet at the end of the year' (36). How does Jenkins balance his income, he wonders, when the costs of his carriage, his dinners, his children's education, and so on, clearly exceed his income as Commissioner of the Tape and Sealing-Wax Office? How is it that he has not been 'outlawed long since'?

The Crawleys, then, are not alone in living beyond their means, and furthermore their speculations – Rawdon's at cards and billiards, Becky's in affairs of the heart – would not be possible in a society which did not sustain and even condone them. Similarly, Becky's social climbing is simply more cunning and ruthless than that of characters on every other rung of the ladder in the novel. Mr Dobbin, the successful City grocer, naturally sends his son to Dr Swishtail's (5), as does Raggles, old Lady Crawley's retired butler, who saves enough to buy a greengrocer's business and the house in Curzon Street (37). As in his early fiction, Thackeray emphasizes the social mobility of those who inhabit Vanity Fair, and subverts social norms in many of his comic episodes. When Becky is engaged as a governess to old Sir Pitt's daughters by his second marriage, she mistakes him, unshaven and dressed in filthy clothes, for the porter, much to his amusement (7). Later in the novel Sir Pitt himself lives with the beribboned Miss Horrocks, the butler's daughter, at Queen's Crawley, and 'the Ribbons' speeds the decline of the estate by dismissing the domestics at her pleasure (39).

Becky's contact with the upper classes is not limited to her in-laws, however, for some of the 'very greatest and tallest doors in the metropolis' are opened to her through her connection with Lord Steyne (51). In satirizing the aristocratic world of the silver-fork novel, Thackeray indicates that he places himself and his readers in the middle ranks of society: 'Dear brethren, let us tremble before those august portals. I fancy them guarded by grooms of the chamber with flaming silver forks with which they prong all those who have not the right of the *entrée*.' Most of the doors which are opened to the reader are those of the middle class, whose increased influence and power in the eighteenth and nineteenth centuries created the conditions in which the novel developed and flourished. Mr Osborne, who has made his fortune in the tallow trade, has the kind of lackey's-eye view of his social superiors which the silver-fork novelists exploited in the 1820s and 1830s: he 'grovels' before a great man as 'only a free-born Briton can do' (13), and adopts a sham coat of arms from the peerage (35). His view of his own class, however, is down-to-earth. Although Sedley helped him to acquire his fortune, and the two men once planned a match between their young children, Osborne now insists that he sees 'Amelia's ten thousand down' before he allows the marriage to proceed, for Sedley's affairs look precarious and he will have 'no lame duck's daughter' in his family (13).

The commercial and familial manoeuvrings of the middle and upper classes are closely scrutinized by the sternest and indeed most influential moralists in the novel: the servants. Lord Steyne's servants point at Becky as 'lost and ruined' as she 'writhes and pushes onward' towards a 'position in society' (44); and her own servants unite with poor Raggles in open revolution against her on the morning that Rawdon leaves her (55). Servants have seen little Rawdon Crawley 'squaring his fists at Lord Steyne's hat in the hall', and his mother reject and abuse him while keeping up a display of humility and virtuousness by taking a little shirt from her work-box from time to time, although it is too small for him long before it is finished (44). Thackeray's own comments on Becky's treatment of her son are uncompromisingly damning: 'Mother is the name for God in the lips and hearts of little children; and here was one who was worshipping a stone!' (37). If, however, Becky follows the broad road which leads to destruction, or to some kind of judgement, Thackeray does not demonstrate elsewhere in the novel that those on a more strait path attain greater happiness, or are not to be brought to judgement. Amelia, whose treatment of her son Georgy is utterly devoted, and whose path through Vanity Fair is clearly quite different from Becky's, might seem a candidate for such rewards. At the end of the novel, however, William Dobbin in effect judges the two women and finds them both wanting.

Of all the major characters, only Dobbin has the courage to say openly that Becky is not a fit companion for Amelia and her son. His anger towards Becky leads him also to express his resentment against Amelia, after fifteen years of selfless service: 'You are not worthy of the love which I have devoted to you' (66). Amelia has treated Dobbin rather as Becky treated her hired 'upper servant and *maître d'hôtel*', Rawdon Crawley (37): Dobbin 'had placed himself at her feet so long that the poor little woman had been accustomed to trample upon him'. At this crucial point in the narrative Thackeray prepares for a highly ambiguous denouement by again hinting that affairs of the heart are conducted like business affairs: for Amelia 'didn't wish to marry' Dobbin, but 'wished to keep him', a 'bargain not unfrequently levied in love'. In the famous passage in the subsequent and last chapter of the novel, in which Becky hands Amelia the note which George Osborne gave her in Brussels, Thackeray makes another of his tactical withdrawals into uncertainty about motivation, when he asks of the weeping Amelia:

> Who shall analyse those tears, and say whether they were
> sweet or bitter? Was she most grieved because the idol of her
> life was tumbled down and shivered at her feet, or indignant
> that her love had been so despised, or glad because the barrier
> was removed which modesty had placed between her and a
> new, a real affection? 'There is nothing to forbid me now,'
> she thought. 'I may love him with all my heart now. Oh, I
> will, I will, if he will but let me and forgive me.' I believe it
> was this feeling rushed over all the others which agitated that
> gentle little bosom. (67)

When Becky encourages her to ask Dobbin to come to her, and she admits that she has already written that morning, the cynical Becky screams with laughter. Although Thackeray believes that Amelia's love for Dobbin rushed over all the other feelings which agitated her gentle little bosom, his reference to George Osborne as her idol reminds us that in her widow-hood she 'consecrated' her night thoughts to her dead husband, and her days to his son (38). The effect that these years of idolatry have on her marriage to Dobbin at the end of the novel is hinted at in Thackeray's penultimate paragraph, in which he states that Colonel Dobbin is fonder of his daughter, little Janey, than of anything in the world: '"Fonder than he is of me," Emmy thinks, with a sigh. But he never said a word to Amelia that was not kind and gentle; or thought of a want of hers that he did not try to gratify' (67). Subtly, almost imperceptibly, Thackeray hints that Amelia has come to judgement, though no casual observer in Vanity Fair would know it.

That Becky has been brought to judgement by society is quite clear as she plies the gambling tables of Pumpernickel, leading the Bohemian exist-ence which Thackeray captures in a detailed observation when Jos Sedley visits her lodgings: 'In that instant she put a rouge-pot, a brandy-bottle, and a plate of broken meat into the bed, gave one smooth to her hair, and finally let in her visitor' (65). Whereas Amelia gets more than she deserves as the wife of Dobbin, Becky's final capitulation to respectability seems in a sense a loss; for, calling herself Lady Crawley, she 'chiefly hangs about Bath and Cheltenham', goes to church, never without a footman, and sub-scribes to the Charity Lists (67). We last see her actually running a charity stall at a London fair, still active, interested, and interesting. If there is no final damnation for her, there is also no Celestial City for Amelia and Dobbin.

Thackeray shapes the careers of Becky and Amelia in such a way that we constantly compare them and the values which they represent, and in a sense have to choose between them. When both are finally brought to judgement, we too are judged. Similar comparisons and choices (for both characters and readers) are often formalized in Victorian fiction by means of a love plot in which a hero or heroine is torn between two lovers. In Thackeray's other novels, for example, the transition of his young men from innocence to experience is generally a painful process both for them-selves and for the several women with whom they fall in love. A com-parison between the partly autobiographical *Pendennis* and *Henry Esmond*, Thackeray's major historical novel, reveals one of the most interesting ex-amples of his reworking of a theme in his work. Arthur Pendennis falls in love with an actress, a lady, and the daughter of a porter, but finally marries Laura Bell, the orphaned daughter of a cousin and old flame of his mother, whom his mother adopted as a child. Henry Esmond is the or-phaned kinsman of the fourth Viscount Castlewood, whose young wife Rachel adopts him as a child. Rachel believes him to be the illegitimate son of the third Viscount, for her husband has concealed the fact that the boy is in fact the legitimate heir to the name and estate of Castlewood. Devoted to Rachel as a boy, Esmond later falls in love with her beautiful daughter Beatrix in early manhood, but eventually marries Rachel herself, renouncing his claim to his inheritance in behalf of her son, Frank. As we will see later, the relationship between Esmond and Rachel, whom he calls both 'mother' and 'mistress', is far more complex than that between Pendennis and Laura Bell, whom Arthur calls 'sister'; and Esmond's spiritual hunger and his subtlety of response to the world are unique in Thackeray's novels.

Thackeray's extraordinary achievement in *Henry Esmond* is to have accommodated this treatment of an individual life in the hero's own historical narrative, in which Esmond gives retrospective first-hand accounts of Marlborough's campaigns in the War of the Spanish Succession and of the Jacobite plots in the reign of Queen Anne. Unlike G. P. R. James, Ainsworth, Bulwer, and Charles Kingsley, Thackeray carries his detailed knowledge of his favourite historical period lightly, and modifies his style to give it the ring of eighteenth-century prose while avoiding the ponderous archaisms and intrusive period detail of his contemporaries. Esmond's descriptions of the barbarities of war are generalized and realistic rather than luridly detailed or heroically idealized, and the big scenes in the novel register important stages in his personal development rather than dramatic moments in the military and political life in which he is engaged.

It is also through Esmond's private life that Thackeray develops his theme of 'no new thing under the sun'. Esmond's Christian name is that of a representative free-born man with whom the reader can identify. He is typically vacillating in his youthful loyalties, rapidly veering from 'Papist' to Protestant to sceptical positions as he reads for holy orders (10), and, like a very Victorian, is dubbed 'Parson Harry' (12) and 'young Killjoy' (16) while in fact, as Rachel later points out, his heart is never in the Church (20). A vulnerable and apparently illegitimate orphan who is blamed for innocently bringing smallpox into the Castlewood family (8) and for failing to save the life of Lord Castlewood in a duel with Lord Mohun (14–15), Esmond feels Rachel's scornful rejection deeply. Yet after he has learned that his mother was actually married to the third Viscount, he is also 'perhaps secretly vain of the sacrifice' he has made (17). Although subtle and at times ambivalent, Thackeray's treatment of Esmond's inner life is placed in the larger and familiar context of the 'old story' of the human condition in a world of suffering through biblical allusions introduced at key moments in the narrative. At the end of Book I, for example, Esmond burns Lord Castlewood's death-bed confession which acknowledges his legitimacy in a fire whose chimney tiles are to be read off like a chapter motto or an emblematic illustration: 'On the Dutch tiles . . . was a rude picture representing Jacob in hairy gloves, cheating Isaac of Esau's birthright. The burning paper lighted it up' (14). After the moving reconciliation of Esmond and Rachel in Winchester Cathedral, Rachel quotes the words of the anthem from Psalm 126: 'And then it went, "They that sow in tears shall reap in joy; and he that goeth forth and weepeth, shall doubtless come again with rejoicing, bringing his sheaves with him"; I looked up from the book, and saw you' (20).

Rachel habitually uses the language of the Bible. Her faith is strong, and, at the time of this reconciliation, she is attracted by the idea of a 'life of penance' as a nun (20). Whereas Beatrix at thirteen is a specifically pagan 'rising young divinity', at one time a Diana, at another a Luna (12), Rachel is described as 'celestial' (e.g. 1, 9) in a Christian angelic sense. Later in her life Beatrix complains that Rachel has withdrawn into the austere daily routine of a religious: 'My mother's life is all for heaven, and mine – all for earth' (32). Rachel's nun-like qualities emphasize her role as Esmond's surrogate mother, for his real mother, Gertrude Maes of Brussels, went into a convent after marrying and being deserted by Thomas Esmond, and took the name of Mary Magdalene (17). From the age of twelve, however, Esmond sees Rachel as the mistress to whom he is first childe and later knight, rather than simply as a mother figure. Her golden hair and smiling lips make the little boy's heart 'beat with surprise' when he first sees her, and he kneels as if at the 'touch of a superior being or angel' (1). When Rachel pays for him to go to Cambridge he again kneels to his 'dearest mistress', and blushes when she laughingly says: 'My knight longs for a dragon this instant that he may fight' (9). Later, however, having poured out his passion for Beatrix to Rachel, Esmond finds himself on his knees and buries his head in her lap:

> 'Oh, pardon me, pardon me, my dearest and kindest,' he said;
> 'I am in hell, and you are the angel that brings me a drop of
> water.'
>   'I am your mother, you are my son, and I love you
> always,' she said, holding her hands over him: and he went
> away, comforted and humbled in mind, as he thought of that
> amazing and constant love and tenderness with which this
> sweet lady ever blessed and pursued him. (24)

This episode is strikingly similar to the betrothal scene at the end of *Pendennis*. Both Helen Pendennis, Arthur's mother, and Laura Bell are described as angels (70–71), and in this highly emotional scene Arthur kneels to Laura and prays for a blessing from their mother: 'Pen's head sinks down in the girl's lap, as he sobs out, "Come and bless us, dear mother!" and arms as tender as Helen's once more enfold him' (74). The adopted sister takes over the role of the adoptive mother. In *Henry Esmond*, of course, the young knight's mistress and the son's 'Mother' is later to become his wife. Rachel and Laura Bell are examples of the one ideal that Thackeray preserved in his mature work: the woman who combines the roles of sister, mother, and lover. He was on difficult ground here, and the ambivalence with which he treats Esmond's relationships with Rachel and Beatrix (or 'Jocasta') suggests that he was aware of this. Thackeray's reference to the Oedipus myth occurs at a crucial stage in the development of the plot early in Book III of the novel, where Esmond's private family life is most closely related to the public history of the early eighteenth century. This section of the novel is worth examining in rather more detail.

In the last chapter of Book II and the first two chapters of Book III (29–31) Esmond's position as the true heir to the title of Viscount Castlewood is brought into sharper focus as Frank, the fifth Viscount, is married and Beatrix plans to marry, and the old Dowager dies, leaving Esmond a small fortune. As a soldier he leaves the theatre of a war fought over the succession of the thrones of Europe, and returns to England where he is to become deeply involved on the Jacobite side in the English succession crisis: 'That a foreign despotic prince, out of Germany, who happened to be descended from King James the First, should take possession of this empire, seemed to Mr Esmond a monstrous *injustice* – at least, every Englishman had a right to protest, and the English prince, the *heir-at-law*, the first of all' (30) (my emphases).

Questions concerning family inheritance and national succession thus provide the context of Chapter 32, entitled 'A Paper out of the "Spectator"', which opens with a reference to any young gentleman of the narrator's progeny who may read his old grandfather's papers. With the help of his friend, Dick Steele, Esmond composes a satirical paper and has it printed exactly like the *Spectator*. He describes the paper as a parable concerning Beatrix ('Jocasta') and himself ('Cymon Wyldoats'). The paper concerning 'Queen' Jocasta is signed by one of her servants, 'Oedipus'. This spoof *Spectator* is then left on Beatrix's breakfast table in order to show her that she is a flirt. Now this is just the kind of playful journalistic enterprise which would have appealed to Thackeray himself, yet we surely cannot ignore the profoundly tragic theme of the source of the jocular classical references, particularly as the story of Oedipus – the royal parentage which later comes to light, the murder of his father, and the marriage to his mother, Jocasta – is broadly similar to that of Esmond. Most significantly, of course, Esmond marries his adoptive 'mother', who is often said closely to resemble her daughter, 'little Mistress Jocasta-Beatrix' as he himself calls her (32). Moreover, Beatrix later claims that her mother was always jealous of her from the time she sat on her father's knee (39). The references to the Oedipus myth suggest that in his private family life, as true heir to the Castlewood name and estates, in his military life, as a soldier in the War of the Spanish Succession, and in his political life, as a supporter of the Prince of Wales, whom he believes to be the true heir to Queen Anne's throne, his story is as old as that of Thebes and that there is no new thing under the sun. His marriage to Rachel and their retirement to Virginia, where they are to enjoy the autumn of their lives, represent a final rejection of the vanities of the world in the consummation of a relationship whose moral integrity denies its earlier tragic possibilities.

Souls enslaved: the Brontës

Of the multitude that has read her books, who has not known and deplored the tragedy of her family, her own most sad and untimely fate? Which of her readers has not become her friend? Who that has known her books has not admired the artist's noble English, the burning love of truth, the bravery, the simplicity, the indignation at wrong, the eager sympathy, the pious love and reverence, the passionate honour, so to speak, of the woman? What a story is that of that family of poets in their solitude yonder on the gloomy northern moors![13]

This eulogy on Charlotte Brontë is part of Thackeray's editorial introduction to her fragmentary last sketch, entitled 'Emma', published in April 1860 in the newly founded *Cornhill Magazine*. Five years after her death, and three years after the publication of Elizabeth Gaskell's *Life of Charlotte Brontë*, which seems to have coloured his view of her, Thackeray comments on the woman as well as the writer, on the life as well as the work. Charlotte Brontë's own and much earlier public tribute to Thackeray, her greatest living literary hero, took the form of the dedication and preface to the second edition of *Jane Eyre*, dated December 1847. Interestingly, there are similarities of emphasis in the two eulogies, for Charlotte Brontë describes Thackeray as a 'dauntless' and 'daring' speaker of truth, and as 'the first social regenerator of the day . . . the very master of that working corps who would restore to rectitude the warped system of things'.

While saluting each other as courageous moralists and lovers of truth, Thackeray and Charlotte Brontë also recognize their differences, the former emphasizing the remoteness of Haworth Parsonage, and the latter commenting on Thackeray's bright wit and attractive humour. An urbane man of the world, a traveller, and a historian, Thackeray wrote with a panoramic vision of English society, both past and present, whereas Charlotte Brontë wrote with the subjectivist concentration of one whose experience of the world was narrower and more intense. Whereas Thackeray was a devoted student of the eighteenth century, the Brontës were admirers of the Romantic art of John Martin, whose prints hung on the parsonage walls, and of the writers of the Romantic period, especially Scott and Byron, and the writers for *Blackwood's Magazine*, who included James Hogg. Unlike Thackeray's realist novels, the work of Charlotte and Emily Brontë is remarkable for its depth rather than its breadth, for its idealist vision rather than its social analysis.

Thackeray himself may have had in mind the Brontës' ability to convey heightened emotion and spiritual experience in their novels when he called them 'that family of poets', though he was probably also referring to the fact that Branwell contributed to the Glasstown and Angrian stories and was a failed painter, and that the three novelists also published a volume of verse in 1846, the year before the appearance of *Agnes Grey*, *Jane Eyre*, and *Wuthering Heights*. In some of the key episodes in the last two mentioned works, prose fiction achieves the intensity of great poetic drama, in which language and action conspire to convey more than their surface meaning. Charlotte Brontë develops what one might call a female poetic in her novels, expressing that characteristic Romantic yearning for oneness or unity which for her cannot be achieved within the constraints of a world shaped by men.

Unlike Helen Huntingdon in Anne Brontë's *The Tenant of Wildfell Hall* (1848), who is comparatively conventional in her religion, Charlotte

Brontë's heroines acknowledge the limitations of patriarchal orthodoxy. Although Charlotte Brontë's novels are religious in two narrow senses of the word – in portraying characters, including several clergymen, who confess a firmly held Christian faith, and in adapting the language and forms of Christianity, such as the journey of the soul, confession, meditation, and the inner voice of conscience, to her own purposes – her heroines also turn to nature, and particularly the moon, as mediators of what one Jungian writer has called 'the feminine principle'.[14] While acknowledging that we must suffer in this 'vale of tears', her heroines find inspiration and release in spiritual experiences which cannot be adequately expressed in the language of orthodox religion. In *Wuthering Heights* we enter a world in which the categories of the Christian scheme of salvation seem to be irrelevant. Whereas Jane Eyre finally achieves equipoise with a chastised Rochester in the sacrament of matrimony, *Wuthering Heights* ends with Lockwood walking past the rapidly disintegrating kirk to find three graves in a remote corner of the kirkyard, where the heath is steadily encroaching on the low wall which divides the graves from the open moors (34, 16).

From one perspective the grave in *Wuthering Heights* represents a prison from which the spirits of the dead seek release, and one of the most significant recurrent metaphors in all the Brontë novels is that of imprisonment, confinement, or restraint. In *Wuthering Heights* both Cathy and Heathcliff are physically restrained by their elders as children, and as adults express their longing to escape from the confines of the two houses in the novel and from the physical shells which imprison the souls which share such a strong affinity, or even identity. The sense of claustrophobic enclosure achieved by limiting the action to the Heights and Thrushcross Grange, with occasional excursions into the free space of the moors, is also characteristic of Charlotte Brontë's fiction. *Shirley* (1849) and *Villette* (1853) are set mainly in one location, and the different stages of Jane Eyre's spiritual journey are marked by her escape from a place in which she feels limited or trapped. When she knows that she has to leave Thornfield, she mechanically oils the lock and escapes in the 'dim dawn' of a new day (27). When Lucy Snowe escapes from the *pensionnat* on the night of the great fête, the spring-bolt on the heavy door 'yields with propitious felicity', and once outside she knows that she cannot stay 'so close under the dungeon' where she can 'hear the prisoners moan', but must go to the park (38). In *Wuthering Heights* intermarriage between the Earnshaws and the Lintons intensifies the sense of a closed and exclusive world. In Charlotte Brontë's novels most of the characters know or have at least heard of most of the others, and many are related. Jane Eyre discovers that the Rivers are her cousins; in *Shirley*, Caroline Helstone is a distant cousin of the Moores, though there is no blood-tie between them; and the son of Lucy Snowe's godmother, Dr John Graham Bretton, whom she knew as a child in England, reappears in Villette and plays a central role in her life there.

Within the confines of these limited locations and tight sets of relationships, some of Charlotte Brontë's women respond by developing an alternative female world-view. Shirley Keeldar shocks Caroline Helstone by suggesting that Milton failed to 'see the first woman' in *Paradise Lost*, and that 'it was his cook that he saw' (18). She suggests that Eve was a 'woman-Titan', 'Jehovah's daughter, as Adam was his son'. In the subsequent chapter, when Robert Gérard Moore's mill is attacked by a mob of workers, she prevents Caroline from making a fool of herself by playing the conventional heroine of romance and rushing forward to be with the man she loves, later explaining how men do not 'read' women in a true light: 'Their good woman is a queer thing, half doll, half angel; their bad woman almost always a fiend' (20). The nature and role of women were recurrent themes in the literature of mid-century, and 'dolls' and 'angels' are familiar categories in discussion on the subject. For example, in Arthur Hugh Clough's pastoral poem of 1848, *The Bothie of Toper-na-Fuosich* (later renamed), society ladies are contrasted with peasant girls who 'feel women, not dolls' II. 92), while the angelic women in Dickens's novels have been much criticized. *Shirley* claims for women the right to be themselves and to act freely, privileges traditionally reserved for men.

Like Cathy in *Wuthering Heights*, Jane Eyre and Lucy Snowe also express a sense of spiritual confinement which is reminiscent of the soul's complaint in Marvell's 'Dialogue between the Soul and the Body', from which I take my title for this section:

> O who shall, from this Dungeon, raise
> A Soul inslav'd so many wayes?
> With bolts of Bones, that fetter'd stands
> In Feet; and manacled in Hands.

Lost in *Villette* during a storm, Lucy Snowe faints, and describes her return to consciousness as the (female) soul's re-entry into 'her prison with pain, with reluctance, with a moan and a long shiver' (16). Where the soul went during her swoon she cannot tell: 'She may have gone upward, and come in sight of her eternal home, hoping for rest now, and deeming that her painful union with matter was at last dissolved.' Like her sisters, Jane Eyre and that most moving of suffering women in Victorian fiction, Hardy's Tess Durbeyfield, who knows that 'our souls can be made to go outside our bodies when we are alive' (*Tess of the d'Urbervilles*, 1891; 18), Lucy Snowe then resumes her pilgrimage down the stony track of her narrow existence.

In *Villette*, her last novel and most ambitious study of female psychology, Charlotte Brontë's portrayal of the mundane reality of Madame Beck's school is cut from what Lucy Snowe describes as the 'homely web of truth' (39). The ghostly nun, whose legend Lucy dismisses as 'romantic rubbish' when she first arrives in Villette (12), turns out to be Miss Fanshawe's flesh and blood suitor in disguise (40). The mysterious ties between the 'secret junta' which plots against her – Madame Walravens, Madame Beck, and Père Silas – prove to be mainly commercial (38–39). Lucy herself believes that providence led her to Madame Beck's (7), and that 'it is God's will' that some travellers, like herself, 'breast adverse winds, are belated and overtaken by the early closing winter night' (32). Whereas Jane Eyre eventually finds happiness in marriage to Rochester, Lucy is left separated from Paul Emmanuel, the lover who claims 'affinity' with her (31), at the end of *Villette*. For Lucy only glimpses the possibility of future married bliss with Monsieur Paul. The joy of the walk home in moonlight such as 'fell on Eden', the night before his departure for the West Indies, is all too fleeting (41). Although the ambiguous ending of the novel leaves 'sunny imaginations hope' in the possibility that Paul Emmanuel's ship might escape the storms which rage in the Atlantic, the drive of the plot is clearly towards Lucy's bowing under the will of God and remaining a lonely but *independent* alien in Villette, working in her own school. This ending suggests that Charlotte Brontë was moving towards a new kind of realism in her fiction, two years before her death, in pregnancy, in 1855.

In turning to a more detailed examination of *Jane Eyre* and *Wuthering Heights*, today probably the two most widely read of all Victorian novels, I want to examine the common centrality of spiritual experience which results, however, in different kinds of artistic freedom from the formal constraints of nineteenth-century prose fiction.

When she tells her own story, the adult Jane Eyre has been happily married to Rochester for ten years. Charlotte Brontë's revolutionary autobiographical novel is distantly related to the older form of the spiritual autobiography, of which Bunyan's *Grace Abounding to the Chief of Sinners* (1666) is the best-known example. The linear plot, tracing Jane's progress from location to location, emphasizes that hers is a spiritual journey or quest, and allusions to the *Pilgrim's Progress* indicate that Bunyan's more famous work, almost as familiar to Victorian readers as the Bible itself, was to be 'read' alongside *Jane Eyre* as a parallel text.[15] When Jane relates how Miss Temple cleared her of the charge of lying levelled at her by Brocklehurst at Lowood, she writes: 'Thus relieved of a grievous load, I from that hour set to work afresh, resolved to pioneer my way through every difficulty: I toiled hard, and my success was proportionate to my efforts' (8). This kind of tough-mindedness in the face of difficulty and suffering runs through all Charlotte Brontë's writing, and is central to her conception of the hero of her first novel, *The Professor*. When Crimsworth arrives in Belgium to take up a teaching post, and compares himself to a morning traveller, the hill he describes is reminiscent of the Hill Difficulty in the *Pilgrim's Progress*: 'What if the track be strait, steep, and stony? . . . Difficulty and toil were to be my lot, but sustained by energy . . . I deemed such a lot no hardship' (7). The rather dull Crimsworth does not, however, share Jane's unique combination of those features which Thackeray recognized in Charlotte Brontë herself – a burning love of truth, bravery, and indignation at wrong – *and* an acute sensitivity to the yearnings of the human spirit. The tension between these two sides of Jane, or the horizontal and vertical aspects of her nature, maintains our interest in her throughout the novel. Both aspects develop in the cold atmosphere of Gateshead-hall and Lowood, where her journey of exploration begins, and are tested in her relationships with Rochester and Rivers.

Jane makes her first truly independent move when she leaves Lowood to take up an appointment as a governess (11). In place of the narrow but predictable Brocklehurst and the closed world of the school, she now has Rochester as a master and Thornfield as a home. Both are to withhold their hideous secret from her until the revelation which follows the fiasco of the wedding ceremony (26). Rochester is a master of disguise, revelling in charades (18) and dressing as an old gipsy woman (19) in order to test Jane and Blanche Ingram, that 'extensive armful' (23), when he entertains a house-party at Thornfield, and Jane is thus introduced to the world of the English upper classes. The house seems to be as ambiguous as its master, its third-storey corridor ironically reminding Jane of Bluebeard's castle (11) and yet its orchard seeming 'Eden-like' (23). Both the Gothic horror of Bertha's nocturnal visitations and the sexually charged emotion of the lovers in their false Eden are firmly controlled through the mediation of Jane Eyre as narrator, ever cool and practical at moments of crisis. Charlotte Brontë demonstrates that Jane and Rochester can achieve true physical and spiritual union only within the natural order. Moments of heightened awareness for both characters are symbolically linked, suggesting that each has to come to terms with the same eternal truths. Like Wordsworth's 'spots of time' in *The Prelude*, these moments are at once unique and related glimpses of a larger scheme of things than is perceived in everyday experience. A closer look at four such episodes will suggest this larger scheme.

After the betrothal scene under the great horse-chestnut tree, in the moonlit, Eden-like orchard on midsummer-eve (23), the splitting of the tree by lightning suggests that Rochester is a fallen Adam, the storm being reminiscent of the first thunderstorm which follows Adam's eating of the fruit in *Paradise Lost* (IX. 1002). The first of the visionary episodes I want to consider occurs a month later, on the eve of their wedding, when Jane is troubled by a 'strange and anxious thought', and returns to the tree in the orchard. It is an 'entire ruin': 'The cloven halves were not broken from each other, for the firm base and strong roots kept them unsundered below; though community of vitality was destroyed – the sap could flow no more' (25). A strong wind blows from the south, the direction from which Richard Mason will arrive in the morning to declare an impediment to the marriage. The blood-red moon, reminiscent of Bertha's eyes like 'red balls' which Jane saw the previous night, briefly appears in the part of the sky which fills the 'fissure' in the tree, to throw on Jane 'one bewildered, dreary glance' before being buried again 'in the deep drift of cloud'. The wind drops for a second, and Jane hears a 'wild, melancholy wail' in the distance. The perturbation of nature, of the wind, the threatening clouds, the moon, and the shattered tree, reinforces in outward and visible forms Jane's intuitive sense of unease concerning her marriage to Rochester.

Rochester himself also speaks of natural omens in his confession to Jane after the abortive wedding, when he describes the second of these episodes. During the four years of Rochester's marriage to Bertha Mason, her madness (often associated with uncontrolled sexuality in the nineteenth century) flourished like the luxuriant plants and fruits that surrounded them in Jamaica: 'Her character ripened and developed with frightful rapidity; her vices sprung up fast and rank' (27). One 'fiery' night, when the air was like 'sulpher-streams', the moon set in the waves 'broad and red, like a hot cannonball', throwing 'her last bloody glance over a world quivering with the ferment of tempest'. Jane's anxiety that the glance of the blood-red moon was a bad omen is thus confirmed, for it appears wherever Rochester's mad wife raves. Rochester then describes how he recognized his life as a hell-on-earth and his wife's yells as 'the sounds to the bottomless pit'. In the heat of Jamaica he expresses the same belief as Helen Burns in the cold and darkness of Lowood, though his interpretation of it is different: 'Of the fanatic's burning eternity I have no fear: there is no future state worse than this present one – let me break away, and go home to God.' Unlike Helen, he contemplates suicide, but is saved by a 'wind fresh from Europe' which blows through his tropical garden. He is shown 'the right path to follow' by Wisdom, and is revived by Hope, who tells him to go and 'live again in Europe', bound though he is to a 'filthy burden'. Thus Rochester describes his dark night of the soul in Jamaica in the very language that Jane has made her own in narrating her spiritual journey: natural description of the moon, the wind, and a garden; and allegorical references to personified abstractions and to the path of the pilgrim who carries a burden. Although they must now part, like the divided halves of the chestnut tree, the 'firm base and strong roots' of their love are 'unsundered below', at the deeper level of their shared humanity.

When Rochester's confession is over, he implores Jane, his 'better self' and 'good angel', not to leave him. Struggling to resist him, Jane admits that she is 'insane – quite insane' in her love for him, and must keep the law, given by God and sanctioned by man, to which she adhered when she was 'not mad'. Rochester fails to seduce her, and acknowledges that by crushing her body, a 'mere reed', he could not possess her: 'If I tear, if I rend the slight prison, my outrage will only let the captive loose. Conqueror I might be of the house; but the inmate would escape to heaven before I could call myself possessor of its clay dwelling-place.' These metaphors of body and soul, familiar to readers of seventeenth-century devotional poetry and prose, were still current in nineteenth-century religious writing on death and the future life.

In the third of the four episodes we are considering, Jane is indeed 'transported' in a dream, immediately after her exchanges with Rochester. The vision is described not in traditional metaphors, however, but in the language of her female poetic of personal experience and external nature. She dreams she is back in the red room at Gateshead-hall (cf. 2). Again a light glides up the wall and passes across the ceiling. This time, however, the roof resolves into clouds from which the moon 'bursts':

> Then, not a moon, but a white human form shone in the
> azure, inclining a glorious brow earthward. It gazed and gazed
> on me. It spoke, to my spirit: immeasurably distant was the
> tone, yet so near, it whispered in my heart –
>   'My daughter, flee temptation!'
>   'Mother, I will.'

As in that moment of grace in Coleridge's 'Ancient Mariner' (1798), when 'the moving Moon went up the sky' and the mariner blessed the water-snakes 'unaware', the beneficent female form in Jane's vision comes to her unheralded, and frees her to continue her journey. No longer orphaned, she seems to be in the presence of the Great Mother, the lunar goddess of pagan religions, later associated with worship of the Virgin Mary in peasant communities in Europe. (Mary, Queen of Heaven, is often portrayed on, or against the background of the moon.) Neither a classical Diana nor a Christian Mary, whose names are those given to the Rivers sisters, this 'white human form' represents the feminine principle to which Jane remains faithful when tempted to submit to Rochester's male will. The following morning she escapes in the dawn, hating herself for injuring her master, the idol who has come between herself and God.

In the horizontal plane of mundane experience, Jane's subsequent wanderings in her Valley of Humiliation, lonely and impoverished, and her arrival at Moor House, which is strongly reminiscent of Bunyan's Palace Beautiful, suggest that she has strayed from the narrow way at Thornfield (28). Although Moor House is inhabited by one who seems to offer her a direct route to the Celestial City, she is later to discover that this phase of her journey has in fact been a detour, albeit a necessary one. The Pauline St John Rivers represents the opposite pole to Rochester in Jane's world, seeing himself as an apostle who is called to self-sacrificial work in India as a missionary. He is a more subtle, more attractive Brocklehurst, a 'cold cumbrous column' (34) of a clergyman who reminds us of that 'black pillar' on the hearth-rug at Gateshead-hall (4). Whereas the resilient pupil at Lowood stood firm under Brocklehurst's regime, the adult Jane's will weakens as the more intelligent and persuasive Rivers tries to persuade her that she too is called to work in India as his wife.

When the climax of the novel comes – the last of our four visionary episodes – it is again described in terms of an earlier event in Jane's life: 'I was almost as hard beset by him now as I had been once before, in a different way, by another' (35). As in the climactic lyric xcv in Tennyson's *In Memoriam* (1850), probably written five years before *Jane Eyre*, in which the poet records his mysterious spiritual reunion with the dead Hallam, the experience which follows is firmly placed in a domestic setting at night: 'All the house was still, for I believe all, except St. John and myself, were now retired to rest. The one candle was dying out: the room was full of moonlight.' At the crucial moment when she hears Rochester's disembodied voice calling her name three times, the feminine principle, represented by the moon, is in the ascendancy over Rivers's smaller light.[16] Jane rushes into the garden: '*My* powers were in play, and in force.' All her earlier readings of her surroundings, and of the people who have tried to dominate her, have prepared Jane for this crucial moment of interpretation. Instinct, tempered with scepticism and balanced judgement developed earlier in the novel, combine to guide her in her reading of the cry: '"Down superstition!" I commented, as that sceptre rose up black by the black yew at the gate. "This is not thy deception, nor thy witchcraft: it is the work of nature. She was roused, and did – no miracle – but her best."' Jane implicitly rejects the literary archetypes and religious formulae on which her sensibilities have been nurtured, recognizing female nature as the agent of her liberation from the suppressive forces of her past life. When she breaks from Rivers and hurries to her room to pray in her own way, she penetrates 'very near a Mighty Spirit', and her soul rushes out 'in gratitude at His feet'. (One is again reminded of the 'Ancient Mariner': 'The self-same moment I could pray.')

Jane intuitively knows that she can and must return to Rochester. She finds him a blinded and mutilated Samson at Ferndean, injured when Thornfield fell in ruins around him in the fire which destroyed his mad wife. Rochester explains that he has suffered God's 'chastisements'. Thus the equality with him which Jane claimed during the betrothal scene, as if they were at God's feet after death (23), has now been realized in the equipoise of God's law and the feminine principle which Rivers's religion excludes. Jane marries her Adam as an equal: 'No woman was ever nearer to her mate than I am: ever more absolutely bone of his bone, and flesh of his flesh' (38; cf. Genesis 2. 23).

The later stages of the plot of *Jane Eyre* were clearly planned to accommodate Charlotte Brontë's vision rather than to fulfil the demands of realism. For example, the coincidence of Jane's stumbling upon her cousins at Moor House and later inheriting a fortune is true to the moral scheme of the novel rather than to the laws of probability in the real world outside it. In a novel which attempts to convey spiritual as well as mundane experience, events such as the telepathic cry have an authenticity which can only be described as poetic truth.[17]

Three years after the publication of *Jane Eyre*, a roaring best-seller, Charlotte Brontë wrote the Editor's Preface to the new (1850) edition of Emily's *Wuthering Heights*, a novel which had been less well received by the reading public when it first appeared in 1847. In her defence of the novel, Charlotte Brontë does not mention the reviewers' appreciative references to the great imaginative power of *Wuthering Heights*, but tacitly responds to some of the criticisms which had been levelled at it by those for whom the people and customs of the West Riding of Yorkshire were 'things alien and unfamiliar': 'To all such *Wuthering Heights* must appear a rude and strange production. . . . the language, the manners, the very dwellings and household customs of the scattered inhabitants of those districts, must be to such readers in a great measure unintelligible, and – where intelligible – repulsive.' Although it is true that the violent feelings and behaviour displayed at the Heights represent in an extreme form a world which Emily Brontë actually knew, whereas her readers were more accustomed to novels set in houses like Thrushcross Grange, her novel is also strange and extreme in other ways. Heathcliff is alien and unfamiliar not only as an aggressive Yorkshire farmer but as a being whose very origins are uncertain. Charlotte Brontë herself hazards the idea that 'he was child neither of Lascar nor gipsy, but a man's shape animated by demon life – a Ghoul – an Afreet'. In contrast, Rochester's humanity is never in question. Whereas Conscience and Reason fight a long, hard battle with Feeling within Jane Eyre, whose reward is married bliss, Cathy Earnshaw's uncompromising desire to marry Edgar Linton without being separated from Heathcliff, and the tragic consequences of her marriage, are reminiscent of the lives and works of Romantic writers such as Byron and Shelley – over-reachers in a world whose narrowness they despise.

Charlotte Brontë firmly places Jane's development in relation to characters and events which her readers could recognize. *Wuthering Heights*, on the other hand, is a self-reflexive novel, referring only to itself as the dialectic between two houses, two families, and two generations is worked through. The 'Reader' in *Jane Eyre* is directly addressed by a fictional narrator whom he learns to trust as a guide. The very mode of narration in *Wuthering Heights* makes the truth seem as elusive as events in the distant past are difficult to recall. Ever since C. P. Sanger quietly revolutionized received critical opinion in 1926 by showing that the organization of *Wuthering Heights* is anything but 'rude', readers and critics have wrestled with the secrets which this elaborately constructed work withholds. A novel which gave Sanger enough information concerning dates, seasons, locations, weather conditions, and genealogy to produce a detailed chronology, and a 'pedigree' described as 'a remarkable piece of symmetry in a tempestuous book',[18] is 'strange' in what it leaves indeterminate: Heathcliff's origins, the elemental quality of Cathy's love for him, the question of the literalness of the Gothic machinery of ghosts and demons, and so on.

Although Jane Eyre explicitly states that hers is not to be a 'regular autobiography', and passes over 'a space of eight years almost in silence' (10), she describes the most significant events of her childhood in vivid detail and the development of her relationships with Rochester and Rivers at considerable length. The narrative of *Wuthering Heights*, on the other hand, is structured in such a way that the relationship between Cathy and Heathcliff, from which everything else in the novel flows, is merely sketched in. The very lack of detail, however, and the inability of Nelly Dean to understand Cathy and Heathcliff, actually make more credible the unfathomable, elemental qualities of their love, as Cathy herself describes it in her crucial conversation with Nelly (9). Before turning to this conversation, let us consider some of the scanty information we glean about Cathy's and Heathcliff's childhood at the Heights earlier in the novel.

The first glimpse we get of their childhood is through Lockwood, where he reads Cathy's diary in her own coffin-like bed, on his ill-fated second visit to his landlord in 1801 (3). The diary is written in the margins of her books, and Lockwood's antiquarian instincts are aroused as he begins to 'decipher her faded hieroglyphics'. Under Hindley's tyrannical regime at the Heights, Cathy and Heathcliff took their first step in planned rebellion by refusing to read Joseph's religious tracts, 'The Helmet of Salvation' and 'The Broad Way of Destruction', the only sabbath fare provided by this Calvinistic fanatic. Cathy was delighted by Heathcliff's plan to escape from their subsequent imprisonment in the back kitchen and have a 'scamper on the moors', thus making Joseph think that 'owd Nick' had indeed fetched them away as he had prophesied. Having fallen asleep, Lockwood wakes up screaming after his second nightmare, in which his own cruelty suggests that he has fallen under the spell of the past and present occupants of the Heights. His comments to Heathcliff on what we later learn must have been the spirit of Cathy, pining for admission to the Heights, are characteristically tactless. He calls her a 'little fiend', a 'changeling', and a 'wicked little soul', adding that she told him she had been walking the earth these twenty years, 'a just punishment for her mortal transgressions, I've no doubt'. The full significance of these comments, and of Heathcliff's fury with Lockwood and subsequent action, throwing open the window and passionately appealing to Cathy to return once more, cannot be weighed until Lockwood has heard Nelly's account of these previous twenty years. (It is no wonder that several Victorian reviewers were confused by the different levels of narrative established in the novel's complex organization.) Already, however, Lockwood and, possibly, the Victorian reader who identifies with him, have re-enacted the judgement passed on Cathy in her childhood by Joseph.

Nelly Dean's oral narrative to the now ailing Lockwood, back at Thrushcross Grange, portrays a flesh and blood Cathy, demanding a whip of her father when he leaves for Liverpool (4) and developing a strong bond with the little alien, Heathcliff, whom he brings back (5). Cathy teaches Heathcliff what she herself has learnt, and they delight in spending whole days together on the moors. Heathcliff's account of their capture at Thrushcross Grange highlights the contrast between their clear-sighted impressions of Edgar and Isabella Linton, fighting over a little dog, and the civilized ideal of order which the Grange and what Nelly calls those 'good children' would appear to represent. From Heathcliff's point of view, Cathy's stay at the Grange, where she nurses an injured leg, represents a tragic fall into knowledge of the world, and the imprisonment of a free spirit. Nelly's comment that Cathy's manners were 'much improved' by the time she returned to the Heights (7) quietly indicates the gulf which yawns between her commonsensical view of the matter and that of the rebellious Heathcliff.

From this point in Nelly's story, Cathy is torn between the attractions of Edgar Linton and the apparent material heaven of the Grange, and her love for Heathcliff, her fellow sufferer in the 'infernal house' (7) which is now ruled by the drunken Hindley Earnshaw. In a world of mutually exclusive moral choices, reflected in the narrative method, Cathy refuses to be limited or imprisoned, demanding a freedom which is symbolically represented by her beloved moors. I have compared the novels of Charlotte and Emily Brontë to poetic drama, and have tried to show what I meant by that with respect to *Jane Eyre*. If we now turn to Chapter 9 in *Wuthering Heights*, we will see that although both novels have as their central theme the yearning for spiritual freedom and wholeness in a hostile and dualistic world, Emily Brontë's treatment of the theme is far more radical than that of her sister.

The chapter opens with Nelly describing to Lockwood how she had to hide little Hareton from his unpredictable father, whose feelings towards him veered alarmingly from one emotional pole to the other. Having threatened Nelly with a knife, Handley accidentally drops Hareton over the banisters and Heathcliff, catching him by a 'natural impulse', is mortified to have missed such a perfect opportunity for revenge. The normal values of family life are here reversed; home, often a symbol of heaven in the nineteenth century, has indeed been reduced to an infernal house. Heathcliff flings himself on a bench in the kitchen, out of sight of Cathy and Nelly, who assumes he has gone out to the barn. The stage is now set for Cathy's confession.

Cathy has accepted Edgar's offer of marriage, yet she knows, in her soul and her heart, that she is wrong. Trying to explain this to Nelly, she recounts a dream, one of those which have gone through her 'like wine through water', and altered the colour of her mind. (She could almost be describing the text itself here, for the third chapter of dreams has a pervasive effect on the narrative which follows, like wine in water, altering its colour.) In spite of Nelly's protests, Cathy tells her that she once dreamt she was 'in heaven', which did not seem to be her 'home': 'I broke my heart with weeping to come back to earth; and the angels were so angry that they flung me out into the middle of the heath on the top of Wuthering Heights, where I woke sobbing for joy.' Again one is reminded of Chapter 3, and Cathy's and Heathcliff's plan to escape their judges and gaolers for a scamper on the moors. Cathy believes that she has no more business to marry Edgar than she has to be in heaven, yet it would 'degrade' her to marry Heathcliff now that Hindley has brought him so low. It is at this point that Heathcliff creeps away, having listened without being seen by Cathy. He therefore misses her next words – 'He shall never know how I love him . . . because he's more myself than I am' – and her statement that she will never be separated from Heathcliff, even after her marriage to Edgar. Cathy's famous description of her love for Linton being 'like the foliage in the woods' and her love for Heathcliff resembling 'the eternal rocks beneath', and her dramatic outburst – 'Nelly, I *am* Heathcliff!' – draw this snappish, commonplace response from Nelly: 'If I can make any sense of your nonsense, Miss . . . it only goes to convince me that you are ignorant of the duties you undertake in marrying, or else that you are a wicked, unprincipled girl.' Consider the difference in emotional and imaginative range between Cathy and Nelly at this point. Like Lockwood and Joseph in their different ways, Nelly judges where she does not begin to understand, applying the standards of a received moral code based on ideas of right and wrong, heaven and hell, salvation and damnation, which are radically challenged by the very nature of the love between Cathy and Heathcliff, nurtured in a hostile environment, and by the lack of a controlling authorial presence in the novel.

Cathy marries the infatuated Edgar three years later, taking Nelly with her to the Grange and leaving Hareton to his fate at the hands of his father at the Heights. It is her daughter Catherine who is eventually to return to the Heights and complete the task of teaching Hareton his letters, aban-

doned by Nelly when she left for the Grange (9). The restoration of peace
and order at the Heights, a kind of exorcism in the eyes of Nelly, Lockwood, and Joseph, is itself achieved through Catherine's rebellion against
Heathcliff, the former prisoner of Hindley and now the vengeful gaoler of
the second generation of Earnshaws and Lintons. Another kind of restoration is also achieved in the spiritual reunion of Cathy and Heathcliff in
death. When Heathcliff seems to smile at Nelly, as he lies dead in the
coffin-bed, he has escaped from his idea of hell – separation from Cathy. For
Nelly, who wonders whether the 'goblin' Heathcliff is a 'ghoul' or a 'vam-
pire', and advises him that he is unfit for the orthodox heaven of the Bible
on the day before he dies, his 'queer end' is an event of pure Gothic horror,
whereas the impending marriage of the young couple and their plans to
return to the Grange, are anticipated with pleasure. Joseph grins at Heathcliff's corpse in mockery, saying that the devil has 'harried off his soul',
and offering prayers of thanks that the lawful master and the ancient stock
are restored to their rights. Several of the novel's first reviewers assumed
that Heathcliff was certain of damnation, and that the restoration of
Hareton to his birthright was to be celebrated. Yet these views, also shared
by Nelly and Lockwood, are put into the mouth of the Pharisaical Joseph in
the last pages of Emily Brontë's novel; and, seen in relation to Heathcliff's
tragic grandeur, Hareton's taming seems an act of emasculation.

Similarly, whereas the opening of the final chapter of *Jane Eyre* –
'Reader, I married him' – announces a closed ending of equipoise achieved
through vision and suffering, the apparent closure of Lockwood's final
paragraph remains questionable. He lingers round the graves of Cathy,
Edgar, and Heathcliff under a 'benign sky', wondering 'how anyone could
ever imagine unquiet slumbers, for the sleepers in that quiet earth'. Yet
Nelly has just reported that 'the country folks, if you asked them, would
swear on their Bible that [Heathcliff] *walks*', and that she has met a little
boy and some sheep who were terrified by what the boy assumed to be
Heathcliff and a woman. The mysteries of Lockwood's second nightmare in
Chapter 3 remain unfathomed to the end.

At a time when other English novelists were responding to both the
positive and negative effects of technology and urbanization (the railways
in *Dombey and Son*, urban poverty in *Mary Barton*), Emily Brontë wrote
out of the Romanticism of earlier generations, drawing on the sublime terror of the Gothic novel, the tragic rebellion of Byron's dark heroes, and
the narrative techniques with which Scott experimented, in *The Black
Dwarf* (1816), for example. Ironically, *Wuthering Heights* is also anach-
ronistic in the quite opposite sense of being more accessible to readers familiar with the techniques of Henry James in *The Turn of the Screw* and
Conrad in *Heart of Darkness*, both published at the turn of the twentieth
century, than to her own contemporaries. An old-fashioned novel, it was
fifty years ahead of its time in its radical indeterminacy.

An environment of circumstances:
Elizabeth Gaskell

By the time Elizabeth Gaskell wrote *The Life of Charlotte Brontë* (1857) she could call her 'my dear friend' (I. 2). This superb biography, which first revealed the 'secret' of the Brontës to the world, also tells us much about its author, whose own life and work were so different from those of the 'little lady in a black-silk gown' whom she met near Windermere in 1850 (II. 7). Charlotte Brontë's upbringing in the remote village of Haworth and her Brussels experiences as pupil and teacher, her shy meetings with leading literary figures and her brief experience of married life before an early death, contrast strongly with Elizabeth Gaskell's childhood in Knutsford, her short spell at a school in Stratford, and her secure and busy family life in Manchester, the Cottonopolis of the Industrial Revolution, from 1832 until her death in 1865. Whereas both Charlotte and Emily Brontë work in the more radical Romantic traditions of Byron and the sublime, Elizabeth Gaskell's chief debt is to Wordsworth. Her domestic realism often focuses upon the 'little, nameless, unremembered, acts/Of kindness and of love' ('Tintern Abbey'). Her untroubled religious beliefs as a Unitarian are founded on the kind of faith which Wordsworth saw as consolation for the loss of visionary power:

> In the soothing thoughts that spring
> Out of human suffering;
> In the faith that looks through death,
> In years that bring the philosophic mind.
>
> ('Intimations of Immortality')

Both Wordsworth and Crabbe (whose verse also influenced her work) are cited when, in 1850, Alton Locke talks of the 'great tide' set towards 'that which is common to the many, not that which is exclusive to the few' in nineteenth-century literature (*Alton Locke*, 9). A few years later Kingsley's hero might easily have added Elizabeth Gaskell to the list of Victorian writers he admired, namely Hood, Dickens, and Tennyson, whose 'handling of the trivial everyday sights and sounds of nature' reveal 'an element especially democratic, truly levelling in him'. Shortly before the publication of Tennyson's early volumes of poetry, Carlyle, translating Goethe, first used the word *environment* in a special sense which can usefully be applied both to Tennyson's 'democratic' verse and Elizabeth Gaskell's fiction: 'In such an element, with such an environment of circumstances' ('Goethe', 1828).[19] Environment, 'the conditions under which any person or thing lives or is developed; the sum-total of influences which modify and determine the development of life or character' (*OED*, 2b), is a concept which many Victorian writers explored, but which is specifically Elizabeth Gaskell's central concern in her fiction.

In *Mary Barton* (1848), which I discussed in Chapter 2, her treatment of character and environment is uneven: the mill-owner's son, Harry Carson, for example, is a shallow representative figure, whereas the working-class Barton and Wilson families are minutely and sympathetically observed in relation to their domestic circumstances. In *North and South* (1854–55), however, written as a pendant to *Mary Barton*, she aims to correct this imbalance in her sensitive treatment of John Thornton, the mill-owner, and his mother, who live within the precincts of the mill, and whose personalities are shaped by their environment. A lover of ghost stories, and described by Dickens as his Scheherazade, Elizabeth Gaskell develops her characters in these novels within simple but strong plots in which the heroine is confronted with a moral dilemma, as a result of a concealed fact or event in the life of somebody close to her; and this formula is followed in later works. With the exception of her one tragic novel, *Sylvia's Lovers* (1863), her attempts at the kind of big dramatic scene for which Dickens and Thackeray were famous were less successful than the accretive effects achieved within the compass of mundane reality, where a sense of place is subtly established and developed. Significantly, her female characters are inseparable from the places in which they live. Miss Matty epitomizes the 'elegant economy' of Cranford (1), and the pathos of her quietly heroic response to the crash at the bank (13) is achieved within the limits of the work's comic sketches of Cranford manners (*Cranford*, 1851–53). Similarly, the novella *Cousin Phyllis* (1863–64) depends heavily on atmosphere in its delicate evocation of emotion at times of stress. As in *Cranford*, the coming of the railway provides a parallel in outward and visible form to personal change and development, and especially the growth of Phyllis from girlhood to womanhood. In contrast, Sylvia Robson's drama is played out in a whaling town in the North-East, where the proximity of the sea reinforces the sense of her vulnerability to the vagaries of fortune.

As a novelist who closely relates her heroines' circumstances as daughters and lovers to their physical environment, Elizabeth Gaskell favours the leisurely opening in her fiction, establishing setting and atmosphere with a light touch. Indeed, she begins her major non-fictional work, the *Life of Charlotte Brontë*, not in the parsonage itself but in the manufacturing town of Keighley, four miles distant from Haworth. From there we approach Haworth as Victorian travellers did, first seeing the village in the distance, set against the background of the moors. We climb the steep hill, turn into the little side-street near the house, and are then taken into the church to read the family memorials, a mute record of the Brontës' brief lives. The second chapter describes the people of Haworth and the surrounding district, and it is only in the third chapter, concerned mainly with Rev. Patrick and Mrs Brontë, that the children are introduced. As in *Mary Barton* (2 vols), *Ruth* (1853; 3 vols) and *Sylvia's Lovers* (3 vols), Elizabeth Gaskell could set her own steady pace in the early chapters of the two-volume *Life*.

The publication of her first mature achievement as a novelist, *North and*

South, presented her with real difficulties, however, for it appeared as a serial in Dickens's weekly *Household Words*, immediately following his own *Hard Times*. Dickens looked for the kind of 'effects' which would give each part of the serial the strong definition which came naturally to him, although he himself complained of the problem of space when writing *Hard Times*. The early serial parts of the two novels provide an illuminating contrast between the two novelists: Dickens's striking schoolroom scene (I. 1), for example, and the 'Key-note' chapter (I. 5), in which Coketown is graphically described in a few bold dashes of colour, and Elizabeth Gaskell's steady accumulative approach as she portrays Margaret Hale first in Harley Street and then at Helstone in Hampshire, before the family's departure for the North. Although comparatively leisurely, the opening chapters successfully convey the impact of her father's sudden announcement to Margaret of his decision to leave the Church of England (4), when her later responsibilities are adumbrated in his weakly asking her to break the news to her mother. Helstone is always associated with natural beauty in Margaret's mind after she has left the South, and when she is finally betrothed to John Thornton he presents her with roses from Helstone (52). The moment at which Margaret braces herself to tell her mother the bad news is described as if for her future recollection: 'Her eye caught on a bee entering a deep-belled flower: when that bee flew forth with his spoil she would begin – that should be the sign' (5). As in all her work, many of Elizabeth Gaskell's best observations are those of a miniaturist.

Rather than transferring her directly from Hampshire to the industrial town of Milton-Northern, Elizabeth Gaskell takes Margaret and her family there via London and Heston, a small northern seaside town, in which Margaret notices the contrast between southern ways and the more 'purposelike' carts, clothes, and shopkeepers. When she and her father finally set off to find a house in Milton (clearly modelled on Manchester, but given a fictitious name to avoid the kind of local controversy stirred up by the sub-title of *Mary Barton*), they first notice a lead-coloured cloud on the horizon, and then 'more a loss of the fragrance of grass and herbage than any positive taste or smell' (7). As the Hales negotiate with the landlord over vulgarly loud wallpapers, and peer through industrial smog, Margaret is firmly established as the novel's focus of feeling and sympathy.

The other woman in John Thornton's life, his mother, figures as a powerful opposite pole in the North/South dialectic of the novel's title, and the descriptions of northern manners mentioned above ensure that we almost know her before we meet her. The quiet realism, however, of the passage in which she is introduced contrasts with Dickens's descriptions of Mrs Sparsit of the Coriolanian nose in *Hard Times* (I. 7), for example, or Mrs Clennam in her widow's weeds in *Little Dorrit* (I. 3). For although, like Dickens, Elizabeth Gaskell relates personality to appearance ('large-boned', features 'strong and massive') and to the room in which Mrs Thornton sits ('a grim handsomely-furnished dining-room' with a 'massive side-board'), subtle touches also suggest other sides to her nature: 'She was mending a large, long table-cloth of the finest texture, holding it up against the light occasionally to discover thin places, which required her delicate care' (9).

Dickens might have re-emphasized the strength of her hands here, and drawn attention to the fact that this proud northerner is 'near', whereas the words 'finest' and 'delicate' work against stereotyping. When her son enters and announces that he is changing his clothes before his visit to the Hales, his mother's jealous suspicion is immediately aroused: 'Take care you don't get caught by a penniless girl, John.' Her son's business at the mill has been built up with the same care and labour which she has devoted to the domestic environment of their home; both are to be invaded by Margaret Hale, the incomer. The initial misunderstanding between Margaret and Thornton, in which each is angered by the other's assumptions about northern and southern manners (10), establishes a theme which runs throughout the novel, including the weak sub-plot concerning Margaret's concealment of her brother Frederick's secret and the central conflict between master and men. (The mutiny in which Frederick was involved also reflects the mill-workers' strike in the main plot, reinforcing the theme of authority and justice.) It is within the central triangle of Thornton, Margaret, and Mrs Thornton, however, that the conflicts of environment and circumstances are most fully developed, in both the private and the public spheres.

Take for example the failures of communication between the three characters. When Margaret discusses the prospect of a strike with Mrs Thornton, soon after her arrival in Milton, her cultural assumptions are expressed in a naive question: 'Does it not make the town very rough?' (15). Mrs Thornton's reply reads like a riposte to Charlotte Brontë's *Shirley*, published six years previously, in which Shirley Keeldar prevented Caroline Helstone from rushing forward at the mill (see p. 58 above): 'I have known the time when I have had to thread my way through a crowd of white, angry men, all swearing they would have Makinson's blood . . . some one had to go and tell him, or he was a dead man; and it needed to be a woman, – so I went.' In the alien environment of Milton, where Margaret hears the workers' views from Nicholas Higgins, her own version of Mrs Hale's intervention in a crowd of angry men leads to further misunderstandings. For when Thornton tells his mother of the blow Margaret has suffered in shielding him from the angry strikers, she is startled by the violence of his emotions: 'It was a mixture of joy, of anger, of pride, of glad surprise, of panting doubt; but she could not read it' (23). In order to gain time and control her own feelings, she turns away from him and wipes up a drop of eau de Cologne she has noticed on the polished arm of the sofa. When she finally speaks, however, her voice seems unusual and constrained.

Although Margaret is the central figure in the drama in front of Thornton's mill, and in his subsequent declaration of love to her (24), Mrs Thornton's role as chorus is also crucial. In the chapter entitled 'Mother and Son' (26) she sits awaiting Thornton's return with the expected news that Margaret has accepted his proposal of marriage. Again she is at her needlework, unpicking initials on linen which he will be needing, her son, 'her pride, her property'. She then takes up Matthew Henry's Bible Commentaries, the only book in the room, and pretends to be absorbed in reading when her son returns. Although Margaret has proudly rejected him, telling him that he has misread her actions outside the mill, and explicitly not caring to understand him or his views on the strike, he loves her more than ever, and turns to his mother for comfort. Mrs Thornton's strong feelings, however, find expression in the words, 'I hate her'.

Thornton's declaration of love, then, is seen quite differently by the two women, not only because of their different relationships to him but also as a result of different social and cultural assumptions. The love interest and the social-problem plot are conflated throughout the narrative, and the final reconciliation between Margaret and Thornton issues from changes of circumstances and of views. For example, Margaret's idea of Helstone as the idyllic repository of childhood memories is modified in the light of real change at the old vicarage, which she visits late in the novel (46). Thornton looks older and careworn after failing in his business (51). As in *Jane Eyre*, the heroine finally marries as the senior financial partner, when the English novelist's oldest piece of machinery – the legacy – allows Margaret to support Thornton in the continuation of the business in which he and his mother were formerly supreme.

Although courtship and marriage remained the main staple of plotting in fiction throughout the Victorian age, the related theme of parenthood is also ubiquitous. For example, further comparisons and contrasts could usefully be drawn between the 'Mother and Son' chapter in *North and South* and two chapters entitled 'Father and Daughter' in different novels by Dickens, to be discussed in the next section. Our present concern, however, is with Elizabeth Gaskell, whose last and finest novel, *Wives and Daughters* (1864–66), has at its centre a father–daughter relationship which is painfully affected by the widowed father's marrying again. Unlike *North and South*, where the love plot is shaped by the larger external forces of the novel's social-problem theme, *Wives and Daughters* focuses upon the evolution of family relationships and of courtships within a domestic environment of circumstances on which the rapid social change of the period before the 1832 Reform Act has only a limited impact. One of the best chapters in the novel, for example – 'Father and Sons' (27) – brings to a head the tensions between old Squire Hamley and his sons, Osborne and Roger, over the question of French influences and ideas. Osborne, secretly married to a Frenchwoman, has earlier infuriated his father by claiming that his 'little whipper-snapper of a French watch', set by the Horse Guards clock two days previously, was more accurate than the Squire's 'old steady, turnip-shaped watch', which had 'given the law' to all the clocks in the neighbourhood in its day (22). (Standard 'railway time' was soon to eclipse such disputes in the mid-nineteenth century.) Now the Squire hears that Lord Hollingford wishes Roger, a scientist, to meet a French savant who is visiting Cumnor Towers: 'What business has Roger . . . to go currying favour with the French? In my day we were content to hate 'em and to lick 'em.' Elizabeth Gaskell's sure handling of the conflicts between different generations, and between different classes, in *Wives and Daughters* is one aspect of the maturity of her last work. When one compares the novel, however, with *Middlemarch: A Study of Provincial Life* (1871–72), a complex novel of ideas which may well have owed something to the structure of *Wives and*

Daughters: An Every-day Story, George Eliot could almost be said to begin where Elizabeth Gaskell left off. One measure of her far greater sophistication is in her references to German scholarship and art as aspects of the intellectual history of the nineteenth century, whereas Elizabeth Gaskell only touches upon the less demanding theme of English Francophobia as a point of reference in her portrayal of the clash between father and son.

Roger Hamley's success as a scientist is, however, a serious nineteenth-century theme, treated intelligently and with tact, and indicating that *Wives and Daughters* is no lightweight comedy of manners. While some of the chapter titles, such as 'The Dawn of a Gala Day' (1), 'Calf-love' (5), 'Making Friendship' (11), and 'The Bride at Home' (16), suggest the kind of subject-matter treated in the Victorian genre tradition of narrative painting, or even in the plates in ladies' annuals of the period, other titles – 'The Widower and the Widow' (9), 'The Half-sisters' (21), 'Father and Sons' (27) – more truly reflect the novel's central subject: the complex systems of roles and relationships within and between families, and the kinds of conflicts and tensions which they generate. These were also Jane Austen's themes, and Elizabeth Gaskell's sanity and balance have often been compared to hers. Indeed, in a limited sense, Elizabeth Gaskell can be said to have mediated between Jane Austen and George Eliot as a mid-Victorian social realist.

As in the works of these greater novelists, moral judgements are often passed silently in Elizabeth Gaskell's fiction: by placing two characters in the same difficult situation and thus implicitly inviting comparison between them; by describing the behaviour of two children and thus implicitly contrasting their parents, whose influence partly determined their early development. Squire Hamley's 'troubles' (22) are paralleled with those of Mr Gibson, whose second wife plans to introduce French furniture and genteel manners into a household in which he had formerly eaten bread and cheese quite happily with his daughter Molly (11, 16). The parallel is clearest when both men are drawn into Mrs Gibson's web through her daughter's engagement to Roger, after Cynthia returns from France. Cynthia, who has previously involved herself with the agent, Mr Preston, and is finally betrothed to Mr Henderson, states that she does not like people of deep feelings (56). Her actions are therefore based on a moral scheme which is diametrically opposed to Molly's, and which reflects the very different environment of circumstances in which she was brought up. Thus the contrast between Cynthia and Molly provides mute commentary upon Mrs Gibson.

Although Molly's dilemma when entrusted with both Osborne's and Cynthia's secrets is similar to that of Margaret Hale, she is at once more vulnerable than the earlier heroine – being the unwilling victim rather than the agent of events – and more consistent: a still point in the turning worlds of both her own and her second home at Hamley Hall. Elizabeth Gaskell suggests her vulnerability in the opening chapters, when, at the age of twelve, she is at the mercy of Clare Kirkpatrick, her future stepmother, whose actions belie the image of unselfish devotion which she projects to her social superiors (2). Discovered asleep at the Cumnors' gala day at the beginning of the novel, she is later discovered in tears by Roger when she learns that her father is to marry Clare (10). Although Elizabeth Gaskell's subtle treatment of the unhappy Gibson family after this marriage indicates that her probing of the idea of family life has now gone deeper than in her portrayal of the mutual weakness of the Hales in *North and South*, her breadth of sympathy extends even to the second Mrs Gibson, who, after her crashing error of judgement over Cynthia and Roger, is shown 'groping about to find the means of reinstating herself in [Gibson's] good graces – really trying according to her lights, till Molly was often compelled to pity her in spite of herself, and although she saw that her stepmother was the cause of her father's increased astringency of disposition' (37). As a Unitarian who denied the doctrines of hell and a Last Judgement, Elizabeth Gaskell found it impossible finally to judge even the characters who most cruelly damage those around them, and this has been seen as a limitation. Mrs Gibson's main function, however, is that of the agent of change in Molly's environment of circumstances, a change to which she responds with the simple nobility which supplies the novel's moral touchstone.

Themes and variations: Dickens at mid-century

Four of the six novels Dickens wrote between 1845 and 1860 – *Dombey and Son* (1846–48), *David Copperfield* (1849–50), *Bleak House* (1852–53), and *Little Dorrit* (1855–57) – were published in the monthly number form which had been familiar to his readers since the early days of *Pickwick Papers* and *Nicholas Nickleby*. They are of the same length as those early novels, and each demonstrates Dickens's extraordinary ability to create dozens of memorable characters in every new work. (Even the shorter novels, *Hard Times* (1854) and *A Tale of Two Cities* (1859), which appeared as weekly serials in Dickens's own journals, are densely populated when compared to, say, the Brontës' novels.) Whereas in *Pickwick* and *Nickleby*, however, the proliferation of characters answered the needs of a loosely constructed picaresque scheme, and allowed Dickens the freedom to do what he did best as he improvised month by month, we find in *Dombey and Son* and *David Copperfield* a new sense of design. Pairs or groups or whole families of characters are now placed in some comparative or contrastive relationship to other significant groupings, in order to explore a central theme; and the static quality of most of Dickens's characters – a feature of his fiction from the beginning – complements this kind of thematic organization in the novels of mid-century.

It is worth examining the views of nineteenth-century critics and fellow novelists on Dickens's method of characterization, and in particular the comments of three writers who all mentioned one of his most famous creations, Mr Micawber. Trollope, who parodied Dickens as 'Mr Popular Sentiment' in *The Warden* (1855), wrote this about his rival's characters in his autobiography:

> I do acknowledge that Mrs Gamp, Micawber, Pecksniff, and
> others have become household words in every house, as
> though they were human beings; but to my judgment they are
> not human beings, nor are any of the characters human which
> Dickens has portrayed. It has been the peculiarity and the
> marvel of this man's power, that he has invested his puppets
> with a charm that has enabled him to dispense with human
> nature.
> (*Autobiography*, 1883; 13)

Trollope chose his examples from the first half of Dickens's career, presumably on the grounds – generally agreed in the nineteenth century – that the novels of the 1850s and 1860s showed evidence of a steady decline in comic invention. But George Gissing implicitly answered Trollope's criticism at the end of the century when he wrote, 'Yes, it is quite true that Mr. Micawber, Mr. Pecksniff, Uriah Heep, and all Dickens's prominent creations say the same thing in the same way, over and over again', and asked his readers to remember that 'for twenty months did these characters of favourite fiction make a periodical appearance, and not the most stupid man in England forgot them between one month and the next'.[20] Dickens certainly uses habits of speech and repeated phrases, as well as physical oddities and mannerisms, as means of identification, but David Masson's mid-century lectures on the British novel, discussed in Chapter 1, touch on a more significant aspect of his characterization: 'There never was a Mr. Micawber in nature, exactly as he appears in the pages of Dickens; but Micawberism pervades nature through and through; and to have extracted this quality from nature, embodying the full essence of a thousand instances of it in one ideal monstrosity, is a feat of invention.' Masson also argued that Thackeray was the leading novelist of 'the Real School' (of which Elizabeth Gaskell was a provincial member) whereas Dickens led the 'Ideal or Romantic school': 'He has characters of ideal perfection and beauty, as well as of ideal ugliness and brutality.'[21]

The key to Dickens's technique often lies in the collective rather than the individual function of his characters. Gamp and Pecksniff, Heep and Micawber, represent various behavioural extremes to which Martin Chuzzlewit and David Copperfield are exposed; and Agnes Wickfield represents an ideal perfection to which David aspires. It is in comparison or in relationship, either to one another or to a central hero or heroine, that Dickens's characters, static and fragmentary in themselves, serve his artistic purposes. In *David Copperfield*, Mrs Micawber's fervent oath that she will never desert Mr Micawber suggests an idea of marriage widely different from Betsey Trotwood's (14), in a novel whose central theme is marriage; and it is characteristic of Dickens to have created a Barkis, who when wooing Peggotty with a double set of pigs' trotters or some Spanish

onions, would stare heavily at her, seldom saying anything (10), and a
tongue-tied Mr Peggotty who breaks an embarrassed silence at Salem
House by producing quantities of seafood for little Davey (7), in the novel
haunted by the loquacious Micawber, that other provider of (liquid) re-
freshment. These are two different kinds of variations upon themes or
ideas. Far more interesting and significant, however, is the brilliant stroke
of having Micawber, expansive, irresponsible, and on the side of the
angels, work for the writhing Heep, the 'umble exemplum of obsessive
labour, self-help, and foresight. The chapter in which Micawber 'ex-
plodes' Heep is one of the novel's great set pieces.

Dickens's fiction works through dramatic interaction between characters
who are essentially fixed, unless and until they undergo some sudden
change of heart, rather than through the exploration of gradual individual
human development, and it is in the central phase of his career that he applies his techniques most successfully to social themes. Of all the critics of
Victorian society in the 1840s and 1850s, Dickens, whose comic genius
assured him of a large and receptive readership, was best placed to capture
the public imagination and thus to educate the public mind. In his early
work he had exposed specific social evils, as other writers did in the social-
problem novels of the mid-century period. Now be began to question the
underlying principles upon which the English systems of law and order,
commerce and industry, education and central administration, were based.
Whereas Rev. Stiggins and Mrs Bardell's lawyers in *Pickwick Papers* represent different and largely unrelated areas of the novel's interests, Rev.
Chadband in *Bleak House* is implicated in Dickens's broad satirical attack
upon the responses of the professions to Tom-all-Alone's, and specifically
to poor Jo, an attack which focuses mainly upon the law; and whereas
Oliver Twist reveals the iniquities which flowed from a particular piece of
legislation, the Poor Law Amendment Act of 1834, *Bleak House* satirizes
the legal system itself. Dotheboys Hall takes up much of the second, third,
and fourth numbers of *Nicholas Nickleby*, and is then largely forgotten until
it is broken up at the end of the novel (64). Dickens's portrayal of
M'Choackumchild's school at the beginning of *Hard Times*, on the other
hand, not only satirizes the products of the new teacher-training establish-
ments of the time, but also introduces education as one of the central
themes in the novel's general critique of Utilitarianism, later developed in
the portrayal of Tom and Louisa Gradgrind and of Sissy Jupe and Bitzer
as adults.

In Dickens's novels of mid-century, individual characters are often confronted with their social responsibilities; family breakdowns are related to
the severing of old ties in a more mobile society, in which cash payment
appears to be what Carlyle called the 'sole nexus'; and, as Dickens's vision
darkens in *Bleak House* and *Little Dorrit*, the effects of individual 'Christian
interventionism'[22] seem more fragile and provisional in the context of the
raw realities of modern urban existence. A number of characters in one
novel are often in themselves variations upon specific social themes. Similarly, as Dickens develops a rhetoric which can accommodate his social
vision, we find him introducing ideas, motifs, and metaphors which, in

terms of theme, convey the essence of a thousand instances, to borrow Masson's phrase. In order to illustrate this I will concentrate in the following pages upon two of Dickens's major themes – marriage and parenthood – and two of his most potent symbols – the river flowing into the sea and the prison. In moving from the treatment of these themes and symbols in *David Copperfield* and *Dombey and Son* to the sombre vision of *Little Dorrit*, I also hope to convey some impression of Dickens's rapid development in a period of only six years.

In *David Copperfield* Dickens writes out, in both senses of those words, some of his most painful memories – the secrets of his unhappy childhood, of the blacking factory, and the imprisonment of his father for debt – and the continuing disappointment of an unhappy marriage. DC is not CD, however, and the failure of the rather dull David to convince in his description of his career as a novelist is striking. David's real theme is marriage, and, as he calls up people and memories from the past, he becomes aware of comparisons and contrasts between his own life and the lives of others. It is in the process of organizing these memories that the shape of the main (David) plot and of the novel's sub-plots emerges.

The complaint of Charlotte Brontë's heroine in *Shirley* (1849) that men's idea of a good woman is a 'queer thing, half doll, half angel' (see p. 58 above) is substantiated in Dickens's novel of the same year. For David Copperfield marries first a doll, Dora Spenlow, a*dora*ble but too fragile to survive in the adult world ('Ah Doady, it's a large place!', 48), and, at the end of the novel, an angel, Agnes Wickfield, named after the saint whose symbol is the lamb, *agnus dei*.[23] Whereas David broods over the inability of his child-wife to change, and realizes that he was infatuated when he proposed to Dora, he sees Agnes's unchanging nature as a stable point of reference in an unstable world: she is 'ever pointing upward' (53, 60). In order, then, to show David in the process of learning through marriage, Dickens makes Dora and Agnes static and has David move.

Dickens develops interesting variations upon his central theme in the two major sub-plots. In the Heep/Wickfield plot, Uriah Heep exploits the weakness of Agnes's father, one of many weak men in the novel, and has designs upon Agnes herself. He also maliciously fuels suspicions in the mind of Dr Strong that Annie, his child-wife, has been the lover of her cousin, Jack Maldon (42). When Mr Dick, the novel's holy fool, movingly effects the reconciliation between the couple, the young wife speaks of how, as she grew up, she looked up to Dr Strong as a father and a guide (45), and David applies her haunting phrases to his own marriage. Whereas Mr Dick brings the Strongs together again, Micawber plans the 'explosion' of Heep, at which David assists (52). In the following number (XVII), to which we will return later, David witnesses another kind of destruction: the shipwreck off Yarmouth which brings the second major sub-plot, concerning Steerforth and the Peggotty family, to its dramatic catastrophe. Although the lessons David learns through his involvement with Steerforth are quite different from those he learns from the Strongs, the central female character of the sub-plot, Little Em'ly, is potentially another child-wife, first to David himself, and later to Ham Peggotty, her betrothed. Unlike Annie, Em'ly is actually seduced, of course; and although a kind of restoration is achieved in her emigration to Australia, David is acutely aware of the damage he has done by introducing his friend Steerforth to the innocent Peggotty family. As Betsey Trotwood commented on his love for Dora earlier in the novel, he was 'blind! blind! blind!' (35).

Both David's marriages reflect the emotional vulnerability of one whose father died before he was born; whose cruel stepfather, Murdstone, came between him and his mother and exiled him to the London warehouse; whose next potential surrogate father, Micawber, proved to be in need of help himself, unlike the Pickwicks, Brownlows, and Cheerybles of the early novels; and who was finally taken in by his great-aunt Betsey, herself decidedly masculine in manner and haunted by the weak husband whose shadowy figure occasionally appears at her door. Having as it were married his 'wax doll' of a mother (1) in the shape of Dora, he finally turns to Agnes, whom he calls 'sister' even at the moment of proposal (62), as an angel who can restore him to the peace he knew formerly in her father's house. The 'idealist' Dickens's evasiveness in his treatment of adult sexuality in general and of David's regression to an earlier stage of development in particular are perhaps no more disturbing to the modern reader than is the 'realist' Thackeray's handling of the relationships between Henry Esmond and Beatrix, his 'sister', and Rachel, his 'mother' (see pp. 54–55 above); although Thackeray at least seems to be aware of the fact that he is on difficult ground, whereas Dickens does not. Certainly Dickens is more effective in his portrayal of his hero's childhood miseries and deprivations, than of the idealized final happy marriage. Let us now compare his exploration of the related themes of parenthood and marriage in *Dombey and Son* and his social novels of mid-century.

Whereas *David Copperfield* is concerned mainly with the private life rather than the social role of its hero and of the characters David calls up from memory, *Dombey and Son* examines the relationship between the private and the public life of Mr Dombey, the wealthy London banker. Dombey's is a representative commercial mind, in an age of *laissez-faire* economic expansion and of sharp social divisions. The conflation of business and family relationships in the title of Dombey's firm is complemented by Dickens's play on the word 'house': 'The house will once again . . . be not only in name but in fact Dombey and Son', says Dombey himself, when baby Paul is less than an hour old (1). Family affections and orders of precedence have no place in the famous house of Dombey and Son where James Carker the Manager taunts his older brother, John the Junior, with the latter's past 'disgrace' in the firm, turning upon him 'with his two rows of teeth bristling as if he would have bitten him' (13). Dombey's large private house, a house of 'dismal state', is as 'blank' inside as outside, after his wife's funeral, for the furniture is buried under 'great winding-sheets' (3). Money, which, as Paul points out to his father, did not save his mother (8), cannot save him either; and after little Paul's death, at the end of only the fifth number, Dombey buries himself in his own rooms, shutting out his daughter Florence, whom he has never loved. The focus now shifts from father and son to 'Father and Daughter', the title of the chapter in which Florence is hauntingly described leaving her room at night to rest her face and press her lips against her father's door, 'in the yearning of her love' (18).

Blind to his daughter's love for him, Dombey also fails to see or to register other people and objects that surround him after Paul's death. When he and that other arch–egoist, Major Joey Bagstock, pace the railway platform before their journey to Leamington, neither of them at first notices Toodle, the stoker, dressed in his grimy working clothes: 'Mr. Dombey habitually looked over the vulgar herd, not at them; and the Major was looking, at the time, into the core of one of his stories' (20). As Dombey looks out of the carriage window at the 'miserable habitations far below', it does not occur to him that 'the monster who has brought him there has let the light of day in on these things'. At Leamington he is introduced to the proud, cold Edith Granger, whom her mother, Mrs Skewton, later 'sells' him by marriage contract (27). When 'The Happy Pair' (35) return from their honeymoon, the 'dark blot on the street is gone', for Dombey has completely refurbished his house, and again he fails to see what lies behind Edith's contempt for these lavish improvements; dinner is announced, and the moment passes.

The marriage market is also one of Thackeray's favourite themes, and some of the similarities and differences between *Dombey* and *Vanity Fair*, which appeared concurrently over a period of sixteen months, are worth noting. For example, whereas Thackeray sets his novel in the Regency period, satirizing mankind in general and thus his own generation indirectly, Dickens places the rawness of the new railway age, and the 'earthquake' caused by the building of the railway in Camden Town (6), in telling juxtaposition with the faded world of Miss Tox, most of whose furniture is of the 'powdered-head and pig-tail period' (7), and of Leamington, with its Regency terraces. Like Thackeray, Dickens relates a financial crash – 'the great House was down' (58) – to the idea of moral bankruptcy: the climactic chapter in which the contents of Dombey's private house are auctioned is entitled 'Retribution' (59), and, as in *Vanity Fair*, the servants, or 'the council downstairs', play the role of chorus. After the sale, however, Dickens the sentimentalist and master of melodrama takes over, as Dombey wanders through his empty house and is rescued from the brink of suicide by Florence, who returns to the house in the nick of time. She is now married to Walter Gay, who, together with Solomon Gills and Captain Cuttle, represents Dickens's ideal of good feeling in the novel. In the final tableau, a white-haired Dombey is seen on the sea-shore with his grandson Paul and little Florence, his granddaughter, whom he 'hoards in his heart' (62). Whereas Thackeray exposes the vanities of the world and dismisses his puppets with an ambivalent farewell, Dickens ends with the change of heart towards which the whole novel has worked.

Thomas Gradgrind also undergoes a conversion late in life at the end of *Hard Times*, where we glimpse him as 'a white-haired decrepit man', now 'making his facts and figures subservient to Faith, Hope, and Charity'

(III. 9). Josiah Bounderby, on the other hand, is to die of a fit in the Coke-town street in five years' time, unrepentant. Louisa Gradgrind, Thomas's daughter and Bounderby's estranged wife, is to care for the children of others, and Dickens ends the novel with a direct personal appeal to his reader: 'Dear reader! It rests with you and me, whether, in our two fields of action, similar things shall be or not.' Unlike *Dombey and Son*, then, *Hard Times* specifically demands some kind of response from the reader to the wrongs which it exposes. Whereas most of the action in *Dombey*, *Bleak House*, and *Little Dorrit* is located in London, Coketown is loosely based on Preston, which Dickens visited briefly at the time of a lock-out. Published in his own weekly, *Household Words*, *Hard Times* presents the alien world of a northern industrial town in bold but often crude colours. Pressed for space, Dickens uses his favourite stylistic techniques of hyper-bole and repetition to convey the monotony of Utilitarian educational methods (I. 1) and of Coketown itself, with its streets 'all very like one another' and its steam engines whose pistons work like 'melancholy mad elephants' in the mills (I. 5). 'Black and White' was one of Dickens's puta-tive titles for the novel, whose working-class hero, Stephen Blackpool, a modern martyr, and the angelic Rachael, remain dazzlingly white through all trials and temptations. Dickens draws stark contrasts between good and evil in order to make a strong appeal to his reader, but his imagination is perhaps more fully engaged in the creation of Mrs Sparsit and James Hart-house, two characters who are tangential to the social-problem plot.

It is in his exploration of the inner hell of Louisa Gradgrind's conscious-ness that Dickens most effectively demonstrates the deadly effects of Util-itarian education; by comparison, her brother Tom's descent into crime is a poor thing. As in *Dombey*, a chapter entitled 'Father and Daughter' (I. 15) is one of the most intense in the novel. An interview between Louisa and her father on the question of her possible marriage to his friend Bounderby – a match that would also be to the advantage of her brother – takes place in Gradgrind's study in Stone Lodge, where 'the most complicated social questions were cast up, got into exact totals, and finally settled – if those concerned could only have been brought to know it'. Gradgrind has no need to look out of his 'Observatory' windows at the 'teeming myriads of human beings around him', for he is surrounded by 'blue books', or govern-ment reports, and can 'settle all their destinies on a slate, and wipe out all their tears with one dirty little bit of sponge' (cf. Revelation 7. 14, 17). The allusion suggests that Gradgrind plays God. When Louisa is merely advised by Gradgrind to consider the available statistics on marriage be-tween young women and older men, her longing for real affection and understanding from her father is reminiscent of Florence Dombey's:

> Perhaps he might have seen one wavering moment in her,
> when she was impelled to throw herself upon his breast, and
> give him the pent-up confidences of her heart. But, to see it,
> he must have overleaped at a bound the artificial barriers he
> had for many years been erecting, between himself and all
> those subtle essences of humanity which will elude the utmost

> cunning of algebra until the last trumpet ever to be sounded
> shall blow even algebra to wreck.

The melodramatic machinery of *Hard Times* – Mrs Sparsit's Staircase, the railway journey in the storm, Old Hell Shaft – and the apocalyptic references to the last trumpet, fires, and furnaces which pervade the novel, outwardly represent the inner hell-on-earth in which Louisa suffers, and the judgement on Utilitarianism which Dickens prophesies. In place of Utilitarianism, Dickens can offer only good-heartedness, individual charity, and Sleary's horse-riding; like other writers on the Condition of England Question, he was better equipped to examine the symptoms of the disease than to suggest a possible cure. As a prophetic work, however, dedicated to that most influential early Victorian sage, Thomas Carlyle, *Hard Times* proves to be more than a social-problem novel or political tract for the times.

As diagnoses of a characteristic psychological malaise in the nineteenth century, namely the inability to communicate or share emotion, the relationships between Dombey and Florence and between Gradgrind and Louisa should be studied alongside John Stuart Mill's *Autobiography* (1873), and Matthew Arnold's poems, such as 'The Buried Life' and 'To Marguerite – Continued', both published in 1852. Whereas Arnold, as a poet, uses metaphor in order to describe the inner, emotional life ('Alas! is even love too weak/To unlock the heart, and let it speak?'; 'With echoing straits between us thrown,/... We mortal millions live *alone*'), Dickens, as a novelist, can suggest that life through external action and description: Florence outside her father's room, Carker's teeth, Gradgrind's Observatory lined with blue books. It is in the two novels published on either side of *Hard Times*, namely *Bleak House* and *Little Dorrit*, that this technique is most effectively applied to social analysis. Whereas *Hard Times*, Dickens's shortest novel, is specialized and schematic, in these far more ambitious works his exploration of social divisions and (often ironic) connections ranges across the whole of the English class structure. The familial relationships of marriage and parenthood not only reflect the nature of society, but are also shown to be paradigms of the way in which the dense social web of the modern world is woven.

The plot of *Bleak House* is organized around the apparently orphaned Esther Summerson's discovery that she is the illegitimate daughter of Lady Dedlock. Mr Jarndyce's role as guardian to Esther is reminiscent of that of earlier surrogate fathers in Dickens; but at the end of the novel he relinquishes his own claim on her as his betrothed, handing her over to the younger Allan Woodcourt, a doctor and the hero at a shipwreck. This deferring of the charitable guardian figure to the healer figure has a social as well as a personal resonance in the novel, for it is Dr Woodcourt who penetrates the slum of Tom-all-Alone's and tends the dying Jo, society's orphan (46–47).

Charity is the theme on which Dickens develops his most brilliant variations early in the novel. In Chapter 4, 'Telescopic Philanthropy', Esther and Ada Clare comfort the injured Peepy Jellyby, when his mother serenely dismisses him and 'fixes her fine eyes on Africa again'. Four chapters later they are comforting the mother of the dying baby at the brickmakers', after Mrs Pardiggle, who drafts her own unwilling children into her charity work, has read the family a tract and left, without noticing what really needed to be done. Mr Jarndyce comments that there are 'two classes of charitable people; one, the people who did a little and made a great deal of noise; the other, the people who did a great deal and made no noise at all'.

Mrs Pardiggle and Mrs Jellyby are two of the several inadequate parents in the novel, the most fully developed of whom is the irresponsible Mr Skimpole, who blithely announces that 'in this family we are all children, and I am the youngest' (43). Dickens's treatment of these bad parents, and of the good surrogates who care for Esther, reflects his views on the 'parents' or 'guardians' of English society. One potential guardian, the childless Sir Leicester Dedlock, represents the old aristocracy; any possibility of male issue is finally buried with Lady Dedlock in the family mausoleum (66). Dickens begins Chapter 16 with an account of Sir Leicester's gout, the old family complaint, and then asks 'what connexion can there be' between his 'place' in Lincolnshire, Chesney Wold (pronounced 'chainy'?), his house in town, and the whereabouts of poor Jo, the crossing-sweeper from Tom-all-Alone's? When at the end of the chapter the disguised lady asks Jo to point out the dismal graveyard where, we later learn, Esther's father is buried, we are given the clues which the family lawyer, Tulkinghorn, and subsequently Inspector Bucket are themselves to follow up. The rotting Tom-all-Alone's is thus connected to Chesney Wold, where the waters of the Flood seem reluctant to subside (2), by ties of nature as well as law; but society's orphan has no connection with the potential father figure of the aristocracy.

Although the different locations of *Bleak House* are widely separated, both topographically and in terms of class, none is immune from the disease, both literal and metaphorical, which ironically connects them. Appropriately, then, it is the middle-class doctor, Allan Woodcourt, rather than one of Disraeli's benevolent aristocrats, who enters Tom-all-Alone's. When Lady Dedlock is found dead there, the 'thick humidity' on the walls of the filthy houses breaks out 'like a disease' (59). While Chancery, the only 'connexion' between aristocrat and pauper, ties up everybody and everything in legal deadlock; while Sir Leicester nurses his gout and fights boundary disputes with Boythorn, in a comic variation on the theme of social divisions and boundaries; and while charitable women mistreat their own children, a diseased English society struggles on in the fog with which the novel opens. When Esther as 'Dame Durden', her household keys at her waist, marries Dr Woodcourt and settles in the new Bleak House, her private pastoral idyll balances the desolation of Chesney Wold, but does nothing to reassure us about the future of England (64, 67).

After Amy's marriage to Arthur Clennam at the end of *Little Dorrit* the couple go down the steps of the church to 'a modest life of usefulness and happiness': 'They went quietly down into the roaring streets, inseparable and blessed; and as they passed along in sunshine and shade, the noisy and the eager, and the arrogant and the froward and the vain, fretted and chafed, and made their usual uproar' (II. 34). Amy is one of Mr Jarndyce's charitable people who make no noise at all. Quietly moving among the dirt and disorder of the Marshalsea prison and the streets of London, she does what she can where she can; but the scope of her usefulness is limited, as the final paragraph of the novel suggests. Here are no dramatic changes of heart or uplifting tableaux; and no simple solutions are offered by Dickens.

Dickens's theme of the inadequate parent is made more explicit in this, his darkest novel, through the parental nicknames he attaches to characters. William Dorrit prides himself on his title of Father of the Marshalsea, yet cannot see the damage he has done to his own family (I. 7). Amy, the Child of the Marshalsea and youngest in the family, takes the role of eldest sister, and is known as Little Mother by Maggy, the large and ungainly simpleton (I. 9). Christopher Casby, the sleek, long-haired 'Patriarch', has remained 'unchanged in twenty years' (I. 13), almost as long as William Dorrit has been in the Marshalsea. Philanthropists of both sexes have asked 'why, with that head, is he not a father to the orphan and a friend to the friendless?'. His sole concern, however, is the rents which Pancks extracts from his 'miserable lettings', including Bleeding Heart Yard. Like Mrs Clennam, he is spiritually and physically static, directing others to move on his behalf. Mrs Clennam has remained in her black, funereal room for twelve of the twenty years Arthur has been away in China, and has conducted her affairs through Flintwinch (I. 3). Later in the novel, as Dickens untangles his overcomplicated mystery story concerning Arthur's true parentage, he reveals Mrs Clennam's motive for her repressive upbringing of the 'otherwise predestined and lost boy' who was not actually her own son (II. 30). In *Little Dorrit*, unlike his early novels, Dickens goes back to the source of his characters' evil or misguided actions. Like William Dorrit, Mrs Clennam is pitiful even as she damages her (adopted) child.

As in *Bleak House*, Dickens uses the complex plot of *Little Dorrit* to suggest connections between characters who at first appear to be widely separated. Amy's sister, Fanny, 'goes into society' by marrying Edmund Sparkler, the son of Mrs Merdle, the 'bosom', by her first marriage (II. 15). When Mr Merdle, the crooked financier, who sprang from 'nothing' (II. 25) and married a bosom on which to hang jewels (I. 21), commits suicide, his ruin takes the Dorrits down with him. Henry Gowan's mother lives with other 'gipsies of gentility' in a squalid warren in Hampton Court (I. 26), yet she disdains the parents of Pet Meagles, whom her son marries. In a novel in which the natural relationships of marriage and parenthood are distorted by social ambition, exploitation, or revenge, characters form surrogate relationships in pairings which often border upon psychological symbiosis: Little Dorrit and the large-boned Maggy; the loquacious Flora Finching and the grimly taciturn Mr F's aunt, who occasionally bursts out with a weighty *non sequitur*; the dirty Pancks and the sleek Casby; Miss Wade and her companion in embittered feminism, Tattycoram; Mrs Clennam and Flintwinch; and many others. Ironically, the two major institutions portrayed in *Little Dorrit*, the Marshalsea and the Circumlocution

Office, are both family concerns: the kindly John Chivery and his love-sick son mind the lock, and a shoal of Barnacles keep a tenacious grip on their sinecures while keeping the world waiting in the outer office.

Although the Circumlocution Office is central to Dickens's intentions, he is less concerned in *Little Dorrit* with specifically social injustices than he is in *Bleak House*. (One only has to compare his treatment of Bleeding Heart Yard with that of Tom-all-Alone's to see this.) Rather, he is interested in the spiritual state of the nation, in the effects of social pressures upon people's inner lives; and he develops two of his recurrent symbols, namely the river flowing into the sea and the prison, in exploring this theme. Before turning to a discussion of this symbolism in *Little Dorrit*, I want briefly to consider how it is used in Dickens's earlier novels of mid-century.

Like Tennyson, whose Merlin says of King Arthur's miraculous birth, 'From the great deep to the great deep he goes',[24] Dickens thought of the sea as the mysterious deep of eternity, to which all life returns. He also introduced into his novels the old idea of life being a journey down a river which begins as a stream, broadens into maturity, and finally flows into the sea. Having spent parts of his boyhood happily in Chatham, on the Thames estuary, and miserably in the blacking factory by Hungerford Stairs in central London, and having later got to know the area around Twickenham and Petersham, where the river becomes tidal, he not only set many important episodes of his fiction in these riverside locations, but also made the Thames itself one of his central symbols.

In both *Dombey and Son* and *David Copperfield*, Dickens applies these analogies of the river and the sea to the judgement, salvation, and immortality of the individual, rather than of society as a whole. For example, little Paul Dombey's question about what the waves are saying is answered in one of Dickens's most famous death-bed scenes: a boat seems to carry him down a river, past green banks, bright flowers, and tall rushes to the sea, where he sees his mother on the shore before him (17). (Those who consider Dickens's treatment of Paul's death to be trite might care to compare it with the lingering death of young William Carlyle in Mrs Henry Wood's *East Lynne* (xx. 3), published in 1861.) The eighteenth number of *David Copperfield*, entitled 'The Emigration No' in Dickens's notes,[25] demonstrates his masterly handling of tragicomic material at this stage of his career. The second chapter in the number, 'Tempest' (55), which Dickens himself considered to be the 'most powerful effect in all the Story', describes Steerforth come to judgement when he is drowned in the shipwreck off Yarmouth and Ham's life is sacrificed in an attempt to save him. To David the sea seems to have 'swelled' since the previous night. The Portuguese schooner has been brought close in to this particular shore as if for David to witness the last fruits of his introduction of Steerforth to the Peggotty family. So David himself is also judged in this melodramatic catastrophe to the sub-plot. In Chapter 56 he sombrely describes Mrs Steerforth's and Rosa Dartle's reception of the news of the drowning. Yet in the outer chapters of the number Dickens plays comic variations on the theme of the sea in Mr Micawber's preparing to launch his 'frail canoe on the ocean of enterprise' (54) and the delightful description of the emigrating Micawber family on Hungerford Stairs, 'cleared for action', with Micawber himself looking 'far more nautical, after his manner, than Mr. Peggotty' (56). As the ship sails away to Australia, however, David is left alone in the encircling gloom of guilt, loneliness, and despair. The sea, the natural element of the Peggotty family and of Steerforth the skilful sailor, is the central symbol of the novel, destroying and restoring, but always taking people away from David.

In his last novel of the Hungry Forties, a decade of mass emigration to the colonies, Dickens sends both Emily and her dark shadow, Martha Endell, off to Australia with the Micawbers, Mr Peggotty and Mrs Gummidge, and Mr Mell. At the end of the sixteenth number, when Rosa Dartle describes Emily as 'this piece of pollution, picked up from the water-side' (50), she echoes the first chapter in the number, entitled 'Martha' (47), in which David and Mr Peggotty follow the suicidal prostitute down to the river at Millbank. As a lurid description of the kind of hell Dickens imagines for the prostitute, a place which looks as if it has 'gradually decomposed into that nightmare condition, out of the overflowings of the polluted stream', the passage raises troubling questions concerning Dickens's own attitude towards the women he worked hard to reclaim with the help of Angela Burdett-Coutts. In a novel in which the Micawbers' imprisonment for debt seems slightly to improve their lot, if not David's (11), and in which the imprisonment of Heep and Littimer simply gives Dickens the opportunity to satirize the new model prison system (61), the most haunting reference to a prison comes in the passage in which he describes the Thames in which Martha would have drowned herself: 'There were neither wharves nor houses on the melancholy waste of road near the great blank Prison. A sluggish ditch deposited its mud at the prison walls. Coarse grass and rank weeds straggled over all the marshy land in the vicinity.' The river and the prison are thus associated as sites of social exclusion and despair.

The marshy land described in *David Copperfield* reminds one of Magwitch and the hulks on the marshes in *Great Expectations*; the prison walls of *Little Dorrit*. The 'Martha' chapter also looks forward to the description of the Thames in the famous second paragraph of *Bleak House*: 'Fog everywhere. Fog up the river, where it flows among green aits and meadows; fog down the river, where it rolls defiled among the tiers of shipping, and the waterside pollutions of a great (and dirty) city. Fog on the Essex marshes, fog on the Kentish heights' (1). Like Chancery, which is at its very heart, the fog seems to envelop everybody and everything. The polluted river flows fast through central London, like the lives of those who hurry past poor Jo: 'There he sits, the sun going down, the river running fast, the crowd flowing by him in two streams – everything moving on to some purpose and to one end – until he is stirred up, and told to "move on" too' (19). That one end is death, of course, and when the aptly named Inspector Bucket searches for Lady Dedlock in the penultimate number of the novel, he orders his men to drag the Thames. Bucket himself gazes into the 'profound black pit of water': 'The river had a fearful look, so overcast and secret, creeping away so fast between the low flat lines of shore: so heavy with indistinct and awful shapes, both of substance and shadow: so deathlike and mysterious' (57). When Wordsworth describes the difficulty of separating distant memories from more recent and present experience as being like one hanging over the side of a boat and trying to 'part/The shadow from the substance', reflections on the surface of the water from realities 'in the bottom of the deep', he affirms that such 'impediments' make his 'task more sweet' (*Prelude*, 1850 version, IV. 256–75). In the following book he recalls 'no soul-debasing fear' when he witnessed the incident of the drowned man at the age of eight, but sees it as a moment of sublime terror:

> . . . from a boat others hung o'er the deep,
> Sounding with grappling irons and long poles.
> At last, the dead man, 'mid that beauteous scene
> Of trees and hills and water, bolt upright
> Rose, with his ghastly face, a spectre shape
> Of terror.
>
> (v. 446–51)

Dickens may well have read and imaginatively responded to these passages from *The Prelude; or, Growth of a Poet's Mind*. In *Bleak House*, however, as in *Little Dorrit,* he explores the world of Blake's 'London'[26]; having traced the growth of David Copperfield's mind, he turned from private to social Experience.

In *Little Dorrit* Dickens describes the Thames as a 'deadly sewer' ebbing and flowing through the heart of London (I. 3), and later uses the analogy of the polluted Thames with reference to Christopher Casby's activities, likening the snorting Pancks to a steam-tug taking in tow the cumbrous Patriarch, adrift with the tide (I. 13). Constantly drawn to the Iron Bridge at Southwark, 'as quiet after the roaring streets as though it had been open country' (I. 9), Little Dorrit seems to Arthur Clennam 'the least, the quietest, and weakest of Heaven's creatures' (I. 13). Meanwhile, further up-stream, Arthur himself returns to Twickenham as obsessively as Amy visits the Iron Bridge. As Arthur persuades himself not to fall in love with Pet Meagles, the repeated analogy of the river, reminiscent of Paul Dombey's death-bed scene, conveys the sense of time passing here steadily and peace-fully: 'Within view was the peaceful river and the ferry-boat, to moralise to all the inmates [of the Meagles' house], saying . . . Year after year, so much allowance for the drifting of the boat, so many miles an hour the flowing of the stream, here the rushes, there the lilies, nothing uncertain or unquiet upon this road that steadily runs away' (I. 16). When he drops Pet's roses into the river at Twickenham, on a day when there has been 'no division' between 'the real landscape and its shadow in the water', the flowers float away in the moonlight, as 'things that once were in our breasts, and near our hearts, flow from us to the eternal seas' (I. 28).

Arthur must work out his salvation with Amy Dorrit in the roaring streets of London, rather than with Pet in Twickenham, and their union follows his own imprisonment in the Marshalsea after the ruin of Merdle.

Before this, however, he falls prey to a more dangerous obsession, or mental imprisonment, than that of the rushes and the lilies, when he cannot get Blandois out of his mind. Dickens, the great prose-poet of Victorian fiction, finds his correlative for the obsessive mind in a simile which reads like a nightmarish distortion of the Wordsworth passages quoted above:

> As though a criminal should be chained in a stationary boat
> on a deep clear river, condemned, whatever countless leagues
> of water flowed past him, always to see the body of the
> fellow-creature he had drowned lying at the bottom,
> immovable, and unchangeable, except as the eddies made it
> broad or long, now expanding, now contracting its terrible
> lineaments. (II. 23)

Restoration is made possible for Arthur not through Nature, as in Wordsworth, but by love, in the small human form of Amy, who, within the Marshalsea, unlocks his imprisoned heart (II. 29).

Much has been written about the prison symbolism in *Little Dorrit*, but perhaps the most interesting commentator on the subject is Daleski, whose demonstration that 'England itself is subject to a state of arrest' in the novel touches on many examples, including Mrs General's 'little circular set of mental grooves or rails' on which she starts 'little trains of other people's opinions', which never overtake one another and never get anywhere (II. 2).[27] Almost every character in the novel seems at once prisoner and gaoler: Mrs Clennam, immobilized in her room and imprisoning Affery; Merdle, whose hands constantly try to take himself into custody and whose ruin puts Clennam into the debtors' prison; Miss Wade, locked into a hatred of men and keeping a tight grip on Tattycoram. Expected by Mrs General and her father to develop a surface, Amy turns inward to the lights and shadows of her inner life. But there is hope of transcendence. On the day that Mrs Clennam is briefly freed from her imprisonment and crosses the river to see Little Dorrit in the Marshalsea, the morning light turns the iron bars of the prison gate into 'stripes of gold': 'Far aslant across the city, over its jumbled roofs, and through the open tracery of its church towers, struck the long bright rays, bars of the prison of this lower world' (II. 30). The hope of a future life was fundamental to Dickens's personal faith, as it was to Tennyson's, and this emblem of the universal human lot implies the possibility of a higher existence. For Amy and Arthur there is at present no escape from the roaring streets of the prison of the lower world; there is no emigrant ship waiting for them at the end of the novel, and no idyllic country cottage. Most of the characters in the novel remain locked into their neuroses and obsessions. Yet in the fallen world of Experience, and in the unpromising context of a society in chains, Dickens affirms limited human possibilities.

Like his treatment of orphaned and alienated children, suppressed women, and imprisoned souls, Dickens's sense of the transcendent is comparable to the Romantic vision of the Brontë sisters. In almost every other respect, of course, Dickens and the Brontës inhabited different worlds, both real and imagined, and his novels of mid-century have a lively contemporaneity which theirs lack. The scandal of Chancery was much discussed in 1851, and the damning report on the Civil Service of 1853 became sharply relevant two years later, when gross maladministration came to light during the Crimean War. Yet in his treatment of the law in *Bleak House* and the Marshalsea in *Little Dorrit*, Dickens developed themes and images which had long haunted him, and which represent much more than the institutions of law and order. By portraying an old prison in *Little Dorrit*, demolished before he wrote the novel, rather than the kind of modern prison satirized in *David Copperfield* (61), he freed himself from the limitations of contemporary satire and social-problem exposé, making the *idea* of imprisonment his central analogy for the human condition in Victorian society. It is in the application of such ideas and analogies to the inner lives of his characters that Dickens the novelist becomes the great prose-poet of his age.

Notes

1. See G. M. Young, 'The Victorian Noon-Time', in *Victorian Essays*, edited by W. D. Hancock (London, 1962); Carl Dawson, *Victorian Noon: English Literature in 1850* (Baltimore and London, 1979); J. B. Priestley, *Victoria's Heyday* (London, 1972).

2. Jean-Paul Sartre, *What is Literature?*, translated by Bernard Frechtman (1950; repr. London, 1967), p. 54.

3. Sartre, p. 32.

4. Douglas Jerrold, *Mrs. Caudle's Curtain Lectures and Other Stories and Essays*, World's Classics, 122 (London, 1907), p. ix.

5. See Robert Lee Wolff, *Gains and Losses: Novels of Faith and Doubt in Victorian England* (London, 1977), p. 511.

6. J. A. Froude, *The Nemesis of Faith*, Victorian Fiction: Novels of Faith and Doubt, 68 (1849; repr. New York and London, 1975), p. 199. (The novel is not divided into numbered chapters.)

7. Froude, pp. 148–9, 158.

8. *Charles Kingsley: His Letters and Memories of his Life*, edited by Fanny Kingsley (London, 1883), p. 162.

9. *Charles Kingsley*, p. 164.

10. G. K. Chesterton, Introduction to Everyman *Edwin Drood & Master Humphrey's Clock*, quoted in Geoffrey Tillotson, *Thackeray the Novelist* (1954; repr. London and New York, 1974), p. 6.

11. Tillotson, p. 6.

12. Earlier in *Vanity Fair* Thackeray comments on novelists having 'the privilege of knowing everything' (3) and on 'the omniscience of the novelist' (15).

13. 'The Last Sketch', *Cornhill Magazine*, 1 (1860), 485–98 (p. 486).

14. 'By "principle" I mean an essence, or inner law, not as a law that is imposed by a legal authority but rather using the term as it is used in science, where we speak of the law of gravity.' M. Esther Harding, *Woman's Mysteries, Ancient and Modern: A Psychological Interpretation of the Feminine Principle as Portrayed in Myth, Story and Dreams* (1955; repr. London, 1971), p. 16. See also Barbara Hannah's Jungian study of the Brontës and Sandra M. Gilbert's and Susan Gubar's feminist study, both listed in the Brontë bibliography (see p. 232 below). Robert B. Heilman, in 'Charlotte Brontë, Reason, and the Moon', *Nineteenth-Century Fiction*, 14 (1960), 283–302, focuses on some of the passages included in my own discussion of the novel, but does not comment on the moon in relation to womanhood.

15. For discussion on the *Pilgrim's Progress* in Charlotte Brontë's novels see Michael Wheeler, *The Art of Allusion in Victorian Fiction* (London, 1979), Chapter 3, and Barry V. Qualls, *The Secular Pilgrims of Victorian Fiction: The Novel as Book of Life* (Cambridge, 1982), Chapter 2. Both refer to earlier articles on the subject.

16. See Heilmann, op. cit., p. 299.

17. See also Ruth Bernard Yeazell, 'More True than Real: Jane Eyre's "Mysterious Summons"', *Nineteenth-Century Fiction*, 29 (1974), 127–43.

18. C. P. Sanger, *The Structure of 'Wuthering Heights'*, Hogarth Essays, 19 (London, 1926), reprinted in *Wuthering Heights: An Anthology of Criticism*, compiled by Alastair Everitt (London, 1967), pp. 193–208 (p. 196).

19. 'Goethe', *Foreign Review*, 2 (1828), reprinted in *Critical and Miscellaneous Essays*, 4 vols (London, 1893), I, 172–222 (p. 192). (*OED* wrongly dates the article 1827.)

20. George Gissing, *Charles Dickens: A Critical Study* (1898; repr. New York, 1904), p. 147.

21. David Masson, *British Novelists and their Styles: Being a Critical Sketch of the History of British Prose Fiction* (Cambridge, 1859), pp. 248–59. For further comment on Masson, see p. 6 above.

22. The phrase is Louis Cazamian's, in *The Social Novel in England, 1820–1850*, translated by Martin Fido (London and Boston, 1973), p. 211.

23. Compare Jane Vogel, *Allegory in Dickens*, Studies in the Humanities, 17 (Alabama, 1977), p. 3. Although Vogel's method throws up some suggestive readings of names it is often over-ingenious.

24. 'The Coming of Arthur' (1869), 410. (One of Tennyson's *Idylls of the King*.)

25. See John Butt and Kathleen Tillotson, *Dickens at Work* (London, 1957), pp. 168–71.

26. 'I wander thro' each charter'd street,/Near where the charter'd Thames doth flow,/And mark in every face I meet/Marks of weakness, marks of woe.//In every cry of every Man,/. . . The mind-forg'd manacles I hear.' 'London', *Songs of Experience* (1794). See also F. R. and Q. D. Leavis, *Dickens the Novelist* (1970; repr. Harmondsworth, 1972), pp. 282–359.

27. See H. M. Daleski, *Dickens and the Art of Analogy* (London, 1970), pp. 195, 207. See also Philip Collins, '*Little Dorrit*: the Prison and the Critics', *TLS*, 18 April 1980, pp. 445–6.

Chapter 4
High Victorian Fiction

Retrospect and prospect: sensational, historical, school and religious novels, fantasy

By the beginning of the 'High Victorian' phase in the development of English fiction (*c.* 1860–75), novel-writing, and the sale and lending of works of fiction, had become highly professionalized, and, in terms of sheer numbers of titles, the novel was booming. Mudie opened a large new hall behind his New Oxford Street premises in 1860 and went on to open other branches of his circulating library in London and the provinces, supplying thousands of commercially safe three-deckers to his customers. In the early 1860s W. H. Smith & Son began to compete with Mudie in the library trade. Cheap 'railway' reprints, available at Smith's station bookstalls from the 1850s, made it possible for many more people to buy complete volumes of fiction. Dickens's new family weekly, *All the Year Round*, was founded in 1859; the highly successful monthly, the *Cornhill Magazine*, appeared in the following year, carrying two serial novels, under Thackeray's editorship; and other magazines carrying serials were founded during the 1860s, including the *Argosy* and the *Graphic*. The demand for fiction in the 1860s and 1870s is also reflected in the massive output of some of the novelists who flourished during this period, including not only Trollope, whose hard-headed professionalism was later to become the subject of controversy, but also R. M. Ballantyne, M. E. Braddon, Margaret Oliphant, and Mrs Henry Wood.

The architecture of these decades, which Robert Furneaux Jordan labels High Victorian, is also characterized by massiveness of output, proportions, and confidence. In the later phases of the Gothic Revival, Jordan argues, commercial architects with their trained draughtsmen now permanently replaced the artist and the dilettante.[1] William Butterfield and Gilbert Scott could forget that Gothic had roots in the Middle Ages, and produced something that was assertively modern and Victorian. In describing the fiction of the period as High Victorian, and thus suggesting broad parallels between developments in literature and the other arts, I want to leave the term undefined, as Jordan does. Certain features can nevertheless be identified; the professionalism of the novel trade has, for example, already been mentioned. Novelists consolidated and developed the Victorian

identity established in the previous two decades, and a second generation
of writers modified received conventions in ways which were ultimately
to lead to a rejection of Victorian ideas. George Meredith, who thought
of the mass reading public as 'the porkers', and George Eliot, whose later
works were criticized for their difficulty, offer a revealing contrast to Dickens's relationship with his broadest of readerships in the early and middle
years of his career. A split between highbrow and middle–brow readerships began to open up as George Eliot and Meredith raised the intellectual
standards by which the novel could be judged, and their respective high
realism and mannerism prepared the ground for a later generation of novelists, including Thomas Hardy, George Moore, and George Gissing, for
whom 'seriousness' and 'thought' were to become keywords.[2]

In the High Victorian phase, then, novelists became more ambitious
intellectually, the novel became more complex and self-aware, and Victorian values were treated more sceptically. All these features are represented in the career of George Eliot, whose development as a novelist
made possible much that followed in late Victorian fiction. George Eliot
also epitomizes an essential feature of High Victorianism in her application
of the lessons of history to the realities of the present and ideals of the
future. Writing in the democratizing era of the Second Reform Act (1867)
and Forster's Education Act (1870), and of rapidly developing communi-
cations (both the telegraph and the telephone were invented in the 1870s),
she set several of her novels in the period of the stage-coach and the first
Reform Act (1832). Like other novelists of the 1860s and 1870s, her treatment of themes explored by former Victorian writers could be described
as a kind of rewriting: earlier ideas and conventions are reworked from a
new agnostic and post-Darwinian position. Yet the larger European dimension of *Daniel Deronda* (1876), her last novel, and especially its concern
with the racial and cultural inheritance of the Jews, looks forward to the
anti-parochial European movement of Modernism. Similarly, Meredith's
ambition as a literary artist, rather than as a novelist merely writing for a
specific market, suggests parallels with French and Russian rather than
English contemporaries.[3]

George Eliot's and Meredith's first novels, *Adam Bede* and *The Ordeal
of Richard Feverel*, were published in 1859, a year as much a literary and
intellectual watershed as 1847–48 had been in the history of English fiction,
painting, and politics. For 1859, described by several recent critics as an
annus mirabilis, was also the year of Darwin's *Origin of Species* and J. S.
Mill's *On Liberty*. H. T. Buckle in his *History of Civilization in England*
(1857–61), and, more radically, Thomas Huxley and Herbert Spencer in
their applications of Darwinian theory to biological and social sciences,
now challenged the intellectual assumptions of earlier generations by applying scientific laws and principles to the study of human institutions and the
natural world. The publication of *Essays and Reviews*, in which seven
liberal writers questioned, among other things, the idea of eternal punishment, caused almost as great a stir in 1860 as the *Origin of Species* had
the previous year. George Eliot not only knew many members of the new
intellectual élite of the High Victorian era; she was also a member herself.

Meanwhile Dickens, whose genius was not that of an intellectual, entered the third and final phase of his career. His last novels, published in the late 1860s, indicate a deepening interest in the psychology of the individual rather than the condition of English society, but at the same time he also attempted to restore his unique rapport with the reading public, which he felt he was losing, through the exhausting reading tours which finally killed him. Trollope's development in the period, though characteristically uneven, was broadly from a conservative quietism to a pessimistic cynicism, in a world which increasingly baffled and disturbed him. Before, however, examining the work of Dickens and Trollope, and of George Eliot and Meredith, I propose to consider five of the principal sub-genres of fiction in the period, each of which, in its different way, exploits the potential of the novel, which was now not only taken more seriously by the heavyweight literary journals, but was also enjoying unrivalled popularity and demand among an increasingly powerful and confident middle class: the sensation novel, the historical novel, the school novel, the fantasy, and the religious novel.

Although the influence of royalty on the national life was considerably diminished after the death of Prince Albert in 1861 and Queen Victoria's retirement into private mourning, the earnestness and high moral tone of Victoria's reign was perpetuated in much of the art and literature of the 1860s. The new decade, however, must have felt very different from previous decades to thinking people, and an indicator of cultural change is the fact that one can hardly imagine Meredith's sonnet sequence on the breakdown of a marriage (based on his own), *Modern Love* (1862), and Swinburne's notorious *Poems and Ballads* (1866) appearing ten or twenty years earlier. Like these poets, although sometimes more covertly, the exponents of the most significant new sub-genre of Victorian fiction in the 1860s, the sensation novel, explored the darker, often forbidden areas of human experience. Drawing on elements of the Gothic novel of the late eighteenth and early nineteenth centuries, the fiction of Poe and Victor Hugo, and the Newgate novel of the 1830s, Wilkie Collins, Charles Reade, M. E. Braddon, and Mrs Henry Wood produced novels which sold in great numbers, and which were widely considered by reviewers to be not only innovatory but also subversive. Working on what Browning's Bishop Blougram calls 'the dangerous edge of things', the sensation novelists challenged both the authority of the realistic tradition and the prudish Grundyism of the age. Collins, the acknowledged leader in the sub-genre and its only true artist, created a fascinating, even attractive villain in Count Fosco (*The Woman in White*, 1859–60). When Mr Pedgift Senior, the wise lawyer in *Armadale* (1864–66), speaks of every guilty woman's 'secret self-possession' and 'neat little lie' (III. 5), his comment on Miss Gwilt could be applied to many of the villainous or corrupt heroines who fascinated the Victorian reading public, including Braddon's doll-like, apparently angelic bigamist, Lady Audley of *Lady Audley's Secret* (1862), and Mrs Henry Wood's adulteress, Lady Isabel Carlyle in *East Lynne* (1861). In *Griffith Gaunt* (1865–66),

Charles Reade brings the dynamic Kate Peyton, a 'scarlet Amazon' who rides like the wind (6), later Mrs Gaunt, into dangerously intimate relations with her passionate confessor, Father Leonard (22f), adding the 'sensation' of religious taboo to a story of suppressed sexual feeling which was attacked by reviewers as immoral.

Unlike the black-and-white characterization and moral judgements of the melodrama, and its equivalent in cheap popular fiction, the Penny Dreadful,[4] character and plot in the sensation novels of the 1860s are often highly ambivalent, and the morality of the novels relativist rather than absolutist. Wilkie Collins's complex plots in *The Woman in White* and *The Moonstone* (1868) – in T. S. Eliot's view 'the first and greatest of English detective novels'[5] – are mediated by relays of narrators, whose function is not unlike that of witnesses in court. The reader is presented with problems of reading or interpretation in which appearance and reality are blurred or contradictory. In *The Woman in White*, whose plot revolves around the identities and origins of near doubles, actually half-sisters, Marian Halcombe reports that all Fosco's smallest characteristics 'have something strikingly original and perplexingly contradictory in them': 'This fat, indolent, elderly man, whose nerves are so finely strung that he starts at chance noises, . . . put his hand on the head of a chained bloodhound . . . so savage that the very groom who feeds him keeps out of his reach' (II. 1. II). *The Moonstone* is littered with written texts – letters, manuscripts, slips of paper found in books – which demand close scrutiny, and the man whose character seems clearly legible in his name, Godfrey Ablewhite, turns out to be the villain (cf. Cain) who dies with his face blacked up (II. 5).

As in *Wuthering Heights*, the reader of the sensation novel often has to interpret not only a trail of clues but also the narrator(s) by whom that trail is set, in an atmosphere of heightened emotion. Braddon's Robert Audley, and Collins's Marian Halcombe and Allan Armadale all have mysterious prophetic dreams which are subsequently validated by events, suggesting that at least parts of the novels' schemes have a non-rational basis. A further problem of interpretation is that of tone and intention, for although the young Henry James, whose own *Turn of the Screw* (1898) owes something to Collins, claimed in a review of 1865 that the latter's works were 'not so much works of art as works of science',[6] Collins is most fascinating when he is, so to say, at play: with Count Fosco; with Sergeant Cuff and his roses, and the tract-distributing Miss Clack, of *The Moonstone*; and, in a quite different way, when he creates a 'sensational' atmosphere through the use of location – the lake at Blackwater Park, the Shivering Sands, Hurle Mere, the Paris morgue.

In his playfulness Collins is the major progenitor of later English detective novelists and thriller writers. In their different ways, and unlike Collins, the other sensation novelists had axes to grind. Mrs Henry Wood, who dutifully supported her own family and that of her brother by writing, was the most conservative, as the famous warning in *East Lynne* to wives thinking of taking a lover suggests. Lady Isabel Carlyle has left her husband and spent nearly a year on the Continent with her lover, never enjoying a moment's calm, or peace, or happiness, and always riddled with guilt. The moral is pressed firmly home: 'Oh, reader, believe me! Lady – wife – mother! should you ever be tempted to abandon your home, so will you awaken! Whatever trials may be the lot of your married life . . . *resolve* to bear them; fall down upon your knees and pray to be enabled to bear them; pray for patience; pray for strength to resist the demon that would urge you so to escape . . .' (XI. 1), and so on. Yet even Mrs Henry Wood makes Lady Isabel a sympathetic figure. Charles Reade combines a serious reformist purpose with sensational material, although his morbid lingering around the instruments of torture in the prison in *It is Never Too Late to Mend* (1856) suggests other reasons for his interest in the subject of penal reform.

More central to the concerns of the sensation novel is Reade's treatment in *Hard Cash* (1863) of the asylum where many of the most memorable episodes take place. Modern criticism on the subject of madwomen in attics and maniacs in cellars has suggested a close correlation between Victorian views on what was considered to be deviant behaviour, particularly in women, and on the nature of insanity.[7] An asylum and a 'sanatorium' figure in Collins's *The Woman in White* and *Armadale*, but perhaps the most interesting treatment of madness is Braddon's in *Lady Audley's Secret*. Lady Audley, whose own 'mad' mother was locked away (35), threatens Robert Audley with the asylum when he is in possession of her secret – her bigamy and the (attempted) murder of her first husband (30). At the end of the novel, however, she herself is 'buried alive' in a madhouse in Belgium (38). Elaine Showalter has suggested that the most radically subversive aspect of the novel lies in the fact that there is *no* madness in Lady Audley's actions, when she is examined in the context of Victorian conventions of marriage and sexual roles: 'As every woman reader must have sensed, Lady Audley's real secret is that she is *sane* and, moreover, representative.'[8] The crimes of passion, bigamous and adulterous relationships, madhouses, and sinister rural locations of the sensation novel are not merely the ingredients of an escapist form of fiction; they provide a context in which human psychology is explored under the stress of extraordinary, heightened emotion, and in which assumptions about the 'ordinary' are questioned or undermined.

Other kinds of fiction published in the 1860s also explored areas beyond the narrow boundaries of domestic realism. The events of Sheridan Le Fanu's fascinating psychological thriller, *Uncle Silas* (1864), a close relation to the sensation novel, are described by the heroine, Maud, whose burden of knowledge becomes almost intolerable when she witnesses one of the most fearful murders in Victorian fiction, a hammer inflicting 'scrunching blows' on the victim's skull (64).[9] Like Maud and her sisters in the sensation novel, it is also the heroines in the love romances of the decade who hold our attention: Lorna Doone in R. D. Blackmore's famous 'Romance of Exmoor' (1869), the fascinating and highly original Cigarette in Ouida's *Under Two Flags* (1867), and the besotted and seduced Kate in Rhoda Broughton's *Not Wisely, but Too Well* (1867).

The period in which the sensation novel and the love romance flourished

also witnessed further developments in the historical novel, the most obvious kind of 'retrospect', with the publication of at least five novels which
at times rival these other sub-genres in dramatic action and sensational effects: Dickens's *A Tale of Two Cities* (1859), Charles Reade's *The Cloister
and the Hearth* (1861), George Eliot's *Romola* (1862–63), Elizabeth Gaskell's
Sylvia's Lovers (1863), and Charles Kingsley's *Hereward the Wake* (1865). As
in the mid-century period, the writing of historical fiction reflected readings
of the present as well as the past, and the period 1860–75 marked not only
a consolidation of economic expansion at home but also expansionism in
the British Empire abroad, culminating in Disraeli's notorious declaration
of Queen Victoria as Empress of India in 1876.

Although very different in style and viewpoint – Dickens and Kingsley
were both strongly influenced by Carlyle, for example, whereas Reade consciously wrote against Carlyle's view of history – various similarities are
worth noting. While Marx worked in the British Museum on a mass of
statistical evidence to support his materialist concept of history, producing
the first volume of *Kapital* in 1867 (trans. 1887), the often laborious researches of these English novelists had the quite different purpose of presenting a detailed and vivid picture of their chosen historical periods. The
dialectic of the most ambitious of the novels is worked out in dramatic
conflicts between different centres of power or influence: Dickens's pairs
of cities – Revolutionary Paris and London, and the earthly city and heavenly city; fifteenth-century Holland, Gerard's 'hearth', and the 'cloister' of
Rome; the two streams of the Italian Renaissance – pagan Greek culture
and Christianity, which converge in Romola's Florence; and the conflict
between Saxon and Norman in Hereward's native fenlands. In each case
the plotting of a central love relationship is shaped by the flow of historical
events. Although these events are often violent and highly coloured, one
contemporary reviewer, writing in 1859, suggested that the attraction of
the sub-genre lay 'not in any facility which it affords for the construction
of a better story, nor any superior interest that attaches to the known and
prominent characters with which it deals, or to the events it describes: but
rather the occasion it gives for making us familiar with the every-day life
of the age and country in which the scene is laid'.[10] It is, then, the combination of a careful attention to detail and a reading of history as a drama
of violent conflicts that characterizes High Victorian historical fiction.

That George Eliot's *Romola*, the novel which turned her into 'an old
woman' in her own eyes, should have been acclaimed as a major work of
serious historical fiction is hardly surprising. Less easy to understand, even
bearing in mind contemporary tastes, is the widely held Victorian view that
Reade's *The Cloister and the Hearth* was the greatest English historical
novel.[11] Reade's pleasure in the freedom of the picaresque form of the narrative is palpable. As Gerard and his companion Denys move from location
to location, their miscellaneous adventures, such as their endurance of filthy
German inns, a fight with a bear, and the attentions of a boastful blood-
letting doctor (24–26), are all comically described in the minutest detail,
fully exploiting the potential bagginess of the long Victorian novel. For all
Reade's encyclopaedic researches into Erasmus's *Compendium* and dozens

of other historical sources, however, it is the scenes of violence which stand out in this novel, as in his others. Severed hands seem to be a speciality, and at one point an enemy's hand is first pinned to a door by the bolt of Denys's crossbow and then briskly cut off by Gerard's sword (33). One of Gerard's first tasks as Brother Clement, an initiate of the Dominican order of friars, is to comfort Roman criminals who are garrotted, drawn, and quartered before his eyes (72). Reade works hard for his sensations, as when Brother Clement suddenly picks out his lover, the mother of his son, in the congregation to which he is preaching: Margaret's 'recognition of that look now made her quiver from head to foot. For that look was "RECOGNITION"' (85). The tone of the novel modulates from straight historical narrative to sentimental love romance to a mock heroic mode which is reminiscent of Byron in *Don Juan*, as in the comments on modern warfare being spoilt by the advent of gunpowder, in Chapter 42. On the other hand, *The Cloister and the Hearth*, and to some extent *Hereward the Wake*, tell us much about that aspect of the Victorian mind which revelled in clutter, ornament, and display, in the Gothic and the outlandish, in crime and its messy punishment. Moreover, modern preferences for the intellectual's marshalling of large forces in *Romola* should not allow us to ignore the more sensational aspects of George Eliot's novel.

The fighting spirit on which Empire was founded in the second half of the nineteenth century, reflected in Kingsley's *Westward Ho!* and *Hereward the Wake*, also gave birth to one of the century's most famous books for boys, *Tom Brown's School Days* (1857), by Kingsley's closest friend and muscular Christian ally in the Christian Socialist movement, Thomas Hughes. Tom Brown epitomizes the kind of stout-hearted English lad whose line runs from Marryat through Ballantyne (*The Coral Island*, 1858) to Henty's novels of the 1880s and beyond. Hughes's best-seller, however, is of special interest as an example of a specific sub-genre: the school novel.[12] Unlike *Vanity Fair* and *Pendennis*, in which Thackeray devotes comparatively little space to public-school life itself, most of Hughes's novel is set in Rugby school, or his own rather strange idea of it, and the enclosed world of Tom, Harry East, little Arthur, and Flashman the School-house bully. The Browns, we learn in the first chapter, are a 'fighting family', and Hughes, in the manner of Kingsley, unselfconsciously holds up the narrative in the climactic chapter entitled 'The Fight' (II. 5) to disabuse his readers of 'the cant and twaddle that's talked of boxing and fighting with fists nowadays'. The sentimental religiosity with which the energy and raw animal life of *Tom Brown's School Days* are treated makes the novel a period piece. At the end of the book Hughes leaves Tom kneeling in front of the altar in Rugby chapel under which Dr Arnold has recently been buried, the altar 'before which he had first caught a glimpse of the glory of his birthright, and felt the drawing of the bond which links all living souls together in one brotherhood' (II. 9). The sequel, *Tom Brown at Oxford* (1861) provides fascinating insight into the world of the undergraduate, again in a more detailed way than Thackeray's treatment of 'Oxbridge' in *Pendennis*, for example, but the novel lacks the verve of the *School Days*, with its roastings, death-beds, and rough games.

The year after Hughes's classic appeared, F. W. Farrar, a master at Harrow and later head of Marlborough and Dean of Canterbury, published the splendidly entitled *Eric; or, Little by Little: A Tale of Roslyn School* (1858), a school story perhaps unique in its ability to draw laughter and tears from the reader simultaneously. More earnest than *Tom Brown's School Days*, *Eric* depicts the decline into sin, mainly in the drinking line, of a public schoolboy whose death-bed is haunted by thoughts of his departed younger brother (fallen off a cliff) and the mother for whose early demise he is partly responsible. Farrar's preface to the twenty-fourth edition (1889) is unequivocal: 'The story of "Eric" was written with but one single object – the vivid inculcation of inward purity and moral purpose by the history of a boy who, in spite of the inherent nobleness of his disposition, falls into all folly and wickedness until he has learnt to seek help from above.' One can hear behind this sentence the echoes of a thousand sermons. Like so many sub-genres of early and mid-Victorian fiction, the school story of the late 1850s and early 1860s is religious in tone and intention. In Farrar's third novel, *St Winifred's; or, The World of School* (1862), his message is conveyed by the bishop in a confirmation sermon in the chapel, after the death of one of the candidates: 'The fair, sweet, purple flower of youth falls and fades, my young brethren, under the sweeping scythe of death, no less surely than the withered grass of age' (20).

Farrar's numerous theological works are more impressive than his novels, and the sermons entitled *Eternal Hope* (1878) caused a major controversy by attacking commonly held ideas on the everlasting punishment of the damned. It is no coincidence that the two most important Victorian fantasy writers, Charles Kingsley and George MacDonald, themselves no strangers to religious controversy, should have produced their best-known works in or around the 1860s. Kingsley and MacDonald turned to the form that Colin Manlove defines as 'a fiction evoking wonder and containing a substantial and irreducible element of the supernatural with which the mortal characters in the story or the readers become on at least partly familiar terms',[13] and that offered a measure of security from the kind of attack each had known in his Christian ministry. One of MacDonald's recurring themes in his creative writing and sermons is the idea of death being a kind friend rather than a fearful enemy, and both the adult fantasy entitled *Phantastes* (1858) and his famous children's book, *At the Back of the North Wind* (1871), suggest ways of imagining death and the future life which differ radically from the orthodox eschatology of other Victorian religious writers. In *The Water-Babies* (1863), written the year before his disastrous clash with Newman, and with greater ease than was usual for him, Kingsley combines a reformist message with his love of natural history while, like MacDonald, illustrating how death is transcended. Manlove follows J. R. R. Tolkein, in suggesting that Lewis Carroll's Alice books, including *Alice's Adventures in Wonderland* (1865) and *Through the Looking-Glass, and What Alice Found There* (1871), are not true fantasies, their 'marvels' being satiric in intention and the whole being presented as a dream. It is interesting to note, however, that it was Charles Dodgson's friend, MacDonald, who persuaded him to send the manuscript of *Alice in Wonderland* to a publisher. Behind the Oxford don's brilliant play with logic and with the Victorian games on which he also wrote manuals – chess, croquet, and playing cards – lies a vision of childhood, adolescence, and adulthood which is as disturbing as it is enchanting, and which, like true fantasy, achieves its effects by reversing the norms of mundane experience and of traditional narrative expectations.

George MacDonald portrayed his own struggles with Scottish Calvinism and later troubles in his ministry at Arundel in his novels, including *David Elginbrod* (1863), *Robert Falconer* (1868), and *Paul Faber, Surgeon* (1879). Perhaps more interesting, if only for its curiosity value, is Eliza Lynn Linton's *The True History of Joshua Davidson* (1872) which, as its title suggests, portrays a Christ-like figure living in the nineteenth century. Scoring several direct hits against the Victorian clergyman who enjoyed the benefits of a fat living, Joshua declares his 'understanding that Christianity is not a creed as dogmatized by churches, but an organization having politics for its means and the equalization of classes as its end. It is Communism' (4). Inevitably he is too good for this world, and is trampled to death by a hostile audience when he tries to lecture on Communism (13).

Both MacDonald and Linton moved away from orthodoxy towards their own very different faiths, in a decade in which many intellectuals lost their faith in the wake of Darwin and German biblical criticism. For several writers, however, the immediate impact on their lives found literary expression only much later in their careers. Samuel Butler did not begin work on *The Way of all Flesh* (1903) until 1873, although he prayed for the last time in 1860; and Hardy, who lost his faith later in the same decade, seriously addressed himself to the subject in fiction only in the 1890s. Winwood Reade, however, author of *The Martyrdom of Man* (1872), portrayed the impact of Malthus and Darwin on a character who eventually goes mad and kills himself, in *The Outcast* (1875). The novel takes the form of letters from Edward Mordaunt, who is ordained but loses his betrothed when he confesses that he has become an 'infidel': 'She started back in horror, clasping her hands. She thought that I was mad' (7). Mordaunt's nadir soon follows: 'O miserable man! two sorrows had stricken me at once. I had lost my love; I had lost my home. I was an OUTCAST; alone and desolate' (8). The capitalization, favoured by Charles Reade and other sensation novelists, suggests the narrowness of the divide between the intense religious fiction of the period and the more extreme secular forms of mid-Victorian fiction.

Sectarian strife continued to fascinate writers and readers alike, and Disraeli rounded on the Roman Catholics, partly for reasons of political expediency, in *Lothair* (1870), written between terms as Prime Minister. The most significant new development in the novel on ecclesiastical themes, however, was Trollope's series of Barsetshire novels (1855–67), to which we will turn later. Less familiar to the modern reader, but widely read in their day, were the 'Chronicles of Carlingford' by the indefatigable Mrs Oliphant, published between 1863 and 1876. That she borrowed the idea for the series from Trollope was always obvious, and was underlined in the sub-title of the last novel, *Phoebe Junior: A Last Chronicle of Carling-ford*. Margaret Oliphant specialized in the comic treatment of sectarian division between Church and Chapel in the insignificant provincial town of Carlingford, where 'to name the two communities . . . in the same breath, would have been accounted little short of sacrilege' (*Salem Chapel*, 1863; 1). In *Salem Chapel* she amusingly portrays the anguished Mr Vincent, the new minister of the chapel, who, stifled by the narrow-minded Tozers and other small tradespeople of his flock, has the misfortune to fall in love with Lady Western, an aristocrat and, of course, a Churchwoman. The rector of Carlingford, Mr Proctor, a timid scholar who delivers a 'smooth little sermon' which nobody much cares about and which disturbs nobody (*The Rector*, 1863; 3), is finally forced to take the same road as Mr Vincent, out of town. Division within the Church of England itself is indicated by the presence of Mr Wentworth, whose High Church ornaments and founding of an order of Sisters of Mercy at St Roque's cause a considerable stir (*The Perpetual Curate*, 1864). Lacking Trollope's broader knowledge of the world, the intelligence of George Eliot's treatment of *Scenes of Clerical Life* (1857), and the satirical bite of Butler in *The Way of all Flesh*, Margaret Oliphant offers a sarcastic but moderate view of the pettiness of mid-Victorian religious life in the dullest of towns. The less dramatic stretches of her writing have a rather awful ring of truth.

The mysteries of identity: late Dickens

1859, the *annus mirabilis* of the *Origin of Species* and *On Liberty*, of *Adam Bede* and *The Ordeal of Richard Feverel*, was also a significant watershed in the careers of Dickens, now aged forty-seven, and Wilkie Collins, twelve years younger, and a close friend since 1851. During the 1850s Collins had accompanied Dickens on foreign tours, had become the most frequent contributor to *Household Words*, joining the staff in 1856, and had collaborated with Dickens in several theatrical productions, including Collins's own play *The Frozen Deep* (1857), in which Dickens took the leading role. As the crisis in Dickens's married life deepened, and he turned increasingly to the histrionic for emotional release, Collins offered him a more sympathetic ear than that of the older and more staid John Forster. In September 1857, a few weeks after Dickens had fallen in love with the eighteen-year-old actress, Ellen Ternan, Collins joined him in the northern walking holiday described in their 'Lazy Tour of Two Idle Apprentices' (*Household Words*). In 1859 Dickens and Collins were drawn even more closely together, both in their private and professional lives. It was probably early in that year that Collins met Mrs Caroline Graves, with whom he is buried in Kensal Green Cemetery, but whom he never married. Stories of the two womanizing writers having been fellow adventurers are probably apocryphal or exaggerated. Both men, however, were now involved in a long-term liaison with a beautiful younger woman, and must have shared confidences.

Collins was also foremost among Dickens's 'young men' who worked on the launching of the new weekly magazine, *All the Year Round*. *A Tale of Two Cities*, which Dickens believed would restore his 'old standing' with his public,[14] led off the magazine from April to November 1859, when Collins's *The Woman in White* took its place, establishing the younger man as a literary celebrity in his own right. It was appropriate that the first sensation novel should have been published in the magazine which marked the severing of Dickens's association with his publishers Bradbury and Evans, and a new phase in his career. For not only was Dickens a major influence upon Collins and the vogue he inaugurated, but his own deepening fascination with the mysteries of identity – especially the split personality and doubles – and with the psychology of passion and crime, reflects in turn his admiration for Collins's work in the 1860s. The sensational combination of violent crime and the destabilizing of individual identity in Dickens's last novels is the subject of this section.

Dickens's 'Hunted Down', a story based partially on that of Thomas Wainewright the poisoner, appeared in *All the Year Round* while *The Woman in White* was the lead serial novel. After the failure of Charles Lever's *A Day's Ride*, Dickens boosted his magazine's sales by writing *Great Expectations* (1860–61) as the main serial, and later also published Collins's *No Name* (1862) and *The Moonstone* (1868), and Charles Reade's *Hard Cash* (1863). The breakdown of the over-complex John Harmon plot in *Our Mutual Friend* (1864–65) suggests that in one respect Collins's influence was counter-productive. In the unfinished *Mystery of Edwin Drood*, however, Dickens successfully challenged Collins on the latter's own ground. Remarkably, the work left half-completed at his death (1870) promised new departures in a career which had already spanned three decades.

Dickens jokingly described himself as Collins's 'obedient disciple' in a letter congratulating him on 'triumphantly' finishing *The Woman in White*, his 'best book'. In an earlier letter he had praised, among other characters, Marian Halcombe and Mr Fairlie, whose polar opposition no doubt appealed to him.[15] Fairlie is described as 'transparently pale' (I. 1. VII). He has a beardless face, dim greyish-blue eyes, soft, scanty hair, white delicate hands, and 'effeminately small' feet. In the previous chapter Miss Halcombe's complexion is described as 'almost swarthy', and the dark down on her upper lip as 'almost a moustache'. 'Masculine' in form and features, she has piercing brown eyes, thick, coal-black hair, and rather large hands. The ambiguity of these sexual inversions complements that of the novel's villain, Count Fosco, while the dark/light contrast reinforces the more central juxtaposition of Marian Halcombe and her fair half-sister Laura, Fairlie's niece, who herself has a 'twin-sister of chance resemblance' (I. 1. XIII) in Anne Catherick, in fact another half-sister. Like *Jane Eyre* in its secrets, dark passions, and death by fire, *The Woman in White* also draws upon the Gothic tradition.[16] Laura Fairlie and Anne Catherick are 'living reflections of one another', and Collins went on to develop the doubles theme in *Armadale*, although it was surely Dickens, the far greater psychological observer, who in the last phase of his career prepared the ground for R. L. Stevenson and *Dr Jekyll and Mr Hyde* (1886). Dickens's world was always violent: consider Sikes and Quilp as examples of the bludgeoner and the sadist in his early novels. In Dickens's violent Gothic tale in 'The Lazy Tour', however, written during the acute emotional crisis of 1857, Harry Stone locates 'massive guilt' in the manner in which he externalizes his relationships with his wife and with Ellen, whose name is given to the central victim in the story.[17] Crime and punishment, externalized forms of individual and corporate passion and guilt, are never far from the centre of Dickens's concerns in his last three novels. Many of those who are somehow involved in crimes of violence in these novels find means of disguise or escape in psychological strategies such as self-division or fantasy, strategies adopted by Dickens himself in the act of writing.

The economy and intensity of vision of the opening of *Great Expectations* immediately indicates a major advance on *David Copperfield*, which Dickens reread in order to ensure that he did not repeat himself in his second novel narrated in the first person. Having described his childhood self-identification ('I called myself Pip') and his attempt to imagine the 'likeness' of his dead parents and brothers from the shape of their gravestones, Pip records that his first 'most vivid and broad impression of the identity of things' seems to have been gained on a 'memorable raw afternoon towards evening' (1). Even before the 'fearful' convict has started up from among the graves and threatened to cut his throat, Pip is in tears, afraid of the threatening external world. The distant sea, for example, is a 'savage lair' from which the wind rushes. Magwitch turns Pip upside down to empty his pockets and then repeatedly tilts him over backwards, glaring down at him and giving him a 'greater sense of helplessness and danger'. Hurrying home, Pip sees Magwitch limp towards a gibbet, as if he were the pirate who was once chained there, and is 'going back to hook himself up again': 'It gave me a terrible *turn* when I thought so' (my emphasis). Having stolen a pork pie from his sister's pantry, everything seems to run at him: 'This was very disagreeable to a guilty mind' (3).

Many of Pip's memorable experiences in the First Stage of his Expectations are assaults upon him. Magwitch, Mrs Joe, and Herbert Pocket assault him physically; Miss Havisham and Estella are psychological antagonists. Violent crime and its punishment (adumbrated in the gibbet on the marshes) and a personal sense of guilt (adumbrated in the stealing of the pie) assume social forms in the Second Stage of the narrative, when he first arrives in London, visits Newgate, and sees Jaggers's grotesque casts of hanged men (20). When Magwitch re-emerges at the end of this Second Stage (39), on a night of winds which shake Pip's house in the Temple 'like discharges of cannon', reminiscent of the warning guns fired on the marshes at the beginning of the novel (2), Pip's sense of being tainted by 'prison and crime' (32) reassumes a shape which threatens him personally. For the discovery of the true identity of his benefactor again turns Pip upside down, as the room begins to 'surge and turn'. In a re-enactment of the graveyard episode, Magwitch bends over Pip, bringing the face he now well remembers very near to his own. Towards the end of the Third Stage, however, Pip temporarily loses his identity altogether. His loathing of Magwitch turns to love, and at the trial he sits holding the condemned man's hand (56). In the eyes of the hanging judge, Abel Magwitch's return from transportation was a yielding to murderous 'passions'. Abel is in reality no Cain, however, and Pip invokes 'the greater Judgement that knoweth all things and cannot err' when the sentence of death is passed. After Magwitch's death in prison, the stress of recent days results in Pip's delirium (57). Magwitch, Compeyson, Orlick, and Miss Havisham haunt him, and he confounds 'impossible existences' with his 'own identity', becoming first a brick high in a house wall, and then part of a vast engine. Having struggled with 'real people', believing them to be murderers, whose faces present 'all kinds of extraordinary transformations' and are 'much dilated in size', he finds that all 'settle down into the likeness of Joe'. As he emerges from his fever and hears the 'dear old home-voice', Pip becomes 'like a child in his hands', and although he returns to his adult self, and is again addressed as 'Sir' by Joe, the discovery that Joe's is the one identity on which he can rely, reinforcing his earlier discovery of Magwitch's true nature, leaves him a changed man.

The published version of the ending of *Great Expectations*, in which Pip and Estella are brought together in the ruins of Satis House, is one indication that the novel is transitional; that Dickens's old anxiety to keep his public happy informed his acceptance of Bulwer's advice to change the original ending. Dickens's first thought, that Pip and the twice-married Estella should meet sadly in a London street, was truer to the openness of the last section of the narrative. For through the dissolution of his identity and his return to the state of childhood in illness, Pip has been reborn, and must begin again, both in his personal life and in his reading of the world. The themes of rebirth and resurrection were to become central in *Our Mutual Friend*, and that of hallucinatory experience in *Edwin Drood*. We have seen that this kind of reworking is typical of Dickens, and that in his variations on themes he often shifts from a tragic to a comic mode, or vice versa. Pip's hallucinations during his illness internalize what has previously been worked out externally, when other characters act as if they are extensions of himself. For example, his covert great expectations are externalized in those of Magwitch, Estella, Miss Havisham, and Herbert Pocket, among others. His sense of the taint of Newgate is personified in Jaggers's neurotic washing of his hands, like Pilate (26). Wemmick's defensive strategy of adopting two identities in his strictly separated Little Britain and Walworth selves is comic in its external manifestations, but provides mute commentary on Pip's own inability to accommodate the taint of prison and crime in his own guilt-ridden identity. The Castle, the Aged, and Miss Skiffins are preserved through Wemmick's willed acts of self-division, disguised as whimsical spontaneity, whereas Satis House is ruined, Miss Havisham burned, and Estella corrupted by Miss Havisham's willed act of arrested development.

Achieving coherence through the controlling consciousness of Pip, and imaginative freedom by relating Pip's inner life to externalized variations on the novel's central theme, Dickens brilliantly exploited the weekly serial form which he had previously found a constraint in the more schematic *Hard Times*. *Our Mutual Friend*, his last completed monthly part novel, was seen by some contemporary critics as the product of a tired mind. At first sight it certainly seems something of a baggy monster, in which the activities of numerous strange characters often appear to be unrelated to one another, and in which the machinery of the main plot creaks and groans. Seen in relation to *Great Expectations* and *Edwin Drood*, the contrast between *Our Mutual Friend* and the satirical social novels of the 1850s marks Dickens's final rejection of the possibility of society's salvation through the reform of its institutions, and his deepening interest in the themes of individual guilt and redemption, and the psychology of the inner life.

This contrast is reflected in changes in Dickens's symbolic method, for whereas the law and the Circumlocution Office were foregrounded as controlling metaphors in *Bleak House* and *Little Dorrit*, *Our Mutual Friend* seems to be loosely constructed around what might be described as a conceit, by no means immediately obvious on a first reading: namely, the idea of rising and falling. This idea is central to the theme of baptism, rebirth, and resurrection developed through a number of drownings and escapes from drowning in the river Thames, and through references to the baptismal and the burial service in the Book of Common Prayer.[18] While Gaffer Hexam and Rogue Riderhood earn a precarious living by pulling corpses out of the Thames, Silas Wegg pokes around in the 'dust' heaps which themselves rise and fall, like the fortunes of the Veneerings, the Lammles, and the Boffins. Wegg's reading of Gibbon's *Decline and Fall* to Boffin is doubly appropriate, when one considers his role of 'official expounder of mysteries' (I. 5) as a comic parallel to that of Charley Hexam's schoolmaster, Bradley Headstone, whose social elevation was achieved through a grinding effort of will in the mill of a reformed education system, and whose suppressed passions destroy him. Further variations, such as Jenny Wren's roof-garden ('Come up and be dead!', II. 5), confirm the pervasiveness of the idea and the fact that its function is to draw parallels between the disparate areas of the anarchic world of the novel, rather than to bind the work together. For the relationship between the many centres of activity in *Our Mutual Friend* tends to be oblique or ironic. Let us briefly consider the parallels between the main Rokesmith/Harmon plot and the Wrayburn/Headstone plot.

The fact that the first of these two pairs is one man with two main identities (a third being 'Julius Handford'), and the second is two men with opposite identities, provides a clue to the nature of Dickens's experiment with the doubles motif in the novel. Halfway through the narrative, Dickens gives up his attempt to emulate Wilkie Collins in the development of the Rokesmith/Harmon plot, and has the novel's central character explain his metamorphosis from John Harmon to John Rokesmith (via, briefly, Julius Handford) in an unconvincing internal dialogue: 'Now, stop, and so far think it out, John Harmon. Is that so? That is exactly so', and so on

(II. 13). Harmon's account, however, of his return to England 'divided in [his] mind', of his change of clothes with the third mate, George Radfoot, who drugged him and appeared to 'swell immensely', and of his escape from drowning in the Thames, externalizes a crisis of identity in a way which anticipates Conrad: 'A heavy horrid unintelligible something vanished, and it was I who was struggling there alone in the water. . . . I was sucked under [a boat], and came up, only just alive, on the other side. . . . So John Harmon died, and Julius Handford disappeared, and John Rokesmith was born.'

It was George Radfoot's body, then, dressed in John Harmon's clothes, that Gaffer Hexam fished out of the river in the dark opening chapter of the novel; and it was John Harmon who examined what was thought to be his own body, in the presence of the Inspector, Eugene Wrayburn, and Mortimer Lightwood (I. 3), and who is later to be accused of murdering himself (IV. 12). When Wrayburn revisits the riverside inn, in search of Gaffer Hexam, and watches Lizzie Hexam through an uncurtained window, his sense of guilt is associated with the taste of cooled burnt sherry: 'Tastes like the wash of the river. . . . I feel as if I had been half drowned, and swallowing a gallon of it' (I. 13). He then witnesses Lizzie's father being pulled out of the Thames, 'baptized unto Death', like one of Gaffer's own finds (I. 14). Although his confession to Lightwood next morning, that he feels he has 'committed every crime in the Newgate Calendar', is reminiscent of Pip's sense of the taint of Newgate, Wrayburn's guilt is specifically associated with his voyeuristic desires. In the subsequent monthly number of *Our Mutual Friend* (VI), Dickens introduces Wrayburn's dark shadow, Bradley Headstone, a man of respectable external appearance. He wears a 'decent black coat and waistcoat, and decent white shirt, and decent formal black tie, and decent pantaloons of pepper and salt, with his decent silver watch in his pocket and its decent hair-guard round his neck', but is 'stiff' in his manner of wearing this dress, 'recalling some mechanics in their holiday clothes' (II. 1). 'Mechanically' acquiring a 'great store of teacher's knowledge', he has risen in the world, yet 'suppression of so much to make room for so much' has given him a 'constrained manner'. The industrious, self-made Headstone represents the opposite extreme from Wrayburn, who is idle, languid, and aristocratic in bearing. Both love Lizzie Hexam. Each, in his own way, is highly dangerous.

Significantly, Dickens's most direct statement in the novel on the nature of the criminal mind immediately follows his description of Headstone performing his 'routine of educational tricks' by day and breaking loose at night 'like an ill-tamed wild animal':

> Under his daily restraint, it was his compensation, not his
> trouble, to give a glance towards his state at night, and to the
> freedom of its being indulged. If great criminals told the truth
> – which, being great criminals, they do not – they would very
> rarely tell of their struggles against the crime. Their struggles
> are towards it. They buffet with opposing waves, to gain the
> bloody shore, not to recede from it. This man perfectly

comprehended that he hated his rival with his strongest and
worst forces, and that if he tracked him to Lizzie Hexam, his
so doing would never serve himself with her, or serve her.

(III. 11)

Meanwhile, his rival Wrayburn studies London's 'No Thoroughfares' in
the course of the day, and becomes gleefully animated only when goading
Headstone after dark by leading him down them and away from Lizzie
(III. 10); and Rogue Riderhood watches both men with interest. When
Headstone watches Wrayburn rise 'like an apparition against the light' as
his boat emerges from Plashwater Weir Mill Lock (IV. 1), he himself is
disguised as a bargeman in clothes identical to Riderhood's. Wearing 'the
clothes of some other man or men, as if they [are] his own', he seems at
ease in the adopted criminal identity of Riderhood. After the attempted
murder, Lizzie 'raises' the drowning Wrayburn 'from death' by applying
the boating skills learned from her father (IV. 6), while Headstone's attempt
to drown his Riderhood identity, by throwing his borrowed clothes into
the river, is foiled by Riderhood's retrieval of them (IV. 7, 'Better to be
Abel than Cain'). In his subsequent illness Wrayburn frequently rises like
'a drowning man from the deep', only to 'sink again' (IV. 10), while Headstone, having 'risen, as it were, out of the ashes of the Bargeman', is
brought face to face with his other self in the form of Riderhood carrying
a bundle of clothes into his schoolroom (IV. 15). Next day Headstone leaves
his decent watch and guard, symbols of his schoolmaster identity, with
Miss Peecher, and walks to the lock, where Riderhood attempts to black-
mail him. Shadowed by Riderhood, twisting and turning for miles as
Wrayburn has previously led him through London, Headstone the pursuer
now becomes the pursued. Riderhood's promise to go wherever Headstone
goes is fulfilled in their deaths, when Headstone answers his claim that he
cannot be drowned:

> 'I can be!' returned Bradley, in a desperate, clenched voice. 'I
> am resolved to be. I'll hold you living, and I'll hold you dead.
> Come down!'
> Riderhood went over into the smooth pit, backward, and
> Bradley Headstone upon him. When the two men were
> found, lying under the ooze and scum behind one of the
> rotting gates, Riderhood's hold had relaxed, probably in
> falling, and his eyes were staring upward. But, he was girdled
> still with Bradley's iron ring, and the rivets of the iron ring
> held tight.

Headstone's cry, 'Come down!', inverts Jenny Wren's 'Come up and be
dead!' Whereas Headstone and Riderhood drown, John Harmon and Eugene Wrayburn both return from the dead to marry the women they love.

Several aspects of the main Rokesmith/Harmon plot could be described
as sensational, and, although unmistakably Dickensian in execution, they
reflect the closeness of Dickens's working relationship with Wilkie Collins

in the 1860s. Consider, for example, the activities of the Inspector, the clues concerning old Harmon's wills, John Harmon's secret identity, and the experiment in interior dialogue. It is in the fascinating antagonism between Wrayburn and Headstone, however, that Dickens's sensational plotting best subserves his larger purpose of exploring the criminal mind. In *Our Mutual Friend* this kind of analysis is only one strand of a multiplot novel of twenty monthly parts, which addresses itself to the broader themes of the insidious power of money to corrupt and the possibility of redemption through love. In contrast, the psychological themes of criminality and doubles provide the *focus* for the much more tightly organized *Edwin Drood*, originally planned to appear in only twelve monthly parts. Again we find continuities between this and Dickens's previous novel, such as his symbolism of dust and bones, and of drowning; his interest in violence and mastering 'affections' (2); and his strange idea of an idyllic roof-garden. In its plotting and use of setting, however, *Edwin Drood* has the narrow concentration of a Wilkie Collins detective novel.

Although the mystery of the novel's title has lured numerous commentators into speculation on the fate of Edwin Drood and the identity of Datchery, few readers have missed Dickens's fairly obvious identification of John Jasper as the murderer, or, according to some theories, would-be murderer of Edwin. That critics have argued that Jasper is a mesmerist, and a member of a Thuggee sect and thus a garrotter, suggests where the novel's true mystery lies: in the divided mind of its villain.[19] Bearing in mind the kinds of externalization and crises of identity we have seen in *Great Expectations* and *Our Mutual Friend*, and Dickens's portrayal of Pip in a fever and John Harmon in a drugged state, the placing of Jasper's opium-induced hallucinations on the first page of *Edwin Drood*, and the recurrent play with the doubles motif in the five chapters of the first monthly number, suggest new priorities in the novel.

By beginning his narrative with the ancient cathedral tower breaking into Jasper's exotic Eastern visions in an opium den, Dickens not only hints at the character's two identities of lay precentor and opium addict, and the possibility that they can merge, but also ensures that the Jasper of Cloisterham (the novel's main setting) is from the first seen by the reader, though not by the other characters, as Jasper the addict. The dream also introduces the theme of perception and vision, in a novel which is full of references to eyes. Jasper, whose 'scattered consciousness' pieces itself together, looks at the Chinaman and the haggard opium woman and notices a strange likeness between them: 'His form of cheek, eye, and temple, and his colour, are repeated in her.' This likeness is also emphasized by Jasper's repeated comment, 'Unintelligible!', which he applies to both of them.

Division and duplication are opposite but related kinds of doubling, and in *Edwin Drood* Dickens examines them as aspects of the same phenomenon in his treatment of Jasper and his groupings of pairs of characters. In the second chapter, however, the emphasis is upon external opposites, for the dark Jasper, who looks older than he is in his sombre room, is juxtaposed with the Minor Canon, Mr Crisparkle, described as 'fair and rosy', an early riser, 'cheerful, kind, good-natured, social, contented, and boylike'. Jasper is ambiguously 'wrapped up in' his 'dear boy', Edwin (13). While Edwin sleeps in one bedroom, Jasper smokes opium in the other (5). Both are potential husbands to Rosa Bud. Characteristically, Dickens introduces a comic parallel to Jasper's changes from his filmy-eyed state to a 'breathing man again', without 'the smallest stage of transition between the two extreme states' (2), in the transition of Miss Twinkleton, owner of the Seminary for Young Ladies attended by Rosa Bud and Helena Landless, from her 'scholastic state of existence' by day to a sprightlier, gossipy Miss Twinkleton every night (3). (She also has a sister who 'matches' her perfectly, like the second figure in a pair of chimneypiece ornaments, 6.) The sexual ambiguity of Jasper's interest in both Edwin and Rosa Bud is comically paralleled in Miss Twinkleton's young ladies' playing the roles of young men (3) and wearing paper moustaches (9). Finally, Jasper's future guide around the cathedral crypt, the stony Durdles, 'often speaks of himself in the third person', perhaps being 'a little misty as to his own identity, when he narrates' (4).

In the second monthly number a pair of young couples – the Landless twins, who are 'much alike' (6), and Edwin and Rosa – establish lines of attraction and repulsion which serve as the central structure of the plot:

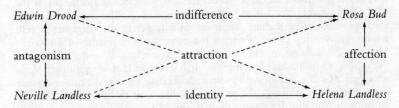

Jasper's influence on these relationships is exerted through the use of secret powers: he mesmerizes Rosa at the piano (7), and he drugs the young men's wine and fuels their mutual hatred (8). (Interestingly, these forms of loss of self-control are specifically mentioned by Dickens in the simile he applies to Miss Twinkleton's two states: 'As, in some cases of drunkenness, and in others of animal magnetism, there are two states of consciousness which never clash . . .', 3.)

We saw earlier how Dickens developed a method of characterization based on the use of pairs of opposite or complementary figures: Micawber and Heep; Micawber and Mr Peggotty; Little Dorrit and Maggy. In *Great Expectations* and *Our Mutual Friend* he adapted this method to various forms of psychological externalization. The tightness of the network of relationships at the core of *Edwin Drood* contributes to the claustrophobic quality of the novel's plotting and setting. In the last chapters Dickens wrote before his death, however, the scene moves from Cloisterham to London, where Neville, suspected of Edwin's murder, escapes from accusing tongues, and Rosa, oppressed by Jasper, begins to fall in love with Mr Tartar. Whereas the subterranean part of Jasper's nature is suggested in 'A Night with Durdles' among the dead in the cathedral crypt (12), the nautical Tartar establishes his light and airy chambers high above 'gritty' London (22). The language of the Gothic novel gives way to the language of transcendence ('a marvellous country that came into sudden bloom', 21), and mesmerism to delightful lovers' glances ('Happening to raise her own eyes, she found that he seemed to be thinking something about *them*', 21). Tartar takes Rosa up the river to some unspecified 'everlastingly-green garden' that seems 'unregainable and far away' (22), while Miss Twinkleton achieves 'a happy compromise between her two states of existence'. Even in the chapter left unfinished where Dickens broke off for the day, a chapter devoted mainly to Jasper's reliving of the murder, in the opium den, and his return to Cloisterham followed by the opium woman, the cathedral city is transformed in the morning sunlight: 'Changes of glorious light . . . from the one great garden of the whole cultivated island in its yielding time – penetrate into the Cathedral, subdue its earthy odour, and preach the Resurrection and the Life' (23). Written within hours of the fatal stroke, this intimation of immortality and the development of the Rosa/Tartar relationship suggest that in the remaining half of the novel Dickens may have planned to experiment with some kind of counterpoint between dark and light, death and life, despair and hope.

Passion, crime, and punishment, however, remain at the centre until the end of the fragment we have, when the old woman, 'as malignant as the Evil One', shakes her fist at Jasper from behind a pillar in the cathedral. Dickens thought of ending the novel with Jasper in the condemned cell, brooding over his crime. Perhaps the most baffling feature of Dickens's vision is the holding in tension of a strong sense of evil, and a faith in the possibility of individual redemption. It is a vision that verges upon Manichaeism. His fascination with violence and crime remained a major driving force behind his writings, however, and there can be little doubt that the addition of the murder from *Oliver Twist*, 'Sikes and Nancy', to his repertoire in the 'Farewell Season' of readings (1868–69) contributed to his virtually self-inflicted death.[20] His rendering of the murder thrilled and horrified his audiences, and many women were carried fainting from halls and theatres around the country. A day or two before his death he was seen in the grounds at Gad's Hill re-enacting the frightful murder of Nancy with an almost manic intensity. His heavily underscored note in the margin of his prompt copy of 'Sikes and Nancy' now reads like a final motto: '*Terror To The End.*'

Truth and a high but gentle spirit: Anthony Trollope

Mention Victorian fiction to your dentist and he may well admit to reading Trollope, probably in bed, like thousands of other 'general educated readers' today. Trollope is now often read for his old-world charm, for his Englishness. Nathaniel Hawthorne, whose own work was of 'quite another class', found that Trollope's novels precisely suited his taste, being 'solid and substantial, written on the strength of beef and through the inspiration of ale', and 'just as English as a beef-steak' (Trollope, *Autobiography*, 1883; 8). Although such talk does not help us to appreciate the subtleties of Trollope, it is perhaps worth dwelling for a moment on his Englishness, and specifically his Victorian Englishness. For, usually without noticing it, general and critical readers alike tend to use Trollope as a touchstone of Victorian fiction.

Though born in the same decade as Dickens, Thackeray, Charlotte Brontë, and Elizabeth Gaskell, Trollope was forty years old before he wrote a successful novel, and most of his best work was published during the High Victorian period of the 1860s and 1870s. Concentrating almost exclusively on middle-class and upper-class circles, he explored the relationships between the individual and society, between private and public lives, the personal and the professional. Clergymen, politicians, and doctors make decisions in their working lives which reflect personal pressures upon them in their domestic lives. When men have to choose between women, and vice versa, the choice is often between love and money. In his treatment of these and other moral dilemmas, which are often the very core of his novels, Trollope's conservatism is underpinned with a deep respect for established conventions and codes of conduct, English traditions of modesty, hard work, and honesty; and with a hostility towards rapid social change and personal ambition.

After early experiments, he soon discovered the value of the multiplot scheme in his novels, although he always admitted that character was more important to him than plot, something for which he was often criticized. In all but two of his novels he addresses the reader as an authorial narrator,[21] and often chats away about his own writing and contemporary literary trends. The second monthly number of *Can You Forgive Her?* (1864–65) begins like this: 'I am not going to describe the Vavasors' Swiss tour. It would not be fair on my readers. "Six Weeks in the Bernese Oberland, by a party of three," would have but very small chance of success in the literary world at present. . . . Ludgate Hill is now-a-days more interesting than the Jungfrau' (5). Trollope's own burning interest in the present is revealed not only in the more obviously polemical novels, such as *The Warden* (1855) and *The Three Clerks* (1858), but also in the steady pressure of a general concern for contemporary issues and problems behind much of his narrative. Trollope combines his quiet realism with plots turning on dramatic events, and, as we have seen, comments interestingly on the critics' division of novelists into the sensational and the non-sensational: 'All this is, I think, a mistake, – which mistake arises from the inability of the imperfect artist to be at the same time realistic and sensational. A good novel should be both, and both in the highest degree' (*Autobiography*, 12).

Taken together, these broad characteristics of Trollope's work add up to our broad idea of what much Victorian fiction is like. Yet we have already seen that Victorian fiction is remarkable for its range and variety. There is variety in Trollope, too, and it is often forgotten that the writer of the six Barsetshire novels also wrote forty-one others. (See the entry on Trollope in 'Individual authors' for a selected list.) These include Irish novels, novels with foreign settings, and another major series, the 'Palliser' novels, which itself includes *The Eustace Diamonds* (1871–73), Trollope's response to Wilkie Collins and the sensation novel. Although it is true that Trollope's vision grew darker over the years, the pattern is by no means uniform.[22] Furthermore, Trollope constantly challenges his own age, and particularly the too easy assumption that the world is progressing, his protest often being in the name of conservatism. His work is unsettling in the way that a good sermon strikes home. The analogy is Trollope's own:

> I have ever thought of myself as a preacher of sermons, and
> my pulpit as one which I could make both salutary and
> agreeable to my audience. I do believe that no girl has risen
> from the reading of my pages less modest than she was
> before, and that some may have learned from them that
> modesty is a charm well worth preserving. I think that no
> youth has been taught that in falseness and flashness is to be
> found the road to manliness; but some may perhaps have
> learned from me that it is to be found in truth and a high but
> gentle spirit.
>
> (*Autobiography*, 8)

If Thackeray's text was 'there is no new thing under the sun', Trollope, who considered Thackeray to be the first novelist of the age, preached on this verse: 'For what shall it profit a man, if he shall gain the whole world, and lose his own soul?' (Mark 8. 36). The road to manliness is to be found in truth and a high but gentle spirit, not in the ambition and success admired by the adulterous and sinful generation satirized in *The Way We live Now* (1874–75). Interestingly, Trollope's comments on the sermon-like quality of his own work, in Chapter 8 of the *Autobiography*, itself written in the mid-1870s when he was acutely conscious of a fall in standards of honesty, were later followed by his statement that he was working in an English tradition of improving fiction, including the works of Maria Edgeworth, Jane Austen, and Walter Scott, and, among contemporaries, Thackeray, Dickens, and George Eliot (12). So Trollope thought of himself as not only typically English, but also typically nineteenth-century in his emphasis upon making 'virtue alluring and vice ugly' while charming readers instead of wearying them (12).

The key to Trollope's success as a novelist and moralist, however, lies in his early invention of a small, almost closed community, the diocese of Barchester, with its own hierarchy, unwritten rules of conduct, and store of shared history and experience: a microcosm in which the subtle shadings of a moral dilemma or small variations of behaviour are magnified in relation to their setting. Trollope himself was fascinated by systems, and did much good work on the postal services of Ireland and England, riding thousands of miles a year on horseback as a surveyor for the Post Office, and thoroughly enjoying it. As the official who introduced the pillar-box, and was an adept at discovering the best short cuts for postmen, Trollope would have been interested in Thomas Pynchon's use of a secret postal service in his novel *The Crying of Lot 49* (1966). It is perhaps no coincidence that it was during the time that Trollope was creating a 'postal *network* which should catch all recipients of letters' (my emphasis) in the South-West of England that he had the idea for his famous series, described in an equally famous sentence from the *Autobiography*: 'In the course of the job I visited Salisbury, and whilst wandering there one mid-summer evening round the purlieus of the cathedral I conceived the story of *The Warden*, – from whence came that series of novels of which Barchester, with its bishops, deans, and archdeacon, was the central site' (5). Like the postal service, with its London headquarters and provincial divisions, the Church of England had its venerable centres of Canterbury and York, its dioceses and its parishes – networks within networks. The various maps of Barsetshire illustrated in the Oxford World's Classics editions of the novels show Barchester at the centre of a web of roads that radiate from it. At the heart of Barchester is the Close, with its own internal network of relationships and power struggles, whereas Rev. Josiah Crawley's parish of Hogglestock, in the north of the diocese, is to Barchester as Siberia is to Moscow, and the perpetual curate's walk to the Bishop's Palace in *The Last Chronicle of Barset* (1866–67) is represented as an epic journey.

In the Palliser series we enter a larger world, but one in which the centres of power and lines of communication are almost as clearly drawn. Trollope sets the action of the novels not only in the chamber and 'passages and halls' of the House of Commons (*Can You Forgive Her?*, 45), where some of the best and, unfortunately, some of the more vulgar Englishmen of the day rub shoulders; in the dingy Cabinet room, where what appear to be 'ordinary gentlemen' meet to discuss the latest crisis (*Phineas Finn*, 1867–69; 29); and Phineas's gorgeous room at the Colonial Office, where his official work is rudely interrupted by a private letter whose contents make further concentration impossible (*Phineas Finn*, 53). Much political business is also carried on in country house parties, where public and private life become inextricably mixed, and where professional favours and the hands of eligible young ladies are to be won or lost.

Like the Barsetshire novels, in which contemporary debates on Darwin or Colenso have very little impact, Trollope's political novels are not novels of ideas, as Disraeli's are, although political affairs, such as reform of the franchise and the question of the secret ballot, are running themes in the series. More central to Trollope's purpose is the examination of human frailties in the working of what he sees as the greatest of human institutions, the English Parliament. For Trollope's interest is in systems, classes, and groupings, and in the nature of community. Although Trollope's concept of community is far broader than what Raymond Williams calls Jane Austen's 'knowable community' (her 'network of propertied houses and families' which can be visited), Williams's term is also suggestive when applied to the Victorian novelist who owed her much.[23] Even in the Barsetshire novels, however, the myth of an organic community, in a century in which the idea of the Church of England as being in organic relation to the State was so powerful,[24] is confronted with the facts of division within and attack from without. Trollope also responded critically to the broad movement of nineteenth-century Europe from what one German sociologist called 'community' to 'association' or 'company', from direct emotional bonds of rural life to acts of exchange in urban life as the basis of human relationship.[25] Trollope's comic resolutions become more difficult as his sense of a decline in contemporary moral standards deepens. The struggles of the 'high but gentle spirit' in an adulterous and sinful generation become more taxing as the age becomes more mercenary, more restless, and more cynical. I will examine the idea of the beleaguered high but gentle spirit in some of the Barsetshire novels, more briefly in the first of the Palliser series, and finally in Trollope's longest and most scathingly satirical novel, *The Way We Live Now*.

Trollope's first idea for *The Warden* was to expose what he saw as opposite but related evils: 'the possession by the Church of certain funds and endowments which had been intended for charitable purposes, but which had been allowed to become incomes for idle Church dignitaries', and 'the undeserved severity of the newspapers towards the recipients of such incomes, who could hardly be considered to be the chief sinners in the matter' (*Autobiography*, 5). *The Warden* is essential reading for the student of the social-problem novel, as much as it is for the student of Trollope; for in failing to resolve the contradiction between these two opposite causes, Trollope at once criticizes contemporary literature 'with a purpose' and finds his own true subject in the interstices between his causes.

As in the social-problem novels I discussed in Chapter 3, Trollope examines the effect of a public issue (Hiram's Hospital and the scandal of Warden Harding's well-paid sinecure) on the private lives of individual characters. The cover of the first edition portrays John Bold, the young 'Barchester Reformer', at a moment of crisis, when his public stance as Mr Harding's critic directly conflicts with his love for the Warden's daughter, Eleanor, who pleads with him to drop the case (11). This classic Trollopian dilemma is quickly resolved in the typically Trollopian manner, with Bold's heart ruling his reformist head. His problems are only just beginning, however, as he later has to visit his friend Tom Towers, editor of the campaigning London newspaper, the *Jupiter*, and explain his new position on the case. Trollope's heavy-handed satire of the *Jupiter* reflects his anger at *The Times*'s recent criticism of inefficiencies revealed in the conduct of the Crimean War. His parodies of Carlyle (Dr Pessimist Anticant) and Dickens (Mr Popular Sentiment) as leading literary social critics, help to define not only his own position on his two original causes, but also the nature of his own text. For Trollope has now introduced three interpolated texts: the *Jupiter* articles which cause Mr Harding such pain; Dr Anticant's pamphlet, written in the style of Carlyle's *Latter-day Pamphlets* (1850); and the first number of Mr Sentiment's latest novel, *The Almshouse*, in which a grotesque, boozy clergyman is crudely and savagely attacked (14–15). Trollope's novel stands in relation to these other, rejected forms as Mr Harding stands in relation to the forces which oppress him: in Barchester, John Bold and, though ostensibly on his own side, his son-in-law, Archdeacon Grantly; and in London, Tom Towers the 'Olympian' journalist, and Sir Abraham Haphazard, the 'great man' of the legal profession.

If the Tom Towers chapters are the worst in the novel, those which follow are probably the best. For John Bold's journey to London is immediately followed by Mr Harding's, as he slips down to Barchester station early in the morning, like some truant schoolboy, in order to avoid detection by the Archdeacon (16). Arriving in London he meekly orders his dinner at a quiet clerical hotel and makes an appointment with Sir Abraham for the following day at 10 pm, a time at which the Close would probably have retired to bed. Next morning he finds that he has the whole day to fill, and he takes 'sanctuary' in Westminster Abbey, like a criminal on the run. While London roars about its business outside, the Warden, also Precentor of Barchester, waits patiently for morning service to begin:

> He longed to get up from his seat, and examine the music-
> books of the choristers, and the copy of the litany from which
> the service was chanted, to see how far the little details at
> Westminster corresponded with those at Barchester, and
> whether he thought his own voice would fill the church well
> from the Westminster precentor's seat. There would,
> however, be impropriety in such meddling, and he sat
> perfectly still, looking up at the noble roof, and guarding
> against the coming fatigues of the day.

This is Trollope at his most perceptive and effective, for the contrasts between the Warden's natural humility and the way the Archdeacon would have behaved in the same circumstances (not that he would attend morning service when in London), and between the beautiful Barchester service and the shabby affair put on in the Abbey, suggest the great divide between Mr Harding's narrow provincial path and the major thoroughfares of the 'world', represented by London. Whereas Chapters 14 and 15 are loud and overstated, Chapter 16 illustrates Trollope's mastery of nicely weighted understatement.

Having endured the horrors of a London shellfish supper-house and fallen asleep in a 'cigar divan', Mr Harding finally keeps his appointment with Sir Abraham, a brilliant public man with no private life, and a man of the world with no time for the soul (17). 'Gallantly fronting' the 'great man', as David confronted Goliath, Mr Harding comes away quietly victorious, having played with bold sweeps on his imaginary cello, to Sir Abraham's bemusement, and unburdened his soul: 'He knew that the attorney-general regarded him as little better than a fool, but that he did not mind.' The chapter ends with him back at his hotel, tempted to escape from the coming interview with the Archdeacon but standing his ground 'manfully'. Unlike the manly great ones who assume that they can bend his will,

Mr Harding's manliness is revealed in his love of truth and in his 'high but gentle spirit' as he decides to resign the wardenship.

Trollope's burlesque of Dickens as Mr Popular Sentiment is a distortion of a writer whose work he never appreciated or really understood, and the lack of sympathy was mutual on Dickens's part. As revealing as the contrast between *The Warden* and *The Almshouse* is that between his treatment of the humble precentor, editor of a collection of ancient church music (1), and Dickens's description of Tom Pinch in Salisbury in *Martin Chuzzlewit* (5). Dickens's long description of the crowded market-day scene and his self-indulgent list of interesting shops would be seen by Trollope as redundant, and his description of Tom at the cathedral organ vulgarly Romantic: 'It was then turning dark, and the yellow light that streamed in through the ancient windows in the choir was mingled with a murky red. As the grand tones resounded through the church, they seemed, to Tom, to find an echo in the depth of every ancient tomb, no less than in the deep mystery of his own heart.' The Warden's love of music is revealed in his modest musical evenings, his extravagant edition of early music, and his longing to examine the little details at Westminster. The mysteries of his spirituality remain discreetly his own.

The contrast between Trollope and Dickens is also partly a matter of scale. At the quiet end of Trollope's 'little story' of one volume (21), Mr Harding has resigned his wardenship and is installed in 'little' rooms at the chemist's (20), with responsibility for the 'smallest possible parish' and a 'singular little Gothic' church (21). While continuing to exploit the narrow focus on Barchester and its diocese, however, Trollope continued the series with longer novels, including the sequel to *The Warden*, the three-volume *Barchester Towers* (1857). Whereas Dickens played variations on his themes with numerous new characters in each novel, Trollope's method was nearer to Thackeray's self-referential habit of bringing familiar characters from earlier novels into his latest work. A series, however, gave Trollope the opportunity not only of giving his readers the pleasure of recognition, but also of making the comic resolution at the end of each novel semi-provisional, a stage reached in the saga of Barset rather than the final full stop of a single novel. Whereas Barsetshire characters go up to London in *The Warden*, the opening chapters of *Barchester Towers* describe the invasion of the Close from London by the new bishop, Dr Proudie, his formidable wife, and his chaplain, Mr Slope. The ground, however, on which Mrs Proudie and Mr Slope fight for supremacy over the weak prelate continues to be that of Hiram's Hospital and its warden, and Mr Harding is again deeply involved in the novel's resolution, handing his future son-in-law, Mr Arabin, his letter of appointment as Dean, and leading Mr Quiverful, the new warden, into the hospital (52). Indeed, at the end of the novel Trollope leaves Mr Harding in the hands of his readers, 'not as a hero' but 'as a good man without guile'(53). The Harding theme is also in a sense carried on in Trollope's treatment of 'the modest country practitioner' in *Doctor Thorne* (3 vols, 1858), while in *Framley Parsonage* (1860–61), which led off the first number of the *Cornhill Magazine*, the Grantlys and the Proudies appear again, Miss Dunstable marries Dr Thorne, and the central figure of the *Last Chronicle*, Rev. Josiah Crawley, makes his first appearance.

Framley Parsonage is not only pivotal in the series, but also well illustrates the way in which the Barsetshire novels approach similar problems from different angles, within a previously known fictional world. Trollope's ability to help 'the heart of man to know itself', as Henry James put it,[26] is typified in his treatment of the financial difficulties into which the hero, Rev. Mark Robarts, gets himself through his interest in good horseflesh and his mishandling of loans. Robarts is no criminal; he is simply a vulnerable human being like the rest of us. His position as a clergyman, however, like that of Edmund Bertram in Jane Austen's *Mansfield Park*, means that he is measured against a higher standard than other men's, as Lady Lufton knows when she asks Mr Crawley to intercede on her behalf with the man who owes his position to her patronage. The interview between Mr Crawley, the impoverished perpetual curate of Hogglestock, and Mark Robarts, the erring young 'brother clergyman' whose breakfast eggs are still brought in by a man in livery, is one of Trollope's minor masterpieces (15). In contrast to Robarts's slangy *bonhomie* ('Oh, Crawley, you are a capital fellow'), Crawley's own language is that of the zealot whose sole reading, apart from the Classics, is the Bible: 'Henceforth let him take a lantern in his hand, and look warily to his path, and walk cautiously among the thorns and rocks, – cautiously, but yet boldly, with manly courage, but Christian meekness, as all men should walk on their pilgrimage through this vale of tears.' With words which resound with the central Victorian religious theme of pilgrimage, the difficult and somewhat unpleasant perpetual curate leaves Robarts to his tears of contrition and stalks 'back on his road to Hogglestock, thus tramping fourteen miles through the deep mud' on the mission on which he has been sent. Mr Crawley, who later solemnly hopes that Mark Robarts's promotion to a stall 'may tend in every way to his advantage here and hereafter' (22), represents the harsh side of the text I quoted earlier from Mark's gospel. Whereas the favoured Robarts is in danger of losing his soul, the Crawleys suffer from their rejection of the world. Whereas Robarts, like the Archdeacon, is attractive in his very worldliness, Crawley is unattractive in his closer adherence to the Gospel's teaching. These contrasts are characteristic of Trollope, whose acceptance of the stubborn resistance of the world to the simple solution of its paradoxes explains much about the nature of his art.

Mr Crawley, then, is a high and in a way a noble spirit, but he lacks the Warden's gentleness. His spiritual pride makes him judge others by his own rigorously ascetic standards, and he imposes his own regimen on a large and suffering family. The victim of a stipendiary system which Trollope deplores, he is sometimes prostrate with a Job-like sense that God has deserted him, and even prays for his own death (*Framley Parsonage*, 14). In his treatment of Mr Crawley, Trollope uses a semi-allegorical mode.[27] For example, early in *The Last Chronicle* Mr Crawley waits in the dark sitting-room at Hogglestock with his daughter, like a benighted Milton, for his wife to come in from the rain (4). As troubles gather around the family after Mr Crawley has been accused of stealing a cheque, he endures a long dark night of the soul. He is sustained, however, by a sense of being in the right, which he sharpens against his enemy, Mrs Proudie. Victorian readers of *The Last Chronicle* would have remembered the bitter encounter between Mr Slope and Mrs Proudie in the bishop's study in *Barchester Towers*, when she was forced to leave the room (26). Trollope sets up a similar confrontation and again uses the pilgrimage metaphor when Mr Crawley is summoned to the palace to discuss the court case that has been brought against him. Ignoring Mark Robarts's warning about appearing before Mrs Proudie with muddy boots, Mr Crawley glories in his dirty state after walking halfway from Hogglestock to Barchester, where he muses on the 'pleasant plate-glass' of the Deanery of his old college friend, Dr Arabin, and compares their present positions in the diocese (17). Soiled only in externals, he 'crushes' the Bishop by refusing to continue their discussion with Mrs Proudie in the room, and, having told her that she debases her husband's high office, walks back to Hogglestock the victor. (Later, after a similar scene with Dr Tempest, Mrs Proudie's interference in her husband's affairs proves to be the death of her, 66.)

Although Mr Crawley unbends somewhat when the question of the cheque is resolved, referring to his 'narrow squeak' (79) and finally accepting Mr Harding's old living of St Ewold's and some new coats (82–83), the contrast between himself and the old Warden is sustained. When his devoted wife breaks down at the good news, he stands 'somewhat apart from her', telling his visitors that 'She was never like this, sirs, when ill news came to us' (74); whereas Mr Harding gains comfort on his death-bed from the physical closeness of his daughters (81). The Barsetshire series dies with the Warden and old Bunce, his favourite bedesman, who soon follows him. The old community that was Hiram's Hospital, scrutinized by reformers in *The Warden* as an 'association' based on acts of exchange, can never regain its former unselfcritical identity, and one senses that it too dies with Mr Harding and Bunce. Although the Archdeacon's often quoted conciliatory words to Mr Crawley at the end of the novel – 'We stand on the only perfect level on which such men can meet each other. We are both gentlemen' (83) – suggest a healing of wounds, the difference between the two men, and between them and Mr Harding remains. Many of the religious novelists of the period would have examined doctrinal differences between the three clergymen. Trollope's interest, however, is in works rather than in faith; in the effect which Crawley's scripturalism has on his behaviour, rather than in his interpretation of Scripture itself; in his manliness, or gentlemanliness, rather than in his position on the Athanasian Creed.

For all the divisions revealed in Barsetshire, *The Last Chronicle* does end with a demonstration, albeit a strained one, that truth will out and that gentlemen can be reconciled. The larger world of the Palliser novels and of *The Way We Live Now* is far more threatening. It is inhabited by dangerous characters such as the 'snake-like' Lizzie Eustace (2), a brilliant actress who is able to achieve metamorphoses of expression and gesture at will (*The Eustace Diamonds*, 19, 74). Although Phineas Finn eventually marries the simple and devoted Mary Flood Jones, his Irish sweetheart, he comes perilously close to abandoning her for three women he meets in English political circles: Lady Laura Standish, Violet Effingham, and Marie Max Goesler. The safe, rather dull gentleman does survive in the Palliser novels, in such figures as John Grey and Plantagenet Palliser, whose contests with their dangerous rivals for the hands of Alice Vavasor and Lady Glencora M'Cluskie are developed in two of the three parallel plots in the first novel of the series, *Can You Forgive Her?*, published before *The Last Chronicle*. (Some characters, such as the Duke of Omnium, figure in both series of novels). John Grey's rival, George Vavasor, with his terrible facial scar and a previous lover who is now a common prostitute (71), behaves like a villain in a sensation novel when he brandishes a pistol at Grey. When a shot has in fact narrowly missed him and Vavasor has escaped, Grey's collected thoughts on his next course of action point the contrast between himself and the would-be murderer: 'That he was called upon by duty to do something he felt almost assured' (72).

Like George Vavasor, Burgo Fitzgerald, who loves and is loved by Glencora, also lives on the 'dangerous edge of things', and is last seen in Baden, desperately trying to recoup his losses at the casino gambling tables. The Pallisers see him there, and Plantagenet, who has turned down the post of Chancellor of the Exchequer in order to take his wife abroad and thus save their marriage (59), goes after him and offers help (76). Burgo, the gambler who risks the lives of his horses when he hunts and the reputation of the woman he loves, bitterly regrets having missed the 'chance' he lost when he failed to win Glencora's hand: with her money behind him, he believes, he would not have gone to the bad. Palliser's quiet response suggests a different view of the world: 'It has been ordered otherwise.' Like Grey he is willing to make sacrifices in order to preserve the standards of honour and fidelity he accepts as the norm in both family and public life. Both the scarred George and the 'beautiful' Burgo become moral desperadoes when frustrated in love and finally virtually destroy themselves.

Trollope explores similar conflicts between high but gentle spirits and those who ruthlessly pursue their own desires and ambitions in *The Way We Live Now*, though the balance of power has shifted towards the latter group of characters. *The Way We Live Now* has often been described as Trollope's *Vanity Fair*: both are panoramic social satires, for example, and both treat human motivation with a profound scepticism, and even cynicism. It is also interesting to compare the treatment of gambling and its parallels to financial speculation in the City and the marriage market in the two novels. As the purveyor of the Beargarden Club, Herr Vossner, bolts with his customers' 'acceptances' (69), and the young bloods, Sir Felix Carbury, Dolly Longestaffe, and Lord Nidderdale, sit in a bemused state, not knowing where the next game of cards and bottle of wine are coming from, the financial empire of Augustus Melmotte, the novel's main villain, is on the brink of collapse, following rumours concerning his corrupt business practices: " 'Here's a go", said Dolly. "One thing atop of another! There'll be nothing left for anybody soon" ' (69). Young Sir Felix hoped to marry

Melmotte's daughter, Marie, whereas his uncle, Squire Roger Carbury, has old-fashioned views on a Jewish family whose head is of uncertain nationality: Roger 'was a gentlemen; – and would have felt himself disgraced to enter the house of such a one as Augustus Melmotte. Not all the duchesses in the peerage, or all the money in the city, could alter his notions or induce him to modify his conduct' (8).

Trollope's emphasis on the fact that Roger Carbury's ideas are old-fashioned complements his disgust at the way we live *now*. In the last chapter of the *Autobiography* he poses questions which challenge his contemporaries' ideas of progress: 'That men have become less cruel, less violent, less selfish, less brutal, there can be no doubt; – but have they become less honest? If so, can a world, retrograding from day to day in honesty, be considered to be in a state of progress?' (20). Trollope's nice distinctions between, for example, selfishness and dishonesty, are certainly questionable, and cruelty and violence are more disturbingly in evidence in the novel than in his earlier works. His main point in both the *Autobiography* and the novel, however, is that a 'certain class of dishonesty', climbing into high places, has become 'so rampant and so splendid' that people will be taught 'to feel that dishonesty, if it can become splendid, will cease to be abominable' (*Autobiography, 20*). This last word, suggestive of the biblical 'abomination', applies to an adulterous and sinful *generation*, a new breed of English men and women who will blink at Melmotte's shady past. Meanwhile Melmotte himself does not understand the ancient English system of inheritance, and his suspicions concerning Sir Felix's claims are well founded (23). Thus the corruption of the new also throws into relief the corruption of the old, against which only the honour of a Roger Carbury can stand.

Unlike Dickens in his treatment of Merdle in *Little Dorrit*, Trollope describes Melmotte's grandiose schemes and speculations in the cool listing detail of the realist (44). Like Dickens in other novels, however, he indicates the heartlessness of the character by showing him tête-à-tête with his daughter, Marie. The topic of their discussion is the old one of parental disapproval of a lover, in this case Sir Felix. Marie's response, which reads like a devalued, secular version of St Mark, is the familiar one of the young woman in love: 'Why can't you let me have the man I love? What's the good of all the money if people don't have what they like?' (50). As Melmotte counts off the good things with which he supplies her, he grasps her by the arm until she cries out. Later, when he is on the brink of ruin, he fails to bully Marie into signing some crucial papers, and tries literally to beat her into submission (77). A few chapters earlier Sir Felix has tried to seduce Ruby Ruggles down a back alley in London, but has been thwarted by the timely arrival of her dull but worthy lover, John Crumb, who hits him repeatedly, 'at every blow obliterating a feature' (71). Where the violence of paternal fury and of young men's sexual passion have previously been only suggested by Dickens and Thackeray, these squalid scenes of naked aggression indicate the depth of the sixty-year-old Trollope's disgust. Where, then, is the high but gentle spirit of the piece?

When Henrietta Carbury expresses surprise that her brother Felix, who was to marry Miss Melmotte, should be interested in Ruby Ruggles, Roger Carbury replies: 'You're old-fashioned, Hetta. It used to be the way, – to be off with your old love before you are on with the new; but that seems to be all changed now' (72). Implicitly he is also commenting on the fact that Paul Montague has continued to see Mrs Hurtle, a former lover, while treating Henrietta as his lover, and that all the time Roger himself has loved Henrietta devotedly. Love in this novel not only leads to deception and violence; it also divides old friends, such as Paul Montague and Roger Carbury (66).

In the final chapters, however, in a variation on Dickens's and Thackeray's treatments of father figures as lovers, Roger Carbury tells Paul that Henrietta shall be his 'daughter', that she shall have his property, or her child shall be his heir ('A True Lover', 93). When the young couple marry, the bride is given away by Roger, and everyone declares that the Squire has not seemed to be 'so happy for many a long year' (100). There is something rather desperate about Trollope's insistence on the magnanimity of his gentleman mouthpiece in *The Way We Live Now*, and for all Roger's nobility under the assaults of disappointment and the abuse of others, it is always emphasized that he is unusual even in his own generation. Melmotte, much more a product of 'now', has killed himself with prussic acid (83). The younger generation are a feckless bunch, and the last sentence of the novel is reserved for Sir Felix Carbury, sent abroad with a young curate to keep an eye on him: 'Happily up to this time Mr. Septimus Blake had continued to keep that gentleman as one of his Protestant population in the German town, – no doubt not without considerable trouble to himself.'

Incarnate history and unhistoric acts:
George Eliot

Writing on George Eliot in 1876, when her last novel, *Daniel Deronda*, was appearing in parts, Trollope concurred with many contemporary critics in describing her as 'the first of English novelists' at the 'present moment' (*Autobiography*, 13). He is particularly interested in characterization, again like other Victorian critics of the 'fiction as a mirror of life' school[28]: 'Seth Bede, Adam Bede, Maggie and Tom Tulliver, old Silas Marner, and, much above all, Tito, in *Romola*, are characters which, when once known, can never be forgotten. I cannot say quite so much for any of those in her later works, because in them the philosopher so greatly overtops the portrait-painter, that, in the dissection of the mind, the outward signs seem to have been forgotten.' The word 'dissection' echoes Trollope's broader criticism that 'her imagination is no doubt strong, but it acts in analysing rather than in creating'; and the reference to her later works is developed in further comments on their difficulty. Perhaps Trollope's most interesting point, however, is that the philosopher overtops the portrait-painter, for recent academic criticism of George Eliot has furthered our own century's rescue work on her later novels from Victorian claims of affected difficulty and an imaginative falling off by acclaiming rather than apologizing for the subtleties of her mature intellect and a complexity of mythic structure which anticipates Joyce.[29] I suggested in the last section that Trollope did not write novels of ideas. His characters, unlike those in novels of religious polemic, for example, do not tend to discuss the major intellectual issues of his own times. This last point also applies to George Eliot's characters in fact, for only *Daniel Deronda* has a contemporary setting, and the discussions of politics in *Felix Holt* (1866) and *Middlemarch* (1871–72), and of scientific and historical research in the latter novel, are carefully placed in the period of the first Reform Act (1832). Even in the early phase of her novel-writing career, however, the period of *Adam Bede* (1859), *The Mill on the Floss* (1860), and *Silas Marner* (1861), the notoriously intrusive authorial narrator is a thinker: meditative, moral, and philosophical.

When one compares George Eliot's own intellect with that of Thackeray (for Trollope an even greater novelist), one is struck not only by its remarkable depth and breadth, but also by the fact that almost all her interests, like Thackeray's, had a historical dimension, in a century obsessed by history. Capable of reading Greek, Latin, French, Italian, and German in her mid-twenties, she had access to ancient historical sources and, particularly through German, which Mr Casaubon in *Middlemarch* lacked (21), to the most advanced modern writings on religious, historical, and philosophical subjects. Although she lost her faith in early womanhood, her respect for and interest in Christianity as the highest expression to date of man's spiritual quest was expressed in and through her fiction. Influenced by Comtean Positivism, aspects of which she embraced, and by the works of Strauss and Feuerbach which she translated from the German, her special interest in Christianity as a phenomenon focused on its origins and, in her view, its waning; in other words, on the history of religion in the West. Like Comte's, her own religion of humanity grew out of historical perceptions. A reader of Buckle, Macaulay, and Froude, George Eliot examined recent English political history, her 'conservative-reforming' impulse[30] being based upon a reading of the history of reform in England and of the German sociologist, Riehl. Her treatment of Lydgate's search for 'certain primary webs or tissue' in *Middlemarch* (15) is rooted in her knowledge of the history of science. Interestingly, she thought that Darwin's development theory, and 'all other explanations of processes by which things came to be, produce a feeble impression compared with the mystery that lies under these processes'.[31] In her examination of the mysteries that lie beneath racial history, in *Daniel Deronda*, and the Renaissance, in *Romola*, she also explores the central social-scientific issue of individual development in relation to the environment which at least partially determines that development.

Like her friend Herbert Spencer, who thought of society as an evolving

organism, George Eliot applies the language of science to the study of society, as in her seminal review article in the *Westminster Review* entitled 'The
Natural History of German Life', on the work of Riehl:

> He sees in European society *incarnate history*, and any attempt
> to disengage it from its historical elements must, he believes,
> be simply destructive of social vitality. What has grown up
> historically can only die out historically, by the gradual
> operation of necessary laws. The external conditions which
> society has inherited from the past are but the manifestation of
> inherited internal conditions in the human beings who
> compose it; the internal conditions and the external are related
> to each other as the organism and its medium, and
> development can take place only by the gradual consentaneous
> development of both.[32]

These comments on Riehl's 'social-political-conservatism' anticipate her
own thinking in *Felix Holt*, a novel in which the lives of individuals are
partially determined by political upheaval. George Eliot refuted the Hon.
Mrs Ponsonby's extreme version of determinism: 'I shall not be satisfied
with your philosophy till you have conciliated necessitarianism – I hate the
ugly word – with the practice of willing strongly, willing to will strongly,
and so on.'[33] As U. C. Knoepflmacher has said of *Middlemarch*, 'by a
characteristic Victorian manipulation, free will coexists with determinism'
in George Eliot.[34] Indeed, moral choice and the idea of a vision which can
be acted upon are central to her thinking in her novels.

Carlyle, Emerson, and J. A. Foude thought of history as biography and
biography as history. The words 'history' and 'story' share common etymo-
logical roots. George Eliot's 'histories' of her characters, as she herself
often called them, demonstrate not only that within the compass of the
private life, in the everyday world of 'unhistoric acts' (*Middlemarch*, 'Finale'), the moral being is determined by and himself determines the 'incarnate history' of his society, but also that that being's own nature and
behaviour determine his future development. Consider, for example,
George Eliot's recurrent emphasis upon the long-term effects of actions,
or 'deeds'. In the best of the three stories in *Scenes of Clerical Life* (1857),
'Janet's Repentance', she says in relation to the Dempsters, who live in
Orchard Street, that 'the seeds of things are very small' (13), and later comments: 'We cannot foretell the working of the smallest event in our own
lot' (18). Mr Irwine's prophetic words to Arthur Donnithorne in *Adam Bede*
– 'Consequences are unpitying. Our deeds carry their terrible consequences'
(16) – are significantly developed by George Eliot as authorial narrator later
in the novel: 'Our deeds determine us, as much as we determine our deeds'
(29). The dark secret in a personal history, which comes to light in the
present, is George Eliot's most characteristic plot motif. She writes of the
'contaminating effect of deeds' in her analysis of Tito's 'guilty secret' in
Romola (9), and comments on lawyer Jermyn's secret in *Felix Holt* through
mottoes such as this: ''Tis grievous, that with all amplification of travel

both by sea and land, a man can never separate himself from his past history' (21). Her motto to Chapter 70 in *Middlemarch* brings together several of these strands from earlier novels: 'Our deeds still travel with us from afar,/And what we have been makes us what we are.'

George Eliot's emphasis upon moral choice and individual responsibility was one element of a secular morality which was even more demanding than that of her earlier Calvinist phase. Her aggressive attacks upon two Christian writers, Dr John Cumming, an Evangelical, and the poet Edward Young, cleared the ground early in her writing career for a religion of humanity in which the egoist's hope of heaven is replaced by what she sees as the nobler call to duty, on the assumption that our highest aspirations must be directed towards the human lot here on earth.[35] As so often in *Felix Holt*, her hero, that most conservative of radicals, speaks for her as he attempts to draw Esther Lyon back from egoism towards duty, in a manner which reminds one of Carlyle: 'The only failure a man ought to fear is failure in cleaving to the purpose he sees to be best. . . . the universe has not been arranged for the gratification of his feelings. As long as a man sees and believes in some great good, he'll prefer working towards that in the way he's best fit for, come what may' (45). For George Eliot the way out of the hell of egoism, where the damned are often haunted by memories of guilty secrets, is through the 'extension of our sympathies' to fellow pilgrims. Her comments on art and our response to it, in the Riehl review, are also applicable to her own artistic intentions: 'The greatest benefit we owe to the artist, whether painter, poet, or novelist, is the extension of our sympathies. . . . Art is the nearest thing to life; it is a mode of amplifying experience and extending our contact with our fellow-men beyond the bounds of our personal lot.'[36] Twenty years later, at the end of her novel-writing career, she has Daniel Deronda counsel the egoistical Gwendolen in similar terms: 'Look on other lives besides your own. See what their troubles are, and how they are borne. . . . Try to care for what is best in thought and action – something that is good apart from the accidents of your own lot' (36). Formerly Gwendolen's conscience, Deronda also becomes her confessor when she tells him of the remorse she feels for marrying Grandcourt when she knew of the existence of Lydia Glasher and her children: 'That is the bitterest of all – to wear the yoke of our own wrongdoing' (36).

We will return to Gwendolen later, but for the moment I want briefly to consider confession in George Eliot, one of the several Christian forms which she effectively adapts to her own purposes. For confession combines an acknowledgement of some yoke of wrongdoing in a personal history with the extension of sympathies through the sharing of that yoke, an act of mutual recognition and (potentially) acceptance. Gwendolen's vulnerability is reminiscent of one of George Eliot's early heroines, Janet in 'Janet's Repentance', whose appeal to Mr Tryan is as direct as Gwendolen's to Deronda: 'I want to tell you how unhappy I am – how weak and wicked. I feel no strength to live or die. I thought you could tell me something that would help me' (18). Tryan replies that perhaps he can, for she is speaking to a 'fellow-sinner who has needed just the comfort and help you are needing'. Janet's confession of her drinking elicits from Tryan a confession of his seduction of a girl in his youth, as a consequence of which he entered the Church so that he might 'rescue other weak and falling souls'. More obviously that other sacraments, such as baptism, for example, confession can draw heavily on the emotional reserves of the confessor, and George Eliot's interest in the form would have flowed naturally from her Feuerbachian interpretation of religion which locates the spiritual life within the human heart, and denies a relationship with a deity outside or beyond human nature.

Confessions take a variety of forms in subsequent works. In *Romola*, for example, George Eliot comments that 'the purifying influence of public confession springs from the fact, that by it the hope in lies is for ever swept away, and the soul recovers the noble attitude of simplicity' (9); yet at the end of the novel Savonarola's confessions and retractions under torture rock his followers' faith in him (71–72). In contrast, Bulstrode's mute confession to his wife in *Middlemarch* is one of the most affirmative moments in George Eliot's work. Dressed in a plain black gown and bonnet-cap, and looking, in fresh garments, 'suddenly like an early Methodist', Harriet Bulstrode is ready to begin a new life with her husband: 'They could not yet speak to each other of the shame which she was bearing with him, or of the acts which had brought it down on them. His confession was silent, and her promise of faithfulness was silent' (74). The contrast between Mrs Bulstrode's moving extension of sympathy, or 'fellowship with shame and isolation', and Rosamond's response to Lydgate's troubles, which are closely linked to Bulstrode's, illustrates George Eliot's idea of duty as the means of 'salvation' from egoism. In treating periods of moral crisis such as this, George Eliot as the 'belated historian' who must concentrate on 'this particular web' of 'human lots' (*Middlemarch*, 15) in her fiction, fulfils as a novelist Macaulay's prescription for the historian in a passage which she transcribed into one of her notebooks: 'He alone reads history aright, who . . . learns to distinguish what is accidental and transitory in human nature, from what is essential and immutable'.[37]

Before 'George Eliot' had been identified as Marian Evans, Elizabeth Gaskell was suspected of having written *Adam Bede*. Both writers were strongly influenced by Wordsworth, whose famous statement of intent in the 1800 Preface to the *Lyrical Ballads* could also be taken as the manifesto of these and other Victorian novelists: 'The principal object . . . which I proposed to myself in these Poems was to make the incidents of common life interesting by tracing in them, truly though not ostentatiously, the primary laws of our nature.'[38] (Compare Macaulay's comment on the essential and immutable in human nature.) Elizabeth Gaskell wrote a short preface to her first work, *Mary Barton*, in which she recorded that, living in Manchester, she had started work on a tale set in a rural scene, when she realized that her true subject was immediately to hand: 'I bethought me how deep might be the romance in the lives of some of those who elbowed me daily in the busy streets of the town in which I resided. I had always felt a deep *sympathy* with the care-worn men, who looked as if doomed to struggle through their lives in strange alternations between work and want' (my emphasis). George Eliot and Lewes read *Mary Barton* in 1858, together with a little Wordsworth, about a year before she wrote this in *The Mill on the Floss*: 'The pride and obstinacy of millers, and other insignificant people, whom you pass unnoticingly on the road every day, have their tragedy too; but it is of that unwept, hidden sort, that goes on from generation to generation, and leaves no record' (III. 1). Similar in their sympathy,[39] Elizabeth Gaskell and George Eliot differ in their emphases, for whereas the former focuses upon a present social tragedy, the latter, in the very process of evoking our sympathy for the common human lot, introduces a historical perspective with her reference to generations which leave no record.

Both Elizabeth Gaskell and George Eliot, however, refer to the every-day nature of their material, implicitly placing their work in what David Masson described as the 'Real school' (see p. 6 above). In 'Janet's Repentance', George Eliot ponderously emphasizes a characteristic descent from the ideal to the real in her first reference to Mr Tryan's study, saying that her reader's 'too active imagination' perhaps 'conjures up a perfect snuggery', in which the 'light is softened by a screen of boughs with a grey church in the background', but that she has to confess it was 'a very ugly little room indeed', with 'an ugly view of cottage roofs and cabbage-gardens from the window' (11). Her continuing discussion of the nature of realism in fiction, into which the reader is generally drawn by the first-person plural, again raises the question of sympathy early in *Adam Bede*: 'We can hardly think Dinah and Seth beneath our sympathy, accustomed as we may be to weep over the loftier sorrows of heroines in satin boots and crinoline, and of heroes riding fiery horses, themselves ridden by still more fiery passions' (3). Her Wordsworthian interest in the incidents of common life, and specifically of what he called low and rustic life, does not, however, result in her fulfilling in *Adam Bede* the aim of the artist as she expresses it in the Riehl essay: 'We want to be taught to feel, not for the heroic artisan or the sentimental peasant, but for the peasant in all his coarse apathy, and the artisan in all his suspicious selfishness.'[40] Adam is heroic, after all, and Dinah's spirituality transcendent.

George Eliot generally attends most closely to the realities of the commonplace in her treatment of the little vanities and narrow-mindedness of the middle classes. The comic chapter in *The Mill on the Floss* entitled 'Enter the Aunts and Uncles' (7) illustrates this, and also provides an early example of the determining effect of accumulated petty constraints on a George Eliot heroine: it is in this chapter that Maggie persuades Tom to cut off her luxuriant black locks. Later in the novel George Eliot again takes up her discussion with the reader: 'It is a sordid life, you say, this of the Tullivers and Dodsons . . . . You could not live among such people; you are stifled for want of an outlet towards something beautiful, great, or noble. . . . I share with you this sense of oppressive narrowness; but it is necessary that we should feel it, if we care to understand how it acted on the lives of Tom and Maggie – how it has acted on young natures in many generations' (IV. 1).

George Eliot's interest in the relationship between the real and the ideal remained with her and deepened. Indeed, it is often articulated in the most strongly imagined episodes in her novels. Take, for example, the moment at which Tito places Romola's crucifix in the triptych on which Piero di Cosimo has painted them as a 'perfect' Bacchus and Ariadne: 'They held each other's hands while she spoke, and both looked at their imaged selves. But the reality was far more beautiful; she all lily-white and golden, and he with his dark glowing beauty above the purple red-bordered tunic' (20, 'The Day of the Betrothal'). We will later see that in *Middlemarch* the real/ideal dialectic informs George Eliot's treatment of many of the novel's themes, ranging from historical research to Dorothea's first marriage. In *Daniel Deronda* she offers a characteristic gloss on the hero's rambles in parts of London most inhabited by 'common Jews', during the long process of discovering his Jewish ancestry:

> The fact was, notwithstanding all his *sense of poetry in common things*, Deronda, where a keen personal interest was aroused, could not, more than *the rest of us*, continuously escape suffering from the pressure of that *hard unaccommodating Actual*, which has never consulted out taste and is entirely unselect. Enthusiasm, we know, *dwells at ease among ideas*, tolerates garlic breathed in the middle ages, and sees no shabbiness in the official trappings of classic processions: it gets squeamish when *ideals press upon it as something warmly incarnate*, and can hardly face them without fainting. . . . the *fervour of sympathy* with which we contemplate a grandiose martyrdom is feeble compared with the enthusiasm that keeps unslacked where there is no danger, no challenge – nothing but *impartial midday falling on commonplace, perhaps half-repulsive, objects which are really the beloved ideas made flesh*. Here undoubtedly lies the chief poetic energy: – in the force of imagination that pierces or exalts the *solid fact*, instead of floating among cloud-pictures.
>
>   (33; my emphases)

Like George Eliot's treatment of her recurrent theme of our deeds determining us, this passage in her last novel illustrates the way in which each of her novels is a form of rewriting, a return to a set of ideas on which she works again and again. Notice how the words and phrases italicized above echo passages I have quoted earlier, on sympathy, the poetry in common things, incarnate history, and so on. Again the discussion naturally turns to history – the Middle Ages, classic processions, grandiose martyrdom – as Deronda's research into his personal history is conflated with his research into the Jewish race. When personal and racial history coincide, and he tells Mordecai that he is a Jew, Deronda enjoys 'one of those rare moments when our yearnings and our acts can be completely one, and the real we behold is our ideal good' (63). Mirah falls on her knees, and a gladness comes over her as if she were beholding a 'religious rite'. In harmonizing personal and racial histories, Deronda experiences a rare moment outside time, a secular version of the believer's experience of eternity, or of the prophecy of the heavenly Jerusalem, when 'former things are passed away' (Revelation 21. 4).

As an agnostic and a realist, George Eliot's reading of history is fundamentally gradualist rather than catastrophist. Her summary of Riehl was quoted earlier – 'What has grown up historically can only die out historically, by the gradual operation of necessary laws' – and one need only turn to *Felix Holt* to find a full treatment of her anxieties concerning revolutionary change. Yet for all the slow accretion of unhistoric acts in the development of her individual characters, her novels sometimes read like Dickens or the sensation novelists at moments of crisis (or revolutionary change) in her characters' personal histories. Gwendolen's 'piercing cry', 'pallid lips', and 'dilated' eyes, when the panel on which a dead face is painted flies open during the tableau (6), suggest in retrospect certain prophetic powers as she stutters, 'a dead face – I shall never get away from it', after Grandcourt's drowning (56). We have seen that secrets are central themes both for George Eliot and the exactly contemporary sensation novel. Her sensational treatment of the Bulstrode/Raffles plot in *Middlemarch* (e.g. 70), of Arthur Donnithorne's reception of the news that Hetty is in prison (*Adam Bede*, 44), and his last-minute arrival at the gallows with 'a hard-won release from death' (47), of the ending of *The Mill on the Floss*, and of Jermyn's grappling with Harold Transome – '*I am your father*' (*Felix Holt*, 47) – reflects the fact that in moments of crisis or catastrophe the softening film of familiarity and everyday assumptions falls away, to reveal reality sharply illuminated in unrelieved and unaccustomed brilliance. At the moment of crisis, Bulstrode, Arthur, and Jermyn are like the man George Eliot describes in 'Janet's Repentance', who 'looks with ghastly horror on all his property aflame in the dead of night' (16). Each of them later has to live like that man, who is doubly destitute in the morning, 'when he walks over the ruins lying blackened in the pitiless sunshine'. For George Eliot, the real is often associated with the light, the day, or the sun, whose rays reveal dark secrets from the past or the special beauty of a moment of vision.

I will now consider George Eliot's fiction in rather more detail by examining *Silas Marner*, with brief reference to *Romola*, and *Middlemarch*, with brief reference to *Daniel Deronda*, as histories.

'This is the history of Silas Marner until the fifteenth year after he came to Raveloe' (2). By the end of the second chapter of *Silas Marner* George Eliot has traced Silas's history to the point at which her main narrative in the first part of the novel is to begin; that is 'about the Christmas of that fifteenth year', when 'a second great change came over Marner's life' (2). The first great change had been his expulsion from the urban church community of Lantern Yard and his move to a stone cottage near the village of Raveloe. Characteristically, however, George Eliot begins her novel not with an account of that move, but with an introductory paragraph on life in country areas in unspecified 'old times' (1). The vagueness of her opening sentence – 'In the days when the spinning-wheels hummed busily in the farmhouses' –

suggests that the superstition she mentions, which surrounded weavers in country districts, had long been deeply ingrained in the corporate consciousness of English country folk. The 'mysterious burden' carried by one of these 'wandering men', regarded as 'aliens' by their rustic neighbours in that 'far-off time', suggests ancient mythic associations, evoking not only Bunyan's *Pilgrim's Progress* but also the alienated Cain (Genesis 4), and the itinerant smith-caste of the nomadic Kenites.[41] The second paragraph introduces Silas as an example of the type of alien-looking men, specifically in the 'early years of this century', and by the fourth paragraph we know that it was fifteen years since he had first come to Raveloe.

The opening of *Silas Marner* reflects the novel's genesis, described by George Eliot in an often quoted letter to Blackwood: 'It came to me first of all, quite suddenly, as a sort of legendary tale, suggested by my recollections of having once, in early childhood, seen a linen-weaver with a bag on his back; but, as my mind dwelt on the subject, I became inclined to a more realistic treatment' (*Letters*, III, 382). For although she decided to write a prose tale rather than the poem she originally thought of, the legendary element of the conception is retained not only in her inversion of the Midas story, but also in the villagers' reading of Silas's activities. Remarkable for his strange fits, when his eyes were 'set like a dead man's', and for his knowledge of medicinal herbs, his daily habits had presented 'scarcely any visible change' to his neighbours; yet his 'inward life' had been 'a history and a metamorphosis'. George Eliot now takes us back to the time before his arrival in Raveloe, when he had been highly thought of in the 'little hidden world' of Lantern Yard, from which he was rejected when falsely accused of stealing church funds. When he moved to Raveloe, reducing his life 'to the unquestioning activity of a spinning insect' (2), his true history was hidden from his neighbours, for whom he became more a figure of legend than an individual with a history. Two signs, however, of a possible brighter future occurred at about the same time. First, when all other purpose was gone, he began to live for his gold. Secondly, his preparation of foxglove for Sally Oates gave him 'a sense of unity between his past and present life, which might have been the beginning of his rescue from the insect-like existence into which his nature had shrunk'. When other cures were thought to have an adverse effect on villagers, however, his isolation was made more complete. His Lantern Yard history has remained buried as he has built up his crock of gold, itself buried in the floor under his loom.

The final sentence in Chapter 2 prepares for the main narrative: 'But about the Christmas of that fifteenth year, a second great change came over Marner's life, and his history became blent in singular manner with the life of his neighbours.' In order to introduce his most significant neighbours, Squire Cass and his sons Godfrey and Dunstan, George Eliot begins Chapter 3 with a brief account of their high station in Raveloe, which contrasts sharply with Silas's. Whereas Silas's simple cottage, with its buried gold, its hearth, its loom, and, outside, the so-called 'stone-pit', filled with water, retains something of the legendary and symbolic quality of a poem such as Wordsworth's 'Michael' (1800), from which the novel's motto is taken,

Squire Cass's Red House, with 'the handsome flight of stone steps in front and the high stable behind', and, within, 'coats and hats flung on the chairs' and 'tankards sending forth a scent of flat ale', brings us firmly into the world of the nineteenth-century realistic novel. Dunstan's attempt to screw money out of his elder brother by threatening to tell the Squire about Molly Farden, Godfrey's secret drunken wife, and the death of Godfrey's hunter after a bargain has been struck on him, are familiar material to the reader of Thackeray and Trollope. It is, however, in the 'blending' of the histories of Silas Marner and of Godfrey Cass, that George Eliot's interest lies. Such a blending raises technical difficulties, and particularly the problem of bringing histories of different characters forward together.

A historian of the English novel from the mid-eighteenth century to the present day might well organize his argument around the changing ways in which writers have confronted the problem of conveying synchronic action ('meanwhile . . . at the same time') within a narrative form which lends itself most readily to the diachronic ('and then . . . and then'). The Victorian multiplot novel would figure in such a history somewhere between Fielding's and Sterne's experiments with epic form and discussions on the value of the digression, and works by Joyce and Woolf in which the events of only twenty-four hours are viewed and reviewed from several narrative points of view. *Middlemarch*, perhaps the greatest Victorian multiplot novel, is particularly interesting and impressive in this respect, yet George Eliot's method of taking up first one and then another strand of her narrative is also an aspect of the novel's difficulty. We sense a pattern in the parallel lives of her characters, but cannot at every point discern it in a mass of local detail. In its clarity of outline and execution the one-volume *Silas Marner* presents no such difficulties, and George Eliot's use of significant transitions from a chapter on Silas to one on the Cass family, or vice versa, in order to suggest contrasts or parallels between their histories, suggests how we should also read her later and more complex works.

The second great change in Silas's life is initiated by Dunstan's robbery of his gold. At the end of Chapter 4 Dunstan steps out of the cottage 'into the darkness'. George Eliot takes up the narrative thread at the beginning of Chapter 5 – 'When Dunstan Cass turned his back on the cottage, Silas Marner was not more than a hundred yards away from it, plodding along from the village' – before briefly sketching what Silas was doing during the robbery. He now discovers that his gold is missing from its hiding place, and, in desperation, wonders whether he might have put it somewhere else: 'A man falling into dark waters seeks a momentary footing even on sliding stones.' At this very moment, as we discover only much later in the novel (18), Dunstan has literally fallen into the dark waters of the stone-pit and become trapped by two great stones, thus reburying Silas's gold only yards from his cottage door.

The night of the great change itself, New Year's Eve, finally brings Silas Marner and Godfrey Cass together. Again George Eliot makes concurrent events illuminate the two histories of the novel, but this time in the sequence of her narrative. After the description of the warm interior at the

Red House, during the party, in Chapter 11, the scene moves to the cold exterior: 'While Godfrey Cass was taking draughts of forgetfulness from the sweet presence of Nancy . . . Godfrey's wife was walking with slow uncertain steps through the snow-covered Raveloe lanes, carrying her child in her arms' (12). Whereas Silas's carefully accumulated gold disappeared by the willed act of Dunstan, its apparent reappearance to the short-sighted weaver, actually the 'soft warm curls' of Molly's child, who has crawled in from the cold, is achieved by 'the invisible wand of catalepsy'. For Silas stands holding the door open, *powerless to resist* either the good or evil that might enter there' (my emphasis). As he falls on his knees and bends his head to examine the 'marvel', he is reminded of his little sister, as if this child were 'somehow a message come to him from that far-off life' associated with Lantern Yard. As she reverses the Midas touch, the child thus initiates the process of repairing the broken threads which might tie his history into his present life.

In the subsequent chapter (13) we return to the Red House, where Silas appears with the child, whose 'advent' is to Godfrey, as it had been to Silas, an 'apparition' from his 'hidden life'. Having checked that Molly is definitely dead in the snow outside the cottage, he knows that his secret is now safely buried, for if Dunstan ever returned he might be 'won to silence'. Silas's great change thus coincides with a change in Godfrey's history. But whereas Godfrey's secret is buried in Molly's pauper grave and, as we later learn, with Dunstan and Silas's gold in the stone-pit, Silas begins the process of bringing his secret Lantern Yard history into living relationship with his present life. For Eppie's interest in the flowers beyond the stone-pits encourages Silas to look for the once familiar herbs again: 'As the child's mind was growing into knowledge, his mind was growing into memory: as her life unfolded, his soul, long stupefied in a cold narrow prison, was unfolding too, and trembling gradually into full consciousness' (14).

George Eliot told Blackwood that her story was intended to set 'in a strong light the remedial influences of pure, natural human relations' (*Letters*, III, 382). In the novel she comments that 'we see no white-winged angels now', but yet men 'are led away from threatening destruction', and the hand that leads 'may be a little child's' (14). Eppie's remedial influence works upon Silas over the sixteen years which separate the first part of the novel (1–15) from its much shorter second part:

> By seeking what was needful for Eppie, by sharing the effect
> that everything produced on her, he had himself come to
> appropriate the forms of custom and belief which were the
> mould of Raveloe life; and as, with reawakening sensibilities,
> memory also reawakened, he had begun to ponder over the
> elements of his old faith, and blend them with his new
> impressions, till he recovered a consciousness of unity between
> his past and present (16).

Significantly, however, the process initiated by natural human relations between Silas and Eppie was completed through his confession to Dolly

Winthrop of 'all he could describe of his early life', for his new human trust led him to think that perhaps some mistake had cast that 'dark shadow over the days of his best years'.

Meanwhile Godfrey Cass's marriage to Nancy Lammeter has been darkened by yet another burial, that of their only child (17). Like Silas, Godfrey confesses, but with quite different results. His confession to Nancy of his own guilty secret follows the discovery of his brother's skeleton in the stone-pit, sixteen years after Dunstan's robbery of the gold. It is prefaced by a statement which is reiterated in different forms in many of George Eliot's works, as we have seen: 'Everything comes to light, Nancy, sooner or later. When God Almighty wills it, our secrets are found out. I've lived with a secret on my mind, but I'll keep it from you no longer' (18). In Godfrey's case confession of a secret fact in his personal history evokes from Nancy the unforeseen observation that they need not have been childless if he had confessed earlier. Thus the results not only of our deeds but also of our confessions of those deeds remain hidden mysteries until they are revealed in crisis. Godfrey's attempt to take Eppie from Silas, leaving him only with the now restored gold, is thwarted by her rejection of his 'natural claim' on her (19). She is Silas's daughter and is being courted by young Aaron Winthrop. Money and status mean nothing to her, as her life is part of the incarnate history of Raveloe's working people.

When Silas later discovers that Lantern Yard has been obliterated by a new factory, he tells Mrs Winthrop that the true history of the robbery will be 'dark' to him to the last: 'The old home's gone; I've no home but this now' (21). In George Eliot's fairy-tale conclusion, Eppie and Aaron are established as newly-weds in Silas's now 'pretty home'. Renewal comes only after the destruction of the old. Having achieved unity between past and present through confession and natural human relations, Silas is now cut off from the dark secret of his own history and must live in the present, his future hope being embodied in Eppie and her husband.

The writing of *Silas Marner* marks a watershed in George Eliot's career, for her sympathetic treatment of country people looks back to *Adam Bede*, while the novel's moral scheme looks forward to her later works, including her next novel, *Romola*. Having completed *The Mill on the Floss* in March 1860, she spent two weeks of a long Continental tour in Florence, where she eagerly seized upon Lewes's idea of writing a historical romance on the life of Savonarola, the fifteenth-century religious and political reformer.[43] It was not, however, until *Silas Marner* had been written, a year later, that the massive task of researching *Romola* began in earnest, necessitating a further four weeks in Florence and months of labour in London libraries before beginning to write on the first day of 1862. Published in the new form, to her, of a *Cornhill Magazine* serial, for a new publisher who paid her an unprecedented £7,000, *Romola* was far more ambitious than any of her earlier works, and was hailed by the English literary élite as a triumph. Yet in spite of the great differences between *Silas Marner* and *Romola*, the first being a short, simply constructed novel, set in early nineteenth-century England, the second being long and complex, and set in fifteenth-century Italy, the parallels between their symbolic plots suggest that the fable had to be written on the way to the historical romance. It may be that George Eliot needed to write a tale in which light comes out of darkness before she could tackle the oppressive materials of *Romola*, through which runs a black thread of corruption, death, and apocalyptic portents.

We do not know when her earliest 'vision' of the plot of *Romola* occurred,[44] but her comments to Sara Hennell after the last episode had been published are unusually revealing: 'The various *strands* of thought I had to work out forced me into a more ideal treatment of Romola [the heroine, not the work] than I had foreseen at the outset – though the "Drifting away" and the Village with the Plague belonged to my earliest vision of the story and were by deliberate forecast adopted as romantic and symbolic elements' (*Letters*, IV, 104). Let us very briefly consider these episodes in their context.

After the execution of her godfather, Bernardo del Nero, Romola flees from Florence in her grey religious habit, nurturing a 'new rebellion' and a 'new despair': 'The bonds of all strong affection were snapped' (61, 'Drifting Away'). Her husband Tito, who, unlike Eppie, has denied his adopted father, Baldassarre, by whom he is hated, now thinks of their marriage as a youthful mistake. She has lost her faith in Savonarola. As she drifts away in a small boat, with the sail tied in a fixed position, she wishes for death, feeling 'orphaned in those wide spaces of sea and sky'.

As 'Drifting Away' is the last chapter in Part XII, and George Eliot keeps her reader in suspense by deferring the next stage of Romola's history until the final Part XIV, and parallels between the events of the intervening Part XIII and Romola's drifting out into the Mediterranean are immediately striking. Like Romola in her boat, Baldassarre, scavenging by the Arno, and Tito, diving into that river when pursued by the mob, in the last chapter of Part XIII (67), are both at the mercy of tides which determine their human lots. Tito is washed up at Baldassarre's feet. The father strangles his faithless son, and then dies himself. At first nobody sees the two bodies, for Florence is preparing for a 'deeper tragedy' as Savonarola cries out under torture: 'I will confess!'

When Baldassarre sees Tito being swept towards him, he leans forward with a start: 'Something was being brought to him.' 'Romola's Waking' (68), the first chapter in Part XIV, describes how a plague-stricken village at first sees her as the Madonna, brought to them across the sea to save and to heal. As in *Silas Marner*, a miraculous advent, apparently a divine intervention, breaking into historical time, proves to be a human marvel, when she is shown to be a 'substantial woman'.[45] Romola has woken 'without memory and without desire'. As in Silas's catalepsy, the suspension of the will has allowed a metamorphosis to take place, and new life to begin in caring for one weaker than herself: an orphaned Jewish child. Like Silas, Romola is cut off from her former home and from her past life, and has to make her home in the here and now.

Each of George Eliot's last three novels explores the question of how to live and work in the nineteenth century. In *Middlemarch*, her masterpiece,

Dorothea Brooke's yearning to act and to work in ways which will be of use to the community, first as the wife and later as the widow of Edward Casaubon, is the most strongly felt of several kinds of spiritual hunger in the novel. Her naive vision of Casaubon as a great scholar and of herself as his helpmate is the product of 'narrow teaching' and an equally narrow social life (3). Miss Brooke is both literally and metaphorically short-sighted, seeing a 'great soul' in Casaubon where her sister Celia sees only white moles, and comparing him with Milton, Locke, and Hooker while others consider him to be merely a misguided pedant (1–2). Walking through a wood when the idea that he might propose to her first enters her mind, she says to herself:

> It would be my duty to study that I might help him the
> better in his great works. There would be nothing trivial
> about our lives. Everyday-things with us would mean the
> greatest things. It would be like marrying Pascal. I should
> learn to see the truth by the same light as great men have seen
> it by. And then I should know what to do, when I got older:
> I should see how it was possible to lead a grand life here –
> now – in England. (3)

The here and now of the novel is the period in English history immediately preceding the First Reform Act of 1832, a period in which Carlyle, who in George Eliot's own opinion had a profound influence on her generation,[46] addressed himself to the subject of vocation in the modern world. In *Sartor Resartus*, Professor Teufelsdröckh records how Goethe's ideas on work and duty rescued him from the 'Centre of Indifference':

> Let him who gropes painfully in darkness or uncertain
> light, and prays vehemently that the dawn may ripen into
> day, lay this . . . precept well to heart, which to me was of
> invaluable service: '*Do the Duty which lies nearest thee*,' which
> thou knowest to be a Duty! Thy second Duty will already
> have become clearer.
>   . . . here, in this poor, miserable, hampered, despicable
> Actual, wherein thou even now standest, here or nowhere is
> thy Ideal: work it out therefrom; and working, believe, live,
> be free. . . .
>   . . . it is with man's Soul as it was with Nature: the
> beginning of Creation is – Light. Till the eye have vision, the
> whole members are in bonds.
>   (II. 9, 'The Everlasting Yea')

George Eliot describes Dorothea's vision, which comes to her near the end of the novel, the morning after she finds Rosamond and Will Ladislaw alone together, in similar terms. In the morning twilight, when all is dim around her, she thinks about Ladislaw, Rosamond, and Lydgate, whose work on the New Fever Hospital she has supported: 'What should I do – how should I act now, this very day if I could clutch my own pain, and compel it to silence, and think of those three!' (80). Light is 'piercing into the room', and she opens the curtains to see 'a man with a bundle on his back and a woman carrying her baby' on the road: 'Far off in the bending sky was the pearly light; and she felt the largeness of the world and the manifold wakings of men to labour and endurance. She was a part of that involuntary, palpitating life, and could neither look out on it from her luxurious shelter as a mere spectator, nor hide her eyes in selfish complaining.' The 'objects of her rescue' are 'chosen for her', as Silas's was for him. (Could the man with the bundle and the woman carrying a baby be an unconscious echo of the earlier novel?) Her acting upon her vision is not determined but is freely willed.

Dorothea's quest for a true vocation has been a long one, from the early idealism of the Pascal passage to the recognition that it is in what Carlyle called the miserable Actual that she must find her Ideal. On her honeymoon in Rome she becomes painfully aware that Casaubon has indeed, in his own words, lived 'too much with the dead' (2). In England Casaubon is untouched by stirring events, when the issue of political reform is on everyone's lips; in Rome he is untouched by its treasures. He merely moves from the library at Lowick to the Vatican library, accompanied by Dorothea down a 'stony avenue of inscriptions' (20). A belated scholar, his wandering among the ruins of dead history contrasts strongly with the sense of living, incarnate history in his nephew Ladislaw and his friend Naumann, whose names punningly emphasize their youthful engagement in the present. Dorothea's own interest in building model cottages at Lowick is frustrated on their return, when she discovers that there is nothing left for her to do. She too is belated, and stalled by a husband who is more interested in the measurements of Egyptian houses than in those on his estate (3).

Casaubon himself, however, as George Eliot insists in one of her most famous authorial intrusions, at the beginning of Chapter 29, is 'spiritually a-hungered like the rest of us', and her treatment of his first brush with death, when he suffers a scholar's heart-attack, clutching a volume on the library steps at Lowick, illustrates the kind of sympathy for a disagreeable character which makes her unique among Victorian novelists. Significantly, it is young Dr Lydgate who is at hand to give medical aid, for he is walking out with Miss Rosamond Vincy at the time. By bringing Lydgate and Dorothea together at this moment of crisis, George Eliot begins the process of interweaving the two stories of 'Miss Brooke' and 'Middlemarch' which she first planned separately. Later it is Lydgate who breaks the news to Casaubon which brings him to the most acute kind of personal crisis: 'When the commonplace "We must all die" transforms itself suddenly into the acute consciousness "I must die – and soon", then death grapples us, and his fingers are cruel' (42). After Casaubon's death, when Dorothea discovers that his will forbids her to marry Ladislaw, her world is thrown into 'a state of convulsive change', as she feels 'a violent shock of repulsion from her departed husband' and a 'sudden strange yearning of heart towards Will Ladislaw' (50). Again Lydgate is at hand: 'At this crisis Lydgate was announced.' Lydgate, like Dorothea, suffers as a partner in an unhappy marriage, and later experiences similar crises himself. That he and Dorothea do not eventually marry, freed by some easy turn of plotting which might have removed the water nixie Rosamond, marks the advance which *Middlemarch* represents on the endings of *Jane Eyre* or *David Copperfield*. Having passed through crises and moments of vision, both Lydgate and Dorothea find that their human lots are *still* constrained within this 'poor, miserable, hampered, despicable Actual'.

Crises in the private lives of George Eliot's characters in *Middlemarch* are related, either implicitly or explicitly, to the sense of convulsive change in English society which pervades the novel. Debates in England on Reform were given sharp focus by the recent revolution in France (1830), which raised the spectre of 1789 and the Terror; and Carlyle's writing of *The French Revolution* (1837) supplied the context for his prophetic essay on *Chartism* in 1839. In the late 1860s and early 1870s, when *Middlemarch* was written, Tennyson's line 'The old order changeth, yielding place to new' ('The Passing of Arthur', 1869) was as resonant as it had been in the earlier version of the poem, the 'Morte d'Arthur' of 1842. The hysterical tone of Carlyle's response to the second Reform Act, 'Shooting Niagara: And After?' (1867), contrasts with Matthew Arnold's treatment of the Hyde Park riots in *Culture and Anarchy* (1869). Yet Arnold's fears were just as real. Frank Kermode argues that *Middlemarch* is a 'novel of . . . crisis', and specifically of 'crisis as a mode of historical explanation', of 'humanised apocalypse'.[47] Like Kermode, Michael Mason emphasizes George Eliot's acknowledgement in her 'historical novel' that 'the two unmistakable contributions of her age to society were the democratic movement and the development of sanitation and medical welfare'.[48] Interestingly, George Eliot brings these two strands of her novel together in the opening paragraph of Chapter 46, immediately following Lydgate's discussion of his vocation with his wife, Rosamond, who prettily complains that she does '*not* think it a nice profession' (45): 'While Lydgate, safely married and with the Hospital under his command, felt himself struggling for Medical Reform against Middlemarch, Middlemarch was becoming more and more conscious of the national struggle for another kind of Reform.'

The juxtaposition is significant, for in *Middlemarch* ideals of innovation and reform, whether Dorothea's cottages, or Lydgate's medical research and New Fever Hospital, or Mr Brooke's political campaign, are effectively punctured by the sturdy Middlemarchers who act as comic chorus. Rosamond's dislike of Lydgate's profession is shared in the town by, among others, Mrs Dollop, landlady of the Tankard in Slaughter Lane, who becomes increasingly convinced that Lydgate means to 'let the people die in the Hospital, if not to poison them, for the sake of cutting them up without saying by your leave' (45). Such suspicions later fuel the gossip concerning the death of Raffles, which ultimately brings down both Lydgate and Bulstrode (71). Mr Brooke's disastrous speech from the balcony of the White Hart is greeted with brayings, an effigy of himself, and a hail of eggs (51). The clever ventriloquist who parrots his phrases to such effect is thought to be Bowyer, of whom Ladislaw indignantly remarks that there is not a more paltry fellow in Middlemarch: 'But it seems as if the paltry fellows were always to turn the scale.' Middlemarch reduces Lydgate's ideal to body-snatching, Brooke's to a 'punch-voiced echo'. Having informed us that in Middlemarch 'railways were as exciting a topic as the Reform Bill or the imminent horrors of Cholera', George Eliot has Fred Vincy intervene in a ludicrous confrontation between four railway agents and a group of men in smock-frocks with hay-forks in their hands (56). Not only the rude provincial, however, brings down the mighty from their seats. Mrs Cadwallader, whose devastating comments on Casaubon reveal the pathetic short-sightedness of Dorothea early in the novel (6), has the last word on Reform just after the House of Lords throws out the Bill at the end of the novel:

> Mrs Cadwallader was strong on the intended creation of peers: she had it for certain from her cousin that Truberry had gone over to the other side entirely at the instigation of his wife, who had scented peerages in the air from the very first introduction of the Reform question, and would sign her soul away to take precedence of her younger sister, who had married a baronet. (84)

The Reform Bill, cholera, and the coming of the railways are weighty issues, fit subject for the serious historian. That George Eliot's study of the provincial mind's response to these subjects is comic reflects her commitment to realism. That Lydgate and Dorothea have noble aims for good which are tragically limited by their environment reflects her commitment to the pursuit of the highest human endeavours.

Besides news of the Franco-Prussian War, George Eliot's reading in 1870 included *The History of Tom Jones* by Fielding, the 'great historian' to whom she refers in *Middlemarch* (15), Froude's *History of England*, and, perhaps most significantly, Carlyle's *French Revolution*.[49] In his famous essay 'On History' (1830) Carlyle had written about the problem I touched on earlier: that of conveying 'simultaneous' events in a 'successive' written history. His attempt to solve the problem in *The French Revolution*, partly by assembling collages of quotations, partly by his use of the present tense and rapid cutting from one area of Paris to another (see e.g. v. 5), would have been of considerable interest to George Eliot, whose 'particular web' in *Middlemarch* is as complex as Carlyle's history, if smaller than what he called the 'magic web' of 'Universal History' ('On History Again', 1833). Carlyle's use of the present tense emphasizes that in a moment of political crisis individuals and groups of forces are sharply confronted with the question 'What should we do?', and that only the future historian can begin to discern the overall pattern of motives and of events. George Eliot also brings her characters to moments of crisis, as we have seen in the cases of Dorothea and Casaubon, in order to show how their actions reveal their moral priorities in relation to other characters. As the lives of her characters intersect, her pattern also emerges.

Bulstrode's past walks jauntily into his apparently secure present in the unwelcome shape of Raffles (53), who initiates a crisis in his life which is to be a central theme in subsequent chapters. The arrival of Raffles follows a series of other crises. Dorothea's world is thrown into a state of convulsive change when she hears about the codicil in Chapter 50; Brooke delivers his speech in Chapter 51; and Farebrother learns that he is to have the Lowick living, and virtually gives up hope of Mary Garth's hand when he visits her on behalf of Fred Vincy, in Chapter 52. In each case a present reality, hard and unaccommodating, displaces the comforts of self-delusion or ignorance. Whereas Dorothea's repulsion from Casaubon, however, like her earlier decision not to carry on his work after his death, works strongly upon her because he is no longer physically present as an object of pity, Bulstrode is confronted, 'as if by some hideous magic', with 'this loud red figure' which has 'risen before him in unmanageable solidity – an incorporate past'. In the denouement of the Bulstrode plot, George Eliot shows both Bulstrode and Lydgate in a state of crisis at a public meeting in the Town Hall on the 'sanitary question' of a burial-ground which is itself critical, having risen into 'pressing importance by the occurrence of a cholera case in the town' (71). Mr Hawley's demand that before discussion begins Bulstrode should make a statement about the rumours surrounding the death of Raffles throws the banker into 'a crisis of feeling almost too violent for his delicate frame to support'. When Bulstrode is advised to leave the room after an exchange of speeches, it is Lydgate's turn to suffer all eyes being turned upon him in a crisis of feeling:

> Bulstrode . . . grasped the corner of the chair so totteringly
> that Lydgate felt sure there was not strength enough in him to
> walk away without support. What could he do? He could not
> see a man sink close to him for want of help. He rose and
> gave his arm to Bulstrode, and in that way led him out of the
> room; yet this act, which might have been one of gentle duty
> and pure compassion, was at this moment unspeakably bitter
> to him. It seemed as if he were putting his sign-manual to
> that association of himself with Bulstrode, of which he now
> saw the full meaning as it must have presented itself to other
> minds. He now felt the conviction that this man who was
> leaning tremblingly on his arm, had given him the thousand
> pounds as a bribe, and that somehow the treatment of Raffles
> had been tampered with from an evil motive.

As Bulstrode's history comes before the public gaze, Lydgate for the first time understands the true history of his own relationship with him. Yet he cannot 'see a man sink *close to him* for want of help', and thus exposes himself to the same Middlemarch stare that Bulstrode endures.

Lydgate's action and feelings at the public meeting illustrate George Eliot's subtlety of touch in exploring a moral dilemma. Her use of physical gestures and movements in her characters at moments of crisis is masterly. Contrast Lydgate's movements towards Bulstrode, for example, with Rosamond's selfish detachment from himself, expressed in physical distance, when he tells her of his financial crisis (58). Lydgate's problem at the meeting is simply put: 'What could he do?' When Dorothea revisits Rosamond, the day after she finds Ladislaw there, Lydgate goes upstairs to find his wife 'languidly wondering what she should do next, her habitual industry in small things . . . prompting her to begin some kind of occupation' (81). Dorothea's heartfelt question to her – 'How can we live and think that any one has trouble . . . and we could help them, and never try?' – makes Rosamond burst into tears. Dorothea tries to master her own emotions by thinking that this might be a 'turning-point in three lives', and that there may be time to rescue 'the fragile creature who was crying *close to her*' (my emphasis) from the misery of 'false incompatible bonds'. This is a 'newer crisis' in Rosamond's experience than even Dorothea can imagine, for her 'dream-world' has been shattered. The two women clasp each other as if in a shipwreck, and Rosamond's 'confession' concerning Will Ladislaw begins. The histories of three lives come together in a shared moment of crisis. Lydgate accepts his 'narrowed lot' with 'sad resignation' (81), and is to die at fifty, a society doctor and an authority on gout (Finale). Many who know Dorothea after her marriage to Ladislaw think it a pity that 'so substantive and rare a creature should have been absorbed into the life of another, and be only known in a certain circle as a wife and mother'.

George Eliot makes a strong feminist point at the end of her novel, implicating her reader, as Dickens does at the end of *Hard Times*, though more covertly: 'But we insignificant people with our daily words and acts are preparing the lives of many Dorotheas, some of which may present a far sadder sacrifice than that of the Dorothea whose story we know.' The last sentence of the novel, however, holds this point in tension with George Eliot's acknowledgement of the moral duty involved in the sacrifice within marriage which is familiar to both Dorothea and Lydgate: 'For the growing good of the world is partly dependent on unhistoric acts; and that things are not so ill with you and me as they might have been, is half owing to the number who lived faithfully a hidden life, and rest in unvisited tombs.'

James Picciotto claimed, in a review of 1876, that George Eliot had passed from the 'realism' of *Middlemarch* to the 'idealism' of *Daniel Deronda*. In the same year R. E. Francillon wrote of *Daniel Deronda* as 'essentially, both in conception and in form, a Romance', and 'absolutely good'.[50] Both critics wrote in the knowledge that many admirers of *Middlemarch* were disappointed in the middle and later books of *Daniel Deronda*. Like claims that *Romola* is overloaded with the minutiae of historical reconstruction, however, claims that *Daniel Deronda* actually contains two narratives that never meet – a good novel on Gwendolen Harleth and an earnest essay on the Jews, focused upon the idealized Deronda's discovery of his ancestry – have perhaps been exaggerated because we have *Middlemarch* always before us. *Daniel Deronda* is in several respects George Eliot's *summa*. It is a novel whose massive simplicity contrasts with the complexity of her study of English provincial life, but which distils many of her profoundest themes and ideas.

Grandcourt, drawling, languid, and indifferent, a heavy smoker of cigars, is an English egoist, the essence or ideal of the more dangerous features of earlier seducers, such as George Eliot's own Stephen Guest and Arthur Donnithorne, or Dickens's Steerforth and Harthouse. Gwendolen, the novel's central and far more interesting egoist, seems to include Hetty Sorrel and Rosamond Vincy. (The couple also look forward to Isabel Archer and Gilbert Osborn in Henry James's *Portrait of a Lady* (1881), as has often been pointed out.) Grandcourt and Gwendolen belong to the world of the 1870s, of Trollope's *The Way We Live Now*, whereas Deronda, who from the first scene in the casino closely observes Gwendolen, looks back, beyond his English forebears, to his ancient Jewish roots. As in *Middlemarch*, however, George Eliot's interest as a moralist is in the problem of living in the here and now, where the histories of her three principal characters intersect.

Whereas Rosamond and Dorothea are brought together briefly at the end of *Middlemarch*, as if in a shipwreck, and Lydgate and Dorothea open their hearts to one another only once, Gwendolen and Deronda are shown together in a series of private confessional interviews after the first confession (36) I quoted earlier (see p. 122 above). Before Grandcourt's drowning she pleads for guidance (48), and afterwards confesses that murder was in her heart, telling Deronda that he must always be near her (57). Later, Deronda speaks to Gwendolen of her duty to her mother, adding, after Carlyle: 'Other duties will spring from it.... What makes life dreary is the want of motive' (65). Deronda's own sense of duty and moral choice represents George Eliot's ideal, expressed in the critical last interview between them, when he tells her he is a Jew and speaks of restoring a 'political existence' to his people, 'making them a nation again' (69). The world suddenly seems to be getting larger round Gwendolen (as it does to Rosamond when she senses the largeness of Dorothea's soul), and she feels 'more solitary and helpless in the midst':

> That was the sort of crisis which was at this moment
> beginning in Gwendolen's small life: she was for the first time
> feeling the pressure of a vast mysterious movement, for the
> first time being dislodged from her supremacy in her own
> world. . . . All the troubles of her wifehood and widowhood
> had still left her with the implicit impression which had
> accompanied her from childhood, that whatever surrounded
> her was somehow specially for her. . . .

Deronda's happiness in his impending marriage to Mirah makes him aware that Gwendolen is the 'victim of his happiness', and they part. This exquisitely painful scene is followed by the 'Fruit and Seed' of the novel's final chapter, in which Daniel and Mirah marry and prepare to leave for Palestine, and Mirah's brother, Ezra dies in their arms. The ending of *Daniel Deronda* is of a higher order than that of any other Victorian death-bed scene, for it gathers into itself as a final consummation not only the joys and sufferings of these three characters, but also of their race. In a century in which the major prose moralists included a historian and an art historian, in Carlyle and Ruskin, George Eliot's career as the greatest moralist among Victorian novelists ended as it had begun, in the study of her characters' unhistoric acts in the incarnate history of the here and now.

Those high notes and condensings:
Meredith

George Meredith often commented upon his reputation as a difficult writer and, when justifying what he called the 'toughness' of his work, also reminded critics that his treatment of certain kinds of material in his novels was actually simple and direct. For example, when George Pierce Baker, then a student at Harvard, sent him a copy of an article on his work, published in the *Harvard Monthly* in 1887, Meredith replied:

> Concerning style, thought is tough, and dealing with
> thought produces toughness. Or when strong emotion is in tide
> against the active mind, there is perforce confusion. Have you
> found that scenes of simple emotion or plain narrative were
> hard to view? When their author revised for the new edition
> [the Collected Edition, 12 vols, 1885–95], his critical judgment
> approved these passages. . . .
>   In the Comedies, and here and there where a concentrated
> presentment is in design, you will find a 'pitch' considerably
> above our common human; and purposely, for only in such a
> manner could so much be shown. Those high notes and
> condensings are abandoned when the strong human call is
> heard – I beg you to understand merely that such was my
> intention.[51]

By the time he wrote this letter Meredith had forty years of novel-writing behind him, and almost as long as chief reader for Chapman and Hall. Approaching sixty years of age, he now evaluated his own work largely in terms of the extent to which it paved the way 'for the firmer footing of those who succeed us', as he put it earlier in the letter to Baker. For the moment our concern is with Meredith the working novelist of the 1860s and 1870s, and with the nature and significance of those high notes and condensings.

Meredith published his first works of fiction, the fantasies entitled *The Shaving of Shagpat* (1856) and *Farina* (1857), when George Eliot was writing her *Scenes of Clerical Life*. Nine years her junior, he lived for twenty-nine years after her death, his last completed novel, *The Amazing Marriage*, appearing in 1895, the year of Hardy's last novel, *Jude the Obscure*. Whereas the devoted Alexander Main's collection of George Eliot's *Wise, Witty, and Tender Sayings* (1871) presented solid evidence that her fiction was indeed 'the vehicle of the grandest and most uncompromising moral truth', Meredith's collections of aphorisms, such as Sir Austin Feverel's 'The Pilgrim's Scrip' and 'The Book of Egoism', are placed in his novels with characteristic self-consciousness, in order to serve his artistic purposes as an ironist.

Some of the differences between these novelists' aims and methods can be gauged by contrasting George Eliot's role of authorial narrator in her novels with that of Meredith, as described by Gillian Beer: 'Meredith, whose central artistic method is equivocation, . . . seems uneasy about the overt presence of the author within his work . . . and often takes up a defensive stance instead of engaging the reader's sympathy.'[52] Although Judith Wilt legitimately applies Virginia Woolf's description of *Middlemarch* as 'one of the few English novels written for grown-up people' to the work of Meredith, the demands he makes upon his educated and sophisticated 'Civilized Reader' are in most respects far greater than George Eliot's.[53] Meredith was the first major Victorian novelist to be consistently attacked for his difficulty, obscurity, and , in some cases, indecency. More radically than George Eliot's novels, the last of which were probably struggled through by devotees of her 'easier' earlier work, Meredith's mark the divide between the comparative accessibility of early Victorian and mid-century fiction and the late Victorian phase from which Modernism developed.

The last major Victorian to be profoundly influenced by Carlyle, for example, Meredith responded to his work with typical ambivalence. The portrayal of Dr Shrapnel in *Beauchamp's Career* (1874–75) indicates the limits of his admiration for the sage who recognized his talent and told him that he should write history.[54] The Prelude to *The Egoist* (1879), written in clotted Carlylese, introduces a novel in which the stripping of a dandiacal unworking aristocrat to his shirt has little political resonance. Although Meredith, like Carlyle, uses a pipe-smoking German professor as a sharp critic of the British in *The Adventures of Harry Richmond* (1870–71), this is only one aspect of a larger European dimension to his whole corpus. Again, Meredith looks forward to the Modernists, and a literary world centred in Paris and Berlin, as well as in London. His novels of father and son, including *The Ordeal of Richard Feverel: A History of a Father and Son* (1859) and *Harry Richmond*, are closer in spirit to Samuel Butler's *The Way of all Flesh*, written in the 1870s and 1880s, and Edmund Gosse's *Father and Son* (1907), than to the novels of Dickens and Thackeray (in which the hero, incidentally, is often fatherless). Similarly, Meredith's radical treatment of women in *The Egoist* and *Diana of the Crossways* (1885) began where Thackeray's ended, and earned him the respect of the emancipated 'New Woman' of the 1880s.[55]

Always alive to the paradoxes and ambiguities of human existence, Meredith commented in his one major piece of critical writing, the lecture *On the Idea of Comedy* (1877), that 'life, we know too well, is not a Comedy, but something strangely mixed'. In his novels he explores such things as strangely mixed ancestries: Richmond Roy, half actor, half king, and his son, Harry, whose maternal grandfather, Squire Beltham, demonstrates his approval of some of his 'performances' by bawling 'Beltham all over!', in the hope of suppressing his Richmond side (*Harry Richmond*, 8). Unlike satire, which works from a comparatively fixed and engaged position on a subject, comedy, as defined by Meredith, is at once mobile and detached. Like his shyness as an authorial narrator, Meredith's experiments with vari-

ous and often strangely mixed subject-matter and forms reflect his awareness of the protean nature of experience and his unwillingness to tie down
both himself and his subject. Beginning his career with the two fantasies
and the experimental *Richard Feverel*, a 'failure' in its day, but since acclaimed as the first modern novel, written by the first highbrow novelist,[56]
Meredith went on to write, among other works, a *bildungsroman*, *Evan
Harrington* (1860) which includes epistolary passages verging upon stream-
of-consciousness narrative; a novel written in the first person, *Harry Richmond*; a political novel, *Beauchamp's Career*; and prose fiction which often
reads like drama, in *The Egoist* and *The Tragic Comedians* (1880). As we
have seen, he rejected the realist/idealist categories to which critics such as
David Masson subscribed: 'Between realism and idealism, there is no natural conflict. This completes that' (*Letters*, I, 160).

Meredith's comment that 'humorists are difficult; it is a piece of their
humour to puzzle our wits', slipped into a parenthesis in the Prelude to *The
Egoist*, is the beginning of one of many long trails in the history of the novel
which lead to Joyce's famous prediction that *Ulysses* (1922) would keep the
professors busy for centuries, arguing over what he meant. The difficulty
of Meredith as a humorist is, as he himself commented, partly a matter of
his style. I have compared the Brontës' novels to poetic drama, described
Dickens as a prose-poet, and discussed George Eliot's sense of 'poetry in
common things'. Meredith, who published more than ten volumes of
verse, considered himself to be as much a poet as a novelist, and often
blurred the conventional boundaries between prose fiction and poetic
forms. *Modern Love* (1862), his sequence of poems on the breakdown of
a marriage, based on his own, invades territory more obviously suited to
the novel form. As in the letters of Gerard Manley Hopkins, many passages
in Meredith's novels which celebrate what he called the 'joy of earth' are
prose-poems, 'readings of earth'. Reminiscent of Keats and Hopkins in his
intensity, Meredith often subordinates the demands of plot and authorial
commentary to the portrayal of character and scene as a 'reading of life',
and, through allusion or synecdoche, a favourite figure, achieves 'condensings' which puzzle the wits and exercise the imagination. Suggestive,
impressionistic, and elliptical in style, he creates characters which Oscar
Wilde described as 'interpretative and symbolic'.[57] Comparable to Keats in
his intensity and his paganism, he is closer to Byron in his mannerism.
Even in one of his most straightforward pieces of narrative, the lively description of the cricket match in *Evan Harrington*, the usual playful personi-
fications and allusions break through:

> Heat and lustre were now poured from the sky, on whose
> soft blue a fleet of clouds sailed heavily. Nick Frim was very
> wonderful, no doubt. He deserved that the Gods should
> recline on those gold-edged cushions above, and lean over to
> observe him. . . .
> . . . Into what a pit had she suddenly plunged! You ask
> why she did not drive away as fast as the horses would carry

> her, and fly the veiled head of Demogorgon obscuring valley
> and hill and the shining firmament, and threatening to glare
> destruction on her? You do not know an intriguer. (13)

Meredith's own form of baroque High Victorianism is far removed from Dickens's style in the description of the match between Muggleton and Dingley Dell in *Pickwick Papers*.

The comparison between Meredith and the second-generation English Romantic poets can be taken a little further by considering a passage in a letter of 1861, in which he writes of his beloved Alpine peaks as part of the unity of nature and not 'a rebuke to us below' (*Letters*, I, 111). The 'error of all religion', he fancies, has been 'to raise a spiritual system in antagonism to Nature'. Meredith's personal encounter with the Alps is not only a cerebral or spiritual meditation on their remote purity, but also springs from his need to walk off the stresses of his personal and professional life. (Dickens was another compulsive walker, but mainly in London and at night.) Vernon Whitford's discussion with Clara Middleton on mountaineering in *The Egoist* (12), a novel which ends with those characters meeting again in the Alps, is reminiscent of Harry Richmond's Meredithian advice to the reader:

> Carry your fever to the Alps, you of minds diseased: not to
> sit down in sight of them ruminating, for bodily ease and
> comfort will trick the soul and set you measuring our lean
> humanity against yonder sublime and infinite; but mount, rack
> the limbs, wrestle it out among the peaks; taste danger, sweat,
> earn rest: learn to discover ungrudgingly that haggard fatigue
> is the fair vision you have run to earth, and that rest is your
> uttermost reward. Would you know what it is to hope again,
> and have all your hopes at hand? – hang upon the crags at a
> gradient that makes your next step a debate between the thing
> you are and the thing you may become.
>
> (*Harry Richmond*, 53)

Climbing, then, is also an encounter with danger, in which the accretions of so-called civilized life in the valleys fall away: 'How the old lax life closes in about you there! You are the man of your faculties, nothing more.' Meredith's interest in stripping his characters down to their faculties is everywhere evident in his use of metaphor, and in his handling of the big scenes in his novels.[58] He stated approvingly that Molière 'strips Folly to the skin' (*On Comedy*), and in his own work drew upon Carlyle's philosophy of clothes from *Sartor Resartus* (the tailor patched). Evan Harrington is the son of a tailor, like Meredith himself. When his father, the great Mel, dies leaving heavy debts, Evan is caught between the promptings of duty (to become a tailor and clear the family debts) and love (of an heiress named Rose). In the chapter entitled 'My Gentleman on the Road', Meredith, as author-narrator, addresses the reader:

> Are you impatient with this young man? He has little
> character for the moment. Most youths are like Pope's
> women; they have no character at all. And indeed a character
> that does not wait for circumstances to shape it, is of small
> worth in the race that must be run. To be set too early, is to
> take the work out of the hands of the Sculptor who fashions
> men.
>   (*Evan Harrington*, 6).

Working in a tradition which runs from Fielding through Scott and Jane
Austen, Victorian novelists often consciously or unconsciously play God to
their characters, whose lives are ruled by the special providence of their
creators (see p. 11 above). Meredith's explanation for Evan's lack of character is complicated by an oblique hint that of course he is the Sculptor who
fashions Evan. Circumstances immediately begin to shape Evan when he
suffers humiliation at the hands of a postilion whom he cannot pay, and
is finally reduced to walking: 'Money is the clothing of a gentleman: he
may wear it well or ill. . . . very few, I imagine, will bear inspection, who
are absolutely stripped of it.' When Evan's sister, the Countess de Saldar,
returns to the old family home ten days after the funeral, she wears her
Portuguese veil and mantilla in order to hide her identity from the towns-
people and to keep up her sense of superiority (9). She is therefore mortified
to find that Evan has shaved off his moustache and, without this 'disguise',
looks disturbingly like 'the very commonest tradesman'. Evan replies that
he has simply parted with the moustache: 'No more disguises for me!'
Rose, his future wife, also refuses to 'put on a mask' (27), and inspires Evan
to confront her mother, Lady Jocelyn, later in the novel: 'Exalted by Love,
he could dread to abase himself and strip off his glittering garments; low-
ered by the world, he fell back upon his innate worth' (34). Like the
climber who hangs upon the crags, Evan finds and reveals his essential self
at a moment of crisis.

As Evan braces himself for the interview, Meredith again lectures the
reader on the subject of the young:

> Religion, the lack of which in him the Countess deplored,
> would have guided him and silenced the internal strife. But do
> not despise a virtue purely Pagan. The young who can act
> readily up to the Christian light are happier, doubtless: but
> they are led, they are passive: I think they do not make such
> capital Christians subsequently. They are never in such
> danger, we know; but some in the flock are more than sheep.
> The heathen ideal it is not so very easy to attain, and those
> who mount from it to the Christian have, in my humble
> thought, a firmer footing.
>   So Evan fought his hard fight from the top of the stairs to
> the bottom. A Pagan, which means our poor unsupported
> flesh, is never certain of his victory. (34)

Meredith's moral theme, apologetically presented here, links two of his most common associations with Paganism: youth, and our poor unsupported flesh. Paganism, like Classicism, offered Meredith the same freedoms of reference previously enjoyed by Keats. Like his treatment of other familiar nineteenth-century themes, such as science, social progress, and the role of women, Meredith's lively and open-minded treatment of religion can be expressed only in metaphor and personification which subvert the received ideas of a male-dominated, bourgeois, Christian culture. Classical allusion, for example, references to the Fates and imps, descriptions of woods and pagan temples, provide him with a vocabulary devoid of specifically Christian, and therefore over-familiar moral overtones. Ironically, then, in the very process of stripping humankind to its barest essentials, Meredith writes with an obliqueness and opacity of reference and style which many of his first readers registered only as 'difficulty'. As he himself explained in the letter to Baker, 'only in such a manner could so much be shown'.

We saw earlier that Charlotte Brontë admired Thackeray as a 'dauntless' and 'daring' speaker of truth (see p. 56 above). The metaphors she applies to her own intentions in *Jane Eyre* and, implicitly, to Thackeray's in *Vanity Fair*, are associated with the exposure of the truth by stripping away disguises: 'To pluck the mask from the face of the Pharisee', 'to scrutinize and expose – to rase the gilding, and show base metal under it', and so on. Thackeray himself, who always strove to portray the world as it is, used a similar metaphor in his famous statement on the effects of censorship at mid-century, in the preface to *Pendennis*, dated 1850:

> Since the author of Tom Jones was buried, no writer of fiction
> among us has been permitted to depict to his utmost power a
> MAN. We must drape him, and give him a certain conventional
> simper. Society will not tolerate the Natural in our Art. Many
> ladies have remonstrated and subscribers left me, because in the
> course of the story, I described a young man resisting and affected
> by temptation. My object was to say, that he had the passions to
> feel, and the manliness and generosity to overcome them.

In Meredith's first full-length novel, *The Ordeal of Richard Feverel*, written nine years after Thackeray's preface, a young man is portrayed with passions to feel, and affected by temptation. Meredith presses beyond the pale of Grundyism, however, to show the hero failing to overcome temptation. Whereas the more cynical Thackeray shows manliness and generosity finally triumphant, Meredith's natural optimism is tempered by the painful recognition that human nature, like life itself, is something strangely mixed. Having first discussed this theme in *Richard Feverel* in more detail, I will briefly examine Meredith's masterpiece, *The Egoist*.

Two years before the publication of *The Ordeal of Richard Feverel*, Meredith's first wife became pregnant by the painter Henry Wallis, and the unhappy couple separated. The obvious autobiographical parallels between Meredith's own painful experience and that of Sir Austin Feverel, whose wife has run off with a poet, are complicated by the fact that the relationship between Sir Austin and his son Richard reflect the mixed emotions of guilt and joy which characterized Meredith's own relationship with his son Arthur. Similarly, to say that the novel begins as a comedy and ends as a tragedy is to over-simplify, for, like realism and idealism, 'this completes that' in ironic play between the comic and the tragic in the novel. The dialectic between the influences of nature and of Sir Austin's mechanical, pseudo-scientific System of Education on his son, though often worked out in counterpoint between successive groups of chapters in the novel, are also interpenetrating or overlapping in their effects upon both father and son.

Sir Austin's ambition as Richard's father is similar to that of the traditional omniscient authorial narrator of a novel: to order the providential scheme in which the child he has created will develop, from the cradle to the grave. Adopting the role of a God the Father figure, he allows his creation free will, observes him carefully and caringly (Sir Austin is always on the watch, day and night), and believes that he has foreseen all. Sir Austin's response to the first solid evidence that his System is working, when Richard goes to Farmer Blaize to confess that he set fire to the rick, is characteristic:

> The wind that bowed the old elms, and shivered the dead
> leaves in the air, had a voice and a meaning for the baronet
> during that half-hour's lonely pacing up and down under the
> darkness, awaiting his boy's return. The solemn gladness of
> his heart gave nature a tongue. Through the desolation flying
> overhead – the wailing of the Mother of Plenty across the
> bare-swept land – he caught intelligible signs of the beneficent
> order of the universe, from a heart newly confirmed in its
> grasp of the principle of human goodness, as manifested in the
> dear child who had just left him. . . .
>   In the dark, the dead leaves beating on his face, he had a
> word for his note-book: 'There is for the mind but one grasp
> of happiness: from that uppermost pinnacle of wisdom,
> whence we see that this world is well designed.'
>   (10, 'The Preliminary Ordeal')

From Sir Austin's pinnacle, his son's action is interpreted as the earnest of a fair springtime and, eventually, a good harvest, giving meaning and purpose to the blighted landscape of his own lonely existence. From the perspective of hindsight which subsequent events provide, however, such a providential view, condensed in the aphorism, is profoundly ironic, for the sibylline leaves are in fact prophetic of eventual decay and destruction.

In later chapters seasonal imagery registers both the natural stages of the young hero's life and his father's preconceived idea of his development. At Raynham it is part of Sir Austin's 'principle of education' that Richard should be 'thoroughly joyous and happy': 'The System flourished. Tall, strong, bloomingly healthy, he took the lead of his companions on land and water' (12, 'The Blossoming Season'). Meredith is as sensitive in his portrayal of the first stirrings of sexual feeling in Richard as he is in his treatment of boyhood – always one of his strongest subjects: 'The passions then are gambolling cubs; not the ravaging gluttons they grow to. They have their teeth and their talons, but they neither tear nor bite. They are in counsel and fellowship with the quickened heart and brain. The whole sweet system moves to music' (12). The dark hints of later developments in this passage are held in reserve as nature's sweet system, unlike Sir Austin's mechanical one, plays some of its grandest chords in Richard when he falls in love at first sight with Farmer Blaize's niece, Lucy Desborough. The chapter entitled 'Ferdinand and Miranda' is one of the most enchanting, in every sense, in English fiction. Only Meredith could have written the episode in which the besotted Richard leaps into the water to save her book, and then shares a hearty laugh with her: 'Better than sentiment, laughter opens the breast to love. . . . These two laughed, and the souls of each cried out to other, "It is I, It is I"' (15). Lucy, however, a Roman Catholic of lower rank than the Feverels, threatens to undermine the System. Having in the following chapter entered London 'with a sad mind', aware that he has 'divorced the world to wed a System' (16), Sir Austin consults two old friends, who recommend for Richard what his father calls the 'Wild Oats theory', immediately rejected on the evidence of their having an imbecile son and consumptive daughters (18). Meredith's change of setting from the magical island, or enchanted Eden, of Raynham, to the 'world', where, it is hinted, the sower of wild oats harvests venereal diseases, prepares for his subsequent exploration of the 'gluttony' of adult sexuality. But for the moment we are taken straight back to the idyll of Ferdinand and Miranda, and their first kiss, in the subsequent chapter:

> Away with Systems! Away with a corrupt World! Let us breathe the air of the Enchanted Island.
> Golden lie the meadows: golden run the streams; red gold is on the pine-stems. The sun is coming down to earth, and walks the fields and the waters. (19)

Meredith accommodates the general and the universal in the novel, a form uniquely, and often exclusively concerned with the particular, by means of his 'poetry'. In the passage quoted above, he captures both the immediacy of the lovers' enchantment and the universality of that experience through his use of the definite article and the present tense. (The definite article is also used to suggest the typicality of the novel's events in several of Meredith's chapter titles, such as 'The Bitter Cup', 'Of the Spring Primrose and the Autumnal', and 'The Last Scene'.) Richard Feverel is a symbolic and representative character, whose experiences, although unique in their detail, are broadly characteristic of boyhood, adolescence, and man-

hood at each stage of his growth. Similarly, Meredith's treatment of such
concepts as free will and foreknowledge in relation to Sir Austin's System
is a measure of the novel's breadth of reference, when compared, for example, to Dickens's Mr Murdstone and his associations with Old Testament law, written upon stone tablets. Whereas Murdstone, Dombey, and
Gradgrind are different types of inadequate father, Sir Austin, in his very
misguidedness, as well as in his love for his son, is a study of father*hood*
in its broadest aspects.

Following a series of alarums and excursions, the young couple are secretly married. Richard's use of a ring borrowed from Mrs Berry, herself
formerly deserted by her husband, is treated so playfully that the parodic
nature of this outward and visible sign of future separation, of a kind
favoured by other Victorian novelists, is revealed. Two of Meredith's most
familiar metaphors, however – the devil and the mask – are applied un-
ironically to Sir Austin's response to the marriage: 'Sir Austin did not battle
with the tempter. He took him into his bosom at once. . . . He must shut
his heart and mask his face; that was all' (33, 'Nursing the Devil'). In mask-
ing himself he causes Richard's final ordeal, for his calculated separation
of the young husband and wife ultimately destroys them.

Richard's infatuation with the aptly named Mrs Mount, 'a glorious
dashing woman' (36), takes place in Richmond and London, while his wife
waits patiently in the Isle of Wight, herself vulnerable to the attentions of
Lord Mountfalcon, Mrs Mount's husband. Whereas Thackeray and Trollope only hint at the existence of the Victorian *demi-monde* in which the lives
of young gentlemen were often ruined, physically and financially, Meredith
follows Richard into the very arms of his *femme fatale*. When Richard first
fell in love with Lucy, Meredith commented: 'His heart will build a temple
here; and the skylark will be its high-priest' (15). Now the analogy of pagan
worship is applied to a woman who looks like 'a superior priestess of Pa-
phos', and who attracts references to Diana and the 'tutorship of Master
Endymion'. The magic of the island of his innocent first love is now fatally
metamorphosed into the spell of 'An Enchantress' (38). Whereas Lucy hid
demurely behind a broad-brimmed hat, Mrs Mount dresses in the male
attire of the dandy, takes Richard on the town, and adopts the slang of the
day. Herself seduced at sixteen, and now only twenty-one, a 'lurid splendour' glances about her 'like lights from the pit', as she seduces Richard.
The language of the melodrama, often associated with the 'gentleman' seducer whose role she now assumes, complements the tawdriness of the
episode, while also hinting strongly that judgement will follow. Whereas
previously in his life a hearty laugh had opened his soul to Lucy, Richard
can now manage only a melancholy laugh at Mrs Mount and her lap-dog.
The final act of seduction breaks new ground in Victorian fiction in its
explicitness and, perhaps more important, its treatment of sex without
love:

> Not a word of love between them!
> Was ever hero in this fashion won?   (38)

Under pressure from complaining customers, Mudie withdrew his order for copies of *Richard Feverel*. Thackeray had confessed in his preface to *Pendennis* that ladies remonstrated and subscribers left him because he showed a young man resisting and affected by temptation. Meredith's hell of sexual union without love, a theme later developed in *Modern Love*, is far more disturbing than anything Thackeray revealed to the ladies about Pen. *Richard Feverel* is a novel of extremes, and Lucy's death, the result of a brain fever which comes on when she wrongly believes that Richard has been killed in a duel with Lord Mountfalcon, leaves the hero in the depths of bereavement, described by Lady Blandish as lying silently on his bed, 'striving to image her on his brain' (45). When 'Nature Speaks' to Richard in the thunderstorm in Germany (42), in the most impressive set piece in the novel, the encounter with the leveret seems to suggest the hope of reconciliation between Richard and Lucy, and lasting happiness with their child. That Meredith insisted upon a tragic ending, as George Eliot was to in *The Mill on the Floss* in the following year, is one of many indications that he intended his novel to be much more than entertainment for the 'porkers' – the general reading public. I said earlier that Meredith looks forward to Joyce in one respect. In his treatment of nature and his interest in the psychology of a symbolic character, he looks forward to D. H. Lawrence.

Juliet Mitchell describes *Richard Feverel* as a 'medley of romantic interludes, prosaic detail, burlesque, melodrama, pathos, fantasy, realism', and, like other Meredith critics, considers it necessary to outline the plot for her readers.[59] In her view, however, the novel is 'not chaotic, but strangely inclusive'. As he cuts from location to location, and from form to form, in his exploration of different facets of human love, Meredith ranges the System against Nature, the Blossoming Season against the Wild Oats theory, and Ferdinand and Miranda against the Enchantress. In contrast, *The Egoist*, published twenty years after *Richard Feverel* and halfway through his long career, is a masterpiece of control, unity, and economy, in which those high notes and condensings are more often in evidence, but have not run to the extremes of obscurity of a late novel like *One of Our Conquerors* (1890–91). Indeed, they perfectly complement the novel's setting, structure, and style.

'Wise men', Meredith says in the Prelude to *The Egoist*, tell us how comedy 'condenses whole sections' of the Book of Egoism 'in a sentence, volumes in a character'. Like the country houses in the novels of Peacock, Meredith's father-in-law, Patterne Hall provides an enclosed arena for 'civilized' conversation, and Meredith emphasizes the condensed style of his characters: Mrs Mountstuart Jenkinson's famous sayings which 'stuck to you, as nothing laboured or literary could have adhered' (2); Dr Middleton's 'humour of sententiousness and doctorial stilts' (27); Vernon Whitford's epigrams (10); and Horace de Craye's aphorisms (18). Conversations within the confines of the House of Patterne are like exchanges of volleys. The action of *The Egoist*, a novel which adopts dramatic conventions in its chapter titles and even at times in its narrative form, is played out mainly in the dialogue. Meredith's high notes, on the other hand, could be described rather as the grace notes of the mannerist narrator, intended to delight and surprise. Take, for example, the description of Clara Middleton's hair, admired by Sir Willoughby Patterne:

> He . . . doted on her cheek, her ear, and the softly dusky
> nape of her neck where this way and that the little lighter-
> coloured irreclaimable curls running truant from the comb and
> the knot – curls, half-curls, root-curls, vine-ringlets, wedding-
> rings, fledgeling feathers, tufts of down, blown wisps – waved
> or fell, waved over or up or involutedly, or strayed, loose and
> downward, in the form of small silken paws, hardly any of
> them much thicker than a crayon shading, cunninger than
> long round locks of gold to trick the heart.   (9)

The subject of this passage, and the later references to the imps which haunt Sir Willoughby and the 'drawing-room sylphides' which guard and restrain Clara (43), are reminiscent of Pope's *Rape of the Lock*, itself a work which brilliantly exploits its self-imposed constraints of space and subject-matter.

The statuesque Sir Willoughby offers Clara an 'enclosed and fortified bower' of egoism, in the form of married life at Patterne Hall (6). The egoist's name, obviously a play upon the familiar willow pattern on china, and possibly upon its story of a lover's escape from imprisonment by her father,[60] also suggests his neurotic need for order: life within the house must be lived to his pattern. He is stone-like, desiring perfect stasis. Clara is reminiscent of Dorothea discovering Casaubon's true nature in *Middlemarch*, when she is chilled by the thought of a lifetime in 'those caverns of the complacent talking man' (7). Married to him, she would be 'tied not to a man of heart, but to an obelisk lettered all over with hieroglyphics, and everlastingly hearing him expound them, relishingly renewing his lectures on them' (10). In Meredith's variations upon a number of related metaphors and references – the house, the bower, imps, the willow pattern, the statue, stone – the constraints of life in Patterne Hall are experienced through the language. Other characters discover the brittleness and fragility of Sir Willoughby's position, as a man already jilted once before, and terrified of a recurrence, and Meredith introduces another object which turns metaphor in order to suggest this: the porcelain vase sent by Horace de Craye as a wedding present. Sir Willoughby takes the accidental smashing of the vase as an omen (17). Later in the novel Mrs Mountstuart can touch him on the quick simply by saying, 'Porcelain again!' (29).

Outside the Hall, the ordered if fragile life of the central character is threatened by Nature and the World. Clara expresses her frustration by shouting 'Marriage!' as she rides her horse into a ford (22). Sir Willoughby himself bursts out in a similar manner in a moment of melodrama: 'He had actually shouted on the rainy road the theatric call "Fooled!" one of the stage-cries which are cries of nature!' (29). For Sir Willoughby, London is the 'burial-place of the individual man' (4), and he is anxious lest Vernon Whitford should move there: 'One has the feeling of the house crumbling when a man is perpetually for shifting and cannot fix himself.' Sir Willoughby's words prove to be prophetic, although not in the way he might have imagined; for Vernon eventually marries Clara, leaving Sir Willoughby in the humiliating position of having to marry the faithful Laetitia Dale on her own terms. Whereas in *Richard Feverel* Meredith had gone beyond Thackeray in the portrayal of a young man's sexual misdemeanours and his rebellion against his father, in *The Egoist* he focuses upon a young woman's sexual liberation through rebellion against her egoistical father and her betrothed. Meredith's famous feminist statement in *The Egoist* – the 'capaciously strong in soul among women will ultimately detect an infinite grossness in the demands for purity infinite, spotless bloom' – is a gloss on Sir Willoughby's desire that Clara should be 'cloistral' and maidenly even in her response to his own 'gluttonous' advances among the laurels in the park (11). The spotless bloom metaphor prepares for her discovery of Vernon under the 'Double-Blossom Wild Cherry-Tree' later in the chapter. Vernon's awakening and stepping out after her, turning his back on what Dr Middleton earlier called the barren 'Vestal of the forest' (9), beautifully represents the joy of earth which Sir Willoughby's system denies. Whereas Sir Willoughby prefers to ride and thus show off his famous 'leg', Clara and Vernon (an alpinist) are walkers; and Clara's 'Flight in Wild Weather' (25) – an abortive dash to the railway station – is the only real action in a statuesque novel. Crucially, the heroine's attempted flight is aided by a boy, Crossjay Patterne, in whom nature is 'very strong', and who has to be 'plucked out of the earth, rank of the soil, like a root', for his lessons with Vernon (4). Hope for future generations lies in Crossjay, and in the union between Clara and Vernon.

Meredith's sympathetic treatment of Clara Middleton in his finest novel helps to explain his disgusted response to Mrs Henry Wood's *East Lynne*, the sensation novel he had rejected as reader for Chapman and Hall almost twenty years previously. Whereas a dense sensational plot was a suitable vehicle for Mrs Wood's lurid treatment of Lady Isabel, the adulteress, Meredith's novel subtly suggests how Clara could break a lesser but clearly defined Victorian taboo while remaining 'spotless'. In *Diana of the Crossways* he was to work out his ideas on the 'woman question' by examining a social system which produced a brilliant girl unequipped to understand the responsibilities – and especially that of discretion – of those who move in the highest political circles; and the theme of the female victim of male egoism recurs in the later and more obscure novels of the 1890s. The high notes and condensings of the early and middle years of Meredith's career as a novelist are aspects of a vigorous critique of the prolixity of his Victorian precursors. In his turn he himself was to become the Grand Old Man of English letters – the hero of a new generation of ambitious young novelists.

Notes

1. Robert Furneaux Jordan, *Victorian Architecture* (Harmondsworth, 1966), p. 137.

2. See Kenneth Graham, *English Criticism of the Novel, 1865–1900* (Oxford, 1965), p. 8.

3. See Walter Allen, *The English Novel: A Short Critical History* (1954; repr. Harmondsworth, 1958), pp. 218–19.

4. See *The Penny Dreadful; or, Strange, Horrid & Sensational Tales!*, edited by Peter Haining (London, 1975).

5. See T. S. Eliot, 'Wilkie Collins and Dickens' (1927), in his *Selected Essays*, third edition (London, 1951), p. 464.

6. *Wilkie Collins: The Critical Heritage*, edited by Norman Page (London and Boston, 1974), pp. 123–4.

7. See Sandra M. Gilbert and Susan Gubar, *The Madwoman in the Attic: The Woman Writer and the Nineteenth-Century Literary Imagination* (New Haven and London, 1979); Winifred Hughes, *The Maniac in the Cellar: Sensation Novels of the 1860s* (Princeton, NJ, 1980).

8. Elaine Showalter, *A Literature of their Own: British Women Novelists from Brontë to Lessing* (Princeton, NJ, 1977), p. 167.

9. Le Fanu himself disliked the term 'sensation novel', and Margaret Bowen's claim in her introduction to *Uncle Silas* (London, 1947, p. 11) that the novel is 'the first (or among the first) of the psychological thrillers' seems justified.

10. Anon, 'The Historical Novel', *Bentley's Miscellany*, 46 (1859), 42–51 (p. 44), quoted in Andrew Sanders, *The Victorian Historical Novel, 1840–1880* (London, 1979), p. 15.

11. See Sanders, p. 22.

12. Humphrey Carpenter disagrees with Isabel Quigly's statement that the 'school story was born with Thomas Hughes', in her *The Heirs of Tom Brown* (London, 1982). Carpenter cites Sarah Fielding, the Lambs, Harriet Martineau, William Adams, and Dorothy Kilner (whose young hero was also called Tom Brown) as precursors: *TLS*, 23 July 1982, p. 787.

13. C. N. Manlove, *Modern Fantasy: Five Studies* (Cambridge, 1975), p. 1.

14. Robert L. Patten, *Charles Dickens and his Publishers* (Oxford, 1978), p. 273. For further details on *All the Year Round* see Patten's Chapter 14, and on Dickens and Collins see Kenneth Robinson, *Wilkie Collins: A Biography* (1951; repr. London, 1974), Chapter 4 *et seq.*

15. *Letters of Charles Dickens to Wilkie Collins, 1851–70*, selected by Georgina Hogarth, edited by Laurence Hutton (London, 1892), pp. 105, 97.

16. See David Punter, *The Literature of Terror: A History of Gothic Fictions from 1765 to the Present Day* (London and New York, 1980).

17. Harry Stone, *Dickens and the Invisible World: Fairy Tales, Fantasy, and Novel-Making* (London, 1979), p. 291. For another treatment of violence in Dickens see John Carey, *The Violent Effigy: A Study of Dickens's Imagination* (London, 1973), Chapter 1.

18. Andrew Sanders argues that in Dickens's later work 'death becomes thematic and it is balanced by a parallel stress on rebirth', in '"Come Back And Be Alive": Living and Dying in *Our Mutual Friend*', *Dickensian*, 74 (1978), 131–43 (p. 134). For Dickens's sacramental references see *Our Mutual Friend*, e.g. II. 9, III. 9, IV. 4, IV. 9, IV. 11.

19. See Fred Kaplan, *Dickens and Mesmerism: The Hidden Springs of Fiction* (Princeton, 1975), pp. 153–6, 204–7, and Howard Duffield, 'John Jasper – Strangler', *American Bookman* (1930), 581–8.

20. See Charles Dickens, *The Public Readings*, edited by Philip Collins (Oxford, 1975), pp. 465–71 and plate II.

21. See P. D. Edwards, *Anthony Trollope, his Art and Scope* (1977; repr. Hassocks, Sussex, 1978), p. 1.

22. The second part of A. O. J. Cockshut's *Anthony Trollope: A Critical Study* (1955) is entitled 'Progress to Pessimism', but see J. R. Kincaid's caveat in his *The Novels of Anthony Trollope* (Oxford, 1977), p. 63, n. 68.

23. Raymond Williams argues that Jane Austen thinks of neighbours as people living not next door but 'a little less near by who in social *recognition* can be visited': *The English Novel: From Dickens to Lawrence* (1970; repr. Frogmore, 1974), p. 21.

24. Coleridge is the seminal thinker here. For discussion of his ideas on Church and State see Stephen Prickett, *Romanticism and Religion: The Tradition of Coleridge and Wordsworth in the Victorian Church* (Cambridge, 1976), p. 255, *et passim*.

25. Laurence Lerner summarizes the ideas of the German sociologist Tönnies in his discussion of Hardy in *Thomas Hardy's The Mayor of Casterbridge: Tragedy or Social History?*, Text and Context (London, 1975), pp. 89–90.

26. Henry James, 'Anthony Trollope' (1883), in *The Trollope Critics*, edited by N. John Hall (London, 1981), p. 19.

27. One of many similar examples of Trollope's semi-allegorical mode is his use of Lizzie Eustace's diamonds and the heavy metal box which she carries around as a burden (*The Eustace Diamonds*, 44, 49).

28. See Graham, *English Criticism of the Novel*, p. 25.

29. See, for example, Felicia Bonaparte, *The Triptych and the Cross: The Central Myths of George Eliot's Poetic Imagination* (Brighton, 1979).

30. Basil Willey, *Nineteenth-Century Studies: Coleridge to Matthew Arnold* (1949; repr. Harmondsworth, 1964), p. 217.

31. Willey, p. 248.

32. 'The Natural History of German Life', *Westminster Review*, 66 (1856), 51–79, repr. in *Essays of George Eliot*, edited by Thomas Pinney (New York and London, 1963), pp. 266–99 (p. 287).

33. Letter quoted in Neil Roberts, *George Eliot: Her Beliefs and Her Art*, Novelists and Their World (London, 1975), p. 167.

34. U. C. Knoepflmacher, *Religious Humanism and the Victorian Novel: George Eliot, Walter Pater, and Samuel Butler* (Princeton, NJ, 1965), p. 42.

35. K. M. Newton discusses the 'egotistic' and the 'organicist' sides of Romanticism, and argues that 'George Eliot has two main aims as a philosophical novelist: first, to attack the nihilistic and egotistic philosophies that could be derived from the set of ideas that she herself accepted, and, second, to support a humanist philosophy similar in many respects to the moral and social thought of the organicist Romantics without denying that set of ideas'. *George Eliot, Romantic Humanist: A Study of the Philosophical Structure of her Novels* (London, 1981), pp. 11–12.

36. *Essays of George Eliot*, pp. 270–1.

37. *George Eliot's Middlemarch Notebooks: A Transcription*, edited by John Clark Pratt and Victor A. Neufeldt (Berkeley, 1979), p. 133.

38. Wordsworth and Coleridge, *Lyrical Ballads*, edited by R. L. Brett and A. R. Jones (London and New York, 1963), pp. 244–5.

39. Compare Barbara Hardy, 'Mrs Gaskell and George Eliot', in *The Victorians*, edited by Arthur Pollard, Sphere History of Literature in the English Language, 6 (London, 1969), pp. 182–3.

40. See Roberts, *George Eliot*, pp. 66–7.

41. See *Dictionary of the Bible*, edited by James Hastings, second edition, revised by Frederick C. Grant and H. H. Rowley (Edinburgh, 1963), p. 548.

42. See Peter K. Garrett, *The Victorian Multiplot Novel: Studies in Dialogical Form* (New Haven and London, 1980).

43. On the writing of *Silas Marner* and *Romola* see Gordon Haight, *George Eliot: A Biography* (Oxford and New York, 1968), pp. 321–73.

44. Possibly in August 1861, when George Eliot 'conceived the plot . . . with new distinctness'. See Haight, *George Eliot*, p. 351.

45. The demythologizing of the miraculous in the plague chapter is characteristically Feuerbachian. Compare David R. Carroll, '*Silas Marner:* Reversing the Oracles of Religion', *Literary Monographs*, I, edited by Eric Rothstein and Thomas K. Dunseath (Madison, Milwaukee, and London, 1967), pp. 165–200.

46. 'There is hardly a superior or active mind of this generation that has not been modified by Carlyle's writings. . . . many of the men who have the least agreement with his opinions are those to whom the reading of *Sartor Resartus* was an epoch in the history of their minds.' *Thomas Carlyle: The Critical Heritage*, edited by Jules Paul Seigel, Critical Heritage series, edited by B. C. Southam (London, 1971), pp. 409–10.

47. Frank Kermode, '*Middlemarch* and Apocalypse', part of essay in *Continuities* (1968), reprinted in *George Eliot, Middlemarch: A Casebook*, edited by Patrick Swinden (London, 1972), pp. 131–43 (pp. 131, 136).

48. Michael Mason, '*Middlemarch* and History', *Nineteenth-Century Fiction*, 25 (1970–71), 417–31 (pp. 417, 421).

49. Haight, *George Eliot*, p. 430.

50. *George Eliot: The Critical Heritage*, edited by David Carroll, Critical Heritage series, edited by B. C. Southam (London, 1971), pp. 415, 383.

51. *The Letters of George Meredith*, edited by C. L. Cline, 3 vols (Oxford, 1970), II, 876–7.

52. Gillian Beer, *Meredith: A Change of Masks. A Study of the Novels* (London, 1970), p. 40.

53. Judith Wilt, *The Readable People of George Meredith* (Princeton and London, 1975), pp. 17–18.

54. See Beer [n. 51 above], pp. 77–8.

55. See Lionel Stevenson, *The Ordeal of George Meredith* (London, 1954), p. 261.

56. Juliet Mitchell, '*The Ordeal of Richard Feverel*: A Sentimental Education', in *Meredith Now: Some Critical Essays,* edited by Ian Fletcher (London, 1971), pp. 69–94 (p. 69).

57. In 'The Soul of Man Under Socialism', quoted in Graham, *English Criticism of the Novel*, p. 41.

58. *The Egoist* is the most obvious example: see John Goode, '*The Egoist*: Anatomy or Striptease?', in *Meredith Now*, pp. 205–30. Also see the famous statue episode in *Harry Richmond* (17), and the heroine's fear of being stripped by hunters in *Diana of the Crossways* (Beer, *Meredith*, p. 155).

59. Mitchell, in *Meredith Now*, p. 69.

60. For a discussion of the willow pattern motif see Michael Wheeler, *The Art of Allusion in Victorian Fiction* (London, 1979), Chapter 7.

Chapter 5
Late Victorian Fiction

Explorations: The new realists and the romance revival, Utopian and religious novels

Although each phase of every age can be said to be 'transitional' in some sense, the last fifteen-year phase of the period 1830–90 is, like the first, clearly transitional in its cultural, social, and political history. At each end of the Victorian period the new mixes uneasily with the old. The 1880s, the decade of Empire and the Queen's Diamond Jubilee, mark the zenith of Victorianism in terms of national identity at home and abroad. Yet in certain respects Britain in the 1880s is more recognizable to us, a hundred years on, than it would have been to people brought up in the 1830s. In the fiction, characters have the gas meter read and admire buildings lit by electric 'globes'. Male novelists were photographed wearing neckties, turn-down collars, and jackets not unlike those worn today. Fashionable ladies smoked cigarettes. Whereas in 1871 female clerks were unheard of, by 1891 the census returns show almost 18,000. (As Gail Cunningham observes, 'the Typewriter Girl had arrived.'[1]) Following the Bradlaugh-Besant case of 1877, when contraception became a matter of public debate, the practice of birth control became fairly widespread in middle-class families.[2]

Although the male franchise was further extended in the 1880s, perhaps the most profound change in the life of the British populace was the emergence of the first generation to be educated under Forster's Education Act of 1870. Journalism soon responded to the new mass readership, and in 1880 George Newnes broke new ground with his light penny paper, *Tit-Bits*. In 1887 Rider Haggard complained of the bad effects of over-production in the novel market, and mentioned the thousands educated at the Board schools as one reason for the 'mental area open to the operations of the English-speaking writer' growing larger day by day.[3] As Haggard points out, most of the huge number of novels published at the time were mere pulp fiction. Whereas Dickens had written great popular novels which were read by most literate people of his day, several quite separate reading publics were now identifiable.[4]

Meanwhile, although Mudie still reigned in the world of the circulating library, the days of the three-decker novel were numbered. Mudie and the publishers had two battles with writers on their hands. First, censorship was a live issue; for example, George Gissing attacked the circulating libraries in a letter to the *Pall Mall Gazette* on 'The New Censorship in Literature' (1884), and George Moore produced a pamphlet entitled *Literature at Nurse; or, Circulating Morals* (1885). Secondly, the exploitative system whereby most novelists paid to have their work published and received little return on their investment was one of several abuses which led to the foundation of the Society of Authors in 1884. The passions raised by the issue of payments can be gauged by the advice given to young novelists in that year by the Society's founder, Walter Besant: '*never*, NEVER, NEVER pay for publishing a novel.'[5] Not for another ten years, however, were novelists to be free of Mudie and the three-decker, and the transition completed from the most common form of Victorian novel publication to forms which would flourish in the early twentieth century. By the mid-1890s Kipling, Wells, and Conrad were launching their careers on shorter forms of fiction: the one-volume novel, the novella, and the short story.

One of Conrad's best novellas, originally published as 'The Heart of Darkness' in *Blackwood's* (1899) and reprinted as 'Heart of Darkness' (1902), is often cited as a seminal Modernist text. It can, however, also be read as a work which takes up the themes of the previous twenty years of fiction, and particularly three kinds of 'exploration' in which novelists had been either interested or themselves engaged. First, and most obviously, the revival of romance in the 1880s coincided with the so-called 'scramble for Africa' (following the exploration of the continent by, among others, Livingstone and Stanley) and the exploitation of its resources – in Conrad's story epitomized by the ivory trade in the Congo. Secondly, Marlow's observations in Brussels, and his earlier comment that the Thames estuary, now the gateway to the centre of a great Empire, had once been itself a place of darkness, a wilderness inhabited by savages, suggest that travellers need not journey to the Congo to find the heart of darkness. Behind these perceptions lie the ironies of imperialism, in Britain's case as much the product of a falling birth-rate, an economic depression, and the growth of the German and American economies in the 1870s, as of other political motives. To the east of the great London streets in which the spoils of Empire were paraded during the Jubilee celebrations of 1887, the masses of the urban poor posed a real threat to domestic peace and stability. William Booth, founder of the Salvation Army, ironically referred to Stanley's *In Darkest Africa* (1890) in the title of his own book, written with the assistance of W. T. Stead and published later the same year – *In Darkest England, and the Way Out*: 'What a satire it is upon our Christianity and our civilisation, that the existence of these colonies of heathens and savages in the heart of our capital should attract so little attention!'[6] Booth meant attention in the sense of something actually being done, particularly by the churches; during the ten years preceding his statement, the plight of the London poor had certainly received the renewed attention of novelists.

Adrian Poole links the themes of Empire and Darkest London when he comments on 'deep and complex changes in consciousness' in the last years of the nineteenth century:

Gissing and the other late Victorians share in a specific
historical consciousness, the key to which is the sense of an
unprecedented *intransigence* in the terms of the opposition
between the inner, personal and subjective, and the outer,
public and objective. In political, social, and economic
spheres, the move towards corporation reflected a general
sense of the massing of forces, the taking of sides in a world
of decreasing options and manoeuvrability. In the literary
world, both writers and publishers organised bodies to protect
their interests; nations became increasingly conscious of their
boundaries; writers such as Kipling thrived on their ability to
define 'us' and 'them'.[7]

The third kind of exploration in Conrad and his late Victorian precursors,
partly in response to this intransigence, is a turning inward, away from the
outer physical world and towards the human psyche and its powers. The
writings of Herbert Spencer and the American William James (brother of
Henry James), and the foundation of the Theosophical Society (1875) and
the Society for Psychical Research (1882), reflected and deepened the interest in psychology and parapsychology, mysticism, and the paranormal
in the period. Stevenson's Dr Jekyll carries out his experiments in a private
laboratory in London. Conan Doyle, himself a Scottish doctor, investigated
the spirit world with the pseudo-scientific rigour of his own Sherlock
Holmes poring over a tricky case.

During the 1880s writers and critics were drawn into a number of overlapping debates on the nature of the novelist's art (rather than craft) and
on the kinds of exploration in which he or she should be engaged. Meredith, James, and Howells, for example, were accused of over-complex
character analysis, at the expense of a plot.[8] I will discuss the larger debate
between the new realists and the writers of romance in relation to the controversies surrounding the main sub-genres of the period (as far as they can
still be defined thus, when narrow generic divisions were breaking down):
the 'slum school' novel, the romance, the Utopian novel, and the religious
novel.

In Gissing's *New Grub Street* (1891) one reviewer reminds the realist, Harold Biffen, author of 'Mr Bailey, Grocer', that 'a work of art must before
everything else afford amusement' (35). As we saw in Chapter 1, this idea
of the novel's primary function was widely accepted throughout the century, although in the 1860s and 1870s particularly, great emphasis was also
placed on the moral function of the novel. During the 1880s both ideas
were challenged by those who argued that the novel, which Gissing's reviewer significantly calls a 'work of art', should be judged by intellectual
and aesthetic criteria similar to those applied to other art forms.[9] Several
of the new generation of writers worked to the higher intellectual standards
for the novel set by George Eliot and George Meredith. (All the religious

novels discussed at the end of this section, for example, can also be described as 'novels of ideas'.) Henry James, in his famous essay on 'The Art of Fiction' (1884), chastised Trollope for 'a betrayal of a sacred office' in conceding to the reader that he was 'only "making believe"'. James further argued that 'artistic preoccupations' do not interfere with the aims of literature to be 'either instructive or amusing', and that while every good novelist must 'possess the sense of reality', reality has 'a myriad forms'.[10]

James's essay was written in response to Walter Besant's Royal Institution letter on *The Art of Fiction*, delivered earlier in 1884, in which Besant also made large claims for the novel, but without James's sophistication. Besant spoke for many of his Victorian precursors when he said:

> The modern novel converts abstract ideas into living models;
> it gives ideas, it strengthens faith, it preaches a higher
> morality than is seen in the actual world; it commands the
> emotions of pity, admiration, and terror; it creates and keeps
> alive the sense of sympathy; it is the universal teacher; it is the
> only book which the great mass of reading mankind ever do
> read; it is the only way in which people can learn what other
> men and women are like. . . .[11]

Besant's own fiction was much admired in its day, and his two slum school novels, *All Sorts and Conditions of Men: An Impossible Story* (1882) and *Children of Gideon* (1886) influenced public opinion much more profoundly than Gissing's novels of the 1880s on working-class life. Gissing, however, who will be discussed in more detail in a later section, thought little of Besant's work; and whereas Gissing's realistic novels have recently received much critical attention, Besant's philanthropic romances are now rarely read.

Besant's slum school fiction is a curious mixture of old and new. Angela Messenger, for example, the wealthy heroine in *All Sorts and Conditions*, is a more liberated and highly educated version of the Lady Bountifuls of early and mid-Victorian social-problem fiction, and particularly Disraeli's, in which he dreamt of uniting rich and poor. For Miss Messenger, 'delight' is the best social cement. Her conversion of Trinity Almshouse, where her 'work-girls' break off their dressmaking for healthy games of tennis, or, if wet, exercises in the gymnasium (11), is only a modest enterprise compared to the Palace of Delight which she opens at the end of the novel (47). (This later took solid form in the building of the People's Palace in Whitechapel, which Besant helped to organize.) Besant's tone is often not only patronizing but also facetious. The suicide leaping into the Thames was for Dickens and Thomas Hood the epitome of oppressed humanity driven to despair. When Daniel Fagg contemplates dropping into the water of the London Docks, Besant allows himself a little joke about the 'sluggish green water, the first drop of which kills almost as certainly as a glass of Bourbon whisky' (22).

Edith Sichel, in her review of Besant's slum school novels and of two by Gissing, describes the two writers as Optimistic and Pessimistic Philanthropists: 'Whereas Mr Besant paints in perpetual *couleur-de-rose*, Mr

Gissing revels in the blues. His descriptions, his thoughts, his characters, abounding as they do in power, are one and all monochromic without relief.'[12] Gissing, certainly, was always an artist, and he put aesthetic values above any specific moral purpose as the first criteria of the novelist. Because the eye of the artist modifies the 'reality' of the external world, he rejected Zola's scientific principles of naturalism, which attempted to neutralize the role of the novelist as observer and commentator. One of the new realists who refused to make allowances for the delicate sensibilities of Mrs Grundy, Gissing nevertheless also rejected Zola's excesses in the description of the sordid and disgusting. In this he was typically English. Rider Haggard wrote of Zola in his essay of 1887, 'About Fiction': 'Whatever there is brutal in humanity – and God knows there is plenty – whatever there is carnal and filthy, is here brought into prominence, and thrust before the reader's eyes.'[13] F. W. Farrar, author of *Eric*, wrote of Gissing's *The Nether World*: 'I have called the book realistic, but happily it is an English book, and the reader will find in it none of that leprous naturalism which disgusts every honourable reader in the works of Zola and his school.'[14]

Farrar's review appeared in 1889, the year after Henry Vizetelly had first answered an indictment charging him with publishing an obscene libel – a translation of Zola's *La Terre*. (He pleaded guilty, withdrew all his Zola translations, and paid the £100 fine, only to reissue slightly expurgated versions in 1889, for which he served three months in prison at the age of sixty-nine.) Detailed descriptions in Zola's novel of a variety of sexual acts between drunken peasants illustrate the large gap between the French novel and the English at this time, a gap which partly explains the frustration of Meredith, Gissing, George Moore, and Hardy at the censorship applied either directly or indirectly to their much less extreme work. Meredith always hated the petty-mindedness of the 'porkers'. In 1885 Gissing was attacked by *Punch* (in which Thackeray published some of his early work) for his comment that Thackeray had 'betrayed his trust' in his confession in the preface to *Pendennis* (see p. 144 above) that no writer since Fielding had been 'permitted to depict to his utmost power a man'.[15] Hardy, of course, gave up novel-writing in disgust at the hostile response of the reviewers to *Jude the Obscure* (1894–95). Only George Moore, however, attempted to emulate Zola in his earlier 'realistic novels' as he himself called them; and his Zolaesque phase was short-lived.

As Moore's first novel, *A Modern Lover* (1883), had been frowned upon by the circulating libraries, his second, *A Mummer's Wife* (1885), was published cheaply by Vizetelly in one volume. It is a novel of the senses, in which the characters' physical needs and frailties are not only portrayed but followed through to their inevitable consequences with a new and disturbing clarity. Repelled by an ailing husband who picks a bad tooth with a hairpin (6) and has thin hairy arms (1), Kate Ede is irresistibly drawn to the sexually attractive Dick Lennox, an actor, or 'mummer', who lodges with the Edes (2). Sex leads to pregnancy, and pregnancy to acute labour pains and 'a piercing scream' that she 'never will again' (22). (In *Esther Waters* Moore draws attention to steel instruments on a table and basins on the floor of a delivery room in hospital, 16.) Kate's heavy drinking causes her to vomit down her dress in a swaying cab (26). James Joyce consciously aimed to improve on Moore, from whom he took and developed a number of episodes. Less specifically, he also pressed the logic of Moore's realism a stage further. In 'Calypso', for example, in *Ulysses* (1922), Leopold Bloom's early morning walk and breakfast of a pork kidney naturally lead to a visit to the jakes, where he wipes himself on an old number of *Tit-Bits*. Joyce's accommodation of Bloomesque realist detail and Stephen Daedalus's aestheticism within the same Homeric scheme is anticipated in Moore's artistic formal structures, reflective of his training as a painter, within which the stages of his principal characters' lives are realistically portrayed. For example, J. E. Dunleavy likens the shape of *A Mummer's Wife* to that of a Greek vase, and compares Moore's treatment of the five flowers of Galway in *A Drama in Muslin* (1886) to a Monet landscape.[16] Moore's descriptions, however, of Hanley and the Potteries in *A Mummer's Wife* (4, 10), look forward to Arnold Bennett, who acknowledged in 1920 that the novel gave him the idea of his own Potteries novels, and to D. H. Lawrence's apocalyptic treatment of Nottingham and its coalfield.

George Moore was fascinated by ruling passions, like the sex drive, and by obsessions: in *A Mummer's Wife*, the theatre; in *A Drama in Muslin*, the marriage market; in *Esther Waters*, gambling. May Gauld, the sensualist in *A Drama in Muslin*, needs sex, and guiltily resorts to sleeping with an old man (III. 8), whereas the deformed Cecilia's desires are sublimated in her taking the veil. By the time Moore wrote his best and most popular novel, *Esther Waters* (1894), in which Esther's seduction and pregnancy change the course of her life, both the public opposition to and his own enthusiasm for Zola had waned. (Balzac was now his acknowledged master.) As P. J. Keating writes: 'We thus have the odd situation that the only English working-class novel of the period that can be said to be profoundly influenced by French naturalism belongs in many ways to a purely English tradition.'[17] The novel's main weakness, in his view, lies in the contradiction between the naturalistic sense of circumstances which Esther cannot combat and the 'Englishness' of her strength to survive. Moore's treatment of the iniquities of wet-nursing (18) and other forms of exploitation of the servant class (21–22) is more reminiscent of nineteenth-century English precursors than of Zola, and Esther's choice between two men is a reworking of a central Victorian theme, from *Jane Eyre* to *Tess of the d'Urbervilles* (1891).

Moore's reading of *Tess* while working on *Esther Waters* only increased his dislike of Hardy's work. His biographer, Joseph Hone, finds comparisons between the two novels strange, *Tess* being 'primarily the statement of a metaphysical grievance, the other a human document'.[18] Although Hone exaggerates the distinction it is revealing to contrast the novels, and especially their seduction scenes and endings. In *Esther Waters* the opening of Chapter 44 exactly reproduces that of Chapter 1, as Esther returns to Woodview having completed a painful circle through 'labour, suffering, disappointment', over a period of eighteen years. Her son remains to her, as does her old employer, Mrs Barfield. Unlike Hardy's extraordinary tragic ending in *Tess*, Moore's is one of ordinary muted sadness. Life goes on, demanding from Esther not violent reactions to the wrongs she has

suffered but quiet resignation: 'Esther seemed to have quite naturally accepted Woodview as a final stage. Any further change in her life she did
not seem to regard as possible or desirable' (45).

When Hall Caine, himself a writer of romances, wrote an article on 'The
New Watchwords of Fiction' in 1890, he was contributing to a debate
which was already about eight years old. His own definitions would in his
view be understood by 'plain people': 'I take realism to mean the doctrine
of the importance of the real facts of life, and idealism the doctrine of the
superiority of ideal existence over the facts of life.'[19] The revival of romance
in the 1880s, particularly after the publication of Robert Louis Stevenson's
Treasure Island in one volume in 1883, helped to sharpen the distinction
between the novel and the 'romance', a term which had generated little
debate in the 1860s and 1870s.[20] Hall Caine believed that the watchwords
of fiction 'for the next twenty years at least' would be 'ROMANTICISM AND
IDEALISM', and argued that 'the true consort of imagination' is enthusiasm:
'Enthusiasm, living with imagination in the hearts of great men, has again
and again set the world aflame, and purified as well as ennobled every
nature it has touched, save only the natures that were touched already with
fanaticism.'[21]

Caine's British readers would have taken his remarks on enthusiasm
setting the world aflame as an oblique reference to the ideal of Empire.
Martin Green argues in his study on adventure and empire that 'the adventure tales that formed the light reading of Englishmen for two hundred
years and more after *Robinson Crusoe* were, in fact, the energizing myth of
English imperialism', and that in the nineteenth century, readers made a
cult of the engineer, the explorer, the missionary, and the Indian soldier,
who 'all in different ways continued and developed the Crusoe image of
heroism'. Green also suggests that at mid-century children's literature became boys' literature (which was captured by the 'aristomilitary caste'),
adventure took the place of fable, and the adventure took on the characteristics of romance.[22] (Consider, for example, Kingsley's *Westward Ho!*
(1855), discussed in Chapter 3 – see p. 41 above.) Most of G. A. Henty's
romances were specifically written for and addressed to English boys. Like
Robinson Crusoe itself, however, some romances of the 1880s, such as Stevenson's *Treasure Island: A Story for Boys* were and still are recognized as
both children's classics and, simply, classics.

The childhood imagination figures prominently in the critical writings
of those who argued for romance and against realism. For example, Stevenson in his 'Humble Remonstrance' to Henry James (who admired his
work and later became a close friend) writes of the 'novel of adventure':
'There never was a child (unless Master James) but has hunted gold, and
been a pirate, and a military commander, and a bandit of the mountains;
but has fought, and suffered shipwreck and prison, and imbrued its little
hands in gore, and gallantly retrieved the lost battle, and triumphantly pro-
tected innocence and beauty.'[23] This passage is reminiscent of Dickens's
famous account of his own childhood reading in *David Copperfield* (4), as

indeed Hall Caine's comments are reminiscent of David Masson's description of Dickens as the leader of the Ideal or Romantic school of mid-century novelists (see p. 6 above). Taken together, Dickens's list of classics, which includes the *Arabian Nights, Don Quixote, Gil Blas, Robinson Crusoe, Roderick Random, Tom Jones*, and *The Vicar of Wakefield*, and Stevenson's, which includes the *Odyssey*, the *Arabian Nights, Pilgrim's Progress, Robinson Crusoe*, and Scott's novels,[24] outline a radically different great tradition from that traced by F. R. Leavis, whose emphasis on the novelist's 'mature' engagement with the 'adult' themes of 'real' life has so profoundly influenced a whole generation of English critics of the novel.[25] Stevenson considered that 'fiction is to the grown man what play is to the child', and that 'in anything fit to be called by the name of reading, the process itself should be absorbing and voluptuous; we should gloat over a book, be rapt clean out of ourselves'.[26] Both Stevenson and Haggard emphasized the central importance of incident in modern as in ancient forms of narrative, including epic – the main function of incident being to take us 'out of ourselves'. Dame Helen Gardner in her Norton lectures *In Defence of the Imagination* (1982) argues along similar lines, and quotes with approval Lionel Trilling's description of being 'set at liberty' in his childhood reading of Hawthorne, the greatest American romance writer of the mid-nineteenth century.[27]

In contrast to the new realists Gissing and Moore, the writers of romance in the 1880s – including Stevenson (the subject of a later section), Haggard, Henty, Doyle, and Marie Corelli – themselves revelled in being set at liberty from the idea that mundane contemporary 'reality' was the proper subject of fiction. Henty's books for boys epitomize the romance writers' penchant for deeds of derring-do, in which our hero (usually a young, upright Briton) escapes from the deepest dungeons of the Inquisition (*Under Drake's Flag: A Tale of the Spanish Main*, 1883; 16) or overpowers a lion unarmed (*Beric the Briton: A Story of the Roman Invasion*, 1893; 15). Clearly the romance had great potential moral influence on its younger readers, especially through a carefully nurtured empathy with the hero, and with the hero's heroes; and old-fashioned virtues could be inculcated upon readers in this way. Manliness was held up for admiration and foppery for ridicule, as for example in Arthur Conan Doyle's historical romance, *Micah Clarke* (1889; 35), at a time when the New Woman novelists – such as Olive Schreiner and 'Sarah Grand' – and Oscar Wilde, one of their most formidable critics, were questioning the traditional ideals of the strong man and the weaker vessel. In concentrating the mind on matters of life and death, fighting liberates the combatant from more trivial concerns. Points can also be scored by writers in passing, however, as when a cowardly Frenchman hides while British gentlemen engage in the 'Slaughter Grim and Great' of 250 Masai warriors in Haggard's *Allan Quartermain* (7).

Following the success of *King Solomon's Mines* (1885) and its sequel *Allan Quartermain* (1887), Rider Haggard produced the apotheosis of late Victorian romance in *She* (1886–87). Another fascinating story of Africa, in which both the penetration of the dark continent and return from it are achieved in conditions of extreme danger and hardship, it tells of a world in which the norms of European life are reversed. Ayesha, known as She-who-must-be-obeyed, rules over a matriarchal society in which women live on equal terms with men of their own choosing, but without binding ties, and in which the line of descent is on the female side (6). The eroticism of the episodes in which Ayesha reveals her apparently timeless beauty to both uncle Holly (13) and Leo (20) illustrates one kind of freedom enjoyed only by romance writers in this period, while the comic figure of Holly, and his references to the 'fossil friends' he has left behind in Cambridge (6), provide a foil to the exotic material of his narrative.

Holly's account of leaving the secure but dull world of a Cambridge mathematician to undertake a dangerous but exciting journey of exploration conforms to a pattern of escapism in many stories of the 1880s and subsequent decades. While Sherlock Holmes unravels 'the scarlet thread of murder running through the colourless skein of life', Dr Watson, his polar opposite in character and habits, leans back in the cab meditating upon 'the manysidedness of the human mind' (*A Study in Scarlet*, 1887; 4). Holmes's indulgence in cocaine and obsessive 'brain-work' are means of escape from the tedium of the 'dreary, dismal, unprofitable world' of fog-bound London in the late nineteenth century (*The Sign of Four*, 1890; 1), which Gissing's characters simply endure. Marie Corelli, who was 'dazzled to [her] very heart's core by the splendour of *She*',[28] explored the double nature of man in *The Sorrows of Satan* (1895), the biggest best-seller of the nineteenth century. Whereas Henty's readers are transported around the world, and back into romantic historical periods, Marie Corelli is interested in the inner world, and particularly 'internal' or 'human electricity', explained in *A Romance of Two Worlds* (1886). A writer whose enormous popularity and high self-esteem are today difficult to comprehend, Marie Corelli is significant mainly in what her bizarre works tell us of the late Victorian taste for escapist sensationalism and the occult.

Late Victorian romance is about extremes, presenting, as Haggard put it, 'ideal existence' rather than the 'facts of life', and sharp contrasts between black and white rather than shades of grey. It is based upon hypotheses rather than empirical observation, and its heroes are explorers rather than the pilgrims of the earlier nineteenth-century fiction. Utopian fiction of the late Victorian period, whether Utopian satire like Butler's *Erewhon* (1872), or a straight Utopian romance like William Morris's *News from Nowhere* (1890), conveys a social or political argument by means of contrasts between the real world and an impossible 'nowhere'. Like the heroes of Haggard's African romances, the unnamed traveller in *Erewhon; or, Over the Range* (later named Higgs in *Erewhon Revisited*, 1901) is suddenly challenged to make a crucial decision on his journey, in this case when he catches a glimpse of distant plains through a mountain pass: 'To stay where I was would be impossible; I must either go backwards or forwards' (4). Once committed he cannot turn back, and finds himself, like Swift's Gulliver, in a world in which the ideas and customs of his own society are either inverted or taken to ludicrous extremes. Illness is a crime, and crime an illness deserving of sympathy (9). A railway carriage, now several hundred years old, is displayed in a museum of machinery, and the narrator is imprisoned for wearing a watch, (7). Victorian religion and education are satirized in the Musical Banks, which are sparsely attended (15), and the Colleges of Unreason, where youths are prepared for adult life by answering questions arising from a 'set of utterly strange and impossible contingencies' (21). The narrator's escape from Erewhon in a balloon, with his beloved Arowhena Nosnibor concealed in the 'car', caps the most fanciful elopements of nineteenth-century fiction (28).

Morris's *News from Nowhere* also satirizes nineteenth-century society and its fiction, but from the quite different perspective of a perfect country of the future. Morris wrote the book in response to *Looking Backward* (1888) by the New England writer Edward Bellamy, in which Julian West is re-suscitated in the year 2000 in Boston, where goods belong to the nation, all have equal shares, and nineteenth-century individualism is scorned. Morris found Bellamy's mechanical 'cockney paradise' bourgeois and ab-horrent. Influenced by Ruskin, who as 'Mr Herbert' in Mallock's *The New Republic* (1877) plans to blow up the industrial towns and railways and found his own Utopia (II. 2), Morris has his own time traveller[29] wake up in a post-revolutionary twenty-first century which conforms to his cre-ator's ideal of the Middle Ages. In a series of attractive Pre-Raphaelite tab-leaux, men and women are shown working on equal terms at pleasurable crafts in rural English scenes.[30] Money and the marriage tie have been abol-ished, and the Thames is clean again. As old Hammond informs 'Guest', there are now no 'factories for making things that nobody wants, which was the chief business of the nineteenth century' (10), and Manchester no longer exists (17). As in *Erewhon*, the institutions of the Victorian estab-lishment are derided: Barry's Houses of Parliament are used as a market and a storage place for manure (5); Eton College, which 'taught rich men's sons to know nothing', is now open to all who wish to work in the library or learn boating on the river (24); the British Museum library contains books describing the time when Africa was 'infected by a man named Stan-ley' (15).

Morris's method of mediating his vision – through Guest's observations and through long interviews with the natives – is simple, even crude. Pa-trick Brantlinger, however, argues persuasively that the artless quality of *News from Nowhere* is part of its message, and that it is a 'conscious anti-novel, hostile to virtually every aspect of "the great tradition" of Victorian fiction'.[31] Clara's attack upon Victorian novelists is certainly scathing:

> Some of them, indeed, do here and there show some feeling
> for those whom the history-books call 'poor', and of the
> misery of whose lives we have some inkling; but presently
> they give it up, and towards the end of the story we must be
> contented to see the hero and heroine living happily in an
> island of bliss on other people's troubles; and that after a long
> series of sham troubles (or mostly sham) of their own

making, illustrated by dreary introspective nonsense about
their feelings and aspirations, and all the rest of it. (22)

For the Marxist the message is more important than the medium. Guest
returns to dingy nineteenth-century Hammersmith happier for having seen
the future and taking back a little hope to 'the struggle' (32). *News from
Nowhere* must be assessed not as a novel but as a political fable.[32]

The sharp contrasts we have noted in secular fiction of the late Victorian
period – between realism and romance, present realities and Utopias – are
also discernible in the most significant fiction on religious themes. J. H.
Shorthouse's *John Inglesant: A Romance* (1880) and Walter Pater's *Marius the
Epicurean: His Sensations and Ideas* (1885) are both elegantly written, are set
in periods of crisis in the history of the Church, and share a religio-aesthetic
emphasis on the sacrament of the eucharist or mass. That Gladstone, a
learned High Churchman, should have been photographed holding a copy
of *John Inglesant* reflects the Prime Minister's interests (although he also fell
for Marie Corelli's romances). That the book should have been the main
talking point at fashionable London dinner-parties reflects a continuing
general interest not only in historical romance but also in one of the central
religious issues of the Victorian age. For as the fictional narrator, Geoffrey
Monk, comments, there were 'numberless parallels' between the seventeenth and nineteenth centuries (3). Inglesant, who negotiates on King
Charles's behalf with Roman Catholics, describes the choice between Rome
and the Church of England as 'a conflict within a man's own nature – nay,
between the noblest parts of man's nature arrayed against each other' (39),
a sentiment familiar to Victorian High Churchmen. He concludes that upon
the altars of the English Church 'the divine presence hovers as surely, to
those who believe it, as it does upon the splendid altars of Rome'. He has
himself been to Rome at the time of a Vatican Conclave (30), has received
the sacrament at a mass (32), and has passed poison to the condemned
Quietist, Miguel de Molinos (38). Shorthouse had not visited Italy, but his
idea of the country, like his idea of seventeenth-century England – conveyed partly through Inglesant's interviews with notables such as Nicholas
Ferrar (4), Hobbes (5), and Archbishop Laud (6) – is sufficiently impressive
to provide a suitable setting for a novel in which the revenge plot is less
significant than the hero's spiritual quest.

Inglesant does not own a Bible, and his Christianity 'concentrate[s] itself
altogether on what may be called the Idea of Christ', that is, a 'lively conception of and attraction to the person of the Saviour' (17). Although
Pater's Marius dies with the Christians' 'mystic bread' between his lips (28),
his reception of the host, being involuntary, is as ambiguous as his drift
towards Christianity and martyrdom. 'Mr Rose', the obviously homosex-
ual Pater figure in Mallock's *The New Republic*, attends Ritualist services
which he admires for their beauty and 'curious old-world effect' (VI. 1).
Although critics of *Marius* have rightly argued that the work has a moral

dimension, and that Marius is drawn to the *community* of Christians, living together in charity, Pater's response to the Oxford Movement was certainly more aesthetic than doctrinal, and in *Marius* Christianity is often discussed in aesthetic terms. Marius, in the second century, is first shown attending pagan services and developing 'the ideal . . . of a religious beauty' (3). It is with a 'singular novelty of feeling' that he later meditates upon the Christian hope in the Roman catacombs, at the shrines of children (21). Pater explains the attraction of Christianity in terms of the art and poetry which it later informed, of a 'graver and higher beauty' than that of the Greeks (22). It is the aesthetic charm of the Catholic Church which finally appeals to Marius, from whom the eucharist draws the exclamation: 'What profound unction and mysticity!' (23). Pater's examination of Cynicism and Cyrenaicism, Stoicism and Epicureanism, in *Marius the Epicurean* is that of the scholar, the fellow of Brasenose; his treatment of Christianity and the emotional and aesthetic power of its primitive liturgy also reveals a writer at once moved and uncommitted.

William Hale White, in his trilogy of 'Mark Rutherford' novels (1881–87), Mary (Mrs Humphry) Ward, in *Robert Elsmere* (1888), and Samuel Butler, in *The Way of all Flesh* (written 1873–87; published 1903), all directly address themselves to the familiar Victorian theme of doubt. Like *Middlemarch*, all these novels are retrospective. White's *The Revolution in Tanner's Lane*, for example, the last of his trilogy, is divided into two parts, cutting from 1821 (15) to the early 1840s (16). Robert Elsmere's intellectual development parallels that of earlier phases of nineteenth-century thought. Butler, in his semi-autobiographical novel, portrays two generations of the Pontifex family (Theobald and Ernest) in detail, but also emphasizes their genetic and cultural inheritance from the previous two generations (John and George), thus covering a longer time-span even than Mary Ward's. Significantly, all three novelists make their heroes begin a new life in London after their loss of faith, in the midst of the physical and spiritual poverty which challenged Christianity to become practical.

Whereas Pater is attracted to the beauty of the ideas of Christianity, William Hale White's theme is the ugliness of narrow forms of dissent in provincial Victorian England. 'Mark Rutherford' (White's pseudonym) comments that 'these notes of mine are autobiographical, and not a romance' (*Mark Rutherford's Deliverance*, 8), and emphasizes the ordinariness of his background: 'My father and mother belonged to the ordinary English middle class of well-to-do shopkeepers' (*The Autobiography of Mark Rutherford*, 1). From the beginning of the *Autobiography* Rutherford is established as a highly critical retrospective commentator on the kinds of hypocrisy and petty-mindedness formerly analysed by Margaret Oliphant in her Carlingford series, and on the Sabbatarian excesses satirized by Dickens. White is unique, however, in his ability to convey the sense of sincere feelings and thoughts in a minister whose depression is as much the product of his dispiriting environment as of doctrinal problems. The quiet honesty of his writing makes his more startling revelations, such as the phoniness of Rutherford's conversion (*Autobiography*, 1) – thought to be the first of its kind in Victorian fiction – and the unusually unsympathetic portrayal of the Unitarians (7) the more credible. Hypocrisy, like Mr Snale's in the *Auto-biography* and John Broad's in *The Revolution*, is a favourite target, and unhappy marriages a recurring theme. The treatment of marriage, like that of Rutherford's depression (e.g. *Autobiography*, 3), is reminiscent of Gissing, whom White sometimes rivals in his handling of the relationship between thought, feeling, and atmosphere.

In *Mark Rutherford's Deliverance* the ex-minister joins a fellow reporter at the House of Commons, M'Kay, in his programme to 'rescue' Drury Lane, both physically and spiritually. Mark Rutherford's descriptions of our civilization as 'nothing but a thin film or crust lying over a volcanic pit' (5) is again strongly reminiscent of Gissing, although the attempt to teach 'Christ in the proper sense of the word', not as something to be written about by the cultured few but as one whom we must strive to become (2), is not. Mark Rutherford sees his new-found love for his unattractive stepdaughter, Marie, after she has nursed his wife during a serious illness, as 'love of God Himself as He is' (9).

This demythologizing and internalizing of the godhead, like the emphasis on social work in London, also characterizes the last stage of Robert Elsmere's spiritual quest, in Mary Ward's best-selling novel of 1888, probably the most wide-ranging and representative work of its type in the nineteenth century. Elsmere's walk away from Westminster Abbey, 'carrying the poetry and grandeur of England's past' with him, eastward 'to the great new-made London on the other side of St. Paul's, the London of the democracy, of the nineteenth century, and of the future' (32), is a ponderously contrived turning-point in a life whose spiritual roots were put down in Mary Ward's own Oxford (4–5), that other great centre in Victorian religious fiction. John Inglesant's Oxford, the centre of learning and High Church, of Parliament and Court, for a period during the Civil War, represents an ideal for Shorthouse (*John Inglesant*, 8–11). Pater, a neighbour of the Wards in Oxford in the 1870s, reviewed *Robert Elsmere*, as Mary Ward had reviewed *Marius*. Her *Writer's Recollections* (1918) contain vivid portraits of Gladstone, with whom she discussed her novel in Oxford, and who wrote a famous review (*Nineteenth Century*, May 1888), and of the Oxford liberals (anathema to Mallock) who shaped her own ideas, including her uncle, Matthew Arnold, Benjamin Jowett, and T. H. Green (on whom Henry Grey in *Robert Elsmere* is partly based).

Robert Elsmere, however, usually discussed as a *roman-à-clef* of the 1880s, in fact incorporates a panoramic survey of nineteenth-century religious thought, and the novel's settings are used to emphasize this, often with subtle effect. Elsmere's courtship of Catherine Leyburn in Wordsworth's Westmorland is later viewed nostalgically from the workaday Surrey rectory in which he develops a form of ministry clearly modelled on Charles Kingsley's muscular Christianity. In his historical researches in the library of a neighbouring sceptic, Squire Wendover, and in conversations with the Squire and his former Oxford tutor, Langham, doubts about his faith turn on the problem of testimony. The books, many of them German, which Mary Ward calls a chart of the Squire's intellectual history (14), also charted the course of such leading intellectuals as George Eliot and Matthew

Arnold. Arnold, however, who never broke with the Church of England, died before he had read the whole of his niece's novel, and, in Mary Ward's view, would not have approved of Elsmere's resignation of his living (*A Writer's Recollections*, 12). Elsmere begins work in the 'human wilderness' of the East End, now emphasizing that '*Miracles do not happen*', and thus echoing Matthew Arnold's summary of 'Hume's old argument' (40). In the last three books of the novel, Elsmere becomes Mary Ward's mouthpiece, whereas earlier he had been a more broadly representative Victorian figure.

It is the narrower, more hypocritical aspects of early and mid-Victorianism which Samuel Butler attacks in *The Way of all Flesh*. He had already parodied the spiritual biography or religious quest narrative in the brilliant spoof memoir of John Pickard Owen which introduces *The Fair Haven* (1873), a mock-defence of 'the miraculous element in our Lord's ministry on earth', which, to Butler's delight, was actually welcomed by Christian reviewers. Owen is in rapid succession an Evangelical, a Baptist, a Roman Catholic, a Deist, and a Broad Churchman, before his death from nervous exhaustion! Ernest Pontifex in *The Way of all Flesh* veers alarmingly from one extreme position to another within the Church of England, and sometimes for reasons similar to Owen's, in the hilarious Cambridge section of the novel (45–50). Butler's sustained interest, however, in the themes of marriage and family life, Darwinism and heredity, as well as religion, make the novel much broader in scope than *The Fair Haven*. Having himself lost his faith in the 1860s, like many of his contemporaries, Butler was free to revalue the kinds of doctrine and religious practice that Charlotte Brontë and Dickens satirized in the 1840s and 1850s, with the colder eye of one who was now outside the fold. Consider, for example, Ernest's parents' attitudes towards missionary work:

> Theobald did not feel any call to be a missionary. Christina
> suggested this to him more than once, and assured him of the
> unspeakable happiness it would be to her to be the wife of a
> missionary, and to share his dangers; she and Theobald might
> even be martyred; of course they would be martyred
> simultaneously, and martyrdom many years hence as regarded
> from the arbour in the Rectory garden was not painful, it
> would ensure them a glorious future in the next world, and at
> any rate posthumous renown in this – even if they were not
> miraculously restored to life again – and such things had
> happened ere now in the case of martyrs. (12)

Charlotte Brontë did not go half as far as this in her treatment of St John Rivers, in *Jane Eyre*. When Christina really is dying, and is alarmed at the thought of the Day of Judgement, her hint that Theobald's professional reputation is at stake annoys him intensely (83). The cruel undertone of such passages suggests the depth of Butler's loathing of his own Christian upbringing.

Ernest is Theobald's victim, as Theobald was formerly the victim of his father, George Pontifex. Butler's critique of Darwinism, however, which he worked out in a number of non-fictional books (see the Butler entry on p. 234 below), is reflected in Ernest's rescue by two surrogate parents from a life determined by heredity and home environment: his godfather, Overton, who also narrates the story, and his aunt Alethea, who represents the good Pontifex genes inherited from Ernest's great-grandfather, John. Himself saved by building and playing organs, like his great-grandfather, and finally by a legacy from his aunt, held for him by Overton, Ernest saves his own children from their father's bad influence by handing them over to working-class surrogate parents: the novel's plot is merely the vehicle for a set of theories. Butler's friend, Miss Savage, encouraged by the success of *The Fair Haven*, had challenged Butler to improve on *Middlemarch*, which he considered to be pompous and heavy. As novels, *The Way of all Flesh* and *Middlemarch* cannot be compared. The comparison with *Jane Eyre* is more illuminating, however, as both novels focus upon the spiritual development of an individual trapped in a hostile and repressive religious milieu. Whereas Jane Eyre finds her own interpretation of Christianity through rebellion against the extreme positions of those who try to dominate her, Ernest Pontifex rejects the whole framework of faith in favour of a belief in man's ability to develop away from the stunted and stunting social and ethical norms of previous generations, while drawing upon what is good in his predecessors through unconscious memory. Unlike Charlotte Brontë and George Eliot, Samuel Butler was not a novelist of genius, but rather an exceptionally interesting man of ideas who adopted the novel form.

Circles of hell: Gissing

Gladstone's comment of 1896 that the doctrine of hell had been 'relegated . . . to the far-off corners of the Christian mind' indicates a radical change in nineteenth-century theology and Christian teaching.[34] Freed from the complication of profound doctrinal significance, the idea of hell takes on a new life in George Gissing's early fiction, and from the opening paragraph of *Workers in the Dawn* (1880), his first novel, to the last paragraph of *The Nether World* (1889) is a recurrent controlling metaphor. Gissing's close examination of physical conditions in the slums of late nineteenth-century London, and his more impressive analysis of psychological impoverishment in the depressing environment of mean streets, broadly correspond to the two basic Western concepts of hell: as a place of physical torment, and as a place of spiritual pain consequent upon the soul's separation from God.

At the beginning of *Workers in the Dawn*, Gissing the traditional author-narrator writes like a latter-day Henry Mayhew – 'Walk with me, reader, into Whitecross Street' – in the role of Virgil in Dante's *Inferno*: flames and

a 'reddish light' contrast with 'deep blackness' overhead; through a 'yawning archway' are 'unspeakable abominations'. Although Gissing soon rejected this familiar guide-book approach, as P. J. Keating has shown, his
metaphor of the abyss reflected a new fear of the masses of the urban poor
in the last decades of the century, and was to recur with this connotation
not only in Gissing's work, but also in that of H. G. Wells, C. F. G. Masterman, and E. M. Forster.[35] The analogy of Dante's circles of hell, most
obviously present in the gradations of poverty which Gissing carefully distinguishes (in the several floors of lodging-houses, for example), also fulfil
various structural functions in his novels. Beginning in the physical pit of
hell which is Whitecross Street, *Workers in the Dawn* completes its own
circle when, on the last page, Arthur Golding throws himself into Niagara
Falls, the last words of the novel being: '. . . and plunged into the abyss'.
Clem Peckover's bullying of Jane Snowden in the first chapter of *The
Nether World* is repeated towards the end of the novel, to Jane's despair
(38). It is in the construction of individual chapters, however, that the
hopeless circularity of the lives of the poor is most strikingly conveyed.
Chapter 12, 'Io Saturnalia!', describes the wedding-day of Bob Hewitt and
'Pennyloaf' Candy, spent on an East End trip to the Crystal Palace on
August Bank Holiday Monday. Pennyloaf's ring is gold, and the pawn-
broker 'would lend her seven-and-sixpence on it, any time'. That time
comes within twenty-four hours, for when they return to the 'black hole'
which is their 'wedding-chamber' in Shooter's Gardens, Bob is drunk,
Pennyloaf's face is 'all blood and dirt', and, as she listens to her drunken
mother being beaten up outside, she realizes that she will have to pawn the
ring in the morning. The diurnal round, varied only by occasional de-
bauchery, is itself part of the large cycle of generations who are born,
marry, and die within earshot of beatings and brawls. Mad Jack's bellowed
prophetic texts, another familiar sound in the Gardens, begin and end the
later chapter in which Bob Hewitt is arrested (37). Before the arrest, Mad
Jack relates a visitation from an angel, who said to him: 'This life you are
now leading is that of the damned; this place to which you are confined
is Hell!'

Gissing was a solidly Victorian novelist in his technique, and slaved
away under the tyranny of the circulating libraries and the three-decker
novel. As we have seen, he also came to 'abhor Zola's grossness', like his
more conservative contemporaries.[36] Although kept within the bounds of
English decorum, his exposure of the hopelessness of the conditions of the
urban poor was less restrained than that of his precursors. Compare, for
example, Dickens's description of Mr Dombey's train journey, and his
comments on the way in which the railway has 'let the light of day in' on
the 'miserable habitations far below' (*Dombey and Son*, 1846–48; 20), with
Gissing's account of Sidney Kirkwood's train journey to the country with
Michael and Jane Snowden:

> Over the pest-stricken regions of East London, sweltering in
> sunshine which served only to reveal the intimacies of
> abominations; across miles of a city of the damned, such as

thought never conceived before this age of ours; above streets
swarming with a nameless populace, cruelly exposed by the
unwonted light of heaven; . . . the train made its way at
length beyond the outmost limits of dread, and entered upon
a land of level meadows.

(*The Nether World*, 19)

There is a new sense of hopelessness here. Whereas Dickens, even in *Little
Dorrit*, clung on to the hope of transcendence, suggested by the light of
heaven on the Marshalsea and Arthur Clennam's escape from his own
hellish circle of self-imprisonment (see p. 87 above), Gissing's sunshine
merely exposes the squalor in a crueller light, and escape from his London
is only a brief 'Retreat'.

The vicious circle or downward spiral of poverty in *The Nether World*
has a profound psychological effect upon those who are caught in it. Clara
Hewitt, living in a barrack-like tenement building as hard and resistant as
necessity itself, is driven to thoughts of suicide by the crushing sense of
the bestiality which surrounds her, and the impossibility, now that her face
has been disfigured, of escaping from this environment through a career
on the stage. Her question, 'Was it a life that could be lived?' (30), is more
fundamental than Dorothea Brooke's question about *how* she should live
in Middlemarch. Life's battles are more deadly in the nether world, as
Gissing shows in Clem Peckover's longing for 'real tooth-and-claw conflict' (1) and her subsequent attack upon Pennyloaf (8). Gissing's emphasis
throughout his early novels upon the animality of the poor, doomed to be
yoked in repetitive labour (where it is available), to endure sordid living
conditions, and to escape only through drunkenness, madness, or death,
reflects a grim determinism. His Hardyesque comment on the impoverished Mr and Mrs Christopherson in *New Grub Street* is characteristic in
its bitter irony: 'They had had three children; all were happily buried' (8).

The Emancipated (1890), which followed *The Nether World*, marks a turning-point in Gissing's career. Following a tour on the Continent, he set Part I
in Italy. Having formerly concentrated on working-class life and poverty,
he now turned his attention to the middle classes and the theme of spiritual
impoverishment. His treatment of Reuben Elgar's elopement from Italy
with Cecily Doran, and their subsequent marriage in London, reveals a
new approach to themes explored in earlier novels. After the birth of their
child the couple set up house in Belsize Park, and Reuben, announcing his
intention to write 'a history of the English mind in its relation to Puritan-
ism', works long hours in the British Museum reading room (II. 3). Bitter
memories of the nonconformist Sabbatarianism of his own childhood in
a Manchester suburb (I. 13) fuel the passion in his claim that his book will
'declare the emancipation of all the better minds'. In Reuben's urge to write
and the pain he experiences in failure lie the seeds of Gissing's next and
finest novel, *New Grub Street* (1891), where Reuben's hypothetical question,
addressed to his wife, was to be answered: 'Suppose, Ciss, we all of a sudden lost everything, and we had to go and live in a garret, and I had to
get work as a clerk at five-and-twenty shillings a week. How soon should

we hate the sight of each other, and the sound of each other's voices?' (II. 3). We have seen how earlier Victorian novelists often used financial difficulties to put their characters under pressure, and thus reveal their strengths and weaknesses. In his novels Gissing returns again and again to the theme of financial necessity, contrasting the ways in which society judges the behaviour of the down-at-heel with that of the comfortably off, who enjoy the freedom of action which flows from financial security.

The Elgars' marriage fails, as Reuben's statistics would seem to have predicted: 'How many wives and husbands love each other? Not one pair in five thousand' (II. 3). Gissing was later to write of Dickens's 'avoidance of the disagreeable', in his critical study of 1898.[37] Although George Eliot and Meredith devoted far more attention to unhappy unions than Dickens did, it was in Gissing's novels that the analysis of marital tension and break-down was most exhaustively pursued. Following the public scandal of Reuben's affair with a music-hall singer, Cecily feels that her home has become a prison, and that she suffers 'the unequal hardships of a woman's lot' (II. 12). Like Samuel Butler in *The Way of all Flesh*, Gissing places an individual character's longing for freedom in the broader context of a rejection of Victorian religious values:

> A woman who belongs to the old education readily believes that it is not to experiences of joy, but of sorrow, that she must look for her true blessedness; her ideal is one of renunciation; religious motive is in her enforced by what she deems the obligation of her sex. But Cecily was of the new world, the emancipated order. For a time she might accept misery as her inalienable lot, but her youthful years, fed with the new philosophy, must in the end rebel.

Gissing's ambivalent attitude towards the so-called New Woman is reflected in several of his novels of the 1890s, including *New Grub Street*.[38]

For Gissing, a non-believer, the idea of hell as separation from God, the ultimate alienation, is scaled down to the separation of man from man, or woman from husband, in miserable loneliness. In *The Unclassed* (1884), Osmond Waymark places in a newspaper the only lonely hearts advertisement I have encountered in Victorian fiction: 'Wanted, human companionship' (6). In *New Grub Street* the grinding poverty of a struggling novelist leads either to the breakdown of his marriage, as in Edwin Reardon's case, or to enforced bachelorhood, as in the case of his friend Harold Biffen, who envies him his wife Amy (10). Reardon's description of the poor writer's lot – 'The abyss . . . Penury and despair and a miserable death' (15) – proves to be prophetic. By the beginning of the third volume he is leaving his garret at night to haunt the streets where Amy lives, returning with feelings of revolt against the circumstances which have 'driven him into outer darkness' (25). Gissing himself considered that his characteristic contribution to fiction was the young, well-educated man without money.[39] The world of the writer working in London without money was, of course, Gissing's own world; and his subtle distinctions between the strata of the literary profession in *New Grub Street*, and the novel's concentration upon books and writers, are unique. The Christian names of Edwin Reardon and Jasper Milvain suggest Victorian hero and villain figures. Milvain, who serves mammon, cynically accepts whatever literary work is offered to him, drops Marian Yule when it emerges that she will not inherit a large fortune, and marries Reardon's wife, Amy, after Reardon's death. Reardon and his friend Biffen, who serve art, are in temper 'rabid idealists' and in their work realists (10). Unlike Reardon, however, whose spirit is crushed by failure, and who does not share his friend's extreme views on art, Biffen believes in his avant-garde naturalism. The history of the writing and publication of Biffen's 'Mr Bailey, Grocer', and of his eventual suicide (35), is Gissing's most interesting variation on his central theme. At the beginning of the chapter in which Biffen saves his manuscript from a burning house, Gissing addresses the reader directly: 'The chances are that you have neither understanding nor sympathy for men such as Edwin Reardon and Harold Biffen. They merely provoke you' (31). He then restates his old theme in a new context: 'Gifted with independent means, each of them would have taken quite a different aspect in your eyes. The sum of their faults was their inability to earn money.'

The Reardon–Milvain contrast is repeated in that between Biffen and Whelpdale, who knows his own limitations and develops a literary advisory service from small beginnings (16) – a sign of the times in literary London. When Whelpdale marries Milvain's sister at the end of the novel, he wonders why he should have come to this prosperity when both Milvain and Biffen are dead. Milvain's cynical answer is that of a man who has moved with the times: 'In the first place, success has nothing whatever to do with moral deserts; and then, both Reardon and Biffen were hopelessly impractical' (37).

The novel's second major theme, that of the New Woman, is woven into the New Grub Street plot by relating private lives to literary matters. Marian Yule eventually refuses to be her father's literary slave (13). In the chapter whose title refers to the Act which came into effect in 1883, 'Married Women's Property' (26), Amy Reardon's evolution from harassed wife to liberated woman is charted in terms of her ideas on literature. She is sickened by novelists' lies about love being a woman's whole life: 'Love is the most insignificant thing in most women's lives. . . . Think of the very words "novel", "romance" – what do they mean but exaggeration of one bit of life?' Alone and independent, she reads the kinds of social-scientific articles which were alien to Reardon's sympathies, and grasps in outline the main theories of Herbert Spencer and Darwin without actually reading their works. As Gissing, who scorned the half-educated, drily suggests: 'She was becoming a typical woman of the new time, the woman who has developed concurrently with journalistic enterprise.'

In Gissing's novels the abyss metaphor suggests potential disaster below; in both Shooter's Gardens and New Grub Street there are no stable, self-supporting structures of hired labour or professional association within which individuals can be truly secure. Rather, in a *laissez-faire* economic and social system, only the exploitative can survive, at the expense of the exploited. Like most of his precursors, Gissing admired Carlyle as a 'prototype of the artist exiled from contemporary culture'.[40] Gissing's artists and writers, prostitutes and unemployed labourers, are exiled to the edge of society, and his novel titles reflect this displacement: *The Unclassed*, *The Nether World*, *The Emancipated*, *The Odd Women* (1893). Biffen, in *New Grub Street*, 'belonged to no class' (35). Unable to suggest ways of reforming society, Gissing leaves the reader with a sense of hopelessness. As Virginia Woolf wrote: 'His books are very sad.'[41]

Significant simplicity: Stevenson

If somebody who had read the major works of George Gissing and Robert Louis Stevenson, but not their biographies, were asked to guess which of them had written much of his fiction in bed, through chronic ill health, the answer would probably be Gissing. In fact it was Stevenson whose heroic struggle against illness became part of the 'RLS' legend after his early death, and whose memorial in St Giles's, Edinburgh, portrays him writing on an elegant couch, covered by a fringed rug. (A chain-smoker, he holds a pen rather than the cigarette of the earlier, medallion version of the portrait, as this was thought to be more suitable for a church.[42]) Paradoxically, however, poor health also forced Stevenson to become a great traveller and eventually an exile from his native Edinburgh. Early in his married life he moved frequently around Scotland, England, and the Continent; later he and his family left Britain for America, and finally settled in Samoa. His true element was the sea, and in this, as in many aspects of his fiction, he invites comparison with Conrad. Whereas the realist Gissing specializes in the well-educated young man without money, and in characters who are exploited, trapped in a claustrophobic circle of despair, Stevenson's young romance heroes, kidnapped or threatened with violent death, and sometimes having to live on whatever comes their way, are caught up in high adventure. It is in participating in their adventures and thus moving beyond the bounds of everyday experience that we are, in the words of Stevenson I quoted earlier, 'rapt clean out of ourselves'. The first readers of *Treasure Island*, which was initially published in serial form in *Young Folks* (1881–82) and then as a volume (1883), could enjoy the 'absorbing and voluptuous' process of empathizing with young Jim Hawkins as he struggles with the unwieldy coracle (23), gets on board the *Hispaniola*, and confronts Israel Hands with a brace of pistols: 'One more step, Mr Hands . . . and I'll blow your brains out!' (26). In *Kidnapped*, too, some of the most stirring episodes occur on board ship, as when David Balfour and Alan Breck Stewart defend the round-house on the *Covenant* against Captain Hoseason and his men, for example (10).

We have seen that whereas George Eliot's Dorothea Brooke wonders how she should live in Middlemarch, Gissing's Clara Hewitt asks 'Was it a life that could be lived?'. Stevenson's emphasis is often different again, being 'not upon what a man shall choose to do, but on how he manages to do it'.[43] The passage in his essay 'A Gossip on Romance' (1882) from which these words are taken is worth quoting at greater length:

> Conduct is three parts of life, but it is not all the four. There is a vast deal in life and letters both which is not immoral, but simply a-moral; which either does not regard the human will at all, or deals with it in obvious and healthy relations; where the interest turns, not upon what a man shall choose to do, but on how he manages to do it; not on the passionate slips and hesitations of the conscience, but on the problems of the body and of the practical intelligence, in clean, open-air adventure, the shock of arms, or the diplomacy of life. . . . it is possible to build, upon this ground, . . . the most lively, beautiful, and buoyant tales.

Stevenson went on to discuss the power of the childhood imagination in 'A Humble Remonstrance', quoted earlier. That essay was written in 1884, between the publication of his early stories, *New Arabian Nights* (1882) and *Treasure Island*, and the Bournemouth period in which he wrote *The Strange Case of Dr Jekyll and Mr Hyde* (1886) and *Kidnapped* (1886). The advice he offers the young writer in the essay ends with these words: 'And as the root of the whole matter, let him bear in mind that his novel is not a transcript of life, to be judged by its exactitude; but a simplification of some side or point of life, to stand or fall by its significant simplicity.'[44] I want to consider Stevenson's significant simplicity, and briefly discuss *The Master of Ballantrae* (1888–89), his most ambitious completed work.

In 'A Humble Remonstrance' Stevenson writes contemptuously of the three-decker novel, 'the stay and bread-winner of Mr. Mudie', and advises the young writer to avoid a sub-plot, unless, 'as sometimes in Shakespeare, the sub-plot be a reversion or complement of the main intrigue': 'Let him not regret if this shortens his book; it will be better so; for to add irrelevant matter is not to lengthen but to bury.'[45] Unlike Gissing, who drove himself along in order to fill three volumes, Stevenson never wrote at great length. Whereas the three-decker, or twenty monthly parts, or eight bimonthly parts, provided the writer of a multiplot novel with space in which to weave the complex webs of relationships which create dense social realism, Stevenson, like other romance writers, achieved within a much smaller compass the intensity of focus required to develop a single plot which follows the fortunes of one or two central characters. Most of the short chapters of *Treasure Island* turn upon a single, sharply realized incident. The sub-title of *Kidnapped* illustrates the simplicity of its romance plot:

> Being memoirs of the adventures of David Balfour in the year MDCCLI. How he was kidnapped and cast away; his sufferings in a desert isle; his journey in the wild Highlands; his acquaintance with Alan Breck Stewart and other notorious Highland Jacobites; with all that he suffered at the hands of his uncle, Ebenezer Balfour of Shaws, falsely so-called; written by himself, and now set forth by Robert Louis Stevenson.

Plot and narrative technique are here explained in a nutshell; the shortest possible summary of *Bleak House* would extend to several pages. *Dr Jekyll and Mr Hyde* has a simple suspense plot, with the central secret being revealed three-quarters of the way through the story. The more complex *Master of Ballantrae* still focuses steadily upon the two Durie brothers, James and Henry, while the unfinished *Weir of Hermiston* (1896) keeps Archie Weir firmly at the centre of the narrative.

Stevenson further advises his young writer to allow 'neither himself in his narrative nor any character in the course of the dialogue, to utter one sentence that is not part and parcel of the business of the story or the discussion of the problem involved'. In concentrating upon how his characters 'manage to do it', Stevenson follows his own advice, thus consciously avoiding the example of Scott, whom he considered to be 'out and away the king of the romantics' but hardly a great artist.[46] One of the most famous examples of his economy in narrative and dialogue is the chapters of *Kidnapped* describing David and Alan in their flight in the heather (20f). A few snatches of conversation, brief references to some of the natural features they pass, and a number of dangerous incidents sketch in the picture which is completed in the reader's own imagination. Without the encumbrances of sub-plots, lengthy descriptions, and character analyses, and, in his early works, without women characters and love interest, Stevenson achieves a sharp clarity of line both in his plots and in the shaping of his ideas.

In 'A Humble Remonstrance' Stevenson argues that 'the novel which is a work of art exists . . . by its immeasurable difference from life', and that the art of narrative is 'bound to be occupied, not so much in making stories true as in making them typical'.[47] *Kidnapped* has been described as 'something like a fable'.[48] Similarly, Jim's fall from innocence into knowledge in *Treasure Island* is typical in the special sense that Stevenson introduces the symbolism of the Eden myth: it is from inside an apple barrel that he overhears Long John Silver plotting with Hands (11); and before witnessing 'The First Blow' three chapters later, when Silver murders a shipmate, he sees a rattlesnake but does not recognize it as a 'deadly enemy'. Fanny Stevenson's criticism of the first sensational draft of *Dr Jekyll and Mr Hyde* also supports the view that stories should be typical: she persuaded Stevenson to produce the version we have on the grounds that the tale should be written as an allegory.

Whereas in the first draft Jekyll's transformations into Hyde were for the purpose of disguise, in the second the transformations, though implausibly effected through chemicals, illustrate the story's main theme – man's dual nature. This is the central theme not only of the story whose title has entered the language as a shorthand description of the split personality, but also of many other works by Stevenson. In his own childhood, his nurse's Calvinism fuelled nightmares of the devil and judgement. Rejecting Scottish Calvinism in early manhood, Stevenson himself lived something of a double life in Edinburgh, and in 1878–79 worked with W. E. Henley on a play about the notorious Deacon Brodie, who in eighteenth-century Edinburgh was a respectable wright and cabinet-maker by day and leader of a gang of thieves by night. Stevenson's abhorrence of the doctrine of predestination (which his Scottish precursor James Hogg had made the subject of *The Confessions of a Justified Sinner*, 1824) contributed to his suspension of judgement upon his characters. In *Dr Jekyll and Mr Hyde*, for example, which touched the nerve of several Victorian anxieties, the reference to Henry Jekyll's unspecified but 'undignified' pleasures hints at the stereotype of the 'respectable' gentleman's secret peccadilloes in the upper regions of the Victorian underworld. Hyde's 'unexpressed deformity' suggests original sin, but the fact that he is also like a monkey introduces a disturbing hint of Darwinism and the beast within. The painful transitions from Jekyll to Hyde, however, underline the fact that the two cannot coexist ; unity and resolution are impossible. When the lawyer Utterson breaks into Jekyll's laboratory with the butler, and finds that Hyde has killed himself, he declares: 'We have come too late . . . whether to save or punish.' The language of judgement is adopted by the lawyer who in breaking down the door is the immediate cause of Hyde's suicide. Long John Silver's return to 'dooty' at the end of *Treasure Island* is as sudden as Jim's earlier discovery of his villainy: 'And there was Silver, sitting back almost out of the firelight, but eating heartily, prompt to spring forward when anything was wanted, even joining quietly in our laughter – the same bland, polite, obsequious seaman of the voyage out' (33). Devilish in his attractiveness, he slips away to a foreign port on the home voyage with a sack of stolen coins in his pocket, allowed by Stevenson to escape the plank or the noose. Jim Hawkins's speculations about him, however, point to future judgement: 'I dare say he met his old negress, and perhaps still lives in comfort with her and Captain Flint. It is to be hoped so, I suppose, for his chances of comfort in another world are very small' (34).

The recent revival of interest in Stevenson, part of a larger revival of interest in romance, centres upon his treatment of 'the tragic ambiguity of the human animal' and his moral ambivalence.[49] We have just seen a simple example of ambivalence in Jim's comment on Silver working against the non-judgemental open ending to the character's life. Most of *Treasure Island* is of course narrated by Jim, a reliable witness of extraordinary events. Although the sequence of narratives in *Dr Jekyll and Mr Hyde* – authorial narrative, Dr Lanyon's Narrative, and Henry Jekyll's Full Statement of the Case – reveal more and more about the Strange Case, the final suicide leaves it only partially explained and the Jekyll/Hyde dualism unresolved.

It is, however, in *The Master of Ballantrae: A Winter's Tale* that Stevenson's simplicity becomes most significantly treacherous.

In *The Master* Stevenson uses the old device of presenting himself as the editor of a packet of papers more than a hundred years old. When he is advised by his friend the lawyer, Mr Johnstone Thomson, that he will only have to work up the scenery, characters, and style, he replies that the papers should be published as they stand, as 'there is nothing so noble as baldness' (Preface). We are asked to believe, then, that this is an edited transcription of written documents (as we are in Rider Haggard's *She*). These documents are personal testimonies or eyewitness accounts, perfect material for a winter's tale, as in Conan Doyle's historical romance, *Micah Clarke, his Statement as made to his Three Grand-Children, Joseph, Gervas, & Reuben During the Hard Winter of 1734*. As in *Wuthering Heights*[50] and James's *The Turn of the Screw*, the central conflict in *The Master*, between James and Henry Durie, is described mainly by a witness who may or may not be reliable. Ephraim Mackellar, steward to the Master of Ballantrae, tells most of the tale, and incorporates comments and corrections, in footnotes, to extracts from Colonel Burke's memoirs. (There are also statements by two other observers towards The end: The trader, Mountain, and Secundra Dass, James's Indian familiar.) Mackellar combines features of Emily Brontë's Nelly Dean and Mr Lockwood, being at once an insider and an outsider at Ballantrae; a fiercely partisan agent in the story he relates and an external observer of the family's affairs; a practical man and a buffoon. Known as 'Square-Toes', he is also called an old maid by Mrs Henry Durie (6); yet he glories in his discovery of James's private correspondence like a true villain, as he now has him at his mercy (5), and suddenly tries to murder him on board ship to America (9).

The eruption of Square-Toes into violence against James mirrors that of 'Mr Henry', and suggests that the narrator, like the two brothers, also has a dual nature. Early in the story the brothers are presented by Mackellar as polar opposites in nature. Henry is 'neither very bad nor yet very able, but an honest, solid sort of lad', while James is popular and wild (1), a prodigal, who on his return to Ballantrae, practises 'transitions' from a dutiful public persona, assumed for his father and sister-in-law, and a private, vindictive persona, shown only to Henry and Mackellar (4). The brothers' *roles*, however, were decided on the spin of a coin when, as in other Scottish families in 1745, the security of the house was ensured by the two brothers taking different sides – James to fight for King James, the Old Pretender, and Henry to stay at home and support the reigning King George (1). Henry, however, also married the kinswoman intended to be James's wife, Alison Graeme. Whereas James effects his transitions at will, being a good actor, like Alan Breck in *Kidnapped*, Henry's own dual nature is revealed involuntarily, under stress, as he 'drifts from his character', and plays 'alternately the ostrich and the bull' (6). In New York he shows himself to be crueller than his devilish brother, whose spirit he systematically tries to break (10). He later becomes addicted to drink (11). In the sensational ending which Stevenson himself acknowledged to be hurried and unsatisfactory, Henry dies of shock when he thinks that James's week-old corpse is coming back to life. It is their mutual antagonism, however, which has kept them both alive; when one dies the other must follow. Like Nelly's and Lockwood's accounts of Heathcliff in *Wuthering Heights*, Mackellar's Christ/Satan model proves to be inadequate as an account of the brothers in *The Master,* and the ambiguities of his 'bald' narrative multiply as he tries to make sense of them. The relationship between the brothers, each of whom is himself divided, is a brilliant reworking of the Jekyll and Hyde theme. At once simple and sophisticated, *The Master of Ballantrae* is the finest of Stevenson's completed works.

Art is a disproportioning: Hardy

In 1940, the centenary of Thomas Hardy's birth, R. L. Purdy revealed that the official *Life*, originally published in two volumes (1928–30) under the name of the writer's second wife, Florence, was in fact almost entirely Hardy's own work. The biography was actually an autobiography, in which Hardy covertly presented to the world the image of himself which he favoured. Curious in its evolution, the book is also strange in its contents and organization, often being no more than a jumble of scraps and notes, observations and reminiscences. But some of these jottings distil a view of the world which is typically Hardyesque. The dated transcriptions from journals and notebooks for 1890, my *terminus ad quem* in this book, are particularly revealing. An entry for 29 January – 'I have been looking for God 50 years, and I think that if he had existed I should have discovered him' – is followed by a wry comment on a 'staid, worn, weak man at the railway station', whose back, legs, hands, and face were 'longing to be out of the world', but whose brain was not, because, 'like the brain of most people, it was the last part of his body to realize a situation'.[51] As Hardy works on his finest novel, *Tess of the d'Urbervilles* (1891) he comments on London society beauties: 'If put into rough wrappers in a turnip-field, where would their beauty be?'

Scattered among these characteristic observations are no fewer than three attempts to express an idea of art which places Hardy, rather unexpectedly, on the idealist side in the debate between the realists and the writers of romance, outlined earlier in this chapter. Here are the salient points from each of the three passages:

> Art consists in so depicting the common events of life as to
> bring out the features which illustrate the author's
> idiosyncratic mode of regard; making old incidents and things
> seem as new.

> Art is a changing of the actual proportions and order of
> things, so as to bring out more forcibly than might otherwise
> be done that feature in them which appeals most strongly to
> the idiosyncrasy of the artist.
>
> Art is a disproportioning – (*i.e.* distorting, throwing out of
> proportion) – of realities, to show more clearly the features
> that matter in those realities, which, if merely copied or
> reported inventorially, might possibly be observed, but would
> more probably be overlooked. Hence 'realism' is not Art.

As Hardy moves towards this last statement on realism in the third passage,
the former emphasis on the artist's idiosyncrasy is dropped in favour of the
more orthodox view that art reveals the features that matter in realities.
In rejecting realism, as understood in 1890, and in emphasizing the need
to portray the features that matter and to make the old seem as new, Hardy
follows a line of argument similar to Stevenson's in his essays on romance.
In his statement, however, that art is a disproportioning – a personal manifesto for the grotesque, which is broadly characterized by distortion or
unnatural combination – Hardy reveals a different cast of mind and
imagination.

One of Hardy's favourite ways of making old things seem as if new was
through the artist's disproportioning achieved by viewing the world in
varying lights or from unusual perspectives. 'If I were a painter', he observes in the gallery of the English Art Club in 1891, 'I would paint a picture of a room as viewed by a mouse from a chink under the skirting'.[52]
Tess Durbeyfield must be portrayed in more different lights than any other
Victorian heroine: candlelight, moonlight, dawn and evening twilight,
bright sunshine, the lights of a railway train and of allotment fires at night,
and so on. She is also viewed from many angles. In Blackmoor Vale, for
example, she stands still 'upon the hemmed expanse of verdant flatness, like
a fly on a billiard-table of infinite length, and of no more consequence to
the surroundings than that fly' (16); whereas at Talbothays, Angel Clare
admires her in a series of close-ups, as when she is yawning and he sees
'the red interior of her mouth as if it had been a snake's' (27).

In the novels the kind of rapid cutting and changes of scale we have seen
in the *Life* – from the absence of God to an old man at a railway station
– reflect both Hardy's ambition and his oddness (he would say idiosyncrasy)
as a writer. Some of the novels which are least familiar to modern readers
are interesting in this respect. In *A Pair of Blue Eyes* (1872–73), for example,
Henry Knight hangs on a cliff-face poised between heaven and earth,
staring a fossilized trilobite in the eyes (22). In *Two on a Tower* (1882)
Hardy's romance on his old theme of the poor man and the lady is played
out mainly on, at the foot of, or in sight of the tower in the title. From a
distance it merely looks like a classical column (1). As Lady Constantine
approaches it for the first time, however, vagueness gives way to detailed
description: 'It had been built in the Tuscan order of classic architecture,
and was really a tower, being hollow with steps inside.' Below the level of

the surrounding treetops the masonry is lichen-stained and mildewed: 'Pads of moss grew in the joints of the stone-work, and here and there shade-loving insects had engraved on the mortar patterns of no human style or meaning; but curious and suggestive.' From the microscopic the eye is led outwards and upwards to the tower rising into the sky above the trees, a 'bright and cheerful thing, unimpeded, clean and flushed with the sunlight'. At the top of the all too obviously phallic tower, which rises out of a 'moaning cloud of blue-black vegetation', sleeps Swithin St Cleeve, his complexion like that of Raphael's infant John the Baptist. St Cleeve, an astronomer, looks upward in the novel, to the vast immensities of space, 'the voids and waste places of the sky' (4), while Lady Constantine's love draws him down from these aerial flights to ground level, where they are watched by the local peasantry.

The plot of *Two on a Tower* is equally bizarre. Lady Constantine marries St Cleeve, discovers that her first husband was actually alive when she re-married, sends St Cleeve away, discovers that she is pregnant, and marries a bishop – the butt of some of Hardy's cheaper anti-clerical jibes. Margaret Oliphant, whose critical views reflect mid-Victorian values, found the work 'so grotesque that the sense of the comic in it goes much too far to be vanquished by any disapproval'.[53] Mrs Oliphant had 'a great many objections to make to Tess', but was positively outraged by *Jude the Obscure* (1894–95):

> The present writer does not pretend to a knowledge of the works of Zola, which perhaps she ought to have before presuming to say that nothing so coarsely indecent as the whole history of Jude in his relations with his wife Arabella has ever been put in English print – that is to say, from the hands of a Master. There may be books more disgusting, more impious as regards human nature, more foul in detail, in those dark corners where the amateurs of filth find garbage to their taste; but not, we repeat, from any Master's hand.[54]

Ironically, then, the novelist who in 1890 stated that realism – in the sense of copying or reporting 'inventorially' – is not art, was to be tarred with the same brush as Zola, whose detailed portrayal of sordid or disgusting realities revolted Victorian sensibilities. Earlier in his career reviewers were baffled rather than scandalized by the curiously mixed forms and techniques of Hardy. His pedantic usages, idiosyncratic turns of phrase, and elaborate sentence structures were compared to those of Meredith, who had been his first literary adviser as reader for Chapman and Hall. I have quoted Meredith's comment that 'life, we know too well, is not a Comedy, but something strangely mixed', and the description of *The Ordeal of Richard Feverel* as a 'medley' (see p. 140, 148 above). Hardy the realist is our finest country novelist, closely observing, regretting the decline of rural communities in the late nineteenth century but without idealizing the old ways; Hardy the connoisseur of the grotesque, much of whose first published novel, *Desperate Remedies* (1871), has been described as unmistakably Gothic,[55] constructed plots whose incongruities and coincidences are often outrageously sensational. It is his attempt to conflate the realistic and the sensational, as Trollope considered a good novelist should, that so often produces in his novels the roughness, crudity, or unevenness for which he has always been criticized. Yet it is also a key to his greatness.

Both sides of Hardy were discussed by contemporary reviewers of *Far from the Madding Crowd* (1874). R. H. Hutton commented that the novel in relation to many of the scenes it describes was 'the nearest equivalent to actual experience which a great many of us are ever likely to boast of', and particularly admired the 'details of the farming and the sheep-keeping, of the labouring, the feasting, and the mourning'.[56] These are not merely set pieces, however, or purple passages suitable for an anthology. For example, one of his finest passages of description, that of 'The Great Barn and the Sheep-shearers' (22), substantiates one of the novel's central themes – 'In comparison with cities, Weatherbury was immutable. The citizen's *Then* is the rustic's *Now*' – and thus prepares the ground for the rivalry between Sergeant Troy and Shepherd Oak. Unlike Richard Jefferies, whose abilities as a *novelist* have recently been overrated,[57] Hardy rarely digresses in his descriptions, which serve his larger purposes. (Indeed, the hand of the careful craftsman is all to active in *Far from the Madding Crowd*.)

Another, unnamed reviewer, argued that in this novel 'sensationalism is all in all', and that even the career of Gabriel Oak, its least sensational major character, is traced through a series of 'sensational scenes'.[58] But it is Troy, of course, whose swagger smacks of the melodrama and the sensation novel, in his display of swordsmanship (28), his disappearance (47), and his reappearance at Boldwood's farm (53). It is also Troy, the intruder figure, who is associated with Hardy's most curious descriptive passage in the novel. Hardy's strange perspectives, mixed forms, and ironic juxtapositions reflect a sensibility trained in the restoration of Gothic churches. As Troy sleeps in the porch of Weatherbury church, having planted flowers in Fanny Robin's grave, Hardy describes with the objectivity of an architect the gargoyles on the tower and the water that cascades from one of them: 'There was, so to speak, that symmetry in their distortion which is less the characteristic of British than of continental grotesques of the period'; 'The base of the liquid parabola has come forward from the wall' (46). The cool precision works against both the 'horrible' nature of the gargoyle and the highly charged emotional scene which follows, when Troy wakes to find that the flowers have been washed away. Again, detailed description is more than a digression or a whimsical piece of padding: it has a specific function in Hardy's art of the incongruous.

The cold eye of the observer, a familiar figure in Hardy, records the futility of Troy's actions. In Hardy's major tragic novels – *The Return of the Native* (1878), *The Mayor of Casterbridge* (1886), *The Woodlanders* (1886–87), *Tess of the d'Urbervilles*, and *Jude the Obscure* – the vanity of human wishes in a universe that fluctuates between neutrality and malevolence is revealed in his plots, in his handling of time and setting, and in his treatment of what he calls the real and the ideal, a theme we have also encountered in George Eliot. Let us first consider *The Return*, *The Mayor*, and *The Woodlanders*.

Far from the Madding Crowd, a novel which seemed increasingly attractive to Victorian reviewers as Hardy's later and more controversial fiction was published, is now generally considered to be his first major achievement. *The Return of the Native* is a far more ambitious work, and marks a turning-point in his career. The novel's setting on Egdon Heath, a pagan place where the people rarely go to church (I. 10), and Clym Yeobright's speech over the bodies of Eustacia and Wildeve – 'But I cannot die. Those who ought to have lived lie dead; and here am I alive!' (V. 9) – suggest that the last paragraph of the 1895 Preface is more than a piece of Hardyesque whimsy: 'It is pleasant to dream that some spot in the extensive tract whose south-western quarter is here described, may be the heath of that traditionary King of Wessex – Lear.' Dozens of references to classical mythology and the Bible, and especially the Promethean references and quotations from the Book of Job, evoke other ancient sources and models. The local plotting of the novel thus unfolds against a huge backcloth. The forces of the Greek tragedians are marshalled in a weekly serial in an illustrated family magazine – the *Graphic*. It is hardly surprising that the effect is sometimes like grand opera performed in a village hall.

Hardy's grandiose literary references have been criticized as mere pretentious display, the kind of thing expected of an autodidact uncertain of his own powers and wishing to get on terms with the better educated reader. There is some truth in this analysis, although Hardy justly resented being thought of as an autodidact. More significantly, the principal effect of, say, the Promethean references, is to make Clym seem a pathetically limited nineteenth-century man (the product of Matthew Arnold's compromise with Christianity[59]), and thus a Victorian precursor of the twentieth-century anti-hero. In Eustacia's eyes his decline from diamond-seller to teacher to furze-cutter – a modern version of the old tragic fall – is simply absurd. Even when she is first drawn to Blooms-End by the curiosity which later impels her to take part in the mumming, she is aware of the incongruity of his imminent arrival: 'This was the obscure, removed spot to which was about to return a man whose latter life had been passed in the French capital – the centre and vortex of the fashionable world' (II. 1). Eustacia's dream in marrying him is to persuade him to return to Paris (IV. 1), and their marriage founders on this ambition. (Ironically, Wildeve is involuntarily in a position to gratify her 'Parisian desires' when he inherits a fortune and plans to spend some time there, VI. 8.) For Clym, however, Paris was the centre and vortex of intellectual life, and he returns to Egdon Heath with ideals based on 'ethical systems popular at the time', possibly a combination of Fourier, Saint-Simon, and Comte.[60]

Hardy's importing of the modern into the primordial heath, an instance of his disproportioning, is a new dimension in his treatment of Wessex. His 'idiosyncratic mode of regard' is also more sophisticated in *The Return*, as the many references to artists suggest. Figures round a bonfire at night, for example, are said to be 'drawn with Düreresque vigour and dash': 'All was unstable. . . . Shadowy eye-sockets, deep as those of a death's head, suddenly turned into pits of lustre: a lantern-jaw was cavernous, then it was shiny' (I. 3). In a remarkable passage at the beginning of the third Book ('The Fascination'), Hardy focuses upon Clym's face:

In Clym Yeobright's face could be dimly seen the typical countenance of the future. Should there be a classic period to art hereafter, its Pheidias may produce such faces. The view of life as a thing to be put up with, replacing that zest for existence which was so intense in early civilizations, must ultimately enter so thoroughly into the constitution of the advanced races that its facial expression will become accepted as a new artistic departure. People already feel that a man who lives without disturbing a curve of feature, or setting a mark of mental concern anywhere upon himself, is too far removed from modern perceptiveness to be a modern type.
Physically beautiful men – the glory of the race when it was young – are almost an anachronism now; and we may wonder whether, at some time or other, physically beautiful women may not be an anachronism likewise.

Strange as Hardy's speculations are, they represent an advance intellectually on Charlotte Brontë's references to phrenology and Dickens's interest in mesmerism. The idea of a characteristic facial expression of the future looks forward to Little Father Time in *Jude the Obscure* (v. 3), and the paragraph which follows sets the tone for Hardy's tragic fiction in general:

The truth seems to be that a long line of disillusive centuries has permanently displaced the Hellenic idea of life, or whatever it may be called. What the Greeks only suspected we know well; what their Aeschylus imagined our nursery children feel. That old-fashioned revelling in the general situation grows less and less possible as we uncover the defects of natural laws, and see the quandary that man is in by their operation.

Nineteenth-century science uncovered laws of evolution which operate over hundreds of thousands of years. In his own rapid mental development Clym is far in advance of any gradual, scarcely discernible development on Egdon Heath: 'The rural world was not ripe for him. A man should be only partially before his time: to be completely to the vanguard in aspirations is fatal to fame' (iii. 2). Those who 'aspire' on the heath – Clym, Wildeve, Eustacia – are brought low, while the slow rustics who see the folly of Clym's educational schemes, and whose ambitions are as limited as their experience, survive. Whereas Swithin St Cleeve peers up a telescope at the heavens, Clym's failing eyesight reduces his daily life as a humble furze-cutter to the 'microscopic', a 'circuit of a few feet from his person' (iv. 2). Eustacia, the 'raw material of a divinity' (i. 7) despairs at her lot and commits suicide. Always aspiring towards an ideal far above the mundane reality of Egdon, she is destroyed by the 'defects of natural laws'. As Wildeve says to Thomasin Yeobright, who is disappointed that their courtship is not 'pretty and sweet', as in a romance: 'Yes, real life is never at all like that' (i. 5).

The endings of Hardy's tragic novels reflect the conflict between his vision and the conventions of Victorian fiction. In the Wessex (1912) edition of *The Return of the Native* he added a note to explain that he had changed his original plan for Thomasin to remain a widow at the end of the novel only because of 'certain circumstances of serial publication', and hinted strongly that the original, 'more consistent' ending was 'the true one' (VI. 3). His intentions, both in the different endings and in the note, have been much discussed. Even if he was later unhappy with the ending we have, however, he succeeded brilliantly in making Diggory Venn's courtship of Thomasin by moonlight and his stooping movements on the green (VI. 1) an unwitting parody of Clym. Thomasin's no-nonsense attitude towards Venn also adds to one's sense of loss. The softened ending is thus ambiguously mixed. In the tragic endings of *The Mayor of Casterbridge* and *The Woodlanders* Hardy achieves quite different effects. In the former novel, Elizabeth-Jane's good fortune in marrying the prosperous Farfrae does not blind her to the fact that this unbroken tranquillity has been accorded to one whose youth 'seemed to teach that happiness was but the occasional episode in a general drama of pain' (45). The novel's full title – *The Life and Death of The Mayor of Casterbridge: A Story of a Man of Character* – announces its focus on the tragic hero, whose selling of his wife, an example of 'the wilful hostilities of mankind' (1), and the inexorable nemesis which eventually destroys him, demonstrate Novalis's idea that 'Character is Fate' (17). This profoundly moral tragic plan is, however, embodied in a plot which one contemporary reviewer considered to be too improbable.[61] Henchard's luck is all bad luck, and his own comment – 'It never rains but it pours!' (10) – proves to be prophetic when a change in the weather later ruins him and makes Farfrae's fortune (27). Hardy's piling of unlucky chance upon unlucky chance, however, and of coincidence upon coincidence, is a disproportioning which reveals the 'features that matter' in the character of Henchard.

The ending of *The Woodlanders* is even darker than that of *The Mayor*. The novel has no tragic hero, and the pain of existence is endured by several members of the community rather than focused in an individual. In the final chapter Melbury predicts that his son-in-law, Fitzpiers, is bound to be unfaithful to Grace again: 'It's a forlorn hope for her; and God knows how it will end!' (48). As he and his men return to Little Hintock by moonlight, they pass Marty South, who walks to the churchyard and the 'last bed of Giles Winterbourne', where she can at last be his sole and faithful lover. As in *The Mayor*, the tight plotting of *The Woodlanders* is achieved through the careful accumulation of small events, often trivial in themselves but fateful in combination. Plotting of this kind is most effective in a highly localized setting. Hardy himself explained his broad strategy in this respect in the general preface to the Wessex (1912) edition of his works:

It has sometimes been conceived of novels that evolve their action on a circumscribed scene – as do many (though not all) of these – that they cannot be so inclusive in their exhibition of human nature as novels wherein the scenes cover large

extents of country, in which events figure amid towns and
cities, even wander over the four quarters of the globe. I am
not concerned to argue this point further than to suggest that
the conception is an untrue one in respect of the elementary
passions. But I would state that the geographical limits of the
stage here trodden were not absolutely forced upon the writer
by circumstances; he forced them upon himself from
judgment. I considered that our magnificent heritage from the
Greeks in dramatic literature found sufficient room for a large
proportion of its action in an extent of their country not much
larger than the half-dozen counties here reunited under the old
name of Wessex, that the domestic throbbed in Wessex nooks
with as much intensity as in the palaces of Europe, and that,
anyhow, there was quite enough human nature in Wessex for
one man's literary purpose.

Hardy's specific tactic in *The Return, The Mayor,* and *The Woodlanders,*
however, is to concentrate on a small area within the circumscribed scene
of Wessex. In *The Return* he had as it were mapped the relationships between his characters by tracing the intersections of their routes between
Egdon locations: Bloom's-End, The Quiet Woman, Mistover, Rainbar-
row. In *The Mayor* and *The Woodlanders* domestic emotions throb intensely
within narrower limits still, where the daily round of work and leisure is
shaped by the demands of specialized trades – corn and hay in Casterbridge,
timber in Little Hintock – and where everybody's movements are observed
by his or her neighbours.

Greek tragedy and Aristotelian tragic theory had a profound influence
on Hardy's major novels,[62] and he no doubt had the tragedians in mind
when he referred to the dramatic literature of the Greeks in the general
preface. Shakespeare's tragedies, however, were also a major source, and
several parallels between Henchard and King Lear in *The Mayor* suggest
that Hardy's imagination was still working on the play he read in 1876
before writing *The Return of the Native.* When only Elizabeth-Jane is left
to Henchard, he loses her to Newson and Farfrae, and his wedding-present
of a goldfinch in a birdcage – 'the little creature's wire prison' (44) – calls
to mind Lear's speech to Cordelia: 'Come, let's away to prison;/We two
alone will sing like birds i' th' cage' (v. 3. 8–9). He dies in a hovel on
Egdon Heath, attended only by Whittle, whom he calls 'a poor fond fool'
(45).[63] In its organization, however, and claustrophobic atmosphere, *The
Mayor* is closer to *Othello* than to *Lear.*

After the opening few chapters Hardy homes in upon Casterbridge, the
scene of Henchard's rise and fall. Looking down from a hill within a mile
of the town, Elizabeth-Jane describes it as 'huddled all together', and 'shut
in by a square wall of trees' (4). The place is 'compact as a box of domi-
noes'. Hardy's descriptions of different areas within the town, and of buildings and rooms within buildings, reinforce a sense of enclosure.
Respectable Casterbridge journeymen, for example, form a snug circle in
the Three Mariners inn after church every Sunday afternoon, when each

takes a half-pint of liquor. Outside and above the ring of forty cups on the great oak table 'came a circle of forty smoke-jets from forty clay pipes; outside the pipes the countenances of the forty church-goers, supported at the back by a circle of forty chairs' (33). This orderly pub contrasts with Peter's Finger in the disorderly but tight-knit Mixen Lane district of Casterbridge (36), from where the fatal skimmity-ride processes to the centre of the town and past Lucetta's balcony (39). Henchard's crucial meetings with Susan and Lucetta take place in the Ring at Casterbridge, the Roman amphitheatre whose associations with the games, and with hangings and burnings add to its gloom at dusk (11, 35). A large square, called Bull Stake, has the town stocks in a corner and a stone post in the centre, where oxen used to be baited with dogs before going to slaughter (27). People and events press in upon Henchard, until he is driven from his house at the heart of the town, and eventually dies far from its walls.

Before his death, however, his return to Weydon-Priors as an act of penance brings back thoughts of Elizabeth-Jane and thus of Casterbridge: 'Out of this it happened that the centrifugal tendency imparted by weariness of the world was counteracted by the centripetal influence of his love for his stepdaughter' (44). His wanderings as a hay-trusser become 'part of a circle' of which Casterbridge forms the centre, and eventually he returns there for the wedding-day before his final exile and death. Movement in *The Mayor*, as in Greek tragedy, tends to be centripetal. Susan's return to Wessex (3) re-enacts the journey described in the opening pages of the novel. Farfrae, who arrives in Casterbridge on the same day as Susan (6), stands at the very boundary of the town, ready to travel on to America, when Henchard persuades him to return to his home (9). Newson's return to Wessex late in the novel (41) applies the final turn of the screw.

Hardy's treatment of time in the novel is also circular, or rather cyclic, and has been analysed in relation to his comments on Comte's 'looped orbit', a forward and thus progressive cyclic movement of history.[64] When Susan returns to the fair at Weydon-Priors, certain mechanical improvements have been made to the roundabouts and high-fliers, but the real business of the fair has considerably dwindled (3). In the same way that Hardy's passing reference to Bull Stake presents us with a vivid emblem of Henchard's plight, so his brief description of the fair embodies one of the novel's main themes, namely the displacement of Henchard's old rule-of-thumb methods by Farfrae's mechanical business methods and new machinery. On Comte's model of the looped orbit, Farfrae traces the same track as Henchard as he takes over the business, the house, Lucetta, Elizabeth-Jane, and the mayorality, always progressing towards a higher point than that reached by Henchard. The extended narrative form of the novel provides a suitable vehicle for such a progression. In the loss felt in Henchard's fall, however, and in the smallness of any 'improvements' in Casterbridge when viewed *sub specie aeternitatis*, against the 'past-marked prospect' in front of Susan's cottage (13) or from the Roman graves under the town's fields and gardens (11), Hardy reminds his reader of the larger perspectives of tragedy.

As in *The Return* and *The Mayor*, *The Woodlanders* opens on a road, so that the reader, like the traveller, approaches the site of the novel's main action as if from a (neutral) distance. The traveller in this instance is no countryman, but the barber, Percomb, who hopes to persuade Marty South to sell him her hair. The incongruity of the interview between the finically dressed Percomb and Marty, who wears a leather apron and a leather glove much too large for her, is characteristic of Hardy (2). So too is his use of the hair later in the novel, when Marty's revelation to Fitzpiers that she was the original owner of Mrs Charmond's 'supplementary locks' (34) eventually causes the quarrel between the lovers, and thus, indirectly, Felice Charmond's death (43). The hair, like Desdemona's handkerchief, has an influence on people's lives which is out of all proportion to its size and intrinsic significance. Similar kinds of disproportioning in the novel include the incident in the lane when, 'as fate would have it', Giles Winterbourne is in no mood to be polite to Felice, whose carriage blocks the way of the timber waggon (13). Ironically, Giles's cutting down of the tall elm, on Fitzpiers's instructions, kills rather than cures John South, thus depriving Giles of his tenancies (13–15); and Felice is not minded to help him by 'disturbing the natural course of things, particularly as she contemplates pulling the houses down' (15). Giles thus loses Grace to Fitzpiers. The demolition of his boyhood home causes Felice to crash her phaeton, which in turn brings Fitzpiers to her boudoir (26). 'Predestination' – the word is Fitzpiers's – is a grim humorist in Hardy.

Fitzpiers's visit to Hintock House in fact renews a relationship which died in the bud years earlier and far from Hintock, in Heidelberg. These outsider figures – a doctor who reads metaphysics, examines his dead patient's brains under a microscope, and is bad with horses, and a former actress who smokes cigarettes, wears another woman's hair, and probably could not distinguish one species of tree from another – have little contact with the organic world of the woodlands. Their liaison serves as ironic commentary on the fact that Giles is the 'natural' husband for Grace Melbury. As soon as Fitzpiers has disappeared over the horizon, riding to see Felice at Middleton Abbey, Grace sees Giles coming towards her with two horses and a cider-apparatus:

> He looked and smelt like Autumn's very brother, his face being sunburnt to wheat-colour, his eyes blue as corn-flowers, his sleeves and leggings dyed with fruit-stains, his hands clammy with the sweet juice of apples, his hat sprinkled with pips, and everywhere about him that atmosphere of cider which at its first return each season has such an indescribable fascination for those who have been born and bred among the orchards. Her heart rose from its late sadness like a released bough; her senses revelled in the sudden lapse back to Nature unadorned. The consciousness of having to be genteel because of her husband's profession, the veneer of artificiality which she had acquired at the fashionable schools, were thrown off, and she became the crude country girl of her latent early instincts. (28)

Circumstances and social laws, however, will not allow the couple to fulfil their natural roles. When Giles later kisses Grace passionately, knowing that she cannot divorce Fitzpiers, he is acutely conscious of committing a 'social sin' (39). Yet the touching innocence of Grace's chaste concealment in One-Chimney Hut, with Giles sleeping outside, causes his death (43).

Giles's death and Grace's reconciliation with a husband whose 'nature' is to betray her corroborates Fitzpiers's view that 'sorrow and sickness of heart' are 'the end of all love, according to Nature's law' (27). Hardy's interpretation of nature's laws is the main source of the profound pessimism in *The Woodlanders*. Grace's revelling in the 'sudden lapse back to Nature unadorned' is predicated on an idea of benign nature which the novel denies. Far from offering an idyllic contrast to the artificialities of Felice and Fitzpiers, the life of the woodlanders, as of the woodlands, reveals the operation of Darwinian natural laws. In the third chapter of *The Origin of Species* (1859),[65] Darwin deduces a 'corollary of the highest importance' from his remarks on the 'struggle for life' being most severe between individuals and varieties of the same species: 'that the structure of every organic being is related, in the most essential yet often hidden manner, to that of all the other organic beings, with which it comes into competition for food or residence, or from which it has to escape, or on which it preys'. In *Under the Greenwood Tree* (1872) 'quaint tufts of fungi' merely add decoration to the ancient tree of the novel's title, under which the nuptial celebrations are held (v. 2). The 'oozing lumps of fleshy fungi', like 'the rotten liver and lungs of some colossal animal', which impede Eustacia's progress on the night of her death, are simply grotesque features of a landscape as nightmarish as Browning's in 'Childe Roland' (*The Return*, v. 7). In *The Woodlanders*, however, Hardy looks much more closely at the trees on which 'lobes of fungus' grow like lungs: 'Here, as everywhere, the Unfulfilled Intention, which makes life what it is, was as obvious as it could be among the depraved crowds of a city slum. The leaf was deformed, the curve was crippled, the taper was interrupted; the lichen ate the vigour of the stalk, and the ivy slowly strangled to death the promising sapling' (7). Whereas Gissing found grounds for pessimism in the nether world of the East End, Hardy found similar grounds in the very setting to which philanthropists might have wished to remove the slum-dweller.

Melbury and Grace pass these trees on the way to a timber auction, where the woodland men carry curious walking-sticks which exhibit 'monstrosities of vegetation, the chief being corkscrew shapes in black and white thorn, brought to that pattern by the slow torture of an encircling woodbine during their growth, as the Chinese have been said to mould human beings into grotesque toys by continued compression in infancy'. Whereas Darwin ends his chapter on the struggle for life with consolation in the belief that 'the war of nature is not incessant, that no fear is felt, that death is generally prompt, and that the vigorous, the healthy, and the happy survive and multiply', Hardy dwells on slow strangulation and torture. Grace Melbury's life is twisted and retwisted by the vagaries of her meddling father, who educates her in an attempt to lift her out of the world of the woodlands and encourages her to marry well, before regretting his attempts at artificial 'improvement'. Cut off from a state of innocence, or from the unthinking animal vigour of a Suke Damson, Grace becomes a victim of both nature's and society's laws. Felice Charmond complains that 'women are always carried about like corks upon the waves of masculine desires' (26). Grace Melbury proves the point.

Hardy's finest study of a victim of masculine desires is of course Tess Durbeyfield. Each of Tess's journeys is in some way a response to the behaviour of men: first her father, and later her two lovers, Alec d'Urberville and Angel Clare, who, like Rochester and Rivers in *Jane Eyre*, exert upon her equal and opposite pressures. But whereas Jane has a strong sense of providential guidance, refuses to become Rochester's mistress, and finally lands in the safe harbour of an idealized marriage, Tess is resigned to a cruel fate, and dies on the gallows: '"Justice" was done, and the President of the Immortals (in Aeschylean phrase) had ended his sport with Tess. And the d'Urberville knights and dames slept on in their tombs unknowing' (59).[66] The President of the Immortals is masculine. So too are the gods who in Gloucester's words (quoted in the preface to the fifth and later editions of *Tess*) 'kill us for their sport' (*King Lear*, IV. 1. 37). Hardy's references to the d'Urberville knights at the end of the novel recall to mind not only the groundwork of the plot – Jack Durbeyfield's obsession with his ancestry and Alec d'Urberville's assumed family name – but also Hardy's crucial gloss on Tess's 'seduction': 'Doubtless some of Tess d'Urberville's mailed ancestors rollicking home from a fray had dealt the same measure even more ruthlessly towards peasant girls of their time' (11). Riding to a fray and raping peasant girls are traditional forms of masculine 'sport', or hunting, and Tess, herself seduced in The Chase, is associated with hunted animals. On her way to Flintcombe Ash, for example, it is the unwelcome attentions of a 'well-to-do boor' which drive her into the plantation where she finds dead and dying pheasant dabbled with blood, the prey of a (male) shooting-party (41). Surrounded by men who have come to arrest her at Stonehenge, she sleeps on, like a small, innocent animal: 'her breathing now was quick and small, like that of a lesser creature than a woman' (58).

Published almost forty years after Elizabeth Gaskell's *Ruth*, which in its day had been hailed as a 'brave book' by Charlotte Brontë, *Tess* was itself highly controversial, especially in its famous sub-title: 'A Pure Woman'. But Hardy's treatment of marriage and the divorce laws in *Jude* roused even more passionate indignation in reviewers such as Margaret Oliphant, whom I quoted earlier. For Jude, the Church's teaching on sexual love seems to be against nature, and he gives up the idea of training for the ministry (IV. 3). When both Sue's and Jude's divorces have been made absolute, Sue explains that she wants to remain his lover, and would begin to be afraid of him the moment she was 'licensed to be loved on the premises' by him as a wife (V. 1). Her subsequent remarriage to Phillotson draws this memorable comment from old Mrs Edlin: 'Weddings be funerals 'a b'lieve nowadays. Fifty-five years ago, come Fall, since my man and I married! Times have changed since then!' (VI. 9).

Mrs Edlin's remarks sum up the contrast between the early Hardy of *Under the Greenwood Tree* and the Hardy of *Jude the Obscure*. The old rural world of community and shared values has given way to a new world of association and acts of exchange (cf. p. 112 above), epitomized in Sue's fear of being licensed to have sex. We have already seen the transitional phases, in Hardy's novels written between two worlds. The breakdown, for example, of a shared sense of reality in the tragic protagonists of *The Return of the Native* and *The Woodlanders* reflects a lack of correspondence between social forms and individual feelings. The instability of Hardy's central characters becomes critical in *Tess*, where sudden changes in Alec and Angel – both half-men – eventually destroy the heroine-victim. Finally, in *Jude*, the novel which seems from our perspective to signal the end of Victorian fiction, the alienation of the protagonist is further intensified. For whereas in Hardy's earlier novels the outsider/intruder figure is generally an antagonist who disrupts the lives of the protagonists in a small community, Jude is both protagonist and outsider – a would-be intruder into the closed world of Christminster who lives and dies in the obscurity of the intellectual artisan. Unlike Tess, whose nadir as an agricultural worker at Flintcombe Ash contrasts with the zenith of Talbothays earlier in the novel, Jude *begins* his working life scaring rooks for a bullying farmer in a 'meanly utilitarian' field, in which the ancient communal life of the kind Tess knew at Marlott seems to have been ploughed under (I. 2). In both novels, however, movement tends to be centrifugal, away from the birthplace; and even those who remain behind no longer represent fixed points in a comparatively stable world. Tess's mother is forced to move from her cottage at a time when migration and depopulation are becoming common features of country life (51); and Jude's Aunt Drusilla is buried in 'new ground, quite away from her ancestors' (IV. 2).

Rootlessness in these last novels contributes to what Angel Clare in *Tess* calls 'the ache of modernism', when he learns that Tess sees all tomorrows as 'very fierce and cruel', and shares with him a fear of 'life in general' (19). Jude's son, Little Father Time, represents a new generation in his Job-like question: 'I ought not to be born, ought I?' (VI. 1). The doctor who examines his corpse says that the boy represents 'the beginning of the coming universal wish not to live' (VI. 2). Hardy's art of disproportioning has developed from a wry sense of life's little ironies and a fascination with the grotesque to a deeply pessimistic vision, reflected in repetitive plots which allow no forward movement or development in his characters. His darkening vision, then, of universal pain and alienation, his sense of a fragmenting society, his portrayal of women, and especially of Sue Brideshead – to whom Jude exclaims 'How modern you are!' (III. 1) – all suggest that a discussion of *Tess* and *Jude* makes a fitting coda to a study of English fiction of the period 1830–90, as these novels point forward to twentieth-century themes.

In other respects, however, both novels firmly belong to our period. The quirks of fate and sensational effects in *Tess* – the letter hidden under the carpet (33), the gigantic ace of hearts formed by Alec's blood on the boarding-house ceiling (56), and so on – are aspects of Hardy's Victorianism. Although *Jude* is aggressively modern in its sombreness and its grim vision of human life, Hardy's idea, for example, that marriage is merely a means of licensing sex is as much a reflection of his own unattractive temperament as of his response to *early* nineteenth-century radical thought; it hardly represents a startling new development. In other respects, too, the themes of *Tess* and *Jude* were familiar to the reader of his earlier work and of his Victorian precursors. Take, for example, the central idea of change and development in *Tess of the d'Urbervilles*. Hardy deploys a wide range of concepts of and terms for change: Protean change, Ovidian metamorphosis, spiritual transfiguration, Evangelical conversion, and biological transmutation. In each case, however, his real interest is in sudden change rather than slow evolution. Following the birth and death of little Sorrow, and Tess's speculation on her own death-day, Hardy writes: 'Almost at a leap Tess thus changed from simple girl to complex woman' (15). Like intimations of mortality, sex takes Hardy's characters by surprise, either passively, as in Tess's case, or actively, as when Jude is provoked by Arabella to rush up the stairs after her (I. 8).

D. H. Lawrence, in his typically energetic 'Study of Thomas Hardy', wrote of Hardy's 'people of Wessex' always 'bursting *suddenly* out of bud and taking a wild flight into flower, always shooting *suddenly* out of a tight convention, a tight, hide-bound cabbage state into something quite madly personal' (my emphasis).[67] For Lawrence, Hardy's heroes and heroines are 'struggling hard to come into being', and the 'first and chiefest factor is the struggle into love and the struggle with love'. Lawrence wrote his 'Study' in 1914, the year which marked the end of an era in European history and culture, and, in his own career, the transition from the novel of the 'old stable *ego* – of the character' to the exploration, in *The Rainbow*, of 'another *ego*, according to whose action the individual is unrecognisable, and passes through, as it were, allotropic states which it needs a deeper sense than any we've been used to exercise, to discover are states of the same single radically unchanged element'.[68] The ten-year gestation of Joyce's *Portrait of the Artist as a Young Man* ended in 1914, also the year in which he published *Dubliners*. In 1914, at the age of seventy-three, Hardy married his literary assistant and published *Satires of Circumstance*, a collection of lyrics which included the great 'Poems of 1912–13', written after the death of Emma, his first wife. After *Jude* he had turned as a writer from novels of Character and Circumstance – his own description, and one which would also serve for much of the Victorian fiction examined in this book – to poetry in which he could explore the ironies of the inner life: of emotion, and the conscious and unconscious mind, and the psychology of love and bereavement, loss and compensation for loss. It was for other writers of the early twentieth century – Joyce, Lawrence, and Woolf among them – to explore similar psychological themes in new, experimental forms of English prose fiction.

Notes

1. Gail Cunningham, *The New Woman and the Victorian Novel* (London, 1978), p. 4.

2. Cunningham, pp. 6–7.

3. Rider Haggard, 'About Fiction', *Contemporary Review*, 51 (1887), 172–80 (p. 173).

4. See Walter Allen, *The English Novel: A Short Critical History* (1954; repr. Harmondsworth, 1958), p. 261; Richard D. Altick, *The English Common Reader: A Social History of the Mass Reading Public, 1800–1900* (1957; repr. Chicago and London, 1963).

5. Walter Besant, *The Art of Fiction: A Lecture Delivered at the Royal Institution* (London, 1884), p. 38.

6. *Into Unknown England, 1866–1913: Selections from the Social Explorers*, edited by Peter Keating (Glasgow, 1976), p. 150.

7. Adrian Poole, *Gissing in Context* (London, 1975), pp. 8–9.

8. See Kenneth Graham, *English Criticism of the Novel, 1865–1900* (Oxford, 1965), pp. 104–5.

9. See Graham, pp. 5–12, *et passim*.

10. Henry James, *Selected Literary Criticism*, edited by Morris Shapira (1963; repr. Harmondsworth, 1968), pp. 80, 81, 85.

11. Besant, *The Art of Fiction*, pp. 8–9.

12. *Gissing: The Critical Heritage*, edited by Pierre Coustillas and Colin Partridge, Critical Heritage series, edited by B. C. Southam (London and Boston, 1972), p. 118.

13. Haggard, *About Fiction*, p. 176.

14. *Gissing: The Critical Heritage*, p. 142.

15. *Gissing: The Critical Heritage*, p. 73.

16. Janet Egleson Dunleavy, *George Moore: The Artist's Vision, The Storyteller's Art* (Lewisburg, 1973), pp. 68, 78.

17. P. J. Keating, *The Working Classes in Victorian Fiction* (London, 1971), p. 134.

18. Joseph Hone, *The Life of George Moore* (London, 1936), p. 195.

19. Hall Caine, 'The New Watchwords of Fiction', *Contemporary Review*, 57(1890), 479–88 (p. 479).

20. See Graham, *English Criticism of the Novel*, p. 62; also pp. 61–70 on 'The Rise of Romance'.

21. Caine, 'The New Watchwords of Fiction', pp. 488, 481.

22. Martin Green, *Dreams of Adventure, Deeds of Empire* (London and Henley, 1980), pp. 3, 214, 220.

23. Robert Louis Stevenson, 'A Humble Remonstrance', *Longman's Magazine*, 5(1884–85), 139–47 (pp. 143–4).

24. See Robert Louis Stevenson, 'A Gossip on Romance', *Longman's Magazine*, 1(1882–83), 69–79.

25. See F. R. Leavis, *The Great Tradition: George Eliot, Henry James, Joseph Conrad* (1948; repr. Harmondsworth, 1962).

26. Stevenson, 'A Gossip on Romance', pp. 77, 69.

27. Helen Gardner, *In Defence of the Imagination*, Charles Eliot Norton Lectures 1979–1980 (Oxford, 1982), p. 43.

28. Peter Berresford Ellis, *H. Rider Haggard: A Voice from the Infinite* (London and Henley, 1978), p. 113.

29. H. G. Wells's literary career began in the 1890s and thus beyond the scope of this study. His Utopian story *The Time Machine* (1895), whose central character is the 'Time Traveller', was of course a seminal work of science fiction.

30. For an interesting contrast to Morris's vision see Richard Jefferies's *After London; or, Wild England* (1885) in which, following the destruction of all towns and cities, a society develops which exhibits some of the worst features of medieval serfdom and autocratic power.

31. Patrick Brantlinger, ' "News from Nowhere": Morris's Socialist Anti-Novel', *Victorian Studies*, 19(1975–76), 35–49 (pp. 38, 35).

32. Patrick Brantlinger describes *News from Nowhere* as 'the best fictional vision of the future according to Marxism in English' (p. 39). Jack Lindsay makes similar claims, and considers the work to be even more 'relevant' today than it was in the nineteenth century: *William Morris: His Life and Work* (London, 1975), pp. 383–6.

33. See, for example, Graham Hough, *The Last Romantics* (1947; repr. London and New York, 1961), p 154.

34. W. E. Gladstone, *Studies Subsidiary to the Works of Bishop Butler* (Oxford, 1896), p. 206; quoted in Geoffrey Rowell, *Hell and the Victorians* (Oxford, 1974), p. 212.

35. P. J. Keating, *The Working Classes in Victorian Fiction*, p. 59, and *Into Unknown England*, ed. Keating, pp. 20–2.

36. See John Halperin, *Gissing: A Life in Books* (Oxford, 1982), p. 145.

37. George Gissing, *Charles Dickens: A Critical Study* (1904; repr. St Clair Shores, Michigan, 1972), p. 90.

38. See Jacob Korg, *George Gissing: A Critical Biography* (London, 1965), Chapter 8; Poole, *op. cit.*, Chapter 7; Cunningham, *op. cit.*, Chapter 4.

39. See Korg, *George Gissing*, p. 66.

40. See Poole, *Gissing in Context*, p. 106.

41. *Gissing: The Critical Heritage*, p. 530.

42. See J. C. Furnas, *Voyage to Windward: The Life of Robert Louis Stevenson* (London, 1952), plate facing p. 368.

43. Stevenson, 'A Gossip on Romance', p. 70.

44. Stevenson, 'A Humble Remonstrance', p. 147.

45. Stevenson, 'A Humble Remonstrance', pp. 139, 147.

46. Stevenson, 'A Gossip on Romance', pp. 77, 79.

47. Stevenson, 'A Humble Remonstrance', pp. 142–3.

48. Jenni Calder, *RLS: A Life Story* (London, 1980), p. 189.

49. David Daiches, *Stevenson and the Art of Fiction* (New York, 1951), p. 12; Douglas Gifford, 'Stevenson and Scottish Fiction: The Importance of *The Master of Ballantrae*', in *Stevenson and Victorian Scotland*, edited by Jenni Calder (Edinburgh, 1981), pp. 62–87 (p. 71).

50. Emily Brontë and Stevenson were both influenced by Scott and James Hogg, and both were exposed in childhood to extreme Calvinist doctrines. For detailed comparisons between *The Master* and *Wuthering Heights* see Edwin M. Eigner, *Robert Louis Stevenson and Romantic Tradition* (Princeton, 1966), pp. 171–4, 178, 180, 193.

51. Florence Emily Hardy, *The Life of Thomas Hardy, 1840–1928* (London and New York, 1962), p. 224.

52. *Life of Thomas Hardy*, p. 235.

53. *Thomas Hardy: The Critical Heritage*, edited by R. G. Cox, Critical Heritage series, edited by B. C. Southam (London and New York, 1970), p. 203.

54. *Thomas Hardy: The Critical Heritage*, p. 257.

55. Michael Millgate, *Thomas Hardy: His Career as a Novelist* (London, 1971), p. 31.

56. *Thomas Hardy: The Critical Heritage*, p. 21.

57. In *Amaryllis at the Fair* (1887), for example, the benign authorial narrator often breaks into the slow-moving narrative with a digression. Charming and highly evocative of atmosphere, this beautiful work was originally intended by Jefferies to form 'a series of scenes from country life. . . . The idea of calling it a novel was secondary': Samuel J. Looker and Crichton Porteous, *Richard Jefferies, Man of the Fields: A Biography and Letters* (London, 1964), p. 142.

58. *Thomas Hardy: The Critical Heritage*, p. 33.

59. See, for example, David J. de Laura, '"The Ache of Modernism" in Hardy's Later Novels', *ELH*, 34(1967), 380–99.

60. See de Laura, p. 383; and Dale Kramer, *Thomas Hardy: The Forms of Tragedy* (Detroit and London, 1975), p. 52.

61. *Thomas Hardy: The Critical Heritage*, p. 134.

62. See Jeannette King, *Tragedy in the Victorian Novel: Theory and Practice in the Novels of George Eliot, Thomas Hardy and Henry James* (Cambridge, 1978), p. 99.

63. J. I. M. Stewart comments that Whittle's name is 'phonetically indistinguishable from an archaic English word for a fool' [see *wittol*, *OED*]: *Thomas Hardy: A Critical Biography* (1971), p. 112.

64. See Kramer, *Thomas Hardy*, p. 71.

65. Gillian Beer's excellent study on *Darwin's Plots: Evolutionary Narrative in Darwin, George Eliot and Nineteenth-Century Fiction* (1983) – published after my section on Hardy was completed – includes detailed analysis of Hardy and Darwinism.

66. The serial (*Graphic*) version of the first sentence quoted reads: '"Justice" was done, and Time, the Arch-Satirist, had had *his* joke out with Tess' (my emphasis). See *Tess of the d'Urbervilles*, edited by Juliet Grindle and Simon Gatrell (Oxford, 1983), p. 542.

67. 'Study of Thomas Hardy', in *Phoenix: The Posthumous Papers of D. H. Lawrence*, edited by Edward D. McDonald (London, 1936), p. 410.

68. *The Collected Letters of D. H. Lawrence*, edited by Harry T. Moore, 2 vols (New York, 1962), I, 282.

Chronology

Note: Dates refer to first publication of works, whether in volume or in serial form.
See notes on Individual Authors (pp. 225–57) for further details of novels first
published as serials in magazines.

DATE	WORKS OF FICTION	OTHER WORKS	HISTORICAL/CULTURAL EVENTS
1830	Bulwer *Paul Clifford*	Carlyle *On History* *Fraser's Magazine*, ed. Maginn Lyell *Principles of Geology* (–1833) Tennyson, *Poems, Chiefly Lyrical*	Accession of William IV Grey PM (Whig), November French 'Revolution of July'
1831	Disraeli *The Young Duke* Peacock *Crotchet Castle* Surtees *Jorrocks' Jaunts and* *Jollities* (–1834)	Carlyle *Characteristics*	
1832	Bulwer *Eugene Aram* G. P. R. James, *Henry Masterton* Marryat *Peter Simple* (–1833) H. Martineau *Illustrations of Political* *Economy* (–1834)	Carlyle *Biography* Tennyson *Poems*	Darwin's voyage on *Beagle* (–1836) First Reform Act

DATE	WORKS OF FICTION	OTHER WORKS	HISTORICAL/CULTURAL EVENTS
1833		Browning *Pauline*	Factory Act ('Children's Charter')
		Bulwer *England and the English*	Oxford Movement begins
		Carlyle *Sartor Resartus* (−1834)	
		Newman *et al.* *Tracts for the Times* (−1841)	
1834	Ainsworth *Rookwood*	Taylor *Philip van Artevelde*	Melbourne PM (Whig), July; Peel PM (Cons.), December
	Bulwer *Last Days of Pompeii*		Abolition of slavery in British dominions
			Poor Law Amendment Act
1835	Bulwer *Rienzi*	Browning *Paracelsus*	Melbourne PM (Whig), April
			Fox Talbot's first photographs
1836	Dickens *Sketches by Boz* *Pickwick Papers* (−1837)		First train in London
	Marryat *Mr Midshipman Easy*		
1837	Bulwer *Ernest Maltravers*	Barham *Ingoldsby Legends*	Accession of Queen Victoria (20 June)
	Dickens *Oliver Twist* (−1839)	Browning *Strafford*	
	Lever *Harry Lorrequer*	Carlyle *French Revolution*	
	Thackeray *Yellowplush Correspondence* (−1838)		

DATE	WORKS OF FICTION	OTHER WORKS	HISTORICAL/CULTURAL EVENTS
1838	Bulwer *Alice, or the Mysteries* Dickens *Nicholas Nickleby* (−1839)	Maurice *Kingdom of Christ*	Anti-Corn Law League founded 'People's Charter' issued by Chartists Brunel's *Great Western* crosses Atlantic
1839	Ainsworth *Jack Sheppard* Martineau *Deerbrook* Thackeray *Catherine* (−1840)	Bailey *Festus* Carlyle *Chartism*	First Afghan War Chartist riots Fox Talbot and Daguerre announce rival photographic processes
1840	Ainsworth *Tower of London* *Guy Fawkes* (−1841) Dickens *Master Humphrey's Clock* *Old Curiosity Shop* (−1841) Lever *Charles O'Malley*	Barham *Ingoldsby Legends,* series I Browning *Sordello* Thackeray *Paris Sketch Book*	Marriage of Victoria and Prince Albert Penny Post introduced Houses of Parliament, by Barry and Pugin (−1852)
1841	Ainsworth *Old St Paul's* Dickens *Barnaby Rudge* Marryat *Masterman Ready* (−1842) Thackeray *Samuel Titmarsh and the Great Hoggarty Diamond*	Boucicault *London Assurance* Browning *Pippa Passes* Carlyle *On Heroes* Newman *Tract XC* *Punch* ed. Lemon	Peel PM (Cons.) September
1842	Ainsworth *Windsor Castle* (−1843)	Dickens *American Notes* Tennyson *Poems,* 2 vols	Mines Act Chartist riots Mudie's Lending Library, London, opened

DATE	WORKS OF FICTION	OTHER WORKS	HISTORICAL/CULTURAL EVENTS
1843	Bulwer *Last of the Barons* Dickens *Christmas Carol* *Martin Chuzzlewit* *(−1844)* Surtees *Handley Cross*	Borrow *Bible in Spain* Carlyle *Past and Present* Mill *System of Logic* Ruskin *Modern Painters*, vol I *(−1860)*	Wordsworth Poet Laureate
1844	Dickens *The Chimes* Disraeli *Coningsby* Thackeray *Barry Lyndon*	E. Barrett *Poems* Chambers *Vestiges of Creation* Kinglake *Eothen* Newman *et al.* *Lives of the English Saints* *(−1845)*	Factory Act (working hours restricted)

1845	Dickens
	Cricket on the Hearth
	
	Disraeli
	Sybil
	
	Thackeray
	Diary of Jeames de la Pluche (−1846)
		Carlyle
		Oliver Cromwell
		
		Jerrold
		Mrs Caudle's Curtain Lectures
		
		Newman
		Essay on Development
			Irish potato famine
			Newman's conversion
			  to Roman Catholicism
			Sir John Franklin's
			  expedition in search of
			  the North-West Passage

1846	Bulwer
	Lucretia
	
	Dickens
	Dombey and Son (−1848)
		C., E. and A. Brontë
		Poems
		
		G. Eliot, trans.,
		Strauss's
		Life of Jesus
		
		Lear
		Book of Nonsense
		
		Thackeray
		Snobs of England (−1847)
			Repeal of Corn Laws
			  (Peel)
			Russell PM (Whig),
			  July

DATE	WORKS OF FICTION	OTHER WORKS	HISTORICAL/CULTURAL EVENTS
1847	A. Brontë *Agnes Grey* C. Brontë *Jane Eyre* E. Brontë *Wuthering Heights* Disraeli *Tancred* Thackeray *Vanity Fair* (–1848) Trollope *Macdermots of Ballycloran*	Keble *Sermons* Tennyson *Princess* Thackeray *Punch's Prize Novelists*	Foundation of Communist League
1848	A. Brontë *Tenant of Wildfell Hall* Bulwer *Harold* Gaskell *Mary Barton* C. Kingsley *Yeast* Newman *Loss and Gain* Thackeray *Pendennis* (–1850)	Clough *Bothie of Toper-na- Fuosich* Kingsley *Saint's Tragedy*	Chartist petition Pre-Raphaelite Brotherhood founded Revolution in France
1849	Bulwer *The Caxtons* C. Brontë *Shirley* Dickens *David Copperfield* (–1850) J. A. Froude *Nemesis of Faith*	M. Arnold *Strayed Reveller*, etc. Clough and Burbidge *Ambarvalia* Macaulay *History of England, vols* I–II (–1861) Mayhew *Labour and the Poor* (–1850) Ruskin *Seven Lamps of Architecture*	

DATE	WORKS OF FICTION	OTHER WORKS	HISTORICAL/CULTURAL EVENTS
1850	C. Kingsley *Alton Locke*	Browning *Christmas Eve and Easter Day* Carlyle *Latter-Day Pamphlets* *The Germ* ed. W. M. Rossetti *Household Words* ed. Dickens Tennyson *In Memoriam* Wordsworth *Prelude*	Wordsworth d. Tennyson Poet Laureate Wiseman made Cardinal; Roman Catholic hierarchy restored in England
1851	Borrow *Lavengro* Gaskell *Cranford* (–1853)	Carlyle *Life of Sterling* Meredith *Poems* Ruskin *Stones of Venice*, vol. I (–1853)	Great Exhibition, Hyde Park Louis Napoleon, *coup d'état*
1852	Dickens *Bleak House* (–1853) Thackeray *Henry Esmond*	M. Arnold *Empedocles on Etna*, etc. Newman *University Education* (later *Idea of a University*)	Derby PM (Cons.), February Wellington d. Aberdeen PM (Coalition), December
1853	C. Brontë *Villette* Bulwer *My Novel* Gaskell *Ruth* C. Kingsley *Hypatia* C. Reade *Peg Woffington* *Christie Johnstone*	M. Arnold *Poems* Landor *Last Fruit off an Old Tree* F. D. Maurice *Theological Essays* Thackeray *English Humourists of the Eighteenth Century*	

DATE	WORKS OF FICTION	OTHER WORKS	HISTORICAL/CULTURAL EVENTS
1853	Surtees *Mr Sponge's Sporting Tour* Thackeray *The Newcomes* (−1855) Yonge *Heir of Redclyffe*		
1854	Ainsworth *Star Chamber* Dickens *Hard Times* Gaskell *North and South* (−1855)	Patmore *Angel in the House* (−1863) G. Eliot, trans., Feuerbach's *Essence of Christianity*	Crimean War (−1856) Working Men's College, London, founded
1855	Dickens *Little Dorrit* (−1857) C. Kingsley *Westward Ho!* Trollope *The Warden*	Browning *Men and Women* Tennyson *Maud*, etc.	Palmerston PM (Lib.), February Livingstone discovers Victoria Falls
1856	Mulock *John Halifax, Gentleman* Newman *Callista* C. Reade *It is Never Too Late to Mend*	J. A. Froude *History of England*, vols. I–II (−1870)	
1857	Borrow *Romany Rye* C. Brontë *The Professor* G. Eliot *Scenes of Clerical Life* Hughes *Tom Brown's School Days*	E. B. Browning *Aurora Leigh* Buckle *History of Civilization in England*, vol I (−1861) Collins *The Frozen Deep* (performed)	Indian Mutiny (−1859)

DATE	WORKS OF FICTION	OTHER WORKS	HISTORICAL/CULTURAL EVENTS
1857	C. Kingsley *Two Years Ago* Thackeray *Virginians* (–1859) Trollope *Barchester Towers*	Gaskell *Life of Charlotte Brontë* Ruskin *Political Economy of Art*	
1858	Ballantyne *The Coral Island* Farrar *Eric; or, Little by Little* MacDonald *Phantastes* Trollope *Three Clerks* *Dr Thorne*	Carlyle *Frederick the Great* vols. I–II (–1865) Clough *Amours de Voyage*	Derby PM (Cons.), February Brunel's *Great Eastern* launched
1859	Collins *Woman in White* (–1860) Dickens *Tale of Two Cities* G. Eliot *Adam Bede* H. Kingsley *Geoffrey Hamlyn* Meredith *Ordeal of Richard Feverel* Trollope *The Bertrams*	*All the Year Round* ed. Dickens Beeton *Book of Household Management* (–1860) Darwin *Origin of Species* Fitzgerald *Rubáiyát of Omar Khayyám* Mill *On Liberty* Smiles *Self-Help* Tennyson *Idylls of the King* (other vols – 1885)	Palmerston PM (Whig- Lib.), June Franco-Austrian War (–1861)
1860	Dickens *Great Expectations* (–1861)	*Cornhill* ed. Thackeray *Essays and Reviews*	Italian unification

DATE	WORKS OF FICTION	OTHER WORKS	HISTORICAL/CULTURAL EVENTS
1860	G. Eliot *Mill on the Floss* Meredith *Evan Harrington* Peacock *Gryll Grange* Thackeray *Lovel the Widower* Trollope *Framley Parsonage* (–1861)	Ruskin *Unto This Last* Thackeray *Four Georges*	
1861	G. Eliot *Silas Marner* Hughes *Tom Brown at Oxford* H. Kingsley *Ravenshoe* C. Reade *The Cloister and the Hearth* Thackeray *Adventures of Philip* (–1862) Trollope *Orley Farm* (–1862) Wood *East Lynne*	Colenso *Commentary on Romans* *Hymns Ancient and Modern* Mill *Utilitarianism* Palgrave *Golden Treasury*	American Civil War (–1865) Prince Albert d. Emancipation of serfs in Russia
1862	Braddon *Lady Audley's Secret* Bulwer *A Strange Story* Collins *No Name* G. Eliot *Romola* (–1863) Farrar *St. Winifred's*	E. B. Browning *Last Poems* Colenso *The Pentateuch Examined* (–1879) Meredith *Modern Love* C. Rossetti *Goblin Market*, etc.	Cricket tour to Australia

DATE	WORKS OF FICTION	OTHER WORKS	HISTORICAL/CULTURAL EVENTS
1862	Trollope *The Small House at Allington* (–1864) Wood *The Channings*		
1863	Gaskell *Sylvia's Lovers Cousin Phyllis* (–1864) C. Kingsley *The Water-Babies* MacDonald *David Elginbrod* Oliphant *The Rector and The Doctor's Family Salem Chapel* C. Reade *Hard Cash*	Huxley *Man's Place in Nature* Lyell *Antiquity of Man*	Football Association founded
1864	Collins *Armadale* (–1866) Dickens *Our Mutual Friend* (–1865) Gaskell *Wives and Daughters* (–1866) Le Fanu *Uncle Silas* Meredith *Emilia in England* (later called *Sandra Belloni*) Thackeray *Denis Duval* Trollope *Can You Forgive Her?* (–1865)	Browning *Dramatis Personae* Newman *Apologia pro Vita Sua* Spencer *Principles of Biology* (–1867) Tennyson *Idylls of the Hearth* (later called *Enoch Arden*)	

DATE	WORKS OF FICTION	OTHER WORKS	HISTORICAL/CULTURAL EVENTS
1865	Lewis Carroll *Alice's Adventures in Wonderland* C. Kingsley *Hereward the Wake* Meredith *Rhoda Fleming* C. Reade *Griffith Gaunt* (−1866) Trollope *The Belton Estate* (−1866) Yonge *The Clever Woman of the Family*	*Argosy* ed. Mrs Henry Wood M. Arnold *Essays in Criticism,* first series Newman *Dream of Gerontius* Ruskin *Sesame and Lilies* Seeley *Ecce Homo* Swinburne *Atalanta in Calydon*	Russell PM (Whig-Lib.), October President Lincoln assassinated
1866	G. Eliot *Felix Holt* Meredith *Vittoria* Oliphant *Miss Marjoribanks* Trollope *The Claverings* (−1867) *Last Chronicle of Barset* (−1867)	*Contemporary Review* ed. Alford Dallas *The Gay Science* Ruskin *Crown of Wild Olive* Swinburne *Poems and Ballads,* first series	Derby PM (Cons.), June
1867	Broughton *Not Wisely but Too Well* MacDonald *Robert Falconer* Ouida *Under Two Flags* Trollope *Phineas Finn* (−1869)	M. Arnold *New Poems* Carlyle *Shooting Niagara: And After?* Marx *Kapital* (trans. 1887)	Second Reform Act Typewriter invented Henry Irving on London stage
1868	Collins *The Moonstone* C. Reade *Foul Play* (with D. Boucicault)	Browning *The Ring and the Book* G. Eliot *Spanish Gypsy*	Disraeli PM (Cons.), February Gladstone PM (Lib.), December Public executions abolished

DATE	WORKS OF FICTION	OTHER WORKS	HISTORICAL/CULTURAL EVENTS
1868	Trollope *He Knew he was Right*	Morris *Earthly Paradise*	
1869	Blackmore *Lorna Doone* Collins *Man and Wife* (−1870)	M. Arnold *Culture and Anarchy* *Graphic* ed. Edwards J. S. Mill *On the Subjection of Women* Tennyson *Holy Grail*, etc.	Girton College, Cambridge, founded Suez Canal opened
1870	Dickens *Edwin Drood* Disraeli *Lothair* Meredith *Adventures of Harry Richmond* (−1871)	Huxley *Lay Sermons* Newman *Grammar of Assent* Spencer *Principles of Psychology* (−1872)	Franco-Prussian War (−1871) Papal Infallibility declared Forster's Education Act
1871	Bulwer *The Coming Race* Lewis Carroll *Through the Looking-Glass* G. Eliot *Middlemarch* (−1872) Hardy *Desperate Remedies* MacDonald *At the Back of the North Wind* Trollope *Eustace Diamonds* (−1873)	Darwin *Descent of Man* Lear *Nonsense Songs and Stories* Lewis *The Bells* (Royal Lyceum Theatre) Ruskin *Fors Clavigera* (−1884) Swinburne *Songs Before Sunrise*	Trade unions legalized Religious tests abolished at Oxford and Cambridge Stanley meets Livingstone

DATE	WORKS OF FICTION	OTHER WORKS	HISTORICAL/CULTURAL EVENTS
1872	Butler *Erewhon* Hardy *Under the Greenwood Tree* *A Pair of Blue Eyes* (–1873) Linton *Joshua Davidson*	Forster *Life of Dickens* (–1874) W. Reade *The Martyrdom of Man* Ruskin *Munera Pulveris*	(Secret) Ballot Act Edison's telegraph
1873	Bulwer *Kenelm Chillingly* Collins *The New Magdalen* Trollope *Phineas Redux* (–1874)	M. Arnold *Literature and Dogma* Butler *The Fair Haven* J. S. Mill *Autobiography* Pater *Studies in the Renaissance*	
1874	Hardy *Far from the Madding Crowd* Meredith *Beauchamp's Career* (–1875) Trollope *The Way We Live Now* (–1875)	G. Eliot *Legend of Jubal*, etc. Lewes *Problems of Life and Mind* (–1879) Thomson *City of Dreadful Night*, etc.	Disraeli PM (Cons.), February Factory Act
1875	Hardy *The Hand of Ethelberta* (–1876) W. Reade *The Outcast* Trollope *The Prime Minister* (–1876)	Gilbert and Sullivan *Trial by Jury* (Royalty Theatre)	Theosophical Society founded

DATE	WORKS OF FICTION	OTHER WORKS	HISTORICAL/CULTURAL EVENTS
1876	Braddon *Joshua Haggard's Daughter* G. Eliot *Daniel Deronda*	Lewis Carroll *The Hunting of the Snark* Spencer *Principles of Sociology* (−1896) Tennyson *Harold*	Bulgarian atrocities Telephone invented Victoria declared Empress of India
1877	Mallock *The New Republic*	Meredith *On the Idea of Comedy* *Nineteenth Century* ed. Knowles	Bradlaugh−Besant case Delane editor of *The Times* Russo-Turkish War
1878	Hardy *Return of the Native* James *The Europeans* Mallock *The New Paul and Virginia*	Farrar *Eternal Hope* Jefferies *The Gamekeeper at Home* Swinburne *Poems and Ballads,* second series	Salvation Army founded Paris Exhibition Ruskin−Whistler case
1879	G. Eliot *Impressions of Theophrastus Such* Meredith *The Egoist* Trollope *The Duke's Children* (−1880)	Browning *Dramatic Idyls,* first series Spencer *Principles of Ethics* (−1893) Stevenson *Travels with a Donkey*	Electric bulb invented
1880	Baring-Gould *Mehalah* Disraeli *Endymion* Gissing *Workers in the Dawn*	Browning *Dramatic Idyls,* second series Tennyson *Ballads,* etc.	Gladstone PM (Lib.), April

DATE	WORKS OF FICTION	OTHER WORKS	HISTORICAL/CULTURAL EVENTS
1880	Hardy *The Trumpet-Major* *A Laodicean* (–1881) James *The Portrait of a Lady* (–1881) Shorthouse *John Inglesant* Trollope *Dr. Wortle's School*		
1881	Mark Rutherford *Autobiography of Mark* *Rutherford* Stevenson *Treasure Island* (–1882) Trollope *Ayala's Angel*	Carlyle *Reminiscences* *Revised Version of New* *Testament* Wilde *Poems*	Browning Society founded
1882	Besant *All Sorts and Conditions* *of Men* Hardy *Two on a Tower* Jefferies *Bevis* Stevenson *New Arabian Nights*	Besant *The Revolt of Man* J. A. Froude *Carlyle: First Forty Years* Swinburne *Tristram of Lyonesse*, etc.	Married Women's Property Act Phoenix Park murders Society for Psychical Research founded
1883	Besant *All in a Garden Fair* Henty *Under Drake's Flag* Moore *A Modern Lover* Stevenson *The Black Arrow*	Jefferies *Story of my Heart* Meredith *Poems and Lyrics of the* *Joy of Earth* Trollope *Autobiography*	

DATE	WORKS OF FICTION	OTHER WORKS	HISTORICAL/CULTURAL EVENTS
1884	Braddon *Ishmael*	J. A. Froude *Carlyle: Life in London*	Third Reform Act
	Gissing *The Unclassed*	H. James *The Art of Fiction*	
	Ward *Miss Bretherton*	*Oxford English Dictionary*, ed. Murray (–1928)	
		Revised Version of Old Testament	
		Tennyson *Becket*	
1885	Haggard *King Solomon's Mines*	*Arabian Nights* trans. Burton (–1888)	Salisbury PM (Cons.), June Fall of Khartoum
	Meredith *Diana of the Crossways*	*Dictionary of National Biography*, I, ed. Stephen	
	Moore *A Mummer's Life*	Ruskin *Praeterita* (–1889)	
	Pater *Marius the Epicurean*	Tennyson *Tiresias*, etc.	
	Mark Rutherford *Mark Rutherford's Deliverance*		
	Stevenson *Prince Otto*		
1886	Besant *Children of Gideon*	Kipling *Departmental Ditties*, etc.	Gladstone PM (Lib.), February
	Burnett *Little Lord Fauntleroy*	Tennyson *Locksley Hall Sixty Years After*	Salisbury PM (Cons.), August Trafalgar Square riots
	Corelli *A Romance of Two Worlds*		
	Gissing *Demos*		

DATE	WORKS OF FICTION	OTHER WORKS	HISTORICAL/CULTURAL EVENTS
1886	Haggard *She* (–1887) Hardy *The Mayor of Casterbridge* *The Woodlanders* (–1887) Moore *A Drama in Muslin* Stevenson *Dr Jekyll and Mr Hyde* *Kidnapped*		
1887	Doyle *A Study in Scarlet* Gissing *Thyrza* Haggard *Allan Quartermain* Jefferies *Amaryllis at the Fair* Mark Rutherford *The Revolution in Tanner's Lane*	Meredith *Ballads and Poems of Tragic Life* Pater *Imaginary Portraits*	Queen Victoria's Golden Jubilee Independent Labour Party founded
1888	Gissing *A Life's Morning* Hardy *Wessex Tales* Kipling *Plain Tales from the Hills* Stevenson *The Master of Ballantrae* (–1889) Ward *Robert Elsmere* Wilde *The Happy Prince*, etc.	Arnold *Essays in Criticism, second series* Doughty *Travels in Arabia Deserta* Meredith *A Reading of Earth* Morris *A Dream of John Ball*	Accession of Kaiser Wilhelm II

DATE	WORKS OF FICTION	OTHER WORKS	HISTORICAL/CULTURAL EVENTS
1889	Doyle *Micah Clarke* Gissing *The Nether World* Jerome *Three Men in a Boat*	C. Booth *Life and Labour in London*, vol. I (–1903) Pater *Appreciations* Shaw *Fabian Essays* Swinburne *Poems and Ballads*, third series Yeats *The Wanderings of Oisin*	London Dock Strike Eiffel Tower
1890	Doyle *The Sign of Four* Gissing *The Emancipated* Kipling *Soldiers Three* Meredith *One of Our Conquerors* (–1891) Morris *News from Nowhere*	W. Booth *In Darkest England* Frazer *The Golden Bough* W. James *Principles of Psychology* Stanley *In Darkest Africa*	Slum clearance

General Bibliographies

Note: Each section is arranged alphabetically. Place of publication is London unless otherwise stated.

(i) English fiction: history and criticism

Allen, W.   *The English Novel: A Short Critical History* (1954; repr. Harmondsworth, 1958). (Better on broad developments than on individual works.)

Baker, E. A.   *The History of the English Novel*, 10 vols (1924–36; repr. New York, 1950–67), with supplement (XI) by L. Stevenson (1967). (Covers major novelists thoroughly, and briefly treats numerous minor figures.)

Booth, W. C.   *The Rhetoric of Fiction* (Chicago and London, 1961). (Highly influential study on rhetorical strategies and narrative technique.)

Culler, J.   *Structuralist Poetics: Structuralism, Linguistics and the Study of Literature* (1975). (Chapter on 'Poetics of the Novel'.)

Hardy, B.   *The Appropriate Form: An Essay on the Novel* (1964). (Interprets narrative 'form' broadly, illustrating with reference to selected novels.)

Iser, W.   *The Implied Reader: Patterns of Communication in Prose Fiction from Bunyan to Beckett* (Baltimore and London, 1974). (Of general significance; includes chapter on *Vanity Fair*.)

Kettle, A.   *An Introduction to the English Novel*, 2 vols (1951–53). (Focuses on selected texts.)

Leavis, F. R.   *The Great Tradition: George Eliot, Henry James, Joseph Conrad* (1948; repr. Harmondsworth, 1962). (Changed the course of novel criticism; establishes small canon of 'serious' writers which excludes most major Victorian novelists.)

Spilka, M., ed.   *Towards a Poetics of Fiction: Essays from 'Novel: A Forum on Fiction', 1967–1976* (Bloomington and London, 1977). (Useful compilation of theoretical essays.)

Stevenson, L.   *The English Novel: A Panorama* (1960; repr. Westport, Conn. 1978). (Literary history which includes brief critical surveys of many minor novelists as well as the major figures in a precise chronological scheme.)

Van Ghent, D.   *The English Novel: Form and Function* (1953; repr. New York, 1961). (Important analytical essays on individual classics, several of them Victorian.)

(ii) Victorian background: historical, intellectual, cultural

Altick, R. D.   *Victorian People and Ideas* (1974). (Broad sweep of Victorian life and thought.)

Best, G.   *Mid-Victorian Britain, 1851–1875* (1971; repr. Frogmore, 1973). (Good social history; illustrated.)

Briggs, A.   *Victorian People: A Reassessment of Persons and Things, 1851–67* (1954; repr. Harmondsworth, 1965). (Chapters on individual figures in relation to aspects of period: Crystal Palace, Crimean War, etc.)
Victorian Cities (1963; repr. Harmondsworth, 1968). (Chapters on individual cities.)

Buckley, J. H.   *The Victorian Temper: A Study in Literary Culture* (1952). (Concentrates on rise and decline of the 'moral aesthetic'.)
The Triumph of Time: A Study of the Victorian Concepts of Time, History, Progress, and Decadence (Cambridge, Mass. and London, 1967).

Chadwick, O.   *The Victorian Church*, 2nd edn, 2 vols, Ecclesiastical History of England, ed. by J. D. Dickinson, vols VII–VIII (1970). (Magisterial study; much more than ecclesiastical history.)

Chandler, A.   *A Dream of Order: The Medieval Ideal in Nineteenth-Century English Literature* (1970; repr. 1971).

Chapman, R.   *The Victorian Debate: English Literature and Society,*

	1832–1901, Literature and Society series, ed. by H. Tint (1968). (Covers many aspects of the age and its literature.)
Cockshut, A. O. J.	*The Unbelievers: English Agnostic Thought, 1840–1890* (1964).
Dyos, H. J. and M. Wolff, eds	*The Victorian City: Images and Realities*, 2 vols (1973). (Includes superb photographic record of the age.)
Halévy, E.	*A History of the English People in the Nineteenth Century*, 2nd edn, 6 vols (1949–52).
Holloway, J.	*The Victorian Sage: Studies in Argument* (1953). (On Carlyle, Disraeli, George Eliot, Newman, Matthew Arnold, Hardy.)
Houghton, W. E.	*The Victorian Frame of Mind, 1830–1870* (New Haven and London, 1957). (The most helpful introduction to the period for students of literature, though some generalizations are too sweeping.)
Marcus, S.	*The Other Victorians: A Study of Sexuality and Pornography in Mid-Nineteenth Century England* (1964; repr. 1969). (Illuminating reflections on Victorian fiction.)
Martin, R. B.	*The Triumph of Wit: A Study of Victorian Comic Theory* (Oxford, 1974). (Traces changes in comic theory during the period.)
Perkin, H.	*The Origins of Modern English Society, 1780–1880* (1969).
Reardon, B. M. G.	*From Coleridge to Gore: A Century of Religious Thought in Britain* (1971).
Trudgill, E.	*Madonnas and Magdalens: The Origins and Development of Victorian Sexual Attitudes* (New York, 1976).
Willey, B.	*Nineteenth-Century Studies: Coleridge to Matthew Arnold* (1949; repr. Cambridge, 1980). (History of ideas.) *More Nineteenth-Century Studies: A Group of Honest Doubters* (1956; repr. Cambridge, 1980).
Williams, R.	*Culture and Society, 1780–1950* (1958; repr. Harmondsworth, 1961). (Influential study on history of the idea of culture.)

Young, G. M., ed. *Early Victorian England, 1830–1865*, 2 vols (1934). (Rich source on Victorian private and public life; illustrated.)

Young, G. M. *Portrait of an Age: Victorian England*, 2nd edn (1953). (Lively historical introduction.)

(iii) Victorian fiction

A. Bibliographies and reference guides

Cockshut, A. O. J., intro. *The Novel to 1900*, Great Writers Student Library, ed. by J. Vinson and D. L. Kirkpatrick (1980). (Student reference guide; author entries list works and selected criticism, and provide brief critical surveys of widely varying quality.)

Ford, G. H., ed. *Victorian Fiction: A Second Guide to Research* (New York, 1978). (Supplements Stevenson, below.)

Harris, W. V. *British Short Fiction in the Nineteenth Century: A Literary and Bibliographical Guide* (Detroit, 1979).

Stevenson, L., ed. *Victorian Fiction: A Guide to Research* (Cambridge, Mass., 1964). (For advanced students; includes general section, and sections on fifteen novelists.)

Watson, G., ed. *The New Cambridge Bibliography of English Literature*, vol. III (1800–1900) (Cambridge, 1969). (The primary work of reference; revises *CBEL*, ed. Bateson, updating to mid-1960s.)

Watt, I., comp. *The British Novel: Scott through Hardy*, Goldentree Bibliographies in Language and Literature, ed. by O. B. Hardison (Northbrook, Ill., 1973). (Useful bibliographical guide; general and author entries.)

B. Readership, publication, and reception

Altick, R. D. *The English Common Reader: A Social History of the Mass Reading Public, 1800–1900* (Chicago and London, 1957). (Standard work.)

Cruse, A. *The Victorians and their Books* (1935). (Covers a wide field.)

Graham, K. *English Criticism on the Novel, 1865–1900* (Oxford, 1965). (Incisive on major literary debates of period.)

Griest, G. L.   *Mudie's Circulating Library and the Victorian Novel* (Newton Abbot, 1970). (On the mogul of Victorian lending libraries.)

Harvey, J. R.   *Victorian Novelists and their Illustrators* (1970).

James, L.   *Fiction for the Working Man, 1830–50: A Study of the Literature Produced for the Working Classes in Early Victorian Urban England* (1963; repr. Harmondsworth, 1974). (Good on popular publishing.)

Leavis, Q. D.   *Fiction and the Reading Public* (1932; repr. 1965). (Pioneering study; from sixteenth to twentieth century.)

Olmsted, J. C., ed.   *A Victorian Art of Fiction: Essays on the Novel in British Periodicals, 1830–1850*, Garland Reference Library of the Humanities, 100 (New York and London, 1979). (Reprints contemporary reviews and essays.)

Sutherland, J. A.   *Victorian Novelists and Publishers* (1976). (Excellent study on period 1830–70, with general chapters and chapters on individual novelists.)

C. History and criticism (general)

Ford, B., ed.   *From Dickens to Hardy*, New Pelican Guide to English Literature, vol. VI (Harmondsworth, 1982). (Includes chapters on novelists; author bibliographies of original Guide updated.)

Karl, F. R.   *An Age of Fiction: The Nineteenth Century British Novel* (New York, 1965). (Critical survey; mainly on major novelists.)

Miller, J. H.   *The Form of Victorian Fiction: Thackeray,Dickens, Trollope, George Eliot, Meredith, and Hardy* (Notre Dame and London, 1968). (On novel as a 'structure of interpenetrating minds'.)

Pollard, A., ed.   *The Victorians*, Sphere History of Literature in the English Language, vol. VI (1969). (Includes helpful introductory chapters on novelists, with short bibliographies.)

Stone, D. D.   *Novelists in a Changing World: Meredith, James and the Transformation of English Fiction in the 1880's* (Cambridge, Mass., 1972). (Argues that decade witnessed ending of the Victorian era and beginning of the modern era.)

Tillotson, K.   *Novels of the Eighteen-Forties* (Oxford, 1954).
(Brought new scholarly rigour to the study of
Victorian fiction by focusing on major and minor
works published in single decade.)

Williams, R.   *The English Novel: From Dickens to Lawrence* (1970;
repr. Frogmore, 1974). (Argues convincingly that
society is main subject of English novel.)

D. Forms and sub-genres

Anderson, R.   *The Purple Heart Throbs: The Sub-Literature of Love*
(1974). (Includes discussion on Braddon, Corelli,
Ouida, Yonge.)

Bratton, J. S.   *The Impact of Victorian Children's Fiction* (London
and Totowa, NJ, 1981). (Covers large field,
including writers such as 'ALOE' and 'Hesba
Stretton'.)

Buckley, J. H.   *Season of Youth: The Bildungsroman from Dickens to
Golding* (Cambridge, Mass., 1974). (Other
Victorian writers discussed include Meredith,
George Eliot, Butler, Pater, Hardy.)

Cazamian, L.   *The Social Novel in England, 1830–1850: Dickens,
Disraeli, Mrs. Gaskell, Kingsley* (1903), trans. M.
Fido (1973). (Pioneering study.)

Fleishman, A.   *The English Historical Novel: Walter Scott to Virginia
Woolf* (Baltimore and London, 1971). (Includes
discussion on Dickens, Thackeray, Reade, George
Eliot, Shorthouse, Pater, Hardy.)

Garrett, P. K.   *The Victorian Multiplot Novel: Studies in Dialogical
Form* (New Haven and London, 1980). (Focuses on
Dickens, Thackeray, George Eliot, Trollope.)

Gilbert, S. M.   *The Madwoman in the Attic: The Woman Writer and
and S. Gubar   the Nineteenth-Century Literary Imagination* (New
Haven and London, 1979). (Massive, fascinating,
wild.)

Haining, P., ed.   *The Penny Dreadful; or, Strange, Horrid &
Sensational Tales!* (1975). (Anthology, with
introductions and original illustrations.)

Hollingsworth, K.   *The Newgate Novel, 1830–47: Bulwer, Ainsworth,
Dickens, & Thackeray* (Detroit, 1963).

Hughes, W.   *The Maniac in the Cellar: Sensation Novels of the*

1860s (Princeton, 1980). (Important study, though overestimates significance of this sub-genre.)

Kiely, R. *The Romantic Novel in England* (Cambridge, Mass., 1972). (From *The Castle of Otranto* to *Wuthering Heights.*)

King, J. *Tragedy in the Victorian Novel: Theory and Practice in the Novels of George Eliot, Thomas Hardy and Henry James* (Cambridge, 1978). (Argues that Victorian novels created a 'total and new version of tragedy'.)

Levine, G. *The Boundaries of Fiction: Carlyle, Macaulay, Newman* (Princeton, 1968). ('As writers of history and autobiography and social analysis their proximity to the writers of nineteenth-century fiction can be seen clearly.')
The Realistic Imagination: English Fiction from Frankenstein to Lady Chatterley (Chicago and London, 1981). (Significant study on elusiveness of realism as an idea, and 'literary practice' of realism in the fiction.)

Lucas, J. *The Literature of Change: Studies in the Nineteenth-Century Provincial Novel* (Hassocks and New York, 1977). (Includes chapters on Gaskell, Mark Rutherford, and Hardy.)

Maison, M. M. *Search Your Soul, Eustace: A Survey of the Religious Novel in the Victorian Age* (London and New York, 1961). (Less facetious than it sounds; epens up large tract of minor fiction.)

Prickett, S. *Victorian Fantasy* (Hassocks, 1979). (Includes discussion on Dickens, Lear, Carroll, Kingsley, MacDonald.)

Punter, D. *The Literature of Terror: A History of Gothic Fictions from 1765 to the Present Day* (London and New York, 1980). (Includes chapters on the nineteenth-century historical novel and the sensation novel.)

Rosa, M. W. *The Silver-Fork School: Novels of Fashion Preceding Vanity Fair* (1936; repr. Port Washington, NY, 1964). (Includes chapters on Bulwer and Disraeli.)

Sanders, A. *The Victorian Historical Novel, 1840–1880* (1978). (Critical accounts of selected novels.)

Showalter, E. *A Literature of their Own: British Women Novelists from Brontë to Lessing* (Princeton, 1977). (Major feminist study.)

Squires, M.   *The Pastoral Novel: Studies in George Eliot, Thomas Hardy, and D. H. Lawrence* (Charlottesville, 1974). (Focuses on seven major novels.)

Terry, R. C.   *Victorian Popular Fiction, 1860–80* (1983). (On fiction as entertainment for 'middle-brow' readership, with special reference to Oliphant, Broughton, and Payn.)

Tomlinson, T. B.   *The English Middle-Class Novel* (1976). (From Austen to Lawrence.)

Williams, I.   *The Realist Novel in England: A Study in Development* (1974). (From Austen to James.)

E. Themes, motifs, and conventions

Auerbach, N.   *Woman and the Demon: The Life of a Victorian Myth* (Cambridge, Mass. and London, 1982). (Examines paradigms of the angel/demon, the old maid, and the fallen woman.)

Basch, F.   *Relative Creatures: Victorian Women in Society and the Novel, 1837–67* (1974).

Beer, G.   *Darwin's Plots: Evolutionary Narrative in Darwin, George Eliot and Nineteenth-Century Fiction* (1983). (Fascinating analysis of Darwin's language and 'plots' in relation to nineteenth-century literature and thought; followed by detailed treatment of George Eliot and Hardy.)

Beer, P.   *Reader, I Married Him: A Study of the Women Characters of Jane Austen, Charlotte Brontë, Elizabeth Gaskell and George Eliot* (1974).

Calder, J.   *Women and Marriage in Victorian Fiction*, World of Literature series (1976).

Colby, V.   *Yesterday's Women: Domestic Realism in the English Novel* (Princeton, 1974). (Includes treatment of several minor figures.)

Cunningham, G.   *The New Woman and the Victorian Novel* (1978). ('New Woman' fiction discussed in relation to Meredith, Hardy, and Gissing.)

Cunningham, V.   *Everywhere Spoken Against: Dissent in the Victorian Novel* (Oxford, 1975). (Individual chapters on Brontës, Gaskell, George Eliot, Dickens, Oliphant, Mark Rutherford; the sympathetic treatment of dissent is main touchstone of judgement.)

Faber, R.   *Proper Stations: Class in Victorian Fiction* (1971). (Concentrates on period *c.* 1830–80.)

Gilmour, R.   *The Idea of the Gentleman in the Victorian Novel* (1981). (Interesting on eighteenth-century legacy; chapters on Thackeray, Dickens, and Trollope.)

Grylls, D.   *Guardians and Angels: Parents and Children in Nineteenth-Century Literature* (London and Boston, 1978). (Defines 'Puritan' and 'Romantic' ideals, and applies them mainly to Austen, Dickens, Butler, Gosse.)

Jay, E.   *The Religion of the Heart: Anglican Evangelicalism and the Nineteenth-Century Novel* (Oxford, 1979). (Thorough treatment of Evangelicalism, followed by analysis of novels by George Eliot, Mrs Worboise, and Butler.)

Keating, P. J.   *The Working Classes in Victorian Fiction* (1971). (Emphasis falls mainly on Gissing and the 1880s.)

Knoepflmacher, U. C.   *Religious Humanism and the Victorian Novel: George Eliot, Walter Pater, and Samuel Butler* (Princeton, 1965). (Good treatment of relationship between literature and history of ideas.)

Kovačević, I., ed.   *Fact into Fiction: English Literature and the Industrial Scene, 1750–1850* (Leicester, 1975). (Introduction followed by anthology; includes passages from works by Harriet Martineau and Charlotte Elizabeth Tonna.)

Ousby, I.   *Bloodhounds of Heaven: The Detective in English Fiction from Godwin to Doyle* (Cambridge, Mass., 1976).

Praz, M.   *The Hero in Eclipse in Victorian Fiction*, trans. Angus Davidson (1956). (Relates 'decline of the hero' to Romanticism turned bourgeois.)

Qualls, B. V.   *The Secular Pilgrims of Victorian Fiction: The Novel as Book of Life* (Cambridge, 1982). (Takes seventeenth-century religious writings and Romantic 'revisionings' as context in which Carlyle, Charlotte Brontë, Dickens, and George Eliot worked.)

Reed, J. R.   *Victorian Conventions* (Athens, Ohio, 1975). (Conventions range from marriage to duelling, from swindles to the occult; illustrated mainly through the fiction.)

Reed, W. L.   *Meditations on the Hero: A Study of the Romantic Hero in Nineteenth-Century Fiction* (New Haven and London, 1974). (Includes Charlotte Brontë in selected examples of European and American literature.)

Sandison, A.   *The Wheel of Empire: A Study of the Imperial Idea in Some Late Nineteenth and Early Twentieth-Century Fiction* (London and New York, 1967). (Focuses on Haggard, Kipling, Conrad, Buchan.)

Smith, S. M.   *The Other Nation: The Poor in English Novels of the 1840s and 1850s* (Oxford, 1980). (Organized by theme; illustrated.)

Stone, D. D.   *The Romantic Impulse in Victorian Fiction* (Cambridge, Mass. and London, 1980). (Major work on the Romantic heritage.)

Thomson, P.   *The Victorian Heroine: A Changing Ideal* (1956: repr. Westport, Conn., 1978). (Important study on subject which has since been discussed exhaustively.)

Wheeler, M.   *The Art of Allusion in Victorian Fiction* (1979). (On the convention of religious and secular allusion, and its use in selected novels.)

Wolff, R. L.   *Gains and Losses: Novels of Faith and Doubt in Victorian England* (New York and London, 1977). (Survey of novels published in large Garland reprint series; limited critically and prone to inaccuracy, but an invaluable point of departure.)

Individual Authors

Notes on biography, major works and criticism

Each entry is divided into three sections:

(a) *Outline of author's life and literary career.* Dates of novels are those of the first published form – in volumes, monthly numbers, magazine serials, etc. Where novels were published serially in both British and American magazines, only the British are cited.

(b) *Selected biographies and letters.* Place of publication is London unless otherwise stated.

(c) *Selected critical works, etc.* Listed chronologically. Place of publication is London unless otherwise stated.

Modern editions of novels are not cited. For information on scholarly editions, such as the Clarendon editions of Dickens, the Brontës and George Eliot, and on reprints, such as the Harvester reprints of Gissing and the large Garland reprint series of 'Novels of Faith and Doubt', see reference works listed in (iii) A. on p. 218 above. The works of major novelists and selected works of minor writers are now widely available in paperback editions, the best of which are edited by specialists in the field and have critical introductions, textual notes, and explanatory notes. English series in paperback include the Penguin English Library, and the World's Classics series (Oxford University Press). American series include the Norton and Riverside editions.

Series of collections of *Victorian reviews and modern critical essays* are not cited. Volumes on the major novelists and some minor writers are included in the excellent Critical Heritage series (Routledge and Kegan Paul), which reprint selected Victorian reviews and critical essays; the useful Casebook series (Macmillan), which reprint selected Victorian reviews and essays, and twentieth-century critical studies; and the Twentieth-Century Views series (Prentice-Hall, Englewood Cliffs, New Jersey).

AINSWORTH, William Harrison (1805–82), son of Manchester solicitor; educated at Manchester Grammar School. Articled to Manchester solicitor, 1821–24. Went to London to complete legal studies, 1824, but turned to publishing, magazine editing and writing. Married Anne Frances Ebers, 1826; three daughters. Following success of *Rookwood* (1834), published almost forty novels, mainly historical romances, several of which appeared in magazines he edited: *Bentley's Miscellany, Ainsworth's Magazine,* the *New Monthly Magazine.* Best-known works are the Newgate novels, *Jack Sheppard* (1839); *The Tower of London* (1840); *Guy Fawkes* (1840–41); *Old St Paul's* (1841); *Windsor Castle* (1842–43); *The Lancashire Witches* (1848). Well known in London literary circles, Ainsworth continued to write until his death, though later novels were less popular.

> Ellis, S. M., *W. H. Ainsworth and his Friends,* 2 vols (1911). (Includes a bibliography.)

> See: Hollingsworth, K., *The Newgate Novel, 1830–1847* (Detroit, 1963). (Discusses *Rookwood* and *Jack Sheppard.*)
> Worth, G. J., *William Harrison Ainsworth,* Twayne's English Authors, 138 (New York, 1972). (First book-length study.)
> Sanders, A., *The Victorian Historical Novel, 1840–1880* (1978). (Chapter on *The Tower of London.*)

BESANT, Sir Walter (1836–1901), son of Portsmouth merchant; educated at grammar schools in Portsea and Stockwell, King's College, London, and Christ's College, Cambridge, 1856–59. Having taught mathematics at Leamington College, gave up plan to enter ministry, and became senior professor at Royal College of Mauritius, 1861–67. Returned to a literary career in London. Married Mary Garrett, 1874; four children. His many novels included a series written with James Rice, editor of *Once a Week,* published 1872–81; *The Revolt of Man* (1882), an attack on feminism; *All in a Garden Fair* (1883), on the literary scene; and *Dorothy Forster* (1884), a historical romance. Two novels on working-class life in London, *All Sorts and Conditions of Men* (1882) and *Children of Gideon* (1886), were popular and influential. Essay on 'The Art of Fiction' (1884) provoked Henry James's famous response in essay with same title. As founder and first chairman of Committee of Society of Authors (1884–85; again, 1887–92), did much to improve position of writers. Elected FSA, 1894, and knighted, 1895. *Autobiography* published posthumously (1902).

> See: Boege, F. W, 'Sir Walter Besant: Novelist', *Nineteenth-Century Fiction,* 10(1955–56), 249–80; 11(1956–57), 32–60. (Free-ranging discussion.)
> Keating, P. J., *The Working Classes in Victorian Fiction* (1971). (Chapter on 'Walter Besant and the "discovery" of the East End'.)

BLACKMORE, Richard Doddridge (1825–1900), son of clergyman who moved to Devon following death of Blackmore's mother, soon after his birth; educated at Blundell's School, Tiverton, and Exeter College, Oxford. Married Roman Catholic, Lucy Maguire (who converted to Anglicanism), 1852, and was called to the Bar, although gave up law due partly to epilepsy. Became classics master, 1853, and then, from 1858, took up market gardening and writing at a large site he bought in Teddington, Middlesex. Here he wrote his romances, including *Clara Vaughan* (1864); *Lorna Doone: A Romance of Exmoor* (1869), best-selling love story set in seventeenth century; *The Maid of Sker* (1871–72), his own favourite; and *Springhaven: A Tale of the Great War* (1886–87).

> Burris, Q. G., *R. D. Blackmore: His Life and Novels* (Urbana, Illinois, 1930).

Dunn, W. H., *R. D. Blackmore, the Author of Lorna Doone: A Biography* (1956).

Budd, K. G., *The Last Victorian: R. D. Blackmore and his Novels* (1960). (Short relaxed biography.)

See: Sutton, M. K., *R. D. Blackmore*, Twayne's English Authors, 265 (Boston, 1979). (Aims to balance former biographical emphasis by relating the fiction to other literature.)

BORROW, George Henry (1803–81), born and brought up in Norfolk, son of Captain of Militia, with whom he travelled widely in Britain as a child. After sporadic education, including periods at Edinburgh High School and Norwich Grammar School, articled to firm of Norwich solicitors, 1819–24. Having then worked for a London publisher and compiled *Celebrated Trials* (6 vols, 1825), took to the road, sometimes travelling with gypsies. As agent and correspondent of Bible Society, travelled to Russia, Spain, Portugal, and Morocco in 1830s. Married a widow, Mary Clarke, 1840, with whom lived at Oulton Broad. Published his *Bible in Spain* (1843), of which almost 20,000 copies sold in a year, and two autobiographical novels: *Lavengro: The Scholar, the Gypsy, the Priest* (1851) and *The Romany Rye: A Sequel to Lavengro* (1857). Also wrote other travel books, including *Wild Wales* (1862), works on gypsy languages and lore, and translations in thirty languages and dialects. Died almost unknown and unread.

Knapp, W. I., *Life, Writings, and Correspondence of George Borrow*, 2 vols (1899).

Collie, M., *George Borrow, Eccentric* (Cambridge, 1982). (Scholarly and detailed.)

Williams, D., *A World of His Own: The Double Life of George Borrow* (Oxford and New York, 1982). (Enthusiastic and lively.)

See: Meyers, R. R., *George Borrow*, Twayne's English Authors, 32 (New York, 1966). (Biographical and critical introduction.)

BRADDON, Mary Elizabeth (1835–1915), daughter of solicitor; educated privately. Acted under assumed name in 1850s, to support mother. Almost a million copies of *Lady Audley's Secret* (1862), one of the first sensation novels, sold during lifetime. *Aurora Floyd* (1863) and other sensation novels followed at the rate of two or three a year during 1860s, when Braddon was living with John Maxwell, a publisher whose wife was in an asylum. The couple had five illegitimate children before their marriage, 1874. A steady flow of novels, totalling over eighty, continued to appear throughout her career, and included historical fiction, such as *Ishmael* (1884), *London Pride* (1896), and *The Infidel* (1900); novels of manners and character, such as *Strangers and Pilgrims* (1873) and *The Rose of Life* (1905); the tragic *Joshua Haggard's Daughter* (1876); and numerous 'penny dreadfuls'. Her publishers called her 'the Queen of the Circulating Libraries'. Edited several magazines, principally Maxwell's monthly *Belgravia*, 1866–93.

Wolff, R. L., *Sensational Victorian: The Life and Fiction of Mary Elizabeth Braddon* (New York and London, 1979). (Exhaustive critical biography.)

See: Showalter, E., *A Literature of their Own: British Women Novelists from
        Brontë to Lessing* (Princeton, 1977). (Chapter on 'Sensationalism and
        Feminine Protest'.)
        Hughes, W., *The Maniac in the Cellar: Sensation Novels of the 1860s*
        (Princeton, 1980). (Chapter on 'The Wickedness of Woman'
        examines Braddon and Mrs Henry Wood.)

BRONTË, Charlotte (1816–55) Emily Jane (1818–48) and Anne (1820–49)
    daughters of Rev. Patrick Brontë. Brought up in Haworth Parsonage
    near their beloved Yorkshire moors with elder sisters Maria and
    Elizabeth and brother Branwell (1817–48) by father and, following
    mother's death, 1821, maternal aunt Branwell, of Methodist persuasion.
    After less than a year of misery at Cowan Bridge School, later portrayed
    in *Jane Eyre*, Charlotte and Emily withdrawn following death by typhoid
    of elder sisters, 1825. Charlotte studied and later taught at Roe Head
    School, followed briefly by Emily, whose place taken by Anne.
    Remarkable Brontë juvenilia included miniature versions of *Blackwood's
    Magazine* and fantastic tales of mythical Glasstown and Angria (mainly by
    Charlotte and Branwell), some of which still extant, and of Gondal (by
    Emily and Anne), now lost, though some of Emily's poems are on Gondal
    subjects. All three sisters became governesses, 1837–39. Rev. William
    Weightman became Patrick Brontë's curate, 1839, but died of cholera three
    years later; Anne's secret love for him reflected in poetry and *Agnes Grey*.
    Charlotte and Emily travelled to Brussels to study at M. Heger's school,
    1842, but returned same year on aunt's death; Charlotte went back to
    Brussels alone to teach for the married Heger, whom she loved, until 1844.
    All three sisters published their *Poems* (1846) by Currer, Ellis, and Acton
    Bell, and Charlotte's first novel, *The Professor* refused by several publishers.
    Charlotte's *Jane Eyre*, Emily's *Wuthering Heights*, and Anne's *Agnes Grey*
    published (1847) under same pseudonyms; whereas *Wuthering Heights*
    revolted most critics, *Jane Eyre* achieved both notoriety and success as best-
    seller. Identity of sisters established with their publisher, George Smith,
    and his reader, W. S. Williams, July 1848. The same month Anne's *The
    Tenant of Wildfell Hall* achieved great success in circulating libraries, along
    with *Jane Eyre*. Charlotte's *Shirley* published October 1849 following three
    bereavements in twelve months: Branwell, long addicted to drink and
    drugs, and Emily, the most private and visionary of the sisters, died at
    Haworth; the quieter Anne died at Scarborough. Charlotte's social sphere
    now widened; met her hero Thackeray and Harriet Martineau (*qq.v.*) in
    London, and Elizabeth Gaskell (*q.v.*), her future friend and biographer,
    near Windermere, 1850. Last and most ambitious novel, *Villette*, published
    1853. Married Patrick Brontë's curate, Rev. A. B. Nicholls, 1854, after her
    father withdrew objections he raised against match two years previously.
    Died in pregnancy, 1855, leaving small fragment of novel entitled 'Emma'
    written in 1853 and published in *Cornhill Magazine*, April 1860. *The
    Professor* published 1857, year in which Victorian readers were first told the
    Brontës' remarkable story by Elizabeth Gaskell in her *Life of Charlotte
    Brontë*.

        Gaskell, E. C., *The Life of Charlotte Brontë*, 2 vols (1857). (One of
        the best Victorian literary biographies; occasionally exaggerates;
        also suppresses awkward facts.)
        Gérin, W., *Anne Brontë* (1959); *Branwell Brontë* (1961); *Charlotte*

Brontë: *The Evolution of Genius* (Oxford, 1967); *Emily Brontë: A Biography* (Oxford, 1971). (The standard biographies.)
Peters, M., *Unquiet Soul: A Biography of Charlotte Brontë* (1975). (Lively; includes useful bibliography.)

See: Ratchford, F. E., *The Brontës' Web of Childhood* (New York, 1941). (Pioneering study of juvenilia.)
Van Ghent, D., *The English Novel: Form and Function* (New York, 1953). (Chapter on the 'window figure' and the 'two children figure' in *Wuthering Heights*.)
Miller, J. H., *The Disappearance of God: Five Nineteenth-Century Writers* (Cambridge, Mass., 1963). (Chapter on Emily Brontë.)
Ewbank, I. S., *Their Proper Sphere: A Study of the Brontë Sisters as Early-Victorian Female Novelists* (1966).
Martin, R. B., *The Accents of Persuasion: Charlotte Brontë's Novels* (1966). (Sound critical introduction.)
Everitt, A., comp., *Wuthering Heights: An Anthology of Criticism* (1967). (Includes C. P. Sanger's crucial essay on *The Structure of Wuthering Heights*, 1926.)
Craik, W. A., *The Brontë Novels* (1968). (Critical introduction.)
Hannah, B., *Striving Towards Wholeness* (1971; repr. 1972). (Jungian reading of Brontës' lives and novels. Also chapters on Mary Webb and R. L. Stevenson.)
Kiely, R., *The Romantic Novel in England* (Cambridge, Mass., 1972). (Chapter on *Wuthering Heights* as a masterpiece of English romantic fiction.)
Auerbach, N., 'Charlotte Brontë: The Two Countries', *University of Toronto Quarterly*, 42(1973), 328–42. (On the 'war within the self' in *Jane Eyre* and *Villette*.)
Winnifrith, T., *The Brontës and their Background: Romance and Reality* (1973). (Important study of Brontës' background and of previous writers' blurring of biography and the Brontë mythology.)
Eagleton, T., *Myths of Power: A Marxist Study of the Brontës* (1975). (Interesting but lacks balance.)
Gilbert, S. M. and S. Gubar, *The Madwoman in the Attic: The Woman Writer and the Nineteenth-Century Literary Imagination* (New Haven and London, 1979). (Feminist criticism which takes *Jane Eyre* and other Brontë novels as central texts.)

BULWER, Edward George Earle Lytton, later BULWER-LYTTON, from 1843; later LORD LYTTON, from 1866 (1803–73), increasingly called Edward Bulwer by modern scholars; son of a General and Elizabeth Lytton, heiress of Knebworth, Herts; educated at schools in Fulham, Rottingdean, and Ealing, and at Trinity College and Trinity Hall, Cambridge. Unhappy marriage to Rosina Doyle Wheeler, 1827 (two children), and subsequent separation, 1836, alienated his mother, losing him almost all private income and forcing him to write. Published over sixty works: novels, plays, poems, essays, etc. Himself a dandy in his twenties, made name with *Pelham* (1828), silver-fork novel which influenced manners and fashions of the day. *Paul Clifford* (1830) and *Eugene Aram* (1832) are Newgate novels; historical romances include *Devereux* (1829), *The Last Days of Pompeii* (1834), *Rienzi* (1835), *The Last of the Barons* (1843), and *Harold* (1848); novels of modern life include *The Caxtons* (1849), *My Novel* (1853), and *Kenelm Chillingly* (1873). Among other works are *England and the English* (1833); the plays *Money* (1840) and *Not so bad as we seem* (1851); and an occult novel, *A Strange Story* (1862). Succeeded to Knebworth estate, 1843; represented several constituencies as MP, changing party; Colonial Secretary in Derby's Tory government, 1858–59; Baron Lytton of Knebworth, 1866; buried in Westminster Abbey.

> Lytton, E. R. B., ed., *The Life, Letters and Literary Remains of Edward Bulwer, Lord Lytton*, 2 vols (1883).
> Lytton, V. A. G. R. B., *The Life of Edward Bulwer, First Lord Lytton*, 2 vols (1913).

See: Sadleir, M., *Bulwer: A Panorama* (1931).
> Rosa, M. W., *The Silver-Fork School: Novels of Fashion Preceding Vanity Fair* (1936: repr. Port Washington, 1964). (Chapter on *Pelham*.)
> Hollingsworth, K., *The Newgate Novel, 1830–1847* (Detroit, 1963). (Discusses *Paul Clifford* and *Eugene Aram*.)
> Christensen, A. C, *Edward Bulwer-Lytton: The Fiction of New Regions* (Athens, Georgia, 1976). (Aims to 'establish a view of Bulwer as dedicated artist rather than facile opportunist'.)
> Eigner, E. M., *The Metaphysical Novel in England and America: Dickens, Bulwer, Melville, and Hawthorne* (Berkeley, 1978). (Good on Bulwer.)
> Sanders, A., *The Victorian Historical Novel, 1840–1880* (1978). (Chapter on *Harold*.)

BUTLER, Samuel (1835–1902), son of rector of Langar, Nottinghamshire; grandson of Dr, later Bishop Samuel Butler, head of Shrewsbury School, where young Butler educated under Kennedy, 1848–54, before going on to St John's, Cambridge. Broke from oppressive family influences when decided against ordination, 1859; successfully bred sheep in New Zealand, 1860–64, read Darwin, and wrote for Christchurch *Press*. Returned to London, where settled in chambers at Clifford's Inn, to be home for rest of his life. Attended art schools (later exhibiting at Royal Academy), wrote articles on religion and science, travelled abroad. Apart from *A First Year in Canterbury Settlement* (1863), first major publication and sole success in his lifetime was *Erewhon; or, Over the Range* (1872), Utopian satire; *Erewhon Revisited* appeared in 1901. *The Fair Haven* (1873) epitomizes Butler's talent as writer of spoofs, in this case on Christ's miracles. Began work on *The Way of all Flesh*, 1873; wrote and revised from time to time until 1887; posthumous publication (1903). Miss Eliza Savage, a close friend, was not physically attractive to Butler, who disliked idea of marriage and preferred to visit a prostitute. Butler's challenge to Darwin's theories published in articles and newspaper correspondence, in *Life and Habit* (1877), *Evolution, Old and New* (1879), *Unconscious Memory* (1880), *Luck, or Cunning?* (1886), and developed in fictional terms in *The Way of all Flesh*. Miscellaneous other writings included studies on and translations of Homer, in Butler's view a woman.

> Jones, H. F., *Memoir of Samuel Butler*, 2 vols (1919). (By closest friend.)
> Keynes, G. and B. Hill, eds, *Samuel Butler's Note Books* (1951).

Henderson, P., *Samuel Butler, the Incarnate Bachelor* (1953). (Biography.)

Silver, A., ed., *The Family Letters of Samuel Butler, 1841–1886* (Stanford, 1962).

See: Furbank, P. N., *Samuel Butler* (Cambridge, 1948). (Critical of Butler's ideas.)

Willey, B., *Darwin and Butler: Two Versions of Evolution* (1960).

Holt, L. E., *Samuel Butler*, Twayne's English Authors, 2 (New York, 1964). (Critical survey of works and ideas.)

Knoepflmacher, U. C., *Religious Humanism and the Victorian Novel* (Princeton, 1965). (Excellent commentary on Butler's evolutionary theories.)

Wolff, R. L., *Gains and Losses: Novels of Faith and Doubt in Victorian England* (New York and London, 1977). (Section on Butler.)

Jeffers, T. L., *Samuel Butler Revalued* (University Park and London, 1981). (Revaluation of Butler as a Victorian intellectual.)

CARROLL, Lewis (pseudonym of Charles Lutwidge Dodgson: 1832–98, son of clergyman; educated at Richmond, Yorkshire, Rugby School, and Christ Church, Oxford, 1851–54. From second year as an undergraduate was a Student (i.e. Fellow) of Christ Church. As lecturer, 1855–81, taught mathematics, on which also wrote voluminiously. Ordained deacon, 1861, but rarely preached and was not priested. Enjoyed the friendship of children, including Alice Liddell, daughter of Dean of Christ Church, for whom wrote *Alice's Adventures in Wonderland* (1865) and *Through the Looking-Glass, and What Alice Found There* (1871). Nonsense verse includes *The Hunting of the Snark* (1876), *Sylvie and Bruno* (1889), and *Sylvie and Bruno Concluded* (1893). Also wrote handbooks on various games and sports, and photographed many Victorian writers and artists.

Collingwood, S. D., *The Life and Letters of Lewis Carroll* (1898).

Hudson, D., *Lewis Carroll: An Illustrated Biography* (1954; rev. 1977).

Cohen, M. N. and R. L. Green, eds, *The Letters of Lewis Carroll*, 2 vols (New York, 1979).

See: Taylor, A. L., *The White Knight: A Study of C. L. Dodgson (Lewis Carroll)* (Edinburgh and London, 1952). (Places 'nonsense' books in relation to Dodgson's intellectual life in Oxford, with special reference to mathematics and religion.)

Hudson, D., *Lewis Carroll*, Writers and their Work, 96 (1958). (Lightweight.)

Blake, K., *Play, Games, and Sport: The Literary Works of Lewis Carroll* (Ithaca, NY, and London, 1974). (Argues that 'play of all sorts infuses Carroll's imaginative literature'.)

COLLINS, William Wilkie (1824–89), son of William Collins, portrait painter; educated in London where, after spell in Italy, was articled to firm of tea merchants, 1841–46. Studied law and called to the Bar, 1849. Having published plays, stories, and a number of novels in 1850s, including favourably reviewed *Antononia; or, The Fall of Rome* (1850) and *Basil: A Story of Modern Life* (1852), established himself as one of most popular novelists of age with *The Woman in White* (1859–60), first published in *All the Year Round*, recently launched by Dickens (*q.v.*), close friend from 1851. The first sensation novel of 1860s, this was followed by other notable successes – *No Name* (1862; in *All the Year Round*); *Armadale* (1864–66; in *Cornhill*), attacked for treatment of bigamy and crime; and *The Moonstone: A Romance* (1868; in *All the Year Round*) – which secured Collins's position as acknowledged leader in sub-genre. Although later attempts to combine propagandist material with sensational plotting, as in *Man and Wife* (1869–70; in *Cassell's Magazine*) and *The New Magdalen* (1873; in *Temple Bar*), were generally considered inferior by reviewers, enormous popularity remained secure in 1870s and 1880s as continued to write in spite of poor health and addiction to laudanum. Like friends Reade (*q.v.*) and Dickens, was also a dramatist, sometimes producing fictional and dramatic versions of same work. Relationships with Mrs Caroline Graves, with whom is buried at Kensal Green, and Martha Rudd, later 'Mrs Dawson', by whom had three children, were frowned upon by many contemporaries, and prejudiced judgements on him after his death.

Robinson, R., *Wilkie Collins: A Biography* (1951; repr. 1974). (Informative on private life and friendships with Dickens and Reade.)

Ashley, R., *Wilkie Collins*, English Novelists (1952). (Short pioneering critical biography.)

See:　Eliot, T. S., 'Wilkie Collins and Dickens' (1927), in his *Selected Essays*, 3rd edn (1951), pp. 460–70. (Interesting comparisons.)

Marshall, W. H., *Wilkie Collins*, Twayne's English Authors, 94 (New York, 1970). (First attempt to place Collins's art in relation to development of the novel.)

Hughes, W., *The Maniac in the Cellar: Sensation Novels of the 1860s* (Princeton, 1980). (Chapter on Collins.)

Lonoff, S., *Wilkie Collins and his Victorian Readers: A Study in the Rhetoric of Authorship*, AMS Studies in the Nineteenth Century, 2 (New York, 1982). (Fullest critical treatment to date.)

CORELLI, Marie (pseudonym of Mary Mackay: 1855–1924), illegitimate daughter of Charles Mackay, journalist and poet, and Mary Mills, née Kirtland; educated privately. Father's second marriage was to her mother; family moved from London to Mickleham, Surrey, 1865, where Meredith (*q.v.*) was a friend and neighbour. On death of Mary's mother, 1876, Bertha Vyver, a childhood friend, joined household, and remained Mary's lifelong companion. A talented musician, took pseudonym of 'Marie Corelli' when contemplating a career as pianist before return to London, 1883. Instead became the best-selling novelist of late nineteenth century. First work was semi-autobiographical *A Romance of Two Worlds* (1886). *Barabbas: A Dream of the World's Tragedy* (1893) received harsh reviews but great popular acclaim, and *The Sorrows of Satan* (1895) sold more copies than any previous English novel. Other romances included *The Mighty Atom* (1896) and *Boy* (1900). Settled in Stratford-upon-Avon, 1901.

Bullock, G., *Marie Corelli: The Life and Death of a Best-Seller* (1940). (Life and works treated with light touch.)

Bigland, E., *Marie Corelli: The Woman and the Legend* (1953).

Scott, W. S., *Marie Corelli: The Story of a Friendship* (1955).

Masters, B., *Now Barabbas Was a Rotter: The Extraordinary Life of Marie Corelli* (1978). (Lively and detailed biography.)

DICKENS, Charles (1812–70), second of eight children of John Dickens, clerk in Navy Pay Office; born Portsea, near Portsmouth, and lived in Chàtham, Kent, 1817–22. From 1822 John Dickens's debts increased until imprisoned in Marshalsea, 1824; during this period young Dickens worked in Warren's Blacking Warehouse and visited his family in prison. Became solicitor's clerk, 1827; then freelance reporter in Doctor's Commons lawcourts, later in House of Commons. Married Catherine Hogarth, 1836; ten children. Early literary pieces collected in two volumes as *Sketches by Boz* (1836), and followed by *Pickwick Papers* (1836–37), which rapidly established his fame. Early instalments of *Oliver Twist* (1837–39) written and published in *Bentley's Miscellany* concurrently with later numbers of *Pickwick*, when Dickens was also very active as a journalist, and in social life and private theatricals, a lifelong passion. Moved to house in Doughty Street, now Dickens museum, 1837. *Nicholas Nickleby* (1838–39), *The Old Curiosity Shop* (1840–41), and *Barnaby Rudge* (1841) published in rapid succession. Moved to Devonshire Terrace, Regent's Park, 1839. Trip to United States recorded in *American Notes* (1842). Comparative unpopularity of *Martin Chuzzlewit* (1843–44) partly compensated by success of Christmas books, such as *A Christmas Carol* (1843) and *The Chimes* (1844). Trip to Italy in 1844–45 first of several trips on Continent in middle years. Wrote *The Life of Our Lord* for his children (published 1934). *Dombey and Son* published 1846–48 and partly autobiographical *David Copperfield*, Dickens's own favourite, 1849–50. Founded and edited weekly family periodical, *Household Words*, 1850, later to be succeeded by *All the Year Round*, 1859. Moved to Tavistock House, Bloomsbury, 1851. Between *Bleak House* (1852–53) and *Little Dorrit* (1855–57), published *Hard Times* as serial in *Household Words* (1854). By 1859, when *A Tale of Two Cities* published in *All the Year Round*, had bought Gad's Hill Place, near Rochester, had separated from his wife, and had befriended actress Ellen Ternan. *Great Expectations* (1860–61) and *Our Mutual Friend* (1864–65) were last completed novels. Taxing reading tours of Britain and America in late 1860s wore him out as he drove himself to re-establish close contact with reading public. Died at Gad's Hill of a stroke suffered after full day's work on last, unfinished novel, *Edwin Drood*, June 1870; buried in Westminster Abbey.

Forster, J., *The Life of Charles Dickens*, ed. by A. J. Hoppé, 2 vols (1966). (Famous biography by Dickens's friend and adviser, first published 1872–74.)

Johnson, E., *Charles Dickens: His Tragedy and Triumph*, 2 vols (1953). (Well-written scholarly biography, also available in abridged version.)

Fielding, K. J., ed., *The Speeches of Charles Dickens* (Oxford , 1960).

House, M. and G. Storey *et al.*, eds, *The Letters of Charles Dickens*, Pilgrim Edition (Oxford, 1965–). (5 vols to date; 12 projected.)

See: House, H., *The Dickens World* (Oxford, 1941). (Places Dickens and work in historical context).

Butt, J. and K. Tillotson, *Dickens at Work* (1957). (Study of planning and writing of several major works.)

Miller, J. H., *Charles Dickens: The World of his Novels* (Cambridge, Mass., 1958). (Pioneering study of Dickens's existential vision.)

Collins, P., *Dickens and Crime*, Cambridge Studies in Criminology, ed. by L. Radzinowicz, 17 (London and New York, 1962).

Collins, P., *Dickens and Education* (London and New York, 1963).

Marcus, S., *Dickens: From Pickwick to Dombey* (1965). (Fascinating study of early Dickens, with special emphasis on mythic quality of his work.)

Johnson, E. D. H., *Charles Dickens: An Introduction to his Novels* (New York, 1969).

Daleski, H. M., *Dickens and the Art of Analogy* (1970). (Interesting approach to use of analogy as a 'structural principle'.)

Leavis, F. R. and Q. D. Leavis, *Dickens the Novelist* (1970; repr. Harmondsworth, 1972). (Essays on six novels and the illustrations.)

Sucksmith, H. P., *The Narrative Art of Charles Dickens* (Oxford, 1970). (On 'the technical means whereby, through structure, effects are created and vision focused'.)

Wilson, A., *The World of Charles Dickens* (1970). (Lively, lavishly illustrated account of Dickens and his age.)

Carey, J., *The Violent Effigy: A Study of Dickens' Imagination* (1973). (Lively and suitably idiosyncratic.)

Thurley, G., *The Dickens Myth: Its Genesis and Structure* (1976). (Challenging if somewhat insistent on Dickens's reworking of his own myth of guilt and ambition.)

Pattern, R. L., *Charles Dickens and his Publishers* (Oxford, 1978).

Walder, D., *Dickens and Religion* (1981). (First book-length study on subject.)

DISRAELI, Benjamin, 1st Earl of Beaconsfield (1804–81), son of Jewish writer and antiquarian Isaac D'Israeli, from whom received much of his education; attended schools at Islington, Blackheath, and Walthamstow. Baptized into Church of England, 1817. Articled to solicitor, 1821, and became notorious for flashy dandyism in London society. Portrayed leading public figures and political manoeuvring in *Vivian Gray* (1826–27). While aspiring to be a poet and to break into political life, continued to write romances and silver-fork novels: *The Young Duke* (1831), *Contarini Fleming* (1832), *Alroy* (1833), *Henrietta Temple* (1837), and *Venetia* (1837). Elected Conservative MP for Maidstone, 1837; later leader of radical Tory 'Young England' group. Married Mrs Wyndham Lewis, 1839 (died 1872). Bought country estate of Hughenden; elected MP for Shrewsbury, 1841, later for Buckinghamshire, 1847. Developed ideas on party politics, Condition of England Question, and religion in trilogy: *Coningsby* (1844), *Sybil* (1845), and *Tancred* (1847). Three times Chancellor of Exchequer and twice PM, 1868 and 1874–80. Wrote two later novels: *Lothair* (1870) and *Endymion* (1880). Created Earl of Beaconsfield, 1876. At his death left a fragment of novel which has been called *Falconet*, in which his arch-rival Gladstone is satirized.

Moneypenny, W. F. and G. E. Buckle, *The Life of Benjamin Disraeli*, 6 vols (1910–20); rev. edn, 2 vols (1929). (The standard biography.)

Blake, R., *Disraeli* (1966). (Definitive modern biography which supplements Moneypenny and Buckle, above.)

See: Speare, M. E., *The Political Novel* (Oxford, 1924).

Rosa, M. W., *The Silver Fork School: Novels of Fashion Preceding Vanity Fair* (New York, 1936). (Discusses *Vivian Gray*.)

Holloway, J., *The Victorian Sage* (1953).

Levine, R. A., *Benjamin Disraeli*, Twayne's English Authors, 68 (New York, 1968). (First book-length critical study; introductory.)

Schwarz, D. R., *Disraeli's Fiction* (1979). (Enthusiastic study of whole corpus.)

Braun, T., *Disraeli the Novelist* (1981). (Combines literary criticism and biography.)

DODGSON, Charles Lutwidge: see CARROLL, Lewis.

DOYLE, Sir Arthur Conan (1859–1930), son of Edinburgh civil servant, Roman Catholic; educated in Lancashire, at Hodder School and Stonyhurst, 1868–75, and in Austria, 1875–76. Studied medicine at University of Edinburgh, 1876–81, and practised as a GP in Southsea, 1882–90. Married Louise Hawkins, 1885; two children. Became a full-time professional writer, 1891. The detective, Sherlock Holmes, modelled partly on Dr Joseph Bell of Edinburgh, first appeared in two 'long stories', *A Study in Scarlet* (1887; in *Beeton's Christmas Annual*) and *The Sign of Four* (1890; in *Lippincott's Magazine*). Not until publication of short stories in *Strand Magazine*, 1891–92, collected as *The Adventures of Sherlock Holmes* (1892), did Holmes seize the popular imagination. Later in career, Doyle also created the figures of Brigadier Gerard and Professor Challenger. Historical romances included *Micah Clarke* (1889), *The White Company* (1891; in *Cornhill*), and *Sir Nigel* (1905–6; in *Strand Magazine*). During Boer War, was senior physician in a field hospital and wrote in defence of British policy, for which was knighted, 1902. LL.D., University of Edinburgh, 1905. Following death of first wife, 1906, married Jean Leckie, 1907; three children. In later years wrote extensively on spiritualism, which had fascinated him since 1880s.

Pearson, H., *Conan Doyle: His Life and Art* (1943; repr. 1977). (Energetic and anecdotal.)

Carr, J. D., *The Life of Sir Arthur Conan Doyle* (1949).

Pearsall, R., *Conan Doyle: A Biographical Solution* (1977).

See: Harrison, M., *The World of Sherlock Holmes* (1973).

Ousby, I., *Bloodhounds of Heaven: The Detective in English Fiction from Godwin to Doyle* (Cambridge, Mass., 1976).

ELIOT, George (pseudonym of Mary Ann(e) or Marian Evans: 1819–80), daughter of Robert Evans, Warwickshire estate manager; educated at several boarding schools, including the Miss Franklins' school, Coventry, where converted to Calvinist Evangelicalism. After death of mother, 1836, moved to Coventry, where continued study of modern languages and music, and where friendship with the Bray and Hennell families contributed to loss of faith. Translation of Strauss's *Life of Jesus, Critically Examined* (1846) was influential in England. Later also translated Feuerbach's *Essence of Christianity* (1854). Following father's death, 1849, lived for a time in Geneva, returning to live in publisher John Chapman's house in Strand, London, where wrote for his *Westminster Review*. As assistant editor, to 1854, worked with William Hale White (*q.v.*) and met leading intellectuals of new generation, including Herbert Spencer and George Henry Lewes, reviewer, writer on science and philosophy, and novelist, with whom she lived as wife from 1854 until his death. (Lewes was married with four sons, but had separated amicably from wife, who had two children by colleague of his on staff of the *Leader*.) Attracted to aspects of Comtean Positivism, she developed her own religion of humanity, whose idea of duty was as demanding as that of earlier Calvinist position. Works of first half of career as novelist published by Blackwood in rapid succession: *Scenes of Clerical Life* (1857), three stories; *Adam Bede* (3 vols, 1859); *The Mill on the Floss* (3 vols, 1860); and *Silas Marner* (1861). Although based in London, always longed for countryside portrayed in this early fiction, and often travelled abroad with Lewes. Having achieved high sales and recognition as a leading writer, published first work of second phase of career, *Romola* (1862–63), a minutely researched historical romance, as serial in *Cornhill Magazine*. Bought the Priory, next to Regent's Canal, London, 1863, where regularly entertained leading thinkers of post-Darwinian era. Returned to Blackwood with *Felix Holt, the Radical* (3 vols, 1866) and *The Spanish Gypsy: A Poem* (1868). Last and most ambitious novels, *Middlemarch* (1871–72) and *Daniel Deronda* (1876), both published by Blackwood in eight books. Shattered by death of Lewes, 1878, worked on his unfinished *Problems of Life and Mind* and published her own *Impressions of Theophrastus Such* (1879), loosely connected series of sketches and essays. Married John Cross, twenty years younger than herself, 1880, but died later that year at their house in Cheyne Walk, Chelsea.

> Cross, J. W., ed., *George Eliot's Life, as Related in her Letters and Journals*, 3 vols (Edinburgh, 1885).
> Haight, G. S., ed., *The George Eliot Letters*, 7 vols (New Haven, 1954–56).
> Pinney, T., ed., *Essays of George Eliot* (1963).
> Haight, G. S., *George Eliot: A Biography* (Oxford and New York, 1968). (Definitive.)

See: Leavis, F. R., *The Great Tradition: George Eliot, Henry James, Joseph Conrad* (1948; repr. Harmondsworth, 1962). (High-handed but influential criticism of Eliot's works, judged according to their 'maturity'.)

Willey, B., *Nineteenth-Century Studies: Coleridge to Matthew Arnold* (1949; repr. Cambridge, 1980). (Two chapters on major influences on Eliot's intellectual development.)

Hardy, B., *The Novels of George Eliot: A Study in Form* (1959). ('Form' is interpreted broadly; emphasizes tragic dimension of the fiction.)

Harvey, W. J., *The Art of George Eliot* (1961). (Relates the moralist to the artist in her historical context.)

Knoepflmacher, U. C., *Religious Humanism and the Victorian Novel: George Eliot, Walter Pater, and Samuel Butler* (Princeton, 1965). (On Eliot's scientific Positivism, religion of humanity and Feuerbachian demythologizing of Christianity.)

Roberts, N., *George Eliot: Her Beliefs and Her Art*, Novelists and their World (London and Pittsburgh, 1975). (Treatment of Eliot's intellectual development informs discussion of each novel.)

EVANS, Mary Ann(e) or Marian: see ELIOT, George.

FARRAR, Frederic William (1831–1905), son of chaplain of Church Missionary Society, Bombay; educated at King William's College, Isle of Man, King's College, London, and Trinity Hall, Cambridge. Ordained priest, 1857, and married Lucy Mary Cardew, 1860; ten children. Having taught at Harrow, 1855–71, became headmaster of Marlborough, 1871–76. Later Canon and Archdeacon of Westminster, and, from 1895, Dean of Canterbury. A disciple of F. D. Maurice, Farrar wrote many religious works, including famous *Life of Christ* (1874) and controversial *Eternal Hope* (1878). His school stories, *Eric; or, Little by Little: A Tale of Roslyn School* (1858) and *St Winifred's; or, The World of School* (1862), were widely read. Other fiction included *Julian Home* (1859) on college life and *Darkness and Dawn; or, Scenes in the Days of Nero* (1891).

> Farrar, R., *The Life of Frederic William Farrar* (1904). (By son Reginald.)

FROUDE, James Anthony (1818–94) youngest son of Archdeacon of Totnes, and brother of Richard Hurrell Froude; educated at Westminster School and Oriel College, Oxford. Fellow of Exeter College, 1842; ordained deacon, 1844; contributed to Newman's (*q.v.*) *Lives of the English Saints* (1844–45). Having lost his faith, published two stories under title *Shadows of the Clouds* (1847). *The Nemesis of Faith* (1849) was publicly burnt in Exeter College; resigned fellowship on same day. Married Charlotte Maria Grenfell, 1849, who died 1860; one daughter. Married Henrietta Elizabeth Warre, 1861; two children. Many essays published in leading journals later collected as *Short Studies on Great Subjects*, 4 series (1867–83). Major historical works included *History of England from the Fall of Wolsey to the Defeat of the Spanish Armada*, 12 vols (1856–70). His controversial life of Carlyle (1882–84) is one of the great Victorian literary biographies. Elected Regius Professor of Modern History at Oxford, 1892.

> Dunn, W. H., *James Anthony Froude: A Biography*, 2 vols (Oxford, 1961–63).

See: Willey, B., *More Nineteenth-Century Studies: A Group of Honest Doubters* (1956; repr. Cambridge, 1980). (Chapter on Froude.)
Wolff, R. L., *Gains and Losses: Novels of Faith and Doubt in Victorian England* (New York and London, 1977). (Section on Froude.)

GASKELL, Elizabeth Cleghorn (1810–65), daughter of William Stevenson, Unitarian minister and Keeper of Treasury Records; after death of her mother, a year after birth, was brought up by aunt in Knutsford, Cheshire, on which Cranford was later based; educated at Stratford-upon-Avon. Married William Gaskell, Unitarian minister, and moved to Manchester, 1832, where she raised four daughters, worked in slum districts, and wrote novels and numerous short stories. After death of her baby, William, she was encouraged to write first novel, *Mary Barton: A Tale of Manchester Life* (1848). *Cranford*, a series of sketches, first appeared in Dickens's (*q.v.*) *Household Words* (1851–53), and has always enjoyed great popularity. Silverdale, North Lancashire, where holidayed most years from 1850, provided one setting in second full-scale work, *Ruth* (1853), which caused controversy by sympathetically presenting an unmarried mother as heroine. *North and South*, a pendant to *Mary Barton*, published in *Household Words* (1854–55). Having been Charlotte Brontë's (*q.v.*) close friend, 1850–55, she wrote her *Life* (1857), revealing the Brontë 'secret' to the world. By this time she was a world-famous literary figure, who welcomed many distinguished visitors to her home in Plymouth Grove, Manchester. Later works included her only tragic novel, *Sylvia's Lovers* (1863); the novella *Cousin Phyllis* (1863–64; in *Cornhill*), a rural idyll; and *Wives and Daughters: An Every-day Story* (1864–66; in *Cornhill*), her longest and most ambitious novel, left unfinished when she died suddenly.

Hopkins, A. B., *Elizabeth Gaskell: Her Life and Work* (1952).

Chapple, J. A. V. and A. Pollard, eds, *The Letters of Mrs Gaskell* (Manchester, 1966).

Gérin, W., *Elizabeth Gaskell: A Biography* (1976). (Makes full use of *Letters* published 1966).

See: Pollard, A., *Mrs Gaskell, Novelist and Biographer* (Manchester, 1965). (Sound introduction.)

Wright, E., *Mrs. Gaskell: The Basis for Reassessment* (1965). (Pioneering critical study.)

Sharps, J. G., *Mrs. Gaskell's Observation and Invention* (Fontwell, Sussex, 1970). (Useful for its minutiae.)

Craik, W. A., *Elizabeth Gaskell and the English Provincial Novel* (1975). (First study to attempt to place Gaskell in a literary tradition.)

Easson, A., *Elizabeth Gaskell* (1979). (Scholarly study of Gaskell's life and work in historical context.)

GISSING, George Robert (1857–1903), son of Wakefield pharmacist; educated on scholarships at private schools (including Lindow Grove, Alderley Edge, Cheshire), and Owens College, Manchester, 1872–76, where he excelled as classical scholar. His dismissal from college and imprisonment for stealing, to rescue Nell Harrison from prostitution, prevented him from pursuing academic career. Travelled to America, 1876, where taught and wrote for newspapers. Returning to England, took the first of dozens of lodgings in London, 1877, where observed hardships of the poor, read Comte, and married Nell Harrison, 1879, who often returned to prostitution to get money for drink. Frederic Harrison, a leading Positivist, engaged him as tutor to his sons, and introduced him to literary circles. First novel, *Workers in the Dawn* (1880), published at own expense. Always a compulsive worker, he abandoned many partially completed novels, and, even after being 'discovered' by Meredith (*q.v.*), reader for Chapman and Hall, who published *The Unclassed* (1884), he accepted low payments for his works and received mixed reviews. Novels of his early phase also include *Demos* (1886), *Thyrza* (1887), *A Life's Morning* (1888), and *The Nether World* (1889), written after death, 1888, of his wife from whom he was now separated. Travelled to France and Italy, 1889, one of settings in *The Emancipated* (1890), a novel of middle-class life. Marriage to Edith Underwood, 1890, uneducated daughter of a small shopkeeper, proved almost as disastrous as his first. Strongly autobiographical *New Grub Street* (1891) revealed hard realities of the professional writer's life in the period. Later novels include *Born in Exile* (1892), *The Odd Women* (1893), on social position of women, *In the Year of Jubilee* (1894), *Eve's Ransom* (1895), *The Whirlpool* (1897), *The Crown of Life* (1899), and *The Private Papers of Henry Ryecroft* (1902–3; in *Fortnightly Review*, as 'An Author at Grass'), his most popular autobiographical novel. Also wrote numerous short stories, an influential critical study on Dickens (1898), and a travel book, *By the Ionian Sea* (1901). Met young H. G. Wells, 1896, when his fame was at last growing. Separated, 1897, from second wife, who was later admitted to an asylum, and lived with Gabrielle Fleury, translator of *New Grub Street*, from 1898. Died in France.

> Gissing, A. and E., eds, *Letters of George Gissing to Members of His Family* (1927).
> Korg, J., *George Gissing: A Critical Biography* (1963; repr. Brighton and Seattle, 1980). (The standard work.)
> Tindall, G., *The Born Exile: George Gissing* (1974).
> Collie, M., *George Gissing: A Biography* (1977).
> Halperin, J., *Gissing: A Life in Books* (Oxford, 1982). (Critical biography; emphasizes parallels between the life and works.)

See: Donnelly, M. C., *George Gissing: Grave Comedian* (Cambridge, Mass., 1954).
> Keating, P. J., *The Working Classes in Victorian Fiction* (1971). (Chapter on Gissing.)
> Poole, A., *Gissing in Context* (1975). (Important work of 'critical reinterpretation'.)
> Collie, M., *The Alien Art: A Critical Study of George Gissing's Novels* (Folkestone and Hamden, Conn., 1978). (On effect of his position as outsider.)

HAGGARD, Sir Henry Rider (1856–1925), son of Norfolk barrister and squire; educated privately and at Ipswich Grammar School. Aged nineteen, became secretary to Lieutenant-Governor of Natal, 1875. On staff of special commissioner during annexation of Transvaal, 1877, Haggard raised the union flag in Pretoria. Having been Master of High Court in Pretoria from 1877, returned to England, 1879, and married Marianna Margitson, Norfolk heiress, 1880; four children. Called to the Bar, 1884. In literary career, produced many romances, including *King Solomon's Mines* (1885) and its sequel, *Allan Quartermain* (1887), *She* (1886–87; in *Graphic*), *Nada the Lily* (1892), and *Ayesha: The Return of She* (1904). Success of early novels allowed him to give up law, 1887. Also wrote on English farming and rural depopulation. Numerous public services included membership of Dominions Royal Commission, 1912–17. Knighted, 1912, and created KBE, 1919. Autobiography, *The Days of My Life* (1926), published posthumously.

> Haggard, L. R., *The Cloak that I Left* (1951). (Biography by youngest daughter.)
> Cohen, M., *Rider Haggard: His Life and Work*, 2nd edn (1968). (Argues that Haggard vacillated between world of affairs and world of literature.)
> Ellis, P. B., *H. Rider Haggard: A Voice from the Infinite* (1978). (Enthusiastic biography; includes bibliography.)

See: Sandison, A., *The Wheel of Empire: A Study of the Imperial Idea in Some Late Nineteenth and Early Twentieth-Century Fiction* (London and New York, 1967). (Chapter on Haggard and evolution.)
> Higgins, D. S., *Rider Haggard: The Great Storyteller* (1981). (Draws on unpublished material, including diaries which Higgins also edited.)

HARDY, Thomas (1840–1928), son of builder and mason of Higher
Bockhampton, Dorset; mother worked as servant and later as cook before
marriage. Educated at village school, then at two schools in Dorchester,
1850–56, second of which, kept by Isaac Last, Hardy later referred to as a
'college'. Articled to Dorchester architect and church-restorer, John Hicks,
1856–62, before working as assistant architect in London, 1862–67, where
continued wide reading and began to write poetry. On returning to Dorset
to assist Hicks and his successor, was involved in some way with a cousin,
Tryphena Sparks. First novel, 'The Poor Man and the Lady' (now lost)
finished 1868, but remained unpublished on advice of Meredith (*q.v.*).
Following publication of early novels – *Desperate Remedies* (1871), *Under the
Greenwood Tree* (1872), *A Pair of Blue Eyes* (1872–73; in *Tinsleys' Magazine*)
– and Leslie Stephen's publication of *Far From the Madding Crowd* as
successful serial in *Cornhill Magazine* (1874), Hardy married Emma Gifford,
1874, four years after they met in Cornwall. In happiest years of marriage
wrote *The Hand of Ethelberta* (1875–76; in *Cornhill*) and *The Return of the
Native* (1878; in *Belgravia*). With move to Upper Tooting, south London,
1878, he became better known in literary circles and published *The Trumpet
Major* (1880; in *Good Words*), and *A Laodicean* (1880–81; in *Harper's
Magazine*, European edn), written during period of serious illness. Back in
Dorset, wrote *Two on a Tower* (1882; in *Atlantic Monthly*) and moved,
1885, to Max Gate, Dorchester, house designed by himself, and home for
rest of life. Wrote *The Mayor of Casterbridge* (1886; in *Graphic*) and *The
Woodlanders* (1886–87; in *Macmillan's Magazine*), and published first of
several collections of short stories: *Wessex Tales* (1888). From late 1880s,
when suffered from depression, regularly visited London in spring, and
made occasional Continental tours. Later novels are *Tess of the d'Urbervilles*
(1891; in *Graphic*), *The Well-Beloved* (1892; in *Illustrated London News*, as
'The Pursuit of the Well-Beloved') and *Jude the Obscure* (1894–95; in
Harper's Magazine, first as 'Hearts Insurgent', later 'as 'The Simpletons').
Hostile critical reception of *Jude* persuaded Hardy to give up novel-writing
and concentrate on poetry. Following *Wessex Poems* (1898), published other
volumes of verse, best of which followed death of wife, Emma, 1912, and
expressed his grief and remorse over later, unhappy phase of marriage.
Married his assistant, Florence Dugdale, 1914. Elected to five honorary
doctorates from British universities, and honorary fellowships at
Magdalene, Cambridge and Queen's, Oxford. Refused offer of knighthood,
but accepted Order of Merit, 1910. His ashes are buried in Westminster
Abbey, his heart in first wife's grave, Stinsford. Florence Hardy's *The
Early Life of Thomas Hardy, 1840–1891* (1928) and *The Later Years of
Thomas Hardy, 1892–1928* (1930) are in fact Hardy's autobiography,
dictated to her in his old age (apart from last four chapters of second vol.);
he suppressed information concerning parentage, early love-life, and first
marriage.

Orel, H., ed., *Thomas Hardy's Personal Writings* (Lawrence, Kansas,
1966).
Stewart, J. I. M., *Thomas Hardy: A Critical Biography* (1971). (More
than half the book is critical discussion of novels.)
Gittings, R., *Young Thomas Hardy* (1975; repr, Harmondsworth,
1978); *The Older Hardy* (1978; repr. Harmondsworth, 1980). (First
vol. to 1876; excellent biography which places special emphasis on
Hardy's sexuality and class-consciousness.)

Purdy, R. L. and M. Millgate, eds, *The Collected Letters of Thomas Hardy* (Oxford, 1978–). (2 vols to date; 7 projected.)

Millgate, M., *Thomas Hardy: A Biography* (Oxford and Melbourne, 1982). (Heavily documented from original sources.)

See: Lawrence, D. H., 'Study of Thomas Hardy', in *Phoenix: The Posthumous Papers of D. H. Lawrence*, ed. by E. D. McDonald (1936), pp. 398–516. (Lawrence's short book on Hardy's novels, written 1914 but unpublished in lifetime.)

Guerard, A. J., *Thomas Hardy: The Novels and Stories* (Cambridge, Mass., 1949).

Brown, D., *Thomas Hardy*, Men and Books (1954). (Gentle introduction to the subject.)

Millgate, M., *Thomas Hardy: His Career as a Novelist* (1971). (Informative critical study on whole corpus; includes data on writing and publication of each novel.)

Williams, M., *Thomas Hardy and Rural England* (1972). (Supplies historical context and argues that Hardy, 'our most important country novelist', had few nostalgic illusions.)

Gregor, I., *The Great Web: The Form of Hardy's Major Fiction* (1974). (Good critical study.)

Kramer, D., *Thomas Hardy: The Forms of Tragedy* (Detroit and London, 1975). (Interesting treatment of Hardy's use of form in each of his tragic novels.)

Bayley, J., *An Essay on Hardy* (Cambridge, 1978). (Lively treatment of fiction and poetry, discussed together; particularly strong on texture of writing and on early fiction.)

King, J., *Tragedy in the Victorian Novel: Theory and Practice in the Novels of George Eliot, Thomas Hardy and Henry James* (Cambridge, 1978). (Argues that Hardy's are 'tragedies of situation', rather than of character'.)

HENTY, George Alfred (1832–1902), born in Trumpington, Cambridgeshire, son of a stockbroker, educated at Westminster School, 1847–52, and Caius College, Cambridge, 1852; left without taking a degree. Served in Hospital Commissariat during Crimean War, 1855; also wrote as war correspondent. Invalided home, became purveyor of the forces; organized Italian hospitals during war with Austria, 1859; resigned commission after further service in Britain. Married Elizabeth Finucane, 1858; four children. Became foreign correspondent on London *Standard*, 1866–76, which, together with military experience, provided much material for over 100 stories and novels. Specialized in adventure books for boys, published mainly from 1880 until his death. Also edited *Union Jack* magazine, 1880–83, and *Beeton's Boy's Own Magazine*, 1888–90. Married Elizabeth Keylock.

Fenn, G. M., *George Alfred Henty: The Story of an Active LIfe* (1907). (Rambling memoir by a close friend; only two brief chapters on Henty as writer.)

See: Arnold, G., *Held Fast for England: G. A. Henty, Imperialist Boy's Writer* (1980).

HUGHES, Thomas (1822–96), son of John Hughes, minor author and country gentleman of Berkshire; educated at Rugby School and Oriel College,

Oxford, where rowed and played cricket for university. Called to the Bar, 1848, and practised law in London. Married Frances Ford, 1848; six children, two of whom died young. *Tom Brown's School Days* (1857) portrays the 'muscular Christianity' of the Rugby Hughes knew under Dr Thomas Arnold; ran through seventy printings during lifetime. The sequel, *Tom Brown at Oxford* (1861), was less successful, as was *The Scouring of the White Horse* (1859), in which idealized country life of his youth. Also published numerous tracts and biographies. With his mentor, F. D. Maurice, and Charles Kingsley (*q.v.*), his closest friend, was active in Christian Socialist and Working Men's College movements in London. A Liberal MP, 1865–74, became QC, 1869, and County Court Judge at Chester, 1882, where lived in old age. A settlement he founded in Tennessee, 1879, and named Rugby, proved abortive.

Mack, E. C. and W. H. G. Armytage, *Thomas Hughes: The Life of the Author of Tom Brown's School Days* (1952).

JAMES, George Payne Rainsford (1801?–1860), son of a London doctor; educated at Putney. Travelled and read widely in his youth. Married Frances Thomas, 1828; five (?) children. Lived in France, 1829–31. During residence at Melrose, Scotland, 1831–33, knew Scott, and James Hogg. Published several works a year, mainly historical romances, including *Richelieu: A Tale of France* (1829) and *Henry Masterton; or, The Adventures of a Young Cavalier* (1832); also popular history books. British Consul in the early 1850s first for Massachusetts, then for Virginia. Finally Consul at Venice, where died.

Ellis, S. M., *The Solitary Horseman; or, The Life & Adventures of G. P. R. James* (1927). (Pieces together fragments of data on early life; on firmer ground from 1830s.)

JEFFERIES, Richard (1848–87), son of Wiltshire yeoman farmer; educated at schools in Sydenham, Kent, and Wiltshire. Travelled in France, 1865, and made abortive attempt to sail to America. Worked as journalist on various West Country newspapers, 1866–70. Travelled in Belgium, 1870. Married Jessie Baden, 1874; three children. Having written two society novels – *The Scarlet Shawl* (1874) and *Restless Human Hearts* (1875) – wrote for *Pall Mall Gazette*, living in London suburbs and Sussex. Ten years 1877–87 proved highly productive, in spite of serious illness (fistula) from 1881. Fiction includes *The World's End* (1877), *Wood Magic: A Fable* (1880) and its sequel, *Bevis: The Story of a Boy* (1882), *The Dewy Morn* (1884), *After London: or, Wild England* (1885), and *Amaryllis at the Fair* (1887). Numerous other works on country life include *The Amateur Poacher* (1879). In *The Story of my Heart: My Autobiography* (1883) ideas predominate over facts.

Thomas, E., *Richard Jefferies* (1909; repr. 1978). (Justly famous biography by poet Edward Thomas; treatment of literary works illustrated with lengthy extracts.)

Looker, S. J. and C. Porteus, *Richard Jefferies, Man of the Fields: A Biography and Letters* (1965).

See: Keith, W. J., *Richard Jefferies: A Critical Study* (1965). (Standard work; includes bibliography.)

Taylor, B., *Richard Jefferies*, Twayne's English Authors, 329 (Boston, 1982). (Critical introduction; argues that keynote to his work is sincerity.)

KINGSLEY, Charles (1819–75), son of Rev. Charles Kingsley brother of Henry Kingsley; educated at Helston Grammar School, Cornwall; King's College, London; Magdalene College, Cambridge. Ordained priest and became curate of Eversley, Hampshire, 1842. Married Fanny Grenfell, 1844; four children. Rector of Eversley, 1844, where introduced many improvements and preached his 'muscular Christianity' for rest of his life. Reformist fiction, including *Yeast* (1848; in *Fraser's*), *Alton Locke, Tailor and Poet* (1850), and sanitary novel *Two Years Ago* (1857), reflect his views as a Christian Socialist, in which movement he worked with his 'master', F. D. Maurice, and his closest friend, Thomas Hughes (*q.v.*). His historical novels, *Hypatia* (1853), the popular *Westward Ho!* (1855), and *Hereward the Wake* (1865; in *Good Words*) reflect other sides of his complex nature, including nationalist fervour and the vehement anti-Catholicism which led him to attack Newman (*q.v.*) with humiliating results, 1864. Also wrote numerous tracts, sermons, poems, a poetic drama (*The Saint's Tragedy*, 1848), and historical works. His interest in natural history is reflected in fantasy, *The Water-Babies* (1863), and *Glaucus; or, The Wonders of the Shore* (1855). Industry and zeal, though causing frequent nervous breakdowns, brought prestigious appointments, including Regius Chair of Modern History at Cambridge, 1860–69, where was also tutor to Prince of Wales; Canon of Chester, 1869–73, and Westminster, 1873–75; and Chaplain to Queen, 1873–75. His younger brother, Henry Kingsley (1830–76), also wrote novels, including *Geoffrey Hamlyn* (1859), an Australian story reflecting his own experiences there, and *Ravenshoe* (1861), on a Protestant's right of succession in a Roman Catholic family.

Kingsley, F. E., ed, *Charles Kingsley: His Letters and Memories of His Life*, 2 vols (1876). (Informative hagiography by wife.)
Martin, R. B., *The Dust of Combat: A Life of Charles Kingsley* (1959). (Critical biography.)
Chitty, S., *The Beast and the Monk: A Life of Charles Kingsley* (1975). (Includes analysis of Kingsley's remarkable religio-sexual fantasies.)
Colloms, B., *Charles Kingsley: The Lion of Eversley* (1975). (Main focus on Kingsley as reformer.)

LE FANU, Joseph Thomas Sheridan (1814–73), son of Church of Ireland clergyman, later Dean of Emly, related to Sheridan family; educated privately and at Trinity College, Dublin. Called to the Irish Bar, 1839. From 1837 worked on staff of *Dublin University Magazine*, which eventually owned and edited, 1861–70; also edited and purchased a number of Dublin newspapers. Married Susanna Bennett, 1843. Early stories, later collected as *The Purcell Papers* (1880), on Irish life in tradition of Maria Edgeworth. Turned to novel-writing after death of much loved wife, 1858. Spate of novels from *The House by the Churchyard* (1863) and *Uncle Silas: A Tale of Bartram-Haugh* (1864) to time of death, loosely of sensation novel school, and mostly printed in *Dublin University Magazine* before going into volumes. His last collection of stories was *In a Glass Darkly* (1872).

Browne, N., *Sheridan Le Fanu* (1951).
McCormack, W. J., *Sheridan Le Fanu and Victorian Ireland* (Oxford, 1980). (Full biographical study, which includes detailed discussion of most significant works of fiction.)

LEVER, Charles James (1806–72), son of Anglo-Irish parents, father a builder; born in Dublin and educated at Trinity College, Dublin. After medical training in Göttingen and again at Trinity, served as surgeon on emigrant ship to Canada and then practised medicine in Ireland in 1830s and Brussels, 1839–42. Married Catherine Baker, 1833; one daughter. His rollicking tales of Irish garrison life include *The Confessions of Harry Lorrequer* (1837) and *Charles O'Malley, The Irish Dragoon* (1840), both published serially in *Dublin University Magazine*, which Lever edited, 1842–45. Lived in Italy from 1845, being Vice-Consul at Spezia and later Consul at Trieste. Wrote numerous Irish novels after 1845, many on provincial and historical subjects, being influenced by Scott and Maria Edgeworth; but although more mature and realistic, these were less widely read than the early popular successes.

Downey, E., *Charles Lever: His Life in His Letters*, 2 vols (1906).
Stevenson, L., *Dr Quicksilver: The Life of Charles Lever* (1939).

MacDONALD, George (1824–1905), son of tenant farmer; educated at Huntly school, Aberdeenshire, and King's College, Aberdeen. After working as tutor in London and training at Highbury Congregationalist College, became minister at Arundel, 1850, and married Louisa Powell; eleven children. Opposition to his liberal views on salvation having finally forced him to resign post, 1853, taught and preached in Manchester, 1855–56 and Hastings, 1857–59. Professor of English Literature at Bedford College, London from 1859. In attempting to convey highly individual vision, which drew upon eclectic legendary and mystical sources, and ideas of friend F. D. Maurice, who drew him into Church of England, MacDonald experimented with many forms, including fairy-tales, novels, sermons, and volumes of verse. Best known for adult fantasies, *Phantastes* (1858) and *Lilith* (1895), and children's stories such as *At the Back of the North Wind* (1870), which influenced C. S. Lewis and J. R. R. Tolkein, he also wrote novels which reflected own rejection of Scottish Calvinism, including *David Elginbrod* (1863), *Robert Falconer* (1868), and *Paul Faber, Surgeon* (1879). Accepted Civil List pension, 1877, and lived in Italy in 1880s and 1890s.

MacDonald, G., *George MacDonald and His Wife* (1924). (Biography by son Greville.)

See: Freemantle, A., *The Visionary Novels of George MacDonald* (1954).
Wolff, R. L., *The Golden Key: A Study of the Fiction of George MacDonald* (New Haven, 1961). (Enthusiastic and detailed account of major works.)

MACKAY, Mary: see CORELLI, Marie.

MALLOCK, William Hurrell (1849–1923), son of rector of Cheriton Bishop, Devon; educated privately (at Littlehampton) and at Balliol College, Oxford, 1869–74. Began work on satirical *roman-á-clef*, *The New Republic*

(1877), at Balliol, whose Master, Jowett, is 'Dr Jenkinson'. The ideas of Tyndall ('Mr Stockton' in *The New Republic*) and Huxley ('Mr Storks') are again parodied in *The New Paul and Virginia* (1878). Other novels include *A Romance of the Nineteenth Century* (1881) and *The Old Order Changes* (1886). Continued to attack various forms of liberalism and socialism in novels and essays throughout his life. Wrote *Memoirs of Life and Literature* (1920).

See: Adams, A. B., *The Novels of William Hurrell Mallock*, University of Maine Studies, second series, 30 (Orono, 1934). (Three chapters on life, followed by nine on individual novels.)

Lucas, J., ed., *Literature and Politics in the Nineteenth Century* (1971). (Chapter of 'Conservatism and Revolution in the 1880s' focuses on Mallock.)

Wolff, R. L., *Gains and Losses: Novels of Faith and Doubt in Victorian England* (New York and London, 1977). (Chapter on Mallock.)

MARRYAT, Captain Frederick (1792–1848), son of MP, banker, later chairman of Lloyd's; educated at Ponders End. Went to sea as midshipman, 1806. Married Catherine Shairp, 1819; eleven children. Elected FRS, 1819. Resigned as a captain, 1830, and bought house and farm at Langham, Norfolk, where lived permanently from 1843. Edited *Metropolitan Magazine*, 1832–35. Wrote lively sea stories based partly on his own experiences, including *The King's Own* (1830), *Peter Simple* (1832–33; in *Metropolitan Magazine*), *Mr Midshipman Easy* (1836), and *Masterman Ready* (1841–42). *Snarleyyow; or, The Dog Fiend* (1836–37; in *Metropolitan Magazine*) and *The Phantom Ship* (1837; in *New Monthly Magazine*) reflect his interest in the supernatural and grotesque. Other works include popular historical novel for children, *The Children of the New Forest* (1847).

Marryat, F., *Life and Letters of Captain Marryat*, 2 vols (1872).
Hannay, D., *Captain Marryat*, English Men of Letters (1889).
Warner, O., *Captain Marryat: A Rediscovery* (1953). (Biography; includes brief discussion of novels.)

MARTINEAU, Harriet (1802–76), daughter of Norwich manufacturer and sister of Rev. Professor James Martineau, Unitarian minister and scholar. Physically infirm, she suffered from deafness and was educated mostly at home. Wrote religious works in her twenties, but later lost her faith and concentrated on mesmerism. Moved to London, 1832, Her interest in Utilitarian economics and political theory led her to write didactic stories entitled *Illustrations of Political Economy*, 9 vols (1832–34) and *Poor Laws and Paupers Illustrated*, 4 parts (1833–34). Also wrote novels, *Deerbrook* (1839) and *The Hour and the Man* (1841), a historical romance, as well as travel books, children's stories, translation of Comte's *Philosophie Positive* (1853), and *Autobiography* (1877). Built a house at Ambleside in Lake District, 1845, her home for rest of her life.

Bosanquet, T., *Harriet Martineau: An Essay in Comprehension* (1927). (Biography.)
Wheatley, V., *The Life and Work of Harriet Martineau* (1957).
Webb, R. K., *Harriet Martineau: A Radical Victorian* (New York and London, 1960). (Scholarly biography, placing Martineau in relation to Victorian radicalism.)

MEREDITH, George (1828–1909), son of Portsmouth tailor, grandson of
Melchizedek Meredith (the Great Mel of *Evan Harrington*); mother died
when he was five. Following father's bankruptcy, lived with relations near
Petersfield; indifferent early education completed during creative period at
enlightened Moravian school in Germany, 1843–44. Articled to dilettante
London lawyer, 1845, but soon turned to writing. Married Mary Ellen
Nicholls, T. L. Peacock's widowed daughter, 1849; one son, Arthur.
Breakdown of marriage, and wife's affair with painter, Henry Wallis,
reflected in his most impressive sequence of poems, *Modern Love* (1862),
and, together with his relationship with his son, in first full-length novel,
The Ordeal of Richard Feverel (1859), widely held to be immoral at the time.
Having launched literary career with two fantasies, *The Shaving of Shagpat*
(1856) and *Farina* (1857), earned regular income as columnist on *Ipswich
Journal* in 1860s, and as chief reader for publishers Chapman and Hall,
1860–94, an onerous but highly influential position, in which he advised
Hardy and Gissing (*qq.v.*) early in their careers. Following death of first
wife, 1861, married Marie Vulliamy, 1864; two children. Moved to Flint
Cottage, near Box Hill, Surrey, 1868, where entertained leading writers
and intellectuals, and where, from 1877, spent most of his time in a chalet
in grounds. Between two further novels including elements of
autobiography – *Evan Harrington* (1860; in *Once a Week*) and *The Adventures
of Harry Richmond* (1870–71; in *Cornhill Magazine*) – published *Emilia in
England* (1864, later called *Sandra Belloni*), *Rhoda Fleming* (1865), and *Vittoria*
(1866; in *Fortnightly Review*). His political novel, *Beauchamp's Career*
(1874–75; in *Fortnightly Review*), was followed by *The Egoist* (1879), and his
only popular success, *Diana of the Crossways* (1884, shortened version in
Fortnightly Review; 1885, complete in 3 vols), based on Lord
Melbourne/Caroline Norton scandal. His later novels include *One of Our
Conquerors* (1890–91; in *Fortnightly Review*) and *The Amazing Marriage*
(1895; in *Scribner's Magazine*). Later poetry includes *Poems and Lyrics of the
Joy of Earth* (1883), *Ballads and Poems of Tragic Life* (1887), *A Reading of
Earth* (1888), and *A Reading of Life* (1901). Only major critical work was
his lecture *On the Idea of Comedy* (1877). After death of second wife, 1885,
suffered increasingly from paralysis. Became President of Society of
Authors, 1892, and elected to Order of Merit, 1905.

Stevenson, L., *The Ordeal of George Meredith: A Biography* (New
York, 1953). (The standard literary life.)

Cline, C. L., ed., *The Letters of George Meredith*, 3 vols (Oxford,
1970).

Williams, D., *George Meredith: His Life and Lost Love* (1977).
(Informal.)

See: Wright, W. F., *Art and Substance in George Meredith: A Study in
Narrative* (Lincoln, Nebraska, 1953).

Kelvin, N., *A Troubled Eden: Nature and Society in the Works of
George Meredith* (Edinburgh and London, 1961). (On the fiction and
poetry.)

Bartlett, P., *George Meredith*, Writers and their Work, 161 (1963).
(Short introduction.)

Beer, G., *Meredith: A Change of Masks. A Study of the Novels* (1970).
(Balanced literary criticism, concentrating on six novels.)

Pritchett, V. S., *George Meredith and English Comedy*, Clark Lectures,
1969 (1970).

Fletcher, I., ed., *Meredith Now: Some Critical Essays* (1971). (Mostly on individual works.)

Wilt, J., *The Readable People of George Meredith* (Princeton and London, 1975). (Focuses on Meredith's creative concern with real reader of and fictional reader in the novels.)

MOORE, George Augustus (1852–1933), son of Irish Roman Catholic landowner, G. H. Moore, MP, of Moore Hall, County Mayo. Educated at Oscott College, Birmingham, 1861–68, and then with an army tutor in London, where family moved, 1869, and where Moore began art training. Father died, 1870, leaving large estate with only small income. Having come of age, 1873, settled in Paris to enjoy his 'café education' among painters (including Manet and Degas) and poets, later recorded in *Confessions of a Young Man* (1888). Poetry published as *Flowers of Passion* (1878) and *Pagan Poems* (1881). Returning to London, 1880, wrote for *Spectator* and *Examiner*, and later as successful art critic for *Speaker* in early 1890s (collected articles published as *Modern Painters*, 1893). At first influenced by Zola, but later acknowledging Balzac as his master, published what he called 'realistic' novels which challenged Victorian social and aesthetic conventions, including *A Modern Lover* (1883, rewritten as *Lewis Seymour and Some Women*, 1917); *A Mummer's Wife* (1885); *A Drama in Muslin* (1886); and *Esther Waters* (1894), which was successful with reading public. Also wrote plays, often collaboratively, including with the American novelist Mrs Pearl Craigie ('John Oliver Hobbes'), who eventually spurned his love. Returned to Ireland, 1901; lived at Moore Hall and in Dublin. Became leading figure in the Celtic revival, converted to Protestantism, and was made High Sheriff of Mayo, 1905. Works of this period include short stories, such as *The Untilled Field* (1903), and his first symbolist novel, *The Lake* (1905). During final phase of his career, lived in Belgravia, London, 1911–33, and travelled. Revised much of his early work; wrote historical novels, including *The Brook Erith: A Syrian Story* (1916), a rewriting of gospel story; and further memoirs and essays, including *Hail and Farewell: A Trilogy* (*Ave, Salve, Vale*), 3 vols (1911–14), and *Conversations in Ebury Street* (1924).

Hone, J., *The Life of George Moore* (1936). (The standard biography; includes bibliography.)

Gerber, H. E., ed., *George Moore in Transition: Letters to T. Fisher Unwin and Lena Milman, 1894–1910* (Detroit, 1968).

See: Brown, M. J., *George Moore: A Reconsideration* (Seattle, 1955).

Jeffares, A. N., *George Moore*, Writers and their Work, 180 (1965). (Brief outline of literary career, drawing heavily on Hone's *Life*.)

Noël, J. C., *George Moore: L'Homme et l'Oeuvre* (Paris, 1966).

Dunleavy, J. E., *George Moore: The Artist's Vision, The Storyteller's Art* (Lewisburg, 1973). (Short study, in which literary technique is related to artistic training.)

Cave, R. A., *A Study of the Novels of George Moore*, Irish Literary Studies, 3 (Gerrards Cross and New York, 1978). (Chronological treatment: 'The Novel of Social Realism', 'A Phase of Experiment', and 'Styles for Consciousness'.)

MORRIS, William (1834–96), son of wealthy stockbroker; brought up in Essex countryside. Educated at local preparatory school; Marlborough College;

and Exeter College, Oxford, 1853–55, where he met Edward Burne-Jones. Father died, 1847, leaving family rich; inherited £900 a year, 1855. Articled to Street, the architect, in London, 1856. Married Jane Burden, 1859; two daughters. Built the Red House, Bexley Heath, designed by Philip Webb, 1859–60. Founded firm of Morris, Marshall, Faulkner & Co., 1861, producing furniture, stained glass, tiles, fabrics, wallpapers, etc. First made literary reputation as a poet, particularly with *The Earthly Paradise* (1868–70). From 1870s, alternated between Kelmscott House, Hammersmith, and Kelmscott Manor, Oxfordshire, his wife having intermittent liaison with D. G. Rossetti (who died 1882). Founded Socialist League, 1884. Many of his leading ideas expressed in Utopian romance, *News from Nowhere*, published (1890) in *The Commonweal*, which he subsidized and edited.

> Mackail, J. W., *The Life of William Morris*, 2 vols (1899). (Still cited by modern authorities.)
> Henderson, P., *William Morris: His Life, Work, and Friends* (1967). (General biography; good illustrations.)
> Lindsay, J., *William Morris: His Life and Work* (1975). (Detailed, lengthy study; enthusiastic treatment of Morris the Marxist.)
> Faulkner, P., *Against the Age: An Introduction to William Morris* (1980). (Concise but informative literary biography.)

See: Brantlinger, P., ' "News from Nowhere": Morris's Socialist Anti-Novel', *Victorian Studies*, 19(1975–76), 35–49. (Interesting article on 'artless' quality of the work.)

NEWMAN, John Henry (1801–90), son of Evangelical banker; educated at Ealing School and Trinity College, Oxford. Fellow of Oriel, 1822; vicar of St Mary's, Oxford, 1828. Leading member of Tractarian or 'Oxford' Movement, writing many of the *Tracts for the Times* (1833–41), including controversial Tract XC (1841). Converted to Roman Catholicism, 1845, and published *Essay on the Development of Christian Doctrine*. Founded Birmingham Oratory. Wrote two novels, *Loss and Gain* (1848) and *Callista: A Sketch of the Third Century* (1856). The leading English Christian apologist of his age, his major works include the *Apologia pro Vita Sua* (1864), a response to an attack by Charles Kingsley (*q.v.*); *The Dream of Gerontius* (1865); *An Essay in Aid of a Grammar of Assent* (1870). Elected Cardinal, 1879.

> Dessain, C. S. *et al.*, eds, *The Letters and Diaries of John Henry Newman* (1961–). (14 vols to date; 31 projected.)
> Trevor, M., *Newman*, 2 vols (1962). (Standard modern biography.)

See: Wolff, R. L., *Gains and Losses: Novels of Faith and Doubt in Victorian England* (New York and London, 1977). (Section on Newman.)
> Wright, T. R., 'Newman as Novelist: *Loss and Gain*', in *John Henry Newman: A Man for our Time?*, ed. by T. R. Wright (Newcastle upon Tyne, 1983), pp. 7–17. (Also on *Callista*, with special reference to Newman's Romanticism.)

OLIPHANT, Margaret Oliphant (1828–97), daughter of Francis Wilson, at one time a customs officer, and Margaret Oliphant. Lived first in Scotland and later Birkenhead, where married her cousin, Francis Wilson Oliphant, designer of stained glass, 1852. Having settled in London, she became regular contributor to *Blackwood's Magazine* for rest of working life, eventually writing her famous *Annals of a Publishing House* (1897) on the Blackwoods. A prolific novelist, literary critic, historian, and biographer, Margaret Oliphant alone supported her three children after husband's death in 1859, and her brother's family from 1864, the year in which her own daughter died. Her novels of Scottish life include *Katie Stewart* (1853) and *Kirsteen* (1890), but her major achievement was series of novels, 'The Chronicles of Carlingford': *Salem Chapel* (1863), *The Rector and The Doctor's Family* (1863), *The Perpetual Curate* (1864), *Miss Marjoribanks* (1866), and *Phoebe Junior: A Last Chronicle of Carlingford* (1876). Lived in Windsor from 1866, to be near sons at Eton, and died at Wimbledon.

Coghill, A. L., ed., *The Autobiography and Letters of Mrs M. O. W. Oliphant* (1899). (Describes slavery of professional woman writer and pain of bereavements.)

See: Cunningham, V., *Everywhere Spoken Against: Dissent in the Victorian Novel* (Oxford, 1975). (Chapter on Oliphant.)

Wolff, R. L., *Gains and Losses: Novels of Faith and Doubt in Victorian England* (New York and London, 1977). (Two sections examine treatment of High Church and dissent in Carlingford series.)

Terry, R. C., *Victorian Popular Fiction, 1860–80* (1983). (Includes Oliphant as writer for 'middle-brow' readership.)

OUIDA (pseudonym of Marie Louise Ramé, later de la Ramée: 1839–1908), born Bury St Edmunds, daughter of Englishwoman and French political refugee, a teacher of French who also educated Marie. Lived mainly in London from 1857 until settled permanently in Italy in 1870s with beloved dogs. Literary career began under guidance of William Harrison Ainsworth (*q.v.*), who published her stories in *Bentley's Miscellany*. Sustained by belief that she rivalled George Eliot (*q.v.*), produced numerous romantic novels, including the highly successful *Under Two Flags* (1867), a story of fated love in the ranks of Life Guards, and *Moths* (1880), a high-society novel. Her work has an international flavour, and was admired by Bulwer (*q.v.*) and Ruskin among others. Civil List pension saved her from abject poverty in her declining years.

ffrench, Y., *Ouida: A Study in Ostentation* (1938). (Biography.)

Bigland, E., *Ouida: The Passionate Victorian* (1950). (Biography.)

Stirling, M., *The Fine and the Wicked: The Life and Times of Ouida* (1957). (Detailed biography, placing Ouida's work in context of Victorian literary scene.)

See: Anderson, R., *The Purple Heart Throbs: The Sub-Literature of Love* (1974). (Chapter on 'Certain Fine and Nasty Books' by Ouida.)

PATER, Walter Horatio (1839–94), born in London, son of a doctor who was formerly Roman Catholic. Educated in Enfield and King's School, Canterbury; then at Queen's College, Oxford, 1858–62. Elected fellow of Brasenose, 1864. Lived in Oxford quietly, with his sisters, regularly attending church services while remaining intellectually sceptical.

Continental travel deepened interest in the Renaissance, on which wrote essays for periodicals, collected as *Studies in the History of the Renaissance* (1873; 2nd rev. edn as *The Renaissance*, 1877), which established literary reputation. Resigned tutorship, 1883, but not fellowship, and moved to London. *Marius the Epicurean: His Sensations and Ideas* (1885), a historical romance, was his major work. Fragment of a similar work, *Gaston de Latour*, published posthumously, 1896. Later works included *Imaginary Portraits* (1887), *Appreciations* (1889), *Plato and Platonism* (1893). Returned to Oxford, 1893.

> Wright, T., *The Life of Walter Pater*, 2 vols (1907). (Unreliable.)
> Evans, L., ed., *Letters of Walter Pater* (Oxford, 1970).
> Levey, M., *The Case of Walter Pater* (1978). ('Very much about the man – and also about his work.')

See: Hough, G., *The Last Romantics* (1949). (Seminal chapter on Pater.)
> Fletcher, I., *Walter Pater*, Writers and their Work, 114 (1959). (Useful short introduction.)
> Knoepflmacher, U. C., *Religious Humanism and the Victorian Novel: George Eliot, Walter Pater, and Samuel Butler* (Princeton, 1965). (Detailed commentary on Pater's thought and beliefs.)
> Monsman, G., *Walter Pater*, Twayne's English Authors, 207 (Boston, 1977). (Introduction to life and works, concentrating on 'the Aesthetic hero'.)

RAMÉ, Marie Louise (later de la Ramée): see OUIDA.

READE, Charles (1814–84), son of Oxfordshire squire; educated by tutor and at private school. Led Bohemian existence at Magdalen College, Oxford, 1831–35, and Lincoln's Inn, 1836–43. Called to the Bar and held senior posts at Magdalen in 1840s, but went on to write plays and novels in 1850s, mainly living with Mrs Laura Seymour, an actress, in London, 1854–79. Having succeeded in 1853 with first two novels, *Peg Woffington* and *Christie Johnstone*, wrote *It Is Never Too Late to Mend* (1856), a sensation novel which exposed worst aspects of penal system. Reade's obsessive research methods were then applied to writing of his major historical novel, *The Cloister and the Hearth* (1861). Further sensation novels followed, including *Hard Cash* (1863), which exposed abuses in asylums, *Griffith Gaunt* (1865–66), attacked for its treatment of sexual relationships, and, with Dion Boucicault, *Foul Play* (1868). A self-publicist with a strong taste for the grotesque, Reade took on numerous adversaries during a stormy career as dramatist and novelist, but died an ill and lonely man, saddened by years of critical attack from reviewers.

> Elwin, M., *Charles Reade: A Biography* (1931).

See: Turner, A. M., *The Making of The Cloister and the Hearth* (Chicago, 1938). (Detailed analysis of sources.)
> Burns, W., *Charles Reade: A Study in Victorian Authorship* (New York, 1961). (Emphasizes significance of psychology in analysis of Reade.)
> Smith, E. E., *Charles Reade*, Twayne's English Authors, 186

(Boston, 1976). (Useful introduction, aware of Reade's weaknesses as well as strengths.)

Hughes, W., *The Maniac in the Cellar: Sensation Novels of the 1860s* (Princeton, 1980). (Chapter on 'Charles Reade and the Breakdown of Melodrama'.)

RUTHERFORD, Mark (pseudonym of William Hale White: 1831–1913), son of Bedford printer and bookseller, a Calvinist dissenter and member of the Old Meeting, to which White himself was 'admitted', 1848. Educated at Bedford Modern School. Training for ministry at Cheshunt College and New College, St John's Wood, ended with expulsion for heresy, 1852. Although later preached to Unitarian congregations, now turned to miscellaneous writing and journalism in London, working at Chapman's, the publishers, with Marian Evans (George Eliot, *q.v.*) whom he loved. Entered Civil Service, working at Somerset House from 1854, later at Admiralty from 1858, where became assistant director of contracts, 1879–91. Married Harriet Arthur, 1856; six children. Built a house at Park Hill, Carshalton, 1868. His semi-autobiographical trilogy – *The Autobiography of Mark Rutherford* (1881), *Mark Rutherford's Deliverance* (1885), and *The Revolution in Tanner's Lane* (1887) – was followed by other novels: *Miriam's Schooling* (1890), *Catharine Furze* (1893), and *Clara Hopgood* (1896). Other works included translation of Spinoza's *Ethic* (1883) and life of *John Bunyan* (1905). First wife died, 1891. Married Dorothy Smith, 1911.

Maclean, C. M., *Mark Rutherford: A Biography of William Hale White* (1955). (Detailed biography which sees White's life as 'almost in itself. an authentic history of the Victorian era'.)

See: Stock, I., *William Hale White (Mark Rutherford): A Critical Study* (1956). (Study of novels; includes three chapters on his life.)

Merton, S., *Mark Rutherford (William Hale White)*, Twayne's English Authors, 53 (New York, 1967). (On 'the writer of distinctive novels and the representative Victorian'.)

Cunningham, V., *Everywhere Spoken Against: Dissent in the Victorian Novel* (Oxford, 1975). (Chapter on White.)

Lucas, J., *The Literature of Change: Studies in the Nineteenth-Century Provincial Novel* (Hassocks and New York, 1977). (Chapter on White.)

SHORTHOUSE, Joseph Henry (1834–1903), son of Birmingham chemical manufacturer, a Quaker; educated at Quaker school, Egbaston, and Grove House, Tottenham. Worked in father's business from age of sixteen until 1900, but kept up intensive private reading. Married Sarah Scott, 1857, and both converted to Church of England, 1861. Attacks of epilepsy, 1862, left him in poor health. *John Inglesant: A Romance* (privately printed, 1880) brought him immediate fame when published by Macmillan, 1881. Later works included *The Little Schoolmaster Mark: A Spiritual Romance* (1883–84) and *Sir Percival: A Story of the Past and Present* (1886).

Shorthouse, S., ed., *The Life and Letters of J. H. Shorthouse*, 2 vols (1905).

See: Polak, M., *The Historical, Philosophical and Religious Aspects of John*

Inglesant (Oxford, 1934). (Attacks Shorthouse as a plagiarizing autodidact.)

Bishop, M., *'John Inglesant* and its Author', in *Essays by Divers Hands*, N. S. 29 (1958), 73–86. (Affectionate thumb-nail sketch.)

Wagner, F. J., *J. H. Shorthouse*, Twayne's English Authors, 275 (Boston, 1979). (Introduction; includes long chapter on *John Inglesant*.)

STEVENSON, Robert Louis (1850–94), son of prosperous Edinburgh lighthouse and harbour engineer, educated at several schools, including Edinburgh Academy. Neglected engineering studies at Edinburgh University, 1867–71, intended to prepare him for family business, and was articled to Edinburgh legal practice, 1871. Declaration of agnosticism alienated parents, 1873, the year in which fell in love with Mrs Frances Sitwell. Chronic ill health, which dogged him throughout life, forced him to escape Edinburgh winters, mainly on Continent, from 1873. (His many travel books include *Travels with a Donkey in the Cévennes*, 1879.) Sidney Colvin, who later married Frances Sitwell, introduced him to London literary circles, 1874. Although called to Scottish Bar, 1875, decided on literary career. Met W. E. Henley, 1875, with whom later wrote unsuccessful plays, and Mrs Frances Osbourne, 1876, becoming her lover. Travelled on emigrant train across America to be with Fanny in Monterey, California, 1879, where married her after her divorce, 1880, and had first haemorrhage from lungs. (He may have suffered from bronchiectasis rather than tuberculosis.) Returned to Britain with wife and stepson, Lloyd Osbourne, later a writer himself. Early stories included *New Arabian Nights* (1882). Made his literary reputation with *Treasure Island* (1881–82; in *Young Folks*), written, characteristically, in three locations: Braemar, near Balmoral, Scotland; Weybridge, Surrey, England; and Davos, Switzerland. Published *The Black Arrow* (1883; in *Young Folks*) and *Prince Otto: A Romance* (1885; in *Longman's Magazine*). At Skerryvore, house bought by father at Bournemouth, was visited regularly by close friend Henry James, to whom his 'Humble Remonstrance' (1884) had been directed. Bournemouth period produced *The Strange Case of Dr Jekyll and Mr Hyde* (1886) and *Kidnapped* (1886; in *Young Folks*). (A sequel, *Catriona*, published 1893.) Left Britain for last time, 1887, travelling to America, where began *The Master of Ballantrae: A Winter's Tale* (1888–89; in *Scribner's Magazine*). With his wife, stepson, and widowed mother, sailed by yacht to South Seas, completing *The Master*. Family finally settled in a large house, built by themselves, in Samoa, where Stevenson wrote unfinished romance, *Weir of Hermiston* (1896). Apart from fiction, wrote poetry (*Collected Poems*, ed. by J. A. Smith, 2nd edn, 1971), numerous essays (*Essays*, ed. by M. Elwin, 1950), and plays.

Colvin, S., ed., *The Letters of Robert Louis Stevenson to his Family and Friends*, 2 vols (1899); rev. edn, 4 vols (1911).

Balfour, G., *The Life of Robert Louis Stevenson*, 2 vols (1901). (Official biography by Stevenson's cousin.)

Elwin, M., *The Strange Case of Robert Louis Stevenson* (1950). (Challenges the Stevenson 'legend'.)

Furnas, J. C., *Voyage to Windward: The Life of Robert Louis Stevenson* (1952). (Painstakingly researched; a pioneering modern biography.)

Hennessy, J. P., *Robert Louis Stevenson* (1974). (Lively, engaged biography.)

Calder, J., *RLS: A Life Study* (1980). (Particularly interested in Stevenson the man, as opposed to the writer.)

See: Daiches, D., *Robert Louis Stevenson* (New York, 1946). (Important work of rehabilitation after long reaction against Stevenson.)

Daiches, D., *Stevenson and the Art of Fiction* (New York, 1951). (Excellent essay, particularly on ambiguity of Stevenson's morality.)

Kiely, R., *Robert Louis Stevenson and the Fiction of Adventure* (Cambridge, Mass., 1964). (Study of five aspects of Stevenson's adventure fiction.)

Eigner, E. M., *Robert Louis Stevenson and Romantic Tradition* (Princeton, 1966). (Places Stevenson in nineteenth-century tradition of 'serious romance', and examines 'man's dual nature' as major theme.)

Calder, J., ed., *Stevenson and Victorian Scotland* (Edinburgh, 1981). (Mixed bag of essays reflecting aspects of current reassessment of Stevenson.)

Good, G., 'Rereading Robert Louis Stevenson', *Dalhousie Review*, 62 (1982), 44–59. (On the romances as reaction against Victorian social novel.)

SURTEES, Robert Smith (1805–64), son of County Durham landowner; educated at Ovingham School and Durham Grammar School. Articled to local solicitor before moving to London law firm, 1825. Joint founder and editor of *New Sporting Magazine*, 1831–36. Abandoned the law, succeeded to father's estate, 1838, and married Elizabeth Jane Fenwick, 1841; three children. Early comic hunting sketches in *New Sporting Magazine*, 1831–34, collected as *Jorrocks' Jaunts and Jollities* (1838), and sporting novels *Handley Cross* (1843), *Hillingdon Hall* (1845), and *Hawbuck Grange* (1846–47; in *Bell's Life*), did not succeed with public until publication of *Mr Sponge's Sporting Tour* (1849; in *New Monthly*; illustrated by John Leech, 1853). Became High Sheriff of County Durham, 1856.

Cooper, L., *R. S. Surtees* (1952). (Biography.)

See: Watson, F., *Robert Smith Surtees: A Critical Study* (1933; repr. 1978). (Covers novels 'in their relation to his life and environment'.)

Johnstone-Jones, D. R., *The Deathless Train: The Life and Work of Robert Smith Surtees*, Salzburg Studies in English Literature: Romantic Reassessment, ed. by J. Hogg, 36 (Salzburg, 1974). (Life and background followed by aspects of the fiction.)

Welcome, J., *The Sporting World of R. S. Surtees* (Oxford, 1982). (Fullest discussion to date of novels in context of life and times.)

THACKERAY, William Makepeace (1811–63), son of prosperous civil servant (East India Company); born in Calcutta. At age of six was sent to England and attended two schools where he was miserably lonely; mother returned to England with second husband, 1820. Education continued at the Charterhouse, 1822–28, and at Trinity College, Cambridge, where he gambled away a fortune and left without a degree. In early 1830s travelled on Continent, staying in Weimar for some months. Made false starts in London legal training and Paris art training; lost much of his inheritance in a bank failure; bought an unsuccessful newspaper. Having contributed stories, articles, and reviews to *Fraser's Magazine* under Maginn's editorship, married Isabella Shaw, 1836, and, having to support himself by writing, he settled happily in London on *Fraser's* staff, 1837. Wife became incurably insane, 1840, following depression after death of second daughter and birth of a third. (She was to survive Thackeray by thirty years.) Thackeray returned to bachelor existence in London, established home for self and daughters in Kensington, 1846. Contributions to *Fraser's* included *The Yellowplush Correspondence* (1837–38), anti-Newgate novel, *Catherine* (1839–40), *The Great Hoggarty Diamond* (1841), and *The Luck of Barry Lyndon* (1844; rev. as *The Memoirs of Barry Lyndon*, 1856). Also wrote travel books in 1840s: *The Paris Sketch Book* (1840), *The Irish Sketch Book* (1843), and *Notes of a Journey from Cornhill to Grand Cairo* (1846). Consolidated connection with *Punch*, 1844, in which published *The Book of Snobs* (1846–47). (Resigned from *Punch*, 1851.) Turning-point in career came in 1847. when published burlesques entitled 'Punch's Prize Novelists' and *Vanity Fair* in monthly parts (1847–48). Now acknowledged to be a leading novelist, went on to produce four major works which, apart from *The History of Henry Esmond*, 3 vols (1852), set in early eighteenth century, were published in monthly parts: *The History of Pendennis* (1848–50), *The Newcomes* (1853–55), and *The Virginians* (1857–59), a sequel to *Esmond*. His last works came out in both monthly *Cornhill Magazine* (founded 1860), under his own editorship, and the American *Harper's Magazine: Lovel the Widower* (1860), *The Adventures of Philip* (1861–62), and unfinished *Denis Duval* (1864). Non-fictional writings of 1850s include famous lectures on *The English Humourists of the Eighteenth Century*, delivered in London, 1851, and subsequently on tours of Britain and America; and lectures on *The Four Georges*, given on tours, 1855–57. Misfortune continued to dog him: fell in love with wife of a close friend, William Brookfield, which led to a breach with couple, 1851; famous 'Garrick Club affair', 1858, opened a rift with Dickens (*q.v.*); was often in pain in later years as result of stomach trouble and urethral stricture.

Ray, G. N., ed., *The Letters and Private Papers of William Makepeace Thackeray*, 4 vols (1945–46).

Stevenson, L., *The Showman of Vanity Fair: The Life of William Makepeace Thackeray* (1947).

Ray, G. N., *Thackeray: The Uses of Adversity, 1811–46* and *Thackeray: The Age of Wisdom, 1847–63* (London and New York, 1955–58). (The standard biographies.)

See: Trollope, A., *Thackeray*, English Men of Letters, ed. by J. Morley (1879). (Unusual case of one Victorian novelist writing at length on another; cf. Gissing on Dickens.)

Thrall, M. M. H., *Rebellious Fraser's* (New York, 1934). (On Thackeray's contributions to the magazine under Maginn.)

Van Ghent, D., *The English Novel: Form and Function* (New York, 1953). (Chapter on *Vanity Fair*.)

Tillotson, G., *Thackeray the Novelist* (Cambridge, 1954). (Organized around salient features of the fiction.)

Dyson, A. E., '*Vanity Fair*: An Irony against Heroes', *Critical Quarterly*, 6 (1964), 11–31. (On sophistication of Thackeray's ironic strategies.)

Hardy, B., *The Exposure of Luxury: Radical Themes in Thackeray* (1972). (Emphasizes the 'big scenes' in major novels.)

Sutherland, J. A., *Thackeray at Work* (1974). (On Thackeray's inventiveness as a 'one-draft writer'.)

Sutherland, J. A., *Victorian Novelists and Publishers* (1976). (Chapter on *Henry Esmond*.)

Carey, J., *Thackeray: Prodigal Genius* (1977). (Presents case for early works as against 'later and staider' novels.)

Colby, R. A., *Thackeray's Canvass of Humanity: An Author and his Public* (Columbus, Ohio, 1979). (Painstakingly places Thackeray as 'a representative Victorian man of letters'.)

TONNA, Charlotte Elizabeth (1790–1846), daughter of Rev. Michael Browne, minor canon of Norwich; became completely deaf in childhood, almost lost sight. Married Captain Phelan when she was young; separated about 1824. Following Phelan's death, 1837, married Lewis Tonna, 1841. As 'Charlotte Elizabeth' wrote many Evangelical tracts, articles, and stories, including *The Wrongs of Women*, 4 parts (1843–44) and the early industrial novel, *Helen Fleetwood* (1839–40).

See: Kovačević, I. and S. B. Kanner, 'Blue Book into Novel: The Forgotten Industrial Fiction of Charlotte Elizabeth Tonna', *Nineteenth-Century Fiction*, 25 (1970–71), 152–73.

Kovačević, I., *Fact into Fiction: English Literature and the Industrial Scene 1750–1850* (Leicester, 1975). (See index for passages on Tonna.)

TROLLOPE, Anthony (1815–82), son of failed barrister and dominating mother, Frances Trollope (*q.v.*); endured a largely unhappy childhood, often neglected by parents and beaten by masters at Harrow, where was ridiculed as an impoverished day boy, and, briefly, at Winchester College. Entered Central Post Office as clerk, 1834, and worked his way up to be head of eastern district of England by time resigned, 1867, having grown to love the Post Office and introduced the pillar-box. From 1841 worked successfully as postal surveyor in Ireland, travelling extensively on horseback. Met Rose Heseltine, whom married, 1844; two sons. Irish period provided material for first novels, *The Macdermots of Ballycloran* (1847) and *The Kellys and the O'Kellys* (1848), as well as for several later works, including sections of 'Palliser' novels. During spell of surveying in south-west England, Trollope hit upon idea for the 'Barsetshire' series of novels, depicting clerical and professional life in a provincial diocese: *The Warden* (1 vol., 1855), *Barchester Towers* (3 vols, 1857), *Doctor Thorne* (3 vols, 1858), *Framley Parsonage* (1860–61; in *Cornhill*), *The Small House at Allington* (1862–64; in *Cornhill*), and *The Last Chronicle of Barset* (weekly parts, 1866–67). *Barchester Towers* made him famous, and he settled into routine of intense labour on two or three novels a year, writing early in morning, and even on trains and ships, to set timetables. *The Three Clerks* (1858), *The Bertrams*, (1859), and *Orley Farm* (1861–62), were among other works published during Barsetshire period. Bought Waltham House, Waltham Cross, Essex, 1859, and continued to pursue his passion for fox-hunting. Became famous clubman and literary figure in London. In early 1860s an intense but platonic friendship began with attractive young

American, Kate Field, later a famous lecturer, whom he loved. Second major series, Palliser novels, first of which appeared before last Barsetshire novel, follows private lives and political careers of wide range of characters from upper-middle and upper classes, loosely centring on Plantagenet Palliser, later Prime Minister and Duke of Omnium: *Can You Forgive Her?* (1864–65), *Phineas Finn* (1867–69; in *St Paul's Magazine*), *The Eustace Diamonds* (1871–73; in *Fortnightly Review*), *Phineas Redux* (1873–74; in *Graphic*), *The Prime Minister* (1875–76), and *The Duke's Children* (1879–80; in *All the Year Round*). Other novels of 1860s include *Rachel Ray* (1863), *The Belton Estate* (1865–66; in *Fortnightly Review*), *The Claverings* (1866–67; in *Cornhill*), *He Knew he was Right* (1868–69), and *The Vicar of Bullhampton* (1869–70). By 1871 Trollope had resigned from Post Office and from editorship of monthly *St Paul's Magazine*, 1867–70, and had failed to be elected MP for Beverley, losing £2,000, 1868. After successful visit to Australia (his several voyages to colonies provided material for travel books), settled in Montague Square, London, and wrote *Autobiography* (published posthumously, 1883), and bitter satire on modern English society, *The Way We Live Now* (1874–75). Later novels include *Is he Popenjoy?* (1877–78; in *All the Year Round*), *Dr Wortle's School* (1880; in *Blackwood's Magazine*), and *Ayala's Angel* (1881). Moved with wife to converted farmhouse in Hampshire, 1880.

Hennessy, J. P., *Anthony Trollope* (1971). (Particularly good on Trollope the man of letters and traveller.)

Snow, C. P., *Trollope* (1975). (Informal, splendidly illustrated biography.)

Hall, N. J., ed., *The Letters of Anthony Trollope*, 2 vols (Stanford, 1983).

See: James, H., 'Anthony Trollope' (1883), repr. in his *Partial Portraits* (1888), pp. 97–133. (Reprinted in several collections of essays on Trollope.)

Cockshut, A. O. J., *Anthony Trollope: A Critical Study* (1955). (Argues for later works and Trollope's 'Progress to Pessimism'.)

Booth, B. A., *Anthony Trollope: Aspects of his Life and Work* (1959).

Roberts, R., *Trollope: Artist and Moralist* (1971). (Argues that his 'art of the ironic perspective' is suitable case for treatment in revaluing art of the novel.)

Skilton, D., *Anthony Trollope and his Contemporaries: A Study in the Theory and Conventions of Mid-Victorian Fiction* (1972). (Informative on reception of Trollope and on Victorian criticism of fiction in general.)

Edwards, P. D., *Anthony Trollope, his Art and Scope* (1977; repr. Hassocks, Sussex, 1978). (Good on the range of Trollope, and suggests interesting ways of grouping his novels.)

Kincaid, J. R., *The Novels of Anthony Trollope* (Oxford, 1977). (Excellent both on Trollope and Victorian fiction as a whole.)

Pollard, A., *Anthony Trollope* (1978). (Useful and thorough survey of his output.)

The Trollopian, later and currently entitled *Nineteenth-Century Fiction*. (American scholarly journal, containing many essays on Trollope.)

TROLLOPE, Frances (1780–1863) born near Bristol, daughter of Rev. William Milton, afterwards vicar of Heckfield, Hampshire, where she was brought up. Married Thomas Trollope, 1809; six children, including Anthony (*q.v.*), and Thomas Adolphus, also a novelist. Husband failed as a London barrister and then as a farmer at Harrow, and the Trollopes' scheme to run an 'emporium' at Cincinnati proved disastrous. During time in America, however, 1827–31, Frances toured country, and, on returning to England, made her name with *Domestic Manners of the Americans*, 2 vols (1832). After husband's death, 1835, wrote to keep her family, energetically researching and writing travel books and miscellaneous works, and many novels, including *The Vicar of Wrexhill* (1837), *The Widow Barnaby* (1839), *Michael Armstrong, the Factory Boy* (1839–40), and *Jessie Phillips* (1842–43). Settled in Florence, 1843.

> Trollope, F. E., *Frances Trollope: Her Life and Literary Work from George III to Victoria*, 2 vols (1895). (By daughter-in-law.)
> Bigland, E., *The Indomitable Mrs Trollope* (1953).
> Johnston, J., *The Life, Manners and Travels of Fanny Trollope: A Biography* (1979). (More detailed than Bigland, above; illustrated, with bibliography.)

WARD, Mary Augusta, née Arnold [Mrs Humphry Ward] (1851–1920), born in Hobart, Tasmania; daughter of Thomas Arnold (Dr Arnold's son and Matthew Arnold's brother), a school inspector until conversion to Roman Catholicism, 1856, when family returned to England. Educated at private boarding schools until father's return to Church of England and move to Oxford, 1865, where she worked on various academic projects including early Spanish Church history. Married Thomas Humphry Ward of Brasenose College, 1872; three children. Moved to London, 1881, where husband worked on *The Times*. Translated Amiel's *Journal Intime* (1885). Second novel, *Robert Elsmere* (1888) became one of biggest best-sellers of the age. Regarded as George Eliot's (*q.v.*) successor in her own time, her later novels included *The History of David Grieve* (1892), *Marcella* (1894), *Helbeck of Bannisdale* (1898), *Sir George Tressady* (1896), and *The Case of Richard Meynell* (1911), sequel to *Robert Elsmere*. Moved to Stocks, large house near Tring, 1892. Numerous public activities included founding a settlement in Gordon Square, London, 1890, and presidency of Women's Anti-Suffrage League, 1908. Always surrounded by leading writers and thinkers from birth, her *A Writer's Recollections* (1918) provides unique insight into intellectual life of late nineteenth century.

> Trevelyan, J. P., *The Life of Mrs Humphry Ward* (1923). (Biography by her daughter.)
> Jones, E. H., *Mrs Humphry Ward* (1973). (Pleasant, short biography.)

See: Peterson, W. S., *Victorian Heretic: Mrs Humphry Ward's Robert Elsmere* (Leicester, 1976). (Exhaustive study of the novel and its background.)
> Smith, E. M. G., *Mrs Humphry Ward*, Twayne's English Authors, 288 (Boston, 1980). (Survey of her corpus of novels; much summary.)

WHITE, William Hale: see RUTHERFORD, Mark.

WOOD, Mrs Henry (1814–87), born Ellen Price, daughter of Worcester glove ve
    manufacturer; suffered from curvature of spine in girlhood and throughout
    adult life. Married Henry Wood, merchant, 1836, with whom lived on
    French Riviera until he lost his job and returned to London, 1856, where
    she turned to professional writing. Her second novel, *East Lynne* (1861),
    one of the first sensation novels, made her famous and outsold almost
    every other Victorian novel. Her fifty or so other novels, most of which
    combine detailed studies of domestic life with sensational material and
    numerous death-bed scenes, include the quieter *The Channings* (1862) and
    Mrs Halliburton's Troubles (1862), both set in same cathedral town, and the
    lurid *Verner's Pride* (1863). Widowed, 1866. Bought monthly *Argosy*, which
    edited herself, 1865–87, and in which published her famous,
    unmelodramatic 'Johny Ludlow' tales.

> Wood, C. W., *Memorials of Mrs Henry Wood* (1894).

> See: Elwin, M., *Victorian Wallflowers* (1934). (Chapter sketches her life
>   and work.)
>   Hughes, W., *The Maniac in the Cellar: Sensation Novels of the 1860s*
>   (Princeton, 1980). (Chapter on 'The Wickedness of Woman'
>   examines M. E. Braddon and Wood.)

YONGE, Charlotte Mary (1832–1901), daughter of country gentleman; born in
    Otterbourne, Hampshire. Educated mainly by father, and prepared for
    ordination by leading Tractarian, John Keble, who later vetted her novels
    and suggested revisions. Published over 150 books, about half of them
    novels. *The Heir of Redclyffe* (1853) made her famous; profits, as on many
    books, went to a charity. Other novels include *Heartsease; or, The Brother's
    Wife* (1854), *The Daisy Chain* (1856), *The Trial: More Links of the Daisy
    Chain* (1864), and *The Clever Woman of the Family* (1865). Also edited *The
    Monthly Packet*, Tractarian periodical for children, 1851–91 (assistant editor,
    1891–95); *The Monthly Paper of Sunday Teaching*, 1860–75; *Mothers in
    Council*, 1890–1900. Lived quietly in Hampshire throughout her life; alone
    from 1868, following death of father, 1854, and mother, 1868.

> Coleridge, C. R., *Charlotte Mary Yonge: Her Life and Letters* (1903).
> (Includes bibliography.)
> Battiscombe, G., *Charlotte Mary Yonge: The Story of an Uneventful
> Life* (1943). (Critical biography.)

> See: Tillotson, K., '*The Heir of Redclyffe*', in G. and K. Tillotson, *Mid-
>   Victorian Studies* (1965), pp. 49–55. (Text of centenary radio talk,
>   1953.)
>   Woolf, R. L., *Gains and Losses: Novels of Faith and Doubt in Victorian
>   England* (New York and London, 1977). (Section on Yonge.)

Index